THEOLOGY AND THE SOCIAL SCIENCES

THEOLOGY AND THE SOCIAL SCIENCES

Michael Horace Barnes

Editor

THE ANNUAL PUBLICATION
OF THE COLLEGE THEOLOGY SOCIETY
2000
VOLUME 46

Maryknoll, New York 10545

The Catholic Foreign Mission Society of America (Maryknoll) recruits and trains people for overseas missionary service. Through Orbis Books, Maryknoll aims to foster the international dialogue that is essential to mission. The books published, however, reflect the opinions of their authors and are not meant to represent the official position of the society. To obtain more information about Maryknoll and Orbis Books, please visit our website at www.maryknoll.org.

Co-published by the College Theology Society and Orbis Books, Maryknoll, NY 10545-0308

Manufactured in the United States of America

Orbis/ISBN 1-57075-355-5

Contents

Acknowledgments

Thanks go to the thirty-six CTS members who offered articles for this volume. It was often hard to choose among them. Special thanks go to the many reviewers, two per essay, who were the major guides in making choices, and often did painstaking analysis in order to help the authors make their good work even better. It has been a pleasant surprise to me once again how many scholars give willingly of their time to serve as reviewers. Even more thanks go to the office staff at the Alumni Chair in Humanities office at the University of Dayton, Carolyn Ludwig in particular for taking care of all the many mailings back and forth, and for her steady and dedicated efforts to put the manuscript in good shape for Orbis Books; with thanks also to students Sarah Utaski, Dan Smith, and Andrew Knight for proofreading, printing, copying, and so on. It made the task of editing enormously easier. Finally, thanks to Susan Perry of Orbis Books, an editor whose pleasant personality makes it easy to follow her clear and highly competent guidance.

Introduction

Michael Horace Barnes

The variety of articles here illustrates well how varied the relations can be between theology and the social sciences. These relations take two major forms. The first invites the social sciences inside the theological tent to work alongside philosophy in a serving role. The second treats the social sciences less as a servant than as an animal to be domesticated, like goats worth milking once in a while but to be tethered outside the tent where their gamey odor will not disturb the finer air of theology. As I will explain, these are, roughly, Rahnerian and Balthasarian approaches. To adequately categorize the many articles in this volume, however, each of these two approaches will be divided further, into weaker and stronger forms.

The goats-in-the-yard approach is understandable. The history of secular social science theorizing has put theologians on guard. From the atheism of Karl Marx and the religious unmusicality of Max Weber to the "methodological atheism" of the early Peter Berger and the reductionistic claims of E. O. Wilson, social theorists have treated religion at best as a useful fiction and at worst as a debilitating distraction from reality. Similar thought prevails among many psychologists, historians, and anthropologists. It is no wonder Milbank argues in his book on social theory that Christians must reject all interpretations of life except a singularly Christian metanarrative, or that Hauerwas in his many writings tells Christians to expect that the traditions and values of their Christian community will sometimes stand in harsh contrast with the secular world. Yet they may both be willing to milk the goats occasionally for practical information. For example, the social sciences can provide demographics relevant for evangelization efforts or economic data important in promoting social justice. But these goats cannot be valid sources for theologizing itself. Both Michael Baxter and Boyd Blundell seek to alert the reader to the danger of letting goats in the tent.

This strong caution toward the social sciences is less typical than the milder approach of, say, von Balthasar, as described expertly by James Voiss. Balthasar looks at the world of secular thought with restrained appreciation (much as Cardinal Ratzinger looks at the major religions of the world). Balthasar says he sees good in this world; some true wisdom and values can be found there. But he also discerns a striking contrast between the grace-filled church with its revelation-based tradition and the ordinary things of the world. Balthasar reads the scriptures, studies the tradition, learns from the mystics, celebrates the sacraments, and finds in these a divine power and beauty missing from the things of the world. The social sciences know little of this approach. They work deliberately by natural knowledge alone, excluding all those elements of faith and wonder and humility that must ground any truly Christian theology.

Just as there is a mild and stronger style of the goats-in-the-yard approach, a similar difference appears in the servants-in-the-tent interpretation. The ordinary mild approach is not to worry very much about the secular character of the social sciences. Theology has long profited from the spoils of the Egyptians, loading up its tent with foreign ideas that prove useful. The interaction over centuries between Christians and pagan philosophers also set a precedent for learning from worldly sources, a precedent that would bear fruit from the late medieval flourishing of theology to contemporary correlational theologies. Victor Matthews and Carol Dempsey show how to draw upon archeological data and sociological theory to interpret scriptural passages in their historical context. Similarly, in their related presentations, James Davidson and Patricia Wittberg comfortably use sociological data to better understand patterns in American Catholic belief and practice. Judith Merkle explores the various meanings of "social teaching" in different contexts, showing layers of theological possibilities. Mathew Schmalz offers an on-the-scene interpretation of some acculturation problems in India with the help of Dan Sperber's anthropological theories. In a rather striking analysis, more difficult to categorize perhaps, Terry Tilley proposes that a sophisticated mode of historical interpretation can rescue belief in the resurrection from the secular implications of the older historical method.

But even the seemingly comfortable cohabitation of theology and the social sciences has raised disturbing challenges from within the tent. The use of secular historical methods for studying scripture and church tradition makes these sources appear rather more secular and less sacred, much more a part of worldly history than of the special order of redemption. Felicidad Oberholzer's comparison of a modern psychological interpretation of the dreams of Perpetua to a traditional hagiographical interpretation nicely illustrates this distinction. So does Peter Phan's use of Granfield's "cybernetic" ecclesiology, which uses social organization theory to analyze church structures and challenge traditional theology on the uses of episcopal and papal authority. Florence Bourg also discerns some potential within the practices of home churches to unsettle aspects of traditional ecclesiology. William Mattison's interpretation of the relation between the emotions and virtuous choices appeals both to Aquinas and neuropsychology, as though neurological studies could correct traditional theology on the operations of the soul. When the social sciences challenge traditional theology in such ways, laying claim to cohabitation in the tent, questions arise about their right to do so. Theology must decide whether there are adequate grounds, including adequate *theological* grounds, to let the social sciences inside.

The theological issue can be cast in Rahnerian terms: are secular human life and thought simply natural, unconnected to the supernatural, or are they already responding in varying ways and degrees to the divine Self-gift? If ordinary life is unconnected to the supernatural, then when social scientists study ordinary life, they are not studying anything with theological content. If, on the contrary, ordinary life is always related in some way to the supernatural offer by God of a relation to God's own Self, then nothing that the social scientists study is theologically irrelevant. Then the social sciences themselves, as human activities carried on as part of ordinary life, are also response in some way to divine grace. While the social sciences follow rules of the secular academy, they are als7o part of what David Tracy once characterized as living by an implicit faith in the ultimate validity of being a knower in the world.

A few concrete examples can illustrate the meaning of these abstract statements. First, consider that Aquinas found Aristotle to be correct that we humans are social animals. This became part of Aquinas's theology of the person. But from earliest Christianity this was not self-evident to all Christians. The earliest desert fathers, as we call them, went out to be alone with God, apart from the world, including the social world. The earliest collections of monks did not arise from a prior theological conviction that monastic communities rather than a hermitic life were more the will of God. Instead the social reality formed the theology. As is natural to us humans, those seeking a new way of life looked for guides or mentors and attached themselves to famous desert ascetics. This social reality appeared; then theology made sense of it. Religious orders appeared, eventually with a theology of contemplative life in community to justify it, partly with the help of social and political theories from that old pagan Aristotle.

A striking example of theology adjusting to social science is the reinterpretation of the traditional doctrine of original sin. Augustine himself could never decide just how original sin was passed on from parents to children. Traducianism—passing on actual soul from parent to child—would account for it. But to Augustine there were also serious reasons to claim that God created each soul anew. In our own time the historical critical method has made it reasonable to take the stories of the Fall in Genesis less literally, which in turn has opened the way for a more sophisticated understanding of the social nature of human existence. It has also provided a framework for speaking of original sin as an aspect of the socio-cultural character of life.

Similarly, speculations about the Roman Catholic Church illustrate a possible interplay between the social sciences and theology. The Roman church is organized hierarchically. This organization has two distinguishable aspects. One is the responsibility of the bishops to preserve and proclaim the faith and celebrate it sacramentally in community. The second is the authoritarian nature of the structure of responsibility and power as it has been traditionally practiced. There has been a great deal of social theorizing about community structures of power and responsibility. Marx thought that full economic justice in a world of economic plenty would result finally in a withering away of the state. So far this theory has fared poorly. The data suggest that authoritarian power attracts power-seekers, that there will always be at least some who strive after it, as part of their human nature, so to speak. If this is a sound psychological and political judgment, it implies that authoritarian modes of assigning political power and responsibility are inferior to more democratic modes. We might thus conclude from sociological and psychological studies of human behavior that it is wiser to build into church practices some of the checks and balances that characterize democracies, such as the local election of bishops, with checks and balances provided by national bishops' councils and the papacy.

This speculation on the church echoes the deeper reflections in Peter Phan's article on cybernetics and the church. That paper can speak for itself. But how a person responds to it depends on the person's approach to the social sciences. If a theology of the church sits alone in its tent, drawing only upon its own inner resources, especially scripture and tradition, then discussions of the social, economic, political, and psychological implications of church organization will seem to be peripheral—just the bleating of the goats out in the yard. But if theology does depend on the various maids and lads living within the tent, then changing theology's life style to accommodate the ideas from these aides makes excellent theological sense.

Though most of the contributions to this volume keep the social sciences in the tent, only a few explicitly acknowledge and support the theological assumption that these social sciences are also a work built upon grace in some way. In the first article, Gregory Baum, long noted for his outreach to religions and to the social sciences, describes his own story of coming into this theological position. I am grateful that he accepted my invitation to contribute to this volume. In confirmation of Baum's general recommendations, John Coleman provides a detailed review of the on-going presence of theology in social science and social science in theology, and lays out practical and theological justifications for accepting this interaction as both inevitable and constructive.

This brings us back to the challenges from Baxter and Blundell to such Rahnerian accommodation with the secular. Milbank's way of pressing the charge was to accuse Rahner of naturalizing the supernatural. It is a somewhat surprising charge. One could as easily grant to Rahner what Milbank grants to de Lubac, that he supernaturalizes the natural. Rahner argues that while we can speculate that human beings might have been created as purely natural beings, in fact the actual universe that God has created is not a purely natural universe. Rahner argues that God has made a Self-gift to the universe from the first, and that in humans this Self-gift is called supernatural grace, the indwelling of God. Though Milbank does not say it in this way, one can suspect that Rahner's fault in Milbank's eyes is that if nature is thus supernaturalized, the supernatural loses some of its differentiation from what is natural and profane. If everything already has God's gift of Self as its underlying character, then what can the Christian vision and truth and inspiration add? Wherein lies the truly special character of grace as extraordinary gift, if it is found in every ordinary thing? One may read Balthasar in the same way. The special beauty of God's presence that Balthasar seeks is quite distinct from the profanities of life. Signs and wonders must be not be dissolved into the everyday. Similarly, but from a moral rather than ontological direction, Hauerwas insists on the radical distinction between the Christian community and the secular world. What Christians need is not to be found in the social sciences; what Christians should preach and give witness to is a properly Christian moral vision that stands contrary to the ways of the world. The sacred and the secular are not the same and should not be commingled.

This approach stands in contrast to Rahner's. He draws his most significant line not between the sacred and the secular, but between the Uncreated Mystery and creation. All that is not God is part of creation, part of the finite, part of the process of the universe. God made creation to be the recipient of God's gift of Self. Many moments and things and persons in creation have in fact taken a specially sacred role as real-symbols of the basic redemptive truth of the call to all creation to union with God, a union that can be fully achieved only in the free decision of consciously reflective beings like us humans. But the moments and things are sacred because they represent what is true for the secular also: that all creation is part of the single process of achieving union with God. Rahner perceives the Incarnation not as redemption from the world but redemption of the world, the uniting of the created to the Uncreated, in full unity but without confusion of the two.

The goats-in-the-yard approach builds upon a revered tradition that emphasizes redemption from what is merely and often evilly worldly. The servants-in-the-tent approach builds upon a more recent retrieval of an Irenaean sensibility, as well as upon awareness of the cosmos as an evolutionary process, celebrated by both Rahner and Teilhard. In spite of the frequent opposition between the goats-in-the-yard and the servants-in-the-tent approaches, it may not be necessary to choose between them. Those taking one or another approach can value each other precisely as "other," and be grateful for the added resources that come from this plurality.

Psychologically speaking, it is obvious that there is more than one type of person. Some people will be best served by a theology that provides them with a degree of refuge from the profane, with a sense of the specifically and specially sacred among the ordinary, and with a special religious inspiration to guide and strengthen their lives. For many hundreds of years those who did not find the ordinary world adequate for their needs could take up monastic life, go on pilgrimages, engage in special devotions, and above all live their life in a sacramental community. This is still true. To turn from the world to the sacred, at least at many and special moments, is still an important mode of religiousness. But other people are better served by a theology that allows them to go into the world to find God. The lesson of Matthew 25 is still valid: those who minister to the earthly needs of the hungry and thirsty and sick and imprisoned are ministering to Christ even if they do not know it. The point, then, is mainly to minister to others' human needs rather than to succeed at being religious in some distinct way. The passage from Matthew says that worldly service is religious also.

Dealing with otherness and plurality is a message in two of the articles in the section on cross-cultural contexts. Reid Locklin uses Victor Turner's anthropological theories to explore similarities between Sankara and Augustine. Here, seemingly quite diverse religious visions turn out to have some common elements. Similarly, perhaps even those who are apparently in disagreement on the relation of the social sciences to theology may share more than they readily perceive. Jeannine Hill Fletcher's use of Rahner likewise carries us toward an appreciation of otherness, and does so for theological reasons. Her message about the value of a plurality of religions could apply also to a plurality of approaches to the relation between theology and the social sciences.

Nonetheless, those who are uneasy with the world and its secular methods will find it difficult to grant to the social sciences any strong influence over theology; they will also find it difficult to understand those who do grant the social sciences an influential role. They will be inclined to argue that Jerusalem must maintain its distance from Athens, and from the Babylon of secular culture, for that matter. Those who cherish the world, however, will find that from the mount of Zion they can look outward to both Athens and Babylon and find grace there, even in the seemingly secular. The question then is how these

Part I

GENERAL ISSUES

Remarks of a Theologian in Dialogue with Sociology

Gregory G. Baum

I am grateful to Michael Barnes, the editor of this collection, for inviting me to write a short article for this volume on the relationship of theology to sociological science. This topic has been of keen interest to me ever since I studied sociology at the New School of Social Research in New York City from 1969 to 1971. In my subsequent work as a Catholic theologian, I have always been, in one way or another, in dialogue with sociology.

Like theology, sociology is a complex field of inquiry, about which one should avoid making rapid generalizations. The manner in which theologians evaluate sociology depends to a large extent, I think, on the perspective from which they have been introduced to it.

The Classic Sources

My encounter with sociology at the New School was a most illuminating time. Studying Durkheim and Weber, I was amazed by the important place assigned to religion in their social theories. After a few months at the New School, I expressed this amazement in an article written for *The Ecumenist.* At the same time, I was being initiated into sociology as a critical science revealing the problematic character of modern industrial society, proposals that were pleasing to my theological ears.

Alexis de Tocqueville enlightened me in regard both to the merit of egalitarian democracy in promoting greater personal freedom and to the danger of egalitarian democracy in creating the possibility of a new tyranny, power exercised over the people through public opinion manipulated by government. Studying the young Karl Marx, I learned about the self-alienation of workers in industrial capitalism, and about ideology as the deformation of truth for the sake of economic interest. Ferdinand Toennies taught me how deeply human consciousness and public culture were being transformed by the advance of industrial society, and how we were all becoming individualists and utilitarians, unless we remained personally attached to an older tradition. Emile Durkheim recognized the "anomie" created by modern society, lamented "the cult of the individual," and denounced "the pathological division of labor" that created malaise among the employed and anguish among the unemployed. Max Weber examined the ongoing "rationalization" of modern society, namely, the growing domination of "formal reason" and the diminishing cultural power of art, religion, and ethical reflection. A more optimistic note was struck by Georg Simmel who tried to show that the forces of life operative in ordinary people have always been able to break the stranglehold of inhibiting institutions. Ernst Troeltsch, the only theologian among these sociologists, questioned the value-free character of social science. He thought that observers, even if they tried, could not separate the "is" from their perception of the "ought." He demonstrated that sociologists, whether they realize it or not, bring with them their own world as they do their research. They can arrive at a reliable reading of their object of study only if they are willing to explore how their world is actually related to the world of their object of study. Troeltsch recognized that the colonizer cannot credibly study the colonized, without first undergoing a change of personal consciousness. Max Scheler raised serious questions regarding the psychological impact of the natural sciences of his day. He showed that they promoted a positivistic mindset that regarded scientific demonstration as the only truth. More than that, Scheler argued that the *superiority* of the natural scientist over the object of his study and his *power* to manipulate this object and, if necessary, destroy it, created the model for the approach to human subjects by social scientists and, with their help, by governments, thus legitimizing their domination of human beings. Karl Mannheim, another critic of positivism, demonstrated, with the help of the categories of "ideology" and "utopia," that all thought and, in fact, all cultural expressions, including religion, are related to particular social conditions and cannot be appropriately understood unless this relationship is clarified.

What impressed me from the very beginning was that the sociological critiques of modernity, diverse though they were, brought out the grain of truth in the Catholic denunciation of modernity. When Pius IX, in his syllabus of errors, repudiated democracy, republicanism, industrial capitalism, and the entire spirit of modernity, he recognized the dark possibilities of the emerging new world. Many years later, I learned how to name this Catholic rejection of modernity from the social thinkers of the Frankfurt School. These thinkers, some of them sociologists, were also critical of modernity. They engaged in what they called the "dialectical negation" of the Enlightenment, namely, *rejecting* the domination of instrumental reason and the imprisonment of the human subject in determinism and, at the same time, *retrieving* the ethical (anti-feudal) values of the early Enlightenment, in particular liberty, equality, and social solidarity. These social thinkers opposed any "non-dialectical negation" of the Enlightenment, since such a negation would not preserve these humanistic and emancipatory values. What the Frankfurt School argued against was not so much the old-fashioned Catholic "non-dialectical" rejection of modernity, but rather the contemporary forms of this unqualified rejection in existentialism, vitalism, and fascism. As a Catholic theologian, I had sympathy for the dialectical negation of modernity, *rejecting* its scientistic and anti-humanist dimension and at the same time *retrieving*, in a theological mode, its humanistic and emancipatory aspirations. This critical openness to the world was well expressed in *Gaudium et Spes* of Vatican Council II.

A Mood of Positivism

Some theologians have been introduced to sociology in a climate of positivism. Because of this, many of them have doubts as to whether the dialogue of theology with sociology is a fruitful undertaking. Sociologists today may not be positivists in the philosophical sense; they may, in fact, never have asked themselves foundational questions in regard to their scientific discipline. Yet what so often characterizes them is the wish to assimilate the social sciences as much as possible to the natural sciences or, better, to what the natural sciences used to be. In doing their research these sociologists look for laws that determine people's action in society. They search for plausible hypotheses, they continue their empirical research to demonstrate these hypotheses, and once a law has been established, they make predictions about human behavior.

This social scientific approach can be characterized by three features: 1) It demands an ever greater quantification of the empirical data, either by inventing a numerical ordering of qualities or by disregarding qualities altogether; 2) it presupposes a deterministic understanding of human beings, their behavior to be defined by a discoverable set of laws; and 3) it assumes the objectivity of social science research and hence pays no attention to the mindset of the researcher nor to his or her insertion in a social setting.

When this approach is applied to the sociological investigation of religion, it overlooks the independent creativity associated with religion. It categorizes religion as a dependent variable, reducible to the social elements on which it depends. In this kind of sociological literature on religion, we often find two different kinds of reductionism: secular reductionism, which holds that religion is really a manifestation of something material, and phenomenological reductionism, which overlooks the inwardness of religion and its orientation toward transcendence.

A professor of political science whom I once met (a very conservative Catholic who thought I was not orthodox enough) actually made use of "rational choice theory" in his scientific research. Rational choice theory interprets people as "utility maximizers." All acts of service to a community, of fidelity to a tradition, and of solidarity with others are explained in terms of sophisticated and often disguised rational self-interest. Rational choice theory thus gives dominance to economics in the investigation of human behavior in all social contexts. This professor made no attempt to relate these presuppositions of his scientific work to his Catholic theological understanding of the human vocation. Like many social scientists, he did not reflect on foundational questions. This is why I prefer to speak of the positivistic *mood* in social and political science departments, rather than suggest that the practitioners embrace positivism as a philosophy. In my opinion, the dominant trend in the social sciences at this time does not generate an adequate critique of present-day society and Western empire. The dominant trend does not serve "the common good" of humanity, to use an old-fashioned Catholic term that is becoming more relevant every day.

Empirical Research and Subjectivity

Empirical research is, of course, of primary importance. Without it sociology would not exist. Quantification and measurement have an indispensable role to play. Powerful institutions sometimes oppose sociological research because they do not want to know the impact of their policies on the population. Over the last decade, governments in Canada have begun to set up a good number of casinos to increase their revenue, yet they have not commissioned any empirical studies to estimate the impact of these gambling institutions on the low-income sector of society. At times the churches, guided by an ingrained conservatism, also oppose sociological research because they do not wish to know how their members actually react to traditional disciplines and institutions.

Empirical research in sociology differs from research in the natural sciences. Max Weber pointed out that human action consists of behavior plus the meaning the actors assign to it. Since behavior is external, it can be studied with methods similar to those used in the natural sciences. But to study what this behavior means to the actors calls for understanding or interpretation, an approach that has no equivalent in the natural sciences. In his opposition to positivism, Max Weber called his scientific approach *verstehende Soziologie*. It is possible to interpret this *verstehen* simply as a work of human intelligence, yet it is also possible to see it as a work demanding empathy, the emotional effort to put oneself in the shoes of others.

If *verstehen* is an essential dimension of sociological research, can a non-religious person undertake reliable research dealing with religious activities? I think so. Weber regarded himself as "religiously unmusical," yet he was able to explore with great sensitivity the inwardness that guided the practice of religious people. He marveled at the creativity of religion. (Yet, I always felt that he did not do justice to Roman Catholicism, a customary failure of German scholars of his day.) It would be excellent, in my opinion, if the sociological study of religion were carried out by two sets of researchers, by outsiders who rely on empathy and by insiders who are participants by faith, each set correcting the blind spots of the other.

While Weber advocated *verstehen*, he did not explore in detail the subjectivity implicit in his own sociological research. In fact, he strongly defended the objectivity of social science. The task of the researcher was to free himself or herself from all prejudgments and leave behind all cultural presuppositions. The empirical data offered in support of a thesis, Weber argued, must be such that they can be checked by any scholar, of any social class or cultural background.

Formal reason, he believed, was universal. Weber realized, of course, that total freedom from ethical prejudice was unreachable, yet he recommended that the scientist do his or her utmost to achieve it. Sociological research had to be value-free.

Without challenging the universality of what Weber called formal reason, I wish to argue that operative in the mind of the researcher are inevitably value-laden presuppositions affecting his or her research. I shall mention four such factors.

1) There is the *question* the researcher asks. The question guiding the research may either be assigned by an institution for its own reason or freely chosen by the researcher because of a special interest. The question asked reveals something about the concern of the institution that assigned it or of the scientist who elected it. The value-orientation implicit in the question is particularly obvious, for instance, if it has to do with racism in the churches or the feminization of poverty in contemporary society.

2) A research project is always carried by an overall *intention* that supplies the energy required to complete it. This intention may be to obtain an academic degree or be financially remunerated, but it may also be based on a vision and thus have an ethical or political character. The intention may be to make a contribution to the transformation or stabilization of the existing society.

3) The researcher has to choose a model or *paradigm* around which to organize the empirical data. Once a paradigm is chosen, it guides research: it draws the researcher's attention to the appropriate empirical data and allows him or her to disregard other information as inappropriate. Paradigms, moreover, have a symbolic significance that is, in one way or another, value-related. How, for instance, does a sociologist define "poverty" in his or her research—in purely economic terms or in terms that include the disintegration of community? Does the sociologist study the church as a religious community, a social organization, a bureaucracy, a movement, an educational institution, or, as some sociologists do, as a commercial firm selling the Christian message? The choice of the paradigm has evaluative implications.

4) Researchers have to choose how familiar they want to be with the social actors whom they study. Do they approach them with a ready-made theory, or are they willing to listen to the actors and run the risk of discovering that their theory is inadequate? When social scientists study subjects belonging to cultures different from their own,

how hard will they try to acquire the appropriate empathy? Decisions of this kind have ethical meaning.

Value-laden presuppositions or options are thus inevitably operative in the mind of the researcher. One can refer to these as the researcher's "subjectivity." Sociological research is "objective" in the sense that the empirically based arguments can be verified by any scientist, whatever his or her social vision or background. Though all social scientists present objective studies in conformity with the scientific method, they operate out of different subjectivities: they ask different questions, they are carried by different intentions, they use different paradigms, and they opt for different levels of familiarity with the people they study. When we ask why social scientists, all using the same scientific approach, come to different results, as they so often do, our attention is drawn to the different subjectivities that sustain their research. We recognize that sociological research has not resolved the truly burning questions of society. It has not made it clear, for instance, whether the globalization of the free market creates wealth that will eventually help the poor or whether this globalization widens the gap between rich and poor with death-dealing consequences. The subjective element in the social sciences deserves to be critically examined, so social scientists can assume intellectual and moral responsibility for the values implicit in their research.

I wish to draw one conclusion and develop one proposal from the above reflections on the subjective dimension of sociological research. They touch upon issues that have been important in my own intellectual activity. The conclusion is that—contrary to Max Weber's supposition—sociological research can be both objective and engaged; in other words it can follow the canons of rationality and also be guided by a social vision. Commitment to an ethical stance, such as the option for the poor, need not in any way reduce the objectivity of the research, meaning the verifiability of the empirically based arguments. Such commitments influence the question asked, the underlying intention, the paradigm chosen, and the willingness to listen to the subjects under study.

I propose that when theologians wish to engage in dialogue with sociology, they be compelled to choose among various sociological orientations. They will do this appropriately, remaining faithful to their own theological perspective, if they turn to social scientific studies produced by sociologists with subjectivities similar to their own. In other words, by engaging in dialogue with sociology, theologians need not embrace a set of criteria foreign to them.

In philosophy and theology, one easily comes to think of ideas as floating above the historical conditions in which they were created and as independent of the social location of those who hold them. It is assumed that if an idea is true, it transcends all historical circumstances. The sociologists who have impressed me have found this impossible to accept. Ideas are always socially grounded and cannot be correctly understood unless this relationship is clarified.

This also applies to sociology itself. For this reason, sociologists have investigated the historical circumstances in which their own truth has emerged. They have argued that the creation of a capitalist industrial society produced conditions in Europe that compelled intellectuals to compare the new world in the making with the old world that was being left behind. The urgency to compare the two conflicting types of society, adjacent to one another, generated sociology as a new branch of rational inquiry. Thus, when sociologists argue that all thought is related to the social base that sustains it, they do not make an exception for their own thought. On the contrary, since sociological ideas have been created to understand Western developments, the encounter with non-Western cultures in our own day has raised the question of whether the classical sociological categories we have inherited have any validity when used to interpret non-Western cultures.

Even in the West alone different social contexts influence social theory. When we learn that Plato and Hellenistic thought after Plato defined human beings in terms of their rationality, we realize that he belonged to a society where an elite was free to engage in rational reflection, while the labor producing the material conditions of human life was done by women and the lower classes. Christian theology tended to followed the Hellenistic tradition. Yet the perspective of the book of Genesis was quite different: here Adam, the human being, is a farmer. The religious vision expressed in Genesis originated in a peasant society. Karl Marx, in solidarity with the emerging proletariat, again defined the human being primarily as worker, not as thinker, an understanding of the human that was adopted in John Paul II's bold encyclical *Laborem exercens*. These few remarks suggest that it is impossible to offer a philosophy of the human without revealing something of one's relationship to society. Abstractness may not be politically innocent.

Even abstract ideas proposed in society sustain certain trends or aspirations operative in that society. Ideas have a cultural weight that affects society, either by stabilizing it or by promoting change. Identical ideas, repeated in different circumstances, may actually acquire different meanings and sustain different cultural impulses. When people are pleased with their society and their location within it, praising God as the lord of history protects their world and their privilege. By contrast, when people regard their society as a place of injustice and see themselves as its victims, then praising God as the lord of history delegitimates their society and creates a yearning for social change.

There exists a reductionist interpretation of this proposal, according to which ideas are simply reflections of existing social relations and therefore inevitably dependent variables. If the meaning of ideas is reduced to their social function, then there would be no need to wrestle with their content and engage in the quest for truth. This sort of reductionism is not at home in the classical sociological tradition, which has always honored the creativity of the human mind and its intellectual power to innovate. Thought is not entirely determined by history! Yet even when thinkers generate new and original ideas, their thought is inevitably marked by their historical location. Their ideas will have a relation to the existing social reality: they either draw attention to the unjust conditions that cause human suffering or, conversely, they withdraw the mind's attention from these problems and their human consequences.

The reason why sociological reflections such as these are so important to me is that they illuminate the fact that thought and its communication participate in the great historical drama of sin and salvation, touching the whole of humanity, revealed to us in Jesus Christ. In this universe, truth rescues, transforms, and saves.

Every Theology Implies a Sociology and Vice Versa

John A. Coleman, S.J.

The title for this essay comes from an evocative and exemplary text—even if it delivers more a promise for a program of correlation than its actual realization. The text, from Robert Bellah's *Beyond Belief*, reads:

> The absolute separation of social science and theology is impossible. Every theology implies a sociology and a psychology and so on. And every sociology implies a theology, or, at least, any definite theological position limits the variety of sociological positions compatible with it and vice versa. To say that they are separate enterprises is not to deny that there is any relation between them, as some have done, or to argue that they operate at levels so different that there is no necessity to integrate them. On the contrary, I would argue that theology and social science are parts of a single intellectual universe. To refuse to relate them is to admit to intellectual bankruptcy.[1]

In much neglected yet still illuminating texts on this question of the correlation of sociology and theology, Emory theologian William Everett, in his study *Christianity, Personality and Society*, illustrates Bellah's point for theology. Everett shows that H. Richard Niebuhr's theology appealed closely to, and even basically implicated, the determinate if controverted sociology of George Herbert Mead.[2] My own teacher, Gibson Winter, in his book *Elements for a Social Ethic*, laid out schematically the not easily resolvable tensions between the anthropological and social presuppositions in the structural-functionalism of Talcott Parsons's sociology, and the sort of theological ethics drawing on hermeneutics and phenomenology that Winter championed. Winter much preferred the background sociology found in the work of Alfred Schütz.[3]

My purposes in this essay are threefold. Drawing upon what constitutes a very finite list of theologians who use sociology as a truly integral (as opposed to a more ancillary or merely illustrative) part of their enterprise—Gregory Baum, Robin Gill, Don Browning—and, similarly, the exceedingly small cadre of sociologists who can be said to be truly tutored in and informed by theology—Bellah, David Martin, Kieran Flanagan, Andrew Greeley—I will try to tease out some methodological presuppositions and implications for a correlation of theology and sociology. It will be my contention that for at least two sub-units of theology—practical theology and theological ethics—a close correlation between theology and the social sciences, far from being a luxury, is an especially integral part of the enterprise. Finally, to keep this essay from being too abstractly methodological and theoretical, I will conclude by looking again at the data and arguments in an exemplary text by a theologian who deftly uses sociology as part of his theological project: Robin Gill's remarkable study, *Churchgoing and Christian Ethics*.[4]

To clear the decks, however, for Gill's close marriage between social science and Christian ethics, I at least have to confront the opposing camp, most notably in the work of John Milbank and Stanley Hauerwas who deny the usefulness or even the possibility of a correlation between theology and sociology. Juxtaposing Milbank's long and stupendously learned wake for the social sciences, *Theology and Social Theory: Beyond Secular Reason*—a wake at which there are absolutely no tears shed or keening heard—with the work of Browning and Gill, Bellah and Baum tempted me at one point to call this essay, "Four Weddings and a Funeral" for the correlation of theology and the social sciences![5]

It is instructive to take note of the theologians cited in the indices of Bellah's work subsequent to his 1970 book *Beyond Belief*, notably those to be found in *Habits of the Heart, The Good Society*, and his writings on the social sciences as a species of practical reasoning and moral sciences. The list includes, inter alia: Augustine, Aquinas, Calvin, Jonathan Edwards, Troeltsch, Barth, Tillich, the brothers Niebuhr, Harvey Cox, Gordon Kauffman, Johannes Metz, Karl Rahner, Gregory Baum, Wayne Meeks, David Tracy, Stanley Hauerwas, and John Courtney Murray. Still, the use of theology in Bellah's work remains much more implicit than an explicitly worked out program of correlation. Key here is Bellah's insistence that "when ordinary reality turns into a nightmare, as it increasingly has in modern society, only some transcendental perspective offers any hope." When religion is seen to be grounded in the structure of the human situation itself, and theology operates as a self-critical, self-revising public system of thought, then, as he claims in *The Good Society*: "Religious traditions, interpreted in a way respectful of the views of others (including those who are entirely secular) have much to contribute to the democratic debate about a good form of life in our society and our world, if only we know how to draw on them."[6] What might be some of the presuppositions and implications of this correlation? How might the dialogue between theology and sociology become, in fact, a two-way street?

Three Theses on Correlating Sociology and Theology

Presupposition 1: No Easy Consensus about Correlating Sociology and Theology Exists or Is Likely to Emerge Because of the Conflictual Nature of Both Disciplines

Neither sociology nor theology is a truly unified discipline. Both are conflict-ridden, with competing methods and theories. In his book of essays, *Reflections on Sociology and Theology*, David Martin contends that "neither sociology nor theology operates according to an undisputed paradigm. There exist a multiplicity of modes of operation and kinds of procedure in each subject."[7] I have often contended that theology properly has no method of its own. I recently discovered an essay by the English Dominican Timothy Radcliffe, who seems to agree: "Theology is not a 'discipline' in any ordinary sense of the word."[8] If theology is *fides quaerens intellectum*, theology does, however, have a distinctive *faith* of its own. If we follow Michael Polanyi, theology is not unique in basing disciplined knowledge on faith, since all knowledge rests on tacit assumptions and unproven bases.[9] Clearly, however, the grounding faith of secular historical and social science differs from that of theology. Typically, the faith behind sociology and history is more truncated and hidden, less explicit about any transcendent reference, more inner-worldly, less given to an open espousal of its ethical thrust. The differing faiths of sociology and theology may or may not conflict, or they may partially overlap. But no method is unique to theology. It draws on literary studies, history, the historical-critical method, philosophy, ethics and, I will argue, necessarily also on social science.

Similarly, for sociology, as Gregory Baum notes in his classic theological reading of the social sciences, *Religion and Alienation*: "Because of the conflictual nature of sociology . . . it is impossible to find a single theoretical formulation of the relationship between sociology and theology."[10] Sociological studies vary widely on a host of issues about the underlying character of human agency (is it open, does it include elements of spontaneity?) and the good society. Sociologists differ about the sense in which—in sociology as well as in other human studies—truth is self-involving and how some important truths can only be discovered from an engaged perspective. Rarely are the social ethical perspectives driving sociological research explicit.

Much sociology still operates from a model of the social sciences as positivistic, mirroring the natural sciences. One current social science paradigm for understanding human agency—the rational actor theory, derived originally from economics but now regnant in much of sociology and political science—includes a kind of a determinism and reductionist, individualist view of how humans operate. Theologians reading such sociological accounts will surely want to claim more for the originating power of grace and God's revelatory Word than they find when these get translated into the language of social needs, compensations, and adjustments. Yet, as David Martin insists, "a given religion takes place within conditions which will yield sociological rules as to the average likelihood of conversion. Religions tend not to phrase their accounts of conversion in this way, but rather to envisage religious change as a *deus ex machina*. The ex is overemphasized."[11]

Martin, both a distinguished sociologist and an Anglican priest, has driven these points home in his two major sociological studies, *A General Theory of Secularization* and *Tongues of Fire*.[12] In the first, Martin draws a carefully constructed map across Europe, displaying where religion is strong, as measured by factors of conscious adherence, church-going practice, and strong identity, and where it has mainly faded into a mere background nod to civic adherence, such as in Britain, France, and Belgium. Where religion flourishes on this map (a map that usually overlaps with cultural islands, some of which are precise geographical nests, some not)—Ireland, Poland, Croatia, Malta,

Slovenia or, within countries, the Basque lands, Brittany, highland Norway and Sweden, the Finnish Lake Country, Flanders—it almost always correlates very nicely, indeed, with: 1) historic opposition of the cultural region to what is now a "secular" capital; 2) the support of a distinctive language and a distinctive historic myth of a "nation" or "nation-enclave" within a wider modern state; and 3) a historic border with another confession or country.

> This can be illustrated by examples. The hinterland of Bergen is sheltered by mountains. It defends a distinctive language and religiosity and resists secular Oslo. The peninsula of Brittany defends a distinctive language and faith against secular Paris; likewise the Basques defend their faith, language and land against what they call "atheist" Madrid. Flemish-speaking Flanders defends itself against French-speaking Brussels. Catholic western Austria resists secular and sometimes socialist Vienna. Croatia offers a very nice illustration of what it is to stand at the border of languages, religions and empires; and, of course, it offered resistance both to Orthodox Belgrade and to communist Belgrade. Alsace also stands at a linguistic, imperial, and confessional frontier. And, perhaps, surprisingly, Catholic Germany has also seen itself as a threatened border area: first, against Protestant and secular Berlin and then against the pressure of the border with the communist east. In all these nests, large and small, history and memory lie semi-intact. Even the British Isles fit into the pattern. The centre and south and south east are part of the secular mainland but religion increases with each move north and west. The influence of religion is more palpable toward the peninsulas of Wessex and Wales (especially North Wales) and towards the Scottish peninsula (especially the highlands and islands). It finally acquires maximum influence in the ultimate island of Ireland. And there, of course, lies the border of the great confessions, as well as a border of ethnic groups and historic myths.[13]

In a way much similar to Martin's mapping of Europe, Rodney Stark and William Bainbridge, in their study *The Future of Religion*, carefully show the statistical probabilities in the United States for conversion to New Age or other innovative forms of cult-formation (most likely in the highly unchurched regions of the western United States) or into evangelical newly break-off sects. They also provide a reliable set of indicators of about who is especially vulnerable to recruitment to new religious groups.[14]

In *Tongues of Fire*, Martin follows the amazing rise of Pentecostal sects throughout Latin America. Here, too, there are decided and precisely identifiable sociological niches (the agrarian hinterland under certain conditions of new development; the new regions circling the great cities made up of displaced migrant peasants) for the likelihood of conversions to Pentecostalism. There is a discernible pattern of penetration by Pentecostalism that can be rather precisely charted. Brazil and Chile are respectively 20 and 13 percent evangelical. Guatemala stands at 30 percent, Mexico at only 6. The Andean republics have been relatively resistant to the evangelical effervescence. There are variations in vulnerability to conversion to Pentecostalism between and within countries. Uruguay, Argentina, and Venezuela are not particularly fruitful grounds for evangelical growth. The mountain people of Ecuador, on the other hand, may convert very quickly, as may the Maya of Guatemala. As Martin notes, "All these variations in time and place are to be understood in terms of social context."[15]

Evangelicalism's massive and explosive growth across Latin America shows its vital response to the modern situation, most obviously to the moral, economic, and demographic avalanche of changes in the Third World. But its growth potential is also evident in the developed world and in the former communist lands. Evangelicalism presumes the individualism or self-expressive self so characteristic of late modernity and both contains and incorporates them into a less individualist context.

> A characteristic evangelical theme is the church family, but it endeavors to restore broken familial membranes or reconstitute them among the mutually supportive brothers and sisters. Alongside the brethren are the leaders in quasi-paternal roles, who restore a sense of direction and mark out the moral boundaries and the boundaries of the group. . . . All the modern tendencies are given scope by evangelicalism: the need for the small cell-like groupings and the yearning for communal support, for tactile communications, emotional release, holistic healing, a fluid language of the body and empowerment.[16]

In the end, Martin suggests that Pentecostals in Latin America, re-enacting a movement very similar to the Weberian Protestant Ethic and the Spirit of Capitalism, may carry the seeds of new forms of modernization. These may ultimately effect separation of church and state and the emergence of a multi-religious culture, as well as facilitate the transition toward more pluralist societies based in part on the mobility of capital and an industrial breakthrough. Clearly, as Martin notes, "the lava of the Spirit runs along the lines of a social fault."[17]

Martin pushes Weber's larger point about the "elective affinity" between certain religious ideas and social carriers of economic and political transformations: "Are theologians happy with the general supposition that the take-off of movements—and the degree of power exhibited in their expansion, minimally includes the ability of the message to resonate with parallel changes in social circumstance?"[18] Patricia Wittburg, in her essay for this volume, recounting data from her studies of some new recruits to Catholic religious orders, makes a cognate point. She insists that the flourishing of congregations, denominations, and religious movements is closely correlated to the innovative way they address the unique strains and hungers of a given society.

University of Santa Barbara sociologist Wade Clark Roof similarly recounts, both in his *Generation of Seekers* and his recent volume *The Spiritual Marketplace*, the emergence in the United States of what he calls "a spiritual quest culture."[19] In his own way, Roof addresses some "unique strains and hungers" in our society. Roof gives abundant data to demonstrate that "a culture of choice and spiritual exploration prevails—both inside and outside the religious establishments. . . ."[20] Boomers maintain, from their earlier days in the 1960s, a deep distrust of institutions and secular and religious authority. They tend to look less at religious institutions as holy spaces or traditions. Now they see religious institutions such as a congregation or a denomination as "a service organization for the fulfillment of its individual members." Roof notes: "Religious communities are seen as depositories of symbols, practices, teachings and moral codes for assembling and re-assembling strategies of faith and action"[21] (much the way in which sociologist Ann Swidler postulates that culture in the situation of high-modernity is increasingly a kind of tool-kit).

Roof draws on Anthony Giddens's notion of a late modern self that is perpetually in danger of becoming dispersed and thus needs constant monitoring and negotiation. Giddens describes a fragmentation and commodification of the self, whose cultivation and maintenance is problematic—Roof sees its religious correlate in religious identities that are increasingly fluid, multi-layered, and personally achieved. The modern religious seeker is heteroglossic—she speaks in many voices. In an open and deregulated spiritual marketplace, "no single religious or spiritual organization any longer can monopolize the symbolization of the sacred."[22]

The preferred language of baby-boomer spiritual seekers or religious adherents is the language of journey, walk, growth: a language privileging the primacy of experience, a lexicon that allows doubt to play an integral role in the spiritual quest. It is also a language that links spirituality to an expansive self—the self as a chooser who speaks of all loyalties as "preferences." In American Protestantism, as University of Southern California's Donald Miller has shown in his study of The Vineyard and Calvary Chapel, movements that respond to this new spiritual-quest culture have been growing apace and virtually redefining American Protestantism in our larger cities.[23]

Martin, Wittburg, and Roof are not denying Max Weber's notion of elective affinity. This is a claim that once a religious message resonates with a set of circumstances, it may actually work to alter partially those circumstances. Theology can and must be seen by the sociologist not just as a dependent variable but as one that itself may have social consequences. Ideas once incorporated in movements have some independent power and are consequential. As the literature on religion and resource mobilization within social movements shows, Weber's elective affinity still resonates.[24] One reason the American bishops' peace pastoral had more secular impact than their pastoral on the economy was that the first was positioned with new religious ideas, in the middle of a strategic re-alignment of policy experts on nuclear policies in the post-war world, and was joined as a critical resource to the growing nuclear-freeze movement of the early 1980s. There was an "elective affinity" between the wider social movement and the bishops' new religious message.

Martin, following Weber, seems more comfortable with a notion of social science as a human science, often narrative in its mode and employing a vocabulary that overlaps with the language actually used by the participants and actors in the story the sociologist tries to tell. Both sociology and theology employ highly metaphorical discourse. At their richest and best, sociological accounts link to and evoke the vocabularies of everyday usage. Sociological concepts are too close to everyday metaphorical language to be able to be translated into thoroughly mathematical terms. They cannot be abstracted from the concrete world or drained of its color and texture without losing explanatory power. Moreover, as Martin claims,

> It is a matter of observation that the language of sociology retains a continuity with the life-world and with its categories. Indeed, one has to admit that not only does it treat of a world of reflective human beings but it is itself almost chronically inclined to import ethical comment into scientific description. All attempts to dehydrate the language of social analysis, to cut off the relationship to ordinary discourse and to drain out the humanity have ended up ludicrously inadequate.[25]

As Gregory Baum notes in his book *Theology and Society*, "since society is a conflictual reality to which we ourselves belong, it is an illusion to think we can examine society from a neutral point of view."[26] Precisely the attempt by sociologists such as Robert Bellah to see the social sciences as moral sciences, as emanating from an exercise of practical reasoning (which always includes an ethical component), allows for an enriched conversation between theology and sociology.

Though both sociologists and theologians try to deploy the kinds of methodological, even distancing, rigor that seem appropriate to the material at hand, both also sift "soft" materials in such a way that "those trying to relate the precarious to the precarious may well lose their footing." Yet Martin does think that, in the end, a correlation between sociology and theology—provided we examine their correspondences and connections with care, and *do not reduce one level or discipline to the other*—may result in " mutual enrichment rather than mutual destruction."[27] Indeed, Gregory Baum can even claim that "sociology and theology move along the same line, and theology appears as the critical prolongation of sociological concepts."[28] After all, much of the territory they map (human agency; socialization; identity formation; the nature of human community; structural constraints on action; ritual; moral dilemmas and their structural settings; the social consequences and rootedness of symbolization) deeply overlaps. As Timothy Radcliffe once put it, "the sociologist is, in reality, neither the theologian's rival nor his executioner."[29]

Presupposition 2: Theology Cannot Avoid a Correlation with Sociology

Theology, willy-nilly, generates some discourse about the polity and the world. Every theology, then, implicitly contains a proto-sociology and even some presuppositions about social action. For example, most theological accounts so privilege face-to-face community that they remain relatively blind to structural sources of alienation and deformation or cultural bias. These accounts might find it difficult to speak in any meaningful terms of social sin. Frequently, theological discourse about the social is highly idealized and gives little attention to either ideological distortions (think of the Catholic social teaching on the common good which seems oblivious to differential power arrangements that ignore diverse social "interests") or opportunity costs in enacting the ideal view of the polity. Robin Gill has suggested that, since theology makes assumptions about the nature of society, we can legitimately ask sociological questions about the social determinants of theology, the social context of theology, and the social significance of theology.[30]

The Social Determinants of Theology

We have already seen abundant evidence of social determinants of theology in dealing with the sociological work of David Martin. But there is also a social context to theology. "Theologians," Gill notes, "tend to make claims about the society or culture within which they operate and then incorporate these claims into their theology. Sociological analysis could provide incisive and rigorous tools for the theologian to understand better the social context within which he operates."[31] As Martin trenchantly puts it, "There is no discipline more salutary to religious vision, or more helpful to understanding the empirical vicissitudes of vision than being forced to ask the basic questions as to what is actually the case and what is most likely to follow from a given course of action."[32]

The Social Context of Theology

Clearly, as we now know, social context has also shaped the forms of theology and their shifts, from a patristic theology rooted in episcopal voice and mainly pastoral concern, to the mystical theology of the Victorines, stemming from a monastic setting, to the more academic scholastic theology with the rise of the university. As Gregory Baum has claimed, theology varies in accord with 1) the social location of the Christian community; 2) the dominant culture to which it belongs; 3) the academic institution in which it is taught; and 4) the socio-economic class with which it is identified.[33] To take one example, Baum evokes the difference between German and French theology. The German theologian, as a university professor, well paid by the government, looks over his shoulder at his colleagues in philosophy and history to demonstrate that his own exercise of *Wissenschaft* conforms to their high standards. In France, where theology is taught in seminaries financed by the faithful, the theologian has the fervent Christian looking over her shoulder and wants to demonstrate that theology remains spiritual, sounds edifying, and nourishes religious sentiment.

David Martin reminds us, "Doctrines . . . do not land like meteorites from outer space but grow organically where they have a supporting, fertile niche or cranny."[34] Lester Kurtz's brilliant sociological study of the Vatican's response to modernism in his book *The Politics of Heresy* shows how some attention to the social context in which theology is done can help it face distortions in the theological tradition.[35] Robin Gill conjures the costs in not addressing the social context for theology. "The consequence of ignoring contemporary plausibility structures is for the theologians to produce work that may appear increasingly anachronistic."[36]

The Social Significance of Theology

Finally, Gill insists that theology needs to assume responsibility for its socio-political impact. It can, for example, add to the forces that stress individualism and the privatization of faith. It has, in history, fed into violence (the Crusades), anti-Semitism, and the attitudes that denigrate the full human dignity of women. Among the questions the sociologist tends to put to the theologian are the following. Is the sociology the theologian uses critically appropriated? On what bases is it chosen? How attentive are theologians to the theoretical and methodological presuppositions of a given sociological study on which they draw? When the theologian speaks of freedom and human agency—to use the terms Anthony Giddens employs in his important book, *The*

Constitution of Society—does she respect both free agency and social structure?[37] Do theologians attend, as a sociologist must, to the issue of the unintended consequences of human actions and social policy? Do preaching and theological teaching lead to any kind of enactment of what is believed, or does the practice of the church mirror the culture's bourgeois mores, for example? Clearly, as Robin Gill claims, when the practical theologian analyzes religious practice as it relates to religious faith, "his task would appear to be identical with that of the sociologist of religion."[38] It would not be too much for the sociologist to expect the practical theologian to have the requisite skills and theoretical acumen for that task.

Presupposition 3: Sociology, Especially a Hermeneutical and Critical Sociology, Has Much to Learn from a Practical Theology That Engages Ethical Reflection

It is easier to see how sociology could become an integral part of theology than vice versa. In his programmatic book, *A Fundamental Practical Theology: Descriptive and Strategic Proposals*, Don Browning argues that practical theology must engage "in close connection with descriptions of situations."[39] What he calls "descriptive theology," as one of the integral components of a fundamental practical theology, is quite close to hermeneutical understandings of sociology. Browning, of course, has a special expertise in both psychology and congregational studies. His more recent and brilliant book, *From Culture Wars to Common Ground: Religion and the American Family Debate*, is both an exemplar of the program he set out in *A Fundamental Practical Theology* and a conspicuously successful model of how to integrate sociology and theology. There Browning engages in structured interviews, mines the literature in socio-biology about the male problematic, conducts surveys of family therapists to show they are not, as Bellah contended in *Habits of the Heart*, merely devotees of "expressive individualism";[40] Browning contends that *From Culture Wars to Common Ground* differs from standard theological texts in that "we work hard not only to state the theological and ethical ideals that should govern families, but also to speak of the actual developmental and social conditions that allow them to be made manifest in the lives of persons."[41]

For Browning, "descriptive theology," the sociological component, is integral to a specialized version of practical theology. Moreover, the method of correlation he espouses, following David Tracy, means that in some sense all of theology must be practical. This is a more integrated view than that found in the Irish sociologist Kieran Flanagan's quirky yet original book, *The Enchantment of Sociology: A Study of Theology and Culture*, where Flanagan suggests that sociology can serve, in an ancillary role, "as fieldwork in theology."[42] In Flanagan's view, sociology's "theological calling" consists in its mission to explain how theologians can protect their cultural capital (in Pierre Bourdieu's sense of the term) from being misappropriated, trivialized, or traduced by commercial interests.[43]

The integration of sociology with theology—except for a few sociologists such as Bellah and Martin—is a tougher sell. In part, as the Cambridge University social scientist Graham Howes puts it: "Most academic sociologists remain, to paraphrase Weber, theologically unmusical, and theology, itself, is rarely read by them, let alone taken into intellectual account. . . . Their students, in turn, tend to see theology as an arcane and archaic sub-discipline, lacking the rigor of 'pure' philosophy, the intellectual chic of contemporary social theory or the breadth and stimulus of religious studies."[44]

With Emile Durkheim, I assume that sociology is, root and branch, a moral science. The great founders of sociology were concerned not just with change but with deformations that attended modernity. Durkheim could speak of an unacceptable level of anomie, Weber could refer to our modern situation as an iron cage, and Simmel (whose sociology Flanagan, by the way, shows to lie behind most of the theology of Hans Urs von Balthasar) could worry about the cultural effects of money in eroding a deep spiritual cultural ethos. From this vantage point, every sociology does have *a priori* assumptions (about the moral life, about human nature, about the desired image of the good society) that need to be teased out. Much of Browning's complaint about sociology as it is practiced (including a gentle critique of Bellah) is that sociologists never ground, in clear and explicit arguments, the choices that lead them to one or another assumption about human nature, the good society, and the moral life.[45]

Implicit Assumptions in Sociologies

As Alvin Gouldner, the pioneer in the United States of a critical, hermeneutical sociology, put it in his book *Enter Plato*, any diagnostic implies a therapeutic.[46] A theologian reading social science, then, will want to notice and make explicit in sociological theories and methods the following four implicit assumptions.

The Image of the Human That Is Employed

Is it mechanistic and deterministic? Does it allow room for human agency? Does it have a sufficient sense of tragedy and sin? I note, for example, that Browning and his co-authors in *From Culture Wars to Common Ground* say that "the best social science descriptions—as important as they are, seem to miss the reality of sin—a harsh and, for some, an incomprehensible concept."[47] David Martin would contest that point. Martin sees sociology attending to particular cramps, limits, distortions, and resistances, akin to the notion of sin. The problem with many of the theological concepts about human agency and sociability, Martin contends, including that of original sin, is their total lack of falsifiability. They explain everything and nothing. What Martin is getting at is a claim that key theological concepts (such as the spirit, original sin, agape) need to be fleshed out in terms of their meaning to concrete situations and limits to freedom, since these are the arenas that the sociologist treats. Martin, however, does yield to Browning's major point. "An acute and aggressive theologian may assist the sociological enterprise by noting the way sociologists 'frame' their understanding of social development, and utilize their social ontology independently of what the subject-matter itself may demand."[48]

The Sufficiency of the Social Science Account of the Primary Evil to Be Addressed

Is the primary evil, with Marx, mainly class injustices? Is it the rise of methodical bureaucracy, as in Weber? Is it the eclipse of the life-world, as in Alfred Schütz? Clearly, most social science studies of any phenomenon—the family, race relations, gender—define the obstacles or the sources of social problems as a species of evil to be eradicated or tamed. In this sense, sociology does have a sense of evil. Indeed, Flanagan thinks that sociology can help picture for theology the face of hell in the modern situation, delivering what Flanagan refers to as a kind of "revelation without grace."[49] Like Virgil to Dante, sociology shows to theology the contours and pathways of the devil and serves as a guide to the modern hell. Max Weber once made a similar point toward the end of his classic essay, "Politics as a Vocation."

The Account of What Is Going Forward in History

What trajectories does sociology project? Is it to late modernity or post-modernity or the end of history or a globalized village? Each of these senses—should I call them more teleological senses?—of where history and society is going, ingredient in sociological accounts, demand critical reflection and scrutiny about whether they are worthy of the human. They also call for a question about their inevitability. Is history, if constrained, nevertheless, always—as the Christian theologian must assert—in some sense open?

The Carriers of Transformation in Society

I assume, with Gregory Baum, that "social science is itself a reliable instrument of knowledge only if it is guided by a commitment to emancipation."[50] Clearly, sociology may not always be capable of an internal ideological critique of its own.

If I had one main quarrel with Browning's attempt to situate sociology as a sub-unit (what he calls descriptive theology) in a broader practical theology, it would be the danger of not seeing how the dialogue between sociology and theology must remain a two-way street. Let me explain with some pithy remarks about Milbank's tour de force but fundamentally wrong-headed book, *Theology and Social Theory*. I know almost no sociologist who is in agreement with Milbank. Martin has said of the book, "For all of its architectonic brilliance, Milbank's book is less useful to practitioners and less convincing because he devised a metadiscourse far above the analyses we actually carry out. Milbank engaged in obliteration bombing in which the whole discipline was obscured in a pall of smoke. We needed liberation, not elimination."[51] Certainly, no one would claim Milbank has much credibility as a commentator on the politically possible!

As those who know Milbank's book realize, he takes on all of modern secular reason, especially as it gets embodied in social science. He would have theology totally auto-generate its own sociology. He thinks that theology always encounters in sociology only another form of theology in disguise. When pushed, Milbank once quipped that he could, in fact, see some role for sociology—with the proviso that it become the instrument of the Christian faith. I think it very significant that, for all the wide sweep of his reading of sociologists, Milbank systematically neglects the British sociologists whose work he well knows, such as Martin and Flanagan, who are publicly Christian and who correlate their sociological work with theology, yet still insist on a rightful autonomy for their discipline.

While I have learned very much, indeed, from Milbank on some subordinate points, I agree with Aidan Nichols's response:

> Despite the numerous true judgments, good maxims and beautiful insights to be found scattered through this book, its overall message is deplorable. My objections can be summed up in two words: "hermeticism" and "theocracy." By hermeticism I mean, the enclosure of Christian discourse and practice within a wholly separate universe of thought and action, a universe constituted by the prior "mythos" of Christianity. . . . For Milbank there can be no such thing as an intellectual indebtedness of the Church to natural wisdom. . . . The church "pro-exists" for all humanity; but in the meanwhile, before her mission is divinely completed, she must co-exist, with other aggregates of the human members of the creation.[52]

In a similar vein, Gregory Baum faults Milbank's total rejection of a quasi-autonomous sociology. The Christian metanarrative, Baum suggests, may have its own deformations (as in anti-Semitism and patriarchy). Thus, argues Baum, "I insist against Milbank that the church [read also theology here] must be open to its critics, whether they be the victims of society [including the victims of the church, I would add] or the modern masters of suspicion and more than this, that the biblical tradition itself will unfold its full meaning and power only through critical interactions of this kind." Again, Baum on Milbank: "I am puzzled by Milbank's inability to marvel at goodness found beyond the community of believers. He seems to have no sense of 'the irony of the gospel.' Like Jonah, Milbank does not want to believe that God can be merciful to Nineveh."[53]

In a recent paper, Jean Porter captures my sentiments exactly about Milbank's and Hauerwas's projects of a Christian ethics auto-generating its own sociological discourse: "The currently popular idea of a purely Christian morality, which is self-contained, self-justifying and unintelligible to everyone else, seems to me to be as unrealistic as the Enlightenment ideal of a universal morality, which is its mirror image."[54]

Clearly, those who would try to auto-generate their own sociology from theology as Milbank does, would, in fact, have to end up doing something like a correlation. They cannot simply reinvent the wheel or engage in a refutation of "secular" sociology without engaging more closely—element by element and methodological avenue by avenue—its theories, methods, and conceptual schemes. It may be that the anthropological presuppositions of a given sociology (such as Weber's radical pluralism of goods that are simply in conflict) are inimical to theology. Theology will need to raise these up and show if and where they contaminate other elements in the sociological account. It strikes me, for example, that Weber's value polytheism has little direct bearing on his phenomenological method in sociology or on his account of bureaucracy or charism and its routinization. It eludes me why one would reject "secular" sociology root and branch, as Milbank suggests we do. You will see from my reaction to Milbank my problem with Browning's proposal to locate sociology almost entirely as a subunit controlled throughout by the larger project of a practical theology. It runs the danger of taming the autonomous voice and critique of sociology to theology. As I understand it, the pre-condition for a fruitful correlational dialogue absolutely presupposes some respect for the different levels and purposes of discourse (and diverging methods) in theology and the social sciences.

An Exemplary Correlational Text Combining Sociology and Theology

Limitations of space allow me merely to sketch the argument and indicate the integral role of sociology in Robin Gill's *Churchgoing and Christian Ethics.* In many ways, Gill is the doyen of those who try to relate sociology and theology. If I were ever again to teach a graduate seminar on theology and sociology—as I once did with Robert Bellah in Berkeley—Gill's book would be required reading as a kind of paradigm. Ethics is a natural meeting point for the two disciplines since the force of any "ought" implicates attention to some "can."

Gill is intrigued by the turn toward an emphasis on character and virtue in ethics. Yet he notes that many Christian ethicists who turn to virtue ethics, principally Hauerwas, exhibit an ambivalence about the moral communities necessary to socialize people in virtue and to anchor character. It is never quite clear, for example, in Hauerwas, whether he is discussing the church as an ideal community or an actual one. It is hard, for example, to see his actual Methodist church as a sanctuary for resident aliens! Like Milbank, Hauerwas shows an increasing exaggeration of both Christian distinctiveness and worldly secularity where never the twain can meet. Hauerwas faces an obvious dilemma: "The church as it ought to be can enshrine Christian virtues properly, but unfortunately it can not socialize Christians in the actual world. The church as it is can indeed socialize Christians but sadly it does not enshrine Christian virtues properly."[55]

Just how well do the Christian churches succeed in socializing in Christian virtue? Sociologists sometimes despair—every bit as much as the Christian virtue ethicists—in finding any interesting distinctiveness in real churches. Yet there is a crucial sociological variable, churchgoing, which, if used as the explanatory or independent variable, actually shows a consistent, if relative, distinctiveness of attitudes and behaviors among active, fully participating church members. Churchgoing seems to have vastly similar effects, whether the church one goes to is evangelical, Catholic, or Anglican. Gill turns to a rich data source in the European Values Surveys and a number of British, American, Irish, and Australian data sets, which allows him a very careful control on the variable of churchgoing: weekly, monthly, several times a year, only to weddings and funerals, not at all but once was a churchgoer, never a churchgoer. Churchgoing, Gill successfully demonstrates, is a socially and morally significant sociological factor. It anchors and predicts belief rather than vice versa. Those who regularly attend church show up in sociological data sets as: 1) showing more concern for the vulnerable and needy than non-churchgoers; 2) more opposed to easy solutions to life issues such as abortion, euthanasia, and capital punishment; 3) more likely to see purpose in life; 4) more liable to support moral and social order; 5) more concerned with the environment; 6) less racist; 7) associated with concern for and a greater sense of being able to make a positive contribution to world problems; 8) more engaged in the political order (such as by voting or by writing representatives in Parliament); 9) more likely to be engaged in voluntary activities within their communities; 10) more likely to show concern for declining moral standards.

Gill's argument is subtle and nuanced, as is his use of sociology. For the sociologist, part of the power of Gill's book is that it builds a cultural theory of religion, linked to churchgoing, contrary to the secularization theory (which mistakenly assumes that the erosion of belief antedates the erosion of church attendance), contrary also to the opposite belief (such as that found in the work of Andrew Greeley) of a total persistence of religion with no real declines, and contrary to those who postulate a break between belief and belonging (which Gill shows to be, largely, an after-effect of earlier churchgoing behaviors, now abandoned). Gill argues, drawing on Giddens's claims about a dispersed self in late modernity, that "churchgoing fosters a distinctive culture, and therefore, can sustain a sense of personal identity" in a culture where that is hard to achieve.[56] It is important to understand well what Gill is trying to do here. He does not, either sociologically or theologically, equate Christianity with churchgoing. Clearly, for example, some groups (such as Hispanics in the United States) may continue to foster a vital family religion in the absence of active churchgoing, although, even in this example, Hispanic churchgoers show a different profile from purely cultural and family Catholics. Yet in cultures that lack the rich religious after-effects of earlier Catholicism, attention to churchgoing becomes a crucial variable to understand the moral impact of churches. Actual churches, in sociological fact, do serve as moral communities. When churchgoing can be controlled carefully as an independent variable (and is tracked directionally by comparing weekly or monthly churchgoers with those who once went to church and those who never did) the evidence seems overwhelming that the distinctiveness of churchgoers is quite real, if relative.

Gill wants us to be careful about making overly grand claims for the church. It remains an earthen vessel. He also warns against assuming—as Hauerwas and Milbank seemingly do—that the "secular" world is more distinctively "secular" than it really is. Like many sociological accounts, the argument is statistical. It does not yield totally zero-sum or either-or pictures of churchgoers and non-churchgoers. Nonetheless, Gill's very careful wedding of theological ethics with close sociological study challenges theologians who do virtue ethics:

> Virtue ethics makes assumptions about moral socialization which do need to be tested empirically. The depictions of idealized

communities are simply inadequate for this task. Of course, actual, as distinct from idealized, communities are likely to be ambiguous and messy moral carriers. People argue and fight, they disagree and conflict, and even in the most conformist communities there are always idiosyncratic non-conformists. Church communities are no exceptions. Making grand claims is just too easy. Making claims which actually fit the ambiguities of church and society is much more difficult. It might be helpful to gain a more accurate picture of churchgoing as it is before deciding what it should be.[57]

Notes

[1]Robert N. Bellah, *Beyond Belief: Essays on Religion in a Post-Traditional World* (New York: Harper & Row, 1970), 206.

[2]William Everett and T. J. Birchmeyer, *Christianity, Personality and Society* (Washington, D.C.: University Press of America, 1971).

[3]Gibson Winter, *Elements for a Social Ethic: Scientific and Ethical Perspectives on Social Progress* (Chicago: University of Chicago Press, 1969).

[4]Robin Gill, *Churchgoing and Christian Ethics* (New York: Cambridge University Press, 1999).

[5]John Milbank, *Theology and Social Theory: Beyond Secular Reason* (New York: Basil Blackwell, 1991).

[6]Bellah, *Beyond Belief*, 245; Robert Bellah et al., *The Good Society: We Live Through Our Institutions* (New York: Alfred Knopf, 1991), 16.

[7]David Martin, *Reflections on Sociology and Theology* (New York: Oxford University Press, 1997), 22.

[8]Timothy Radcliffe, "A Theological Assessment of Sociological Explanation," in *Theology and Sociology: A Reader*, ed. Robin Gill (London: Cassell, 1996), 170.

[9]Michael Polanyi, *Personal Knowledge: Towards a Post-Critical Philosophy* (Chicago: University of Chicago Press, 1958).

[10]Gregory Baum, *Religion and Alienation: A Theological Reading of Sociology* (New York: Paulist Press, 1979), 258.

[11]Martin, *Reflections on Sociology and Theology*, 101.

[12]David Martin, *A General Theory of Secularization* (New York: Macmillan, 1970); David Martin, *Tongues of Fire: The Explosion of Protestantism in Latin America* (New York: Basil Blackwell, 1990).

[13]Martin, *Reflections on Sociology and Theology*, 227-228.

[14]Rodney Stark and William Bainbridge, *The Future of Religion: Secularization, Revival and Cult Formation* (Berkeley: University of California Press, 1985).

[15]Martin, *Reflections on Sociology and Theology*, 6.

[16]Ibid., 242.

[17]Ibid., 67.

[18]Ibid., 36.

[19]Wade Clark Roof, *A Generation of Seekers: The Spiritual Journeys of the Baby Boom Generation* (San Francisco: Harpers, 1992); Wade Clark Roof, *Spiritual Marketplace: Baby Boomers and the Remaking of American Religion* (Princeton, N.J.: Princeton University Press, 1999), 309.

[20]Roof, *Spiritual Marketplace*, 53.

[21]This description, cited by Roof (*Spiritual Marketplace,* 64), is from Robert Wuthnow, *The Restructuring of American Religion* (Princeton, N.J.: Princeton University Press, 1988), 55.

[22]Anthony Giddens, *Modernity and Self Identity: Self and Society in the Late Modern Age* (Cambridge: Polity Press, 1990).

[23]Donald Miller, *Re-Inventing American Protestantism: Christianity in the New Millennium* (Berkeley: University of California Press, 1977).

[24]Meyer Zald and John McCarthy, eds., *Social Movements in an Organizational Society: Collected Essays* (New Brunswick: Transaction Books, 1987).

[25]Martin, *Reflections on Sociology and Theology*, 51.

[26]Gregory Baum, *Theology and Society* (New York: Paulist, 1987), 169.

[27]Martin, *Reflections on Sociology and Theology*, 73.

[28]Baum, *Religion and Alienation*, 263.

[29]Radcliffe, "A Theological Assessment of Sociological Explanation," 166.

[30]Robin Gill, "Social Variables Within Applied Theology," in Robin Gill, ed., *Theology and Sociology: A Reader* (New York: Paulist Press, 1987), 329-330.

[31]Robin Gill, "Sociology Assessing Theology," in Gill, *Theology and Sociology*, 147.

[32]Martin, *Reflections on Sociology and Theology,* 18.

[33]Gregory Baum, "The Sociology of Roman Catholic Theology," in David Martin, John Mills, and W. S. F. Pickering, eds., *Sociology and Theology: Alliance and Conflict* (New York: St. Martin's Press, 1980), 127.

[34]Martin, *Reflections on Sociology and Theology*, 69.

[35]Lester Kurtz, *The Politics of Heresy: The Modernist Crisis in Roman Catholicism* (Berkeley: University of California Press, 1986).

[36]Gill, "Sociology Assessing Theology," 148.

[37]Anthony Giddens, *The Constitution of Society: Outline of the Theory of Structuration* (Palo Alto, Calif.: Stanford University Press, 1989).

[38]Gill, "Social Variables Within Applied Theology," 325. Clearly, the work of Princeton sociologist Robert Wuthnow is quite germane to this dialogue between theology and social science. His books, *Acts of Compassion: Caring for Others and Helping Ourselves* (Princeton, N.J.: Princeton University Press, 1991); *Sharing the Journey: Support Groups and America's New Quest for Community* (New York: Basic Books, 1994); *God and Mammon in America* (New York: The Free Press, 1994); *After Heaven: Spirituality in America Since the 1950s* (Berkeley: University of California Press, 1998), have much to teach the practical theologian about religious voluntarism, small group formations in congregations, stewardship teaching in churches, and spirituality. I have not lifted up his work in the body of this essay

because he does not explicitly try to correlate theology and sociology, although his sociology of religion does feed into concerns of practical theology.

[39]Don S. Browning, *A Fundamental Practical Theology: Descriptive and Strategic Proposals* (Minneapolis: Fortress Press, 1991).

[40]Don S. Browning et. al., *From Culture Wars to Common Ground: Religion and the American Family Debate* (Louisville: Westminster/John Knox, 1997).

[41]Ibid.

[42]Kieran Flanagan, *The Enchantment of Sociology: A Study of Theology and Culture* (New York: St. Martin's Press, 1996), 6.

[43]Cf. Pierre Bourdieu and Loic Wacquant, *An Invitation to Reflexive Sociology* (Chicago: University of Chicago Press, 1992).

[44]Graham Howes, "Surprised by Grace: The Sociologist's Dilemma," *New Blackfriars* 78:913 (March 1997): 136. This whole issue is devoted to review articles of Flanagan's book.

[45]This was the brunt of Browning's paper, "The Turn to the Practical in Social Science and Theology," given in November 1997 at a special session of the American Academy of Religion devoted to Bellah's work.

[46]Alvin Gouldner, *Enter Plato: Classical Greece and the Origins of Social Theory* (New York: Basic Books, 1965).

[47]Browning et al., *From Culture Wars to Common Ground*, 70.

[48]Martin, *Reflections on Sociology and Theology*, 25.

[49]Flanagan, *The Enchantment of Sociology*, 8.

[50]Baum, *Theology and Society*, 72.

[51]David Martin, "Theology and Sociology: The Irish Flaneur's Account," *New Blackfriars* 78:913 (March 1997): 110.

[52]Aidan Nichols, O.P., "*Non Tali Auxilio*: John Milbank's Suasion to Orthodoxy," in *New Blackfriars* 73:836 (January 1992): 327. This whole issue is devoted to review articles of Milbank's book.

[53]Gregory Baum, "For and Against John Milbank," in *Essays in Critical Theology*, ed. Gregory Baum (Kansas City: Sheed & Ward, 1994), 70, 75.

[54]Jean Porter, "Catholic Social Thought and the Natural Law Tradition," unpublished paper delivered at the *Commonweal* magazine symposium on "Catholics in the Public Square," May 13, 2000.

[55]Gill, *Churchgoing and Christian Ethics*, 19.

[56]Ibid., 197.

[57]Ibid., 261, 30.

Whose Theology? Which Sociology?

A Response to John Coleman

Michael J. Baxter, C.S.C.

As a way of demonstrating the validity of the statement that "every theology implies a sociology and vice versa," John Coleman takes us on a tour "of theologians who use sociology as a truly integral . . . part of their enterprise," and "of sociologists who can be said to be truly tutored in and informed by theology." The tour features several landmark figures whose work recognizes the interdependence of theology and sociology: Gregory Baum, David Martin, Patricia Wittberg, Wade Clark Roof, Don Browning, Robert Bellah, and especially Robin Gill, "the doyen of those who try to relate sociology and theology" (p. 28), whose recent book, *Churchgoing and Christian Ethics*, Coleman commends as an example of how to do it well. The tour also warns us away from one theologian who does not relate theology and sociology very well at all, namely, John Milbank, whose work functions as a counter-example in Coleman's paper. In my response, I focus on this counter-example.

It is in the context of stating his "one main quarrel with [Don] Browning's attempt to situate sociology as a sub-unit . . . in a broader practical theology" that Coleman offers his "pithy remarks about Milbank's tour de force but fundamentally wrong-headed book, *Theology and Social Theory*" (p. 26). Browning runs "the danger of not seeing how the dialogue between sociology and theology must remain a two-way street," and the same is true of Milbank, who "would have theology totally auto-generate its own sociology. He thinks that theology always encounters in sociology only another form of theology in disguise." It is true, Coleman acknowledges, that "when pushed, Milbank once quipped that he could, in fact, see some role for sociology—with the proviso that it become the instrument of the Christian faith." But this concession does not allay Coleman's concern because, in his view, it is only by correlating the findings of theology and sociology, not subordinating one to the other, that the two can learn from each other, yet still retain their autonomy as academic disciplines. Indeed, Coleman maintains that "those who would try to auto-generate their own sociology from theology, as Milbank does, would, in fact, have to end up doing something like a correlation"; that is to say, they would have to engage secular sociology "more closely—element by element and methodological avenue by avenue—its theories, methods, and conceptual schemes," and this means not rejecting it "root and branch," but presupposing "some respect for the different levels and purposes of discourse (and diverging methods) in theology and the social sciences" (p. 28).

Coleman's call for a more careful engagement of theology with the methods and specific findings of sociology is certainly appropriate, but his criticism as a whole does not address the central concerns of Milbank's argument and thus does not effectively refute his critique of sociology. Milbank's argument is directed, first, against the tendency in sociology to provide explanations of actions and events in terms of causes (market forces, dynamics of bureaucratic culture, psychological alienation) that are external to theology and work to supplant theologically informed explanations, and second, against the habit of theologians to allow such functional explanations to control their own explanations of socio-religious phenomena. The result has been that genuine theological explanations are excluded from consideration; either explicitly as in the case of Weber or Durkheim, or implicitly, as in the case with sociologists of religion who confine theology to a interior realm of religious "belief" or to an ahistorical sphere of religious "meaning." The problem, in Aristotelian-Thomistic terms, is that final and formal causes are ruled out of explanations altogether, in favor of efficient causes, deemed to be the only causes that meet scientific standards of empirical demonstration and verification. And for Milbank, the solution, in these same terms, is to retrieve this medieval vision of causality such that events and actions can be explained in terms of the complex interrelationship of final, formal, and efficient causes, the overall operation of which is ultimately mysterious and can only be accounted for in traditional theological categories. Hence the declaration at the outset of the final chapter of *Theology and Social Theory*:

> Theology has frequently sought to borrow from elsewhere a fundamental account of society or history, and then to see what theological insights cohere with it. But it has been shown that no such fundamental account, in the sense of something neutral, rational and universal, is really available. It is theology itself that will have to provide its own account of the final causes at work in human history, on the basis of its own particular, and historically specific faith.[1]

Granted, this argument, scattered as it is throughout *Theology and Social Theory*,[2] does not provide us with many clues as to how, specifically, final, formal, and efficient causes are to be related in the explanation of concrete events. There is a need for more specificity here, and Coleman is right to point it out. But when he goes on to assert the necessity, indeed the inevitability, of a "correlation" between theology and sociology, he misunderstands or simply neglects a leading emphasis in Milbank's argument.

Let me explain. A method of correlation assumes a division of labor between the fields of sociology and theology, with sociology providing empirically based descriptions and explanations of social phenomena and theology reflecting on these descriptions and explanations.[3] Milbank contends that sociology's descriptions and explanation are always already value-laden, hence always already informed by a theology of one sort or another, and therefore open to theological interrogation. Coleman, if I read him rightly, would respond that this is true, but that the relationship is dialogical, in which case theology's assertions are open to sociological interrogation as well. Here Milbank would agree, but only to a point. He would agree that sociology can assist in the work of theology, and he says so explicitly when he acknowledges a place for sociological (and Marxist) critiques of religion in terms of what he call an "*ad hoc* reductive suspicion."[4] But he would also argue that the validity of all sociological descriptions and explanations and their position within the overall Christian narrative must ultimately be determined by theology. This is not a simple task, according to Milbank; the process of "dealing with suspicion," he explains, is "a matter of complex narrative negotiations," which involves "retelling the ecclesial story so as to accept some external criticisms, now made into self-criticisms, and to rebut others. . . ."[5] But it is, he insists, a properly theological task, which is why theology must be restored to its position of "queen of the sciences."[6]

Herein lies the conflict. Coleman opposes granting theology this position of primacy over the social sciences and proposes instead that we look at their relationship as a two-way street. But he provides no account of how traffic is to be regulated on this two-way street. Indeed, for Coleman, it seems that no traffic regulations are necessary. "As I understand it," he writes, "the pre-condition for a fruitful correlational dialogue absolutely presupposes some respect for the different levels and purposes of discourse (and diverging methods) in theology and the social sciences" (p. 28). The image of different levels, purposes, and methods seems to imply that theology and sociology travel in different lanes, but on different streets. But Milbank says they travel on the same street, that more often than not they collide, and that the fault lies primarily with sociology, which from its founding has consistently reached beyond the limited tasks of purely data-based description and no-more-than-partial explanation to put forth full-blown (albeit implicit) accounts of the nature and purpose of human society. Now, if Coleman wants to argue that "dialogue" between theology and the social sciences need not be so conflicted, that we should dismiss Milbank's critique of sociology and embrace his notion of "correlational dialogue," then he will have to pursue two lines of argumentation.

First, he will have to show that Milbank's account of the nature of the discipline of sociology is fundamentally flawed. Specifically, he will have to show that the leading practitioners in the field—from its founders (Weber, Durkheim), to more recent leading lights (Parsons, Geertz), to those who have directly delved into the areas of bibilical studies and the sociology of religion (Gottwald, Meeks, Bellah, Luhmann, Berger, Turner)—do not privilege sociological descriptions and explanations of society over theological ones and therefore do not foreclose a genuine dialogue between theology and sociology, correlational or otherwise. In addition to providing a close reading and rebuttal of the comprehensive and rather complex argument set forth in chapter 5 of *Theology and Social Theory*, Coleman will have to explain why we should not interpret the widespread neglect of theology by sociologists working in the field today as evidence in support of Milbank's argument. In order to ensure that we are dealing here with "hard data," perhaps the place to begin would be with a poll that queries the membership of the American Sociological Association as to the place of theology in their own sociological research. This poll might include such questions as: What is the relevance of the doctrine of the

Trinity to your conception of society? How does the doctrine of the two natures of Christ inform your view of the possibility of moral achievement? What role does the Eucharist play in your understanding of resurrection and the immortality of the soul? Do these beliefs and practices have any place in your scholarship? Do you have even a basic understanding of these beliefs and practices? If such questions were to be asked of the sociologists *doing* the research (not, please note, the people *being* researched), I think we would find that the field of sociology as a whole affords little place for dialogue with theology. It is true that Coleman himself is not happy with the state of the field in this regard, but nowhere in his paper does he entertain the possibility that this situation might be connected to the secular conceptions of society of which Milbank is so critical.

Second, he will have to provide a theological account of "correlational dialogue." Presumably, this account would draw on theologians such as Schleiermacher, Tillich, Tracy, and others whose work has contributed in some way to a method of correlation in theology and the accompanying notion of functional specialties proffered by Lonergan.[7] It would also have to defend this approach against the criticisms of Frei, Lindbeck, and others associated with the so-called "Yale School" in theology.[8] Moreover, and more importantly for our purposes, it would have to respond to the well-developed critique of the trend in Catholic theology to underwrite the discourses of social science in the name of mediation, when in fact what occurs is a full-scale supplanting of a genuine theological conception of the social by a totalizing secular conception.[9] But Coleman does not offer any such account. The paper is virtually devoid of theological argumentation. No references are made to theological works, except those critical of Milbank, and these brief criticisms are cited but not supported (p. 27).[10] No issues are taken up by means of the terms and categories of pneumatology, ecclesiology, eschatology, or soteriology. No perspective is advanced on the basis of the Trinity. No appeal is made to the person and work of Jesus Christ (who is never mentioned by name). Given the title of the paper, one might reasonably expect a theological account of "correlational dialogue" and a defense against Milbank's implicit but unmistakable critique of it, but there is none. So in what sense can Coleman's view of the relationship between theology and sociology be described as dialogical?

It might be pointed out, of course, that Coleman is working within the limits of a short paper, which does not afford a full-length treatment of things theological. But this is beside the point, inasmuch as his paper concludes with an enthusiastic endorsement of Robin Gill's *Churchgoing and Christian Ethics*, which, according to Coleman, serves as a model of how to integrate theology and sociology; for this book is not deeply shaped by theological terms and categories either. This is not to say that the book lacks any theological reference. On the contrary, there is a lengthy presentation of the relationship among Christian beliefs, practices, virtues, and churchgoing.[11] Nevertheless, the book as a whole is not a work of theology per se, but of "ethics," which, as Coleman explains, "is a natural meeting point for the two disciplines [theology and sociology] since the force of any 'ought' implicates attention to some 'can' " (p. 21). Consider this conception of ethics. For Coleman and Gill, theology has to do with beliefs, doctrines, ideals, moral norms, all of which are classified under the heading of "ought"; sociology measures the level of adherence to these beliefs, doctrines, ideals, and moral norms by actual Christian communities, which is classified under the heading "is"; and ethics mediates between the two, as the discipline that negotiates the tension of the "is" and "ought" of Christian life. What is crucial to note here is that while theology has a function in this framework, it is a function that recedes as we move from ought to is, from the ideal to the real, from moral principles to practical applications. This is why Gill can engage in an extended discussion of moral conflict in the Anglican Church (thirty pages) without explicating in detail the theological reasons why one would believe, for example, that polygamy, homosexuality, and divorce are contrary to the natural law, impediments to human flourishing that are morally prohibited. Rather, the emphasis is on whether or not Christians actually do conform to such moral norms; and if not, whether the Anglican Church will have the foresight and flexibility to change its teaching accordingly, or will succumb to the machinations of the small faction of conservatives within its own ranks.[12] The implication throughout this discussion is that such moral prohibitions are ideals that for many people are not realizable in practice. This is a widely held position in the field of Christian ethics, but it is hardly the only one; and yet Gill does not address the moral-theological arguments for subscribing to a "conservative" position, such as the one put forth by Pope John Paul II who, in *Veritatis Splendor*, argues against the notion that it is impossible to fulfill the com-

descriptions have explanations embedded into them, and all sociological explanations are nothing more than a certain kind of historical description. In this case, both history and sociology are dedicated to constructing narratives of various sorts, in which case there is no ultimate difference between the two disciplines. See Milbank, *Theology and Social Theory*, 110-12.

[4]Ibid., 119.

[5]Ibid., 268.

[6]Ibid., 380.

[7]Friedrich Schleiermacher, *The Christian Faith*, 2 vols., ed. H. R. Mackintosh and J. S. Stewart (New York: Harper & Row, 1963); Paul Tillich, *Systematic Theology*, Vol. 1 (Chicago: University of Chicago Press, 1951); David Tracy, *Blessed Rage for Order: The New Pluralism in Theology* (New York: Seabury, 1975); Bernard Lonergan, *Method in Theology* (1972; Toronto: University of Toronto Press, 1990), 125-45.

[8]Hans Frei, *The Eclipse of the Biblical Narrative: A Study in Eighteenth and Nineteenth Century Hermeneutics* (New Haven: Yale University Press, 1974); George Lindbeck, *The Nature of Doctrine: Religion and Theology in a Postliberal Age* (Philadelphia: Westminster, 1984); Bruce Marshall, *Christology in Conflict: The Identity of a Savior in Rahner and Barth* (Oxford: Basil Blackwell, 1987).

[9]See Milbank, *Theology and Social Theory*, 206-55.

[10]Some of the criticisms to which Coleman appeals are quite misleading. For example, Coleman cites Nichols's contention that "for Milbank there can be no such thing as an intellectual indebtedness of the Church to natural wisdom" (p. 27). But this is a misleading criticism. While it is true that Milbank is certainly suspicious of the "wisdom" produced by secular disciplines of the social sciences, it should be noted that this modern "wisdom" is by no means "natural"; indeed, the case can be made on christological grounds that it should be seen as profoundly "*un*natural." On the other hand, Milbank makes extensive use of Platonic and neo-Platonic themes, which can be rightly regarded as containing "natural" wisdom. Indeed, he has been criticized for relying too heavily on Platonism and not enough on distinctively Christian themes.

To take another example, Coleman also cites Gregory Baum's critique of Milbank for his lack of openness to critics of the church, his inability to find goodness beyond the community of believers, his lack of any sense of the irony in the gospel, and his refusal to believe that God is merciful to Nineveh, i.e., those beyond the boundaries of Israel and the church. Each of these charges can be traced to Baum's misreading of Milbank's understanding of the church, which, as Baum reads it, is sectarian (though he does not use the word). Baum writes: "The true Church, for Milbank, is an egalitarian, pacifist community, pacifist not only in the refusal to take up arms but more profoundly in extending love and forgiveness to the perpetrators of evil—an Anabaptist, Mennonite ecclesial project, expressed today in the work of John Howard Yoder and Stanley Hauerwas" (Gregory Baum, "For and Against John Milbank," in *Essays in Critical Theology* [Kansas City, Mo.: Sheed & Ward, 1994], 54). This is a distortion of Milbank's position. Milbank's ecclesiology is not Anabaptist. To the contrary, he presses toward a vision of a restored Christendom; not, however, along the lines of the restored monarchy, but a restored Christian community as implied in a renewed Christian socialism. Accordingly, Milbank is not a pacifist either, and nothing in his writing explicitly says otherwise. Indeed, as is clear by the end of the book, Milbank regards himself as an Augustinian and, in good Augustinian fashion, he is willing to justify the use of coercion to curb the deleterious effects of sin during this interval of time when worldly *dominium* and worldly peace are unavoidable. And yet, also in good Augustinian fashion, this readiness to employ discipline is done in the name of charity and enfolded into the larger and more comprehensive reality of the forgiveness of sins, so that the recipient of discipline, once transformed, will be able to look back upon it, retrospectively, as an instance of divine mercy. The argument here is nuanced and complex (various portions of it can be found in Milbank, *Theology and Social Theory*, 290-2, 398-406, 412-15, 417-22). Suffice it to say that Baum does not go into the intricacies of Milbank's argument.

[11]Robin Gill, *Churchgoing and Christian Ethics* (New York: Cambridge University Press, 1999), 197-229.

[12]Ibid., 230-60.

[13]Pope John Paul II, *Veritatis Splendor*, 102-3.

[14]For Gill's dependence on Troeltsch, see *Churchgoing and Christian Ethics*, 204, 241, 243, 259.

[15]Milbank, *Theology and Social Theory*, 116.

Theological Manners

How Theologians Should Behave in Public

Boyd Blundell

In the past forty years, there has been a significant shift in American Catholic theology toward an attitude that is resolutely *public*. This phenomenon has so much moral momentum that the common antonym for "public" is no longer "private," but rather "sectarian." Those unwilling to give publicly accessible theological arguments are considered not so much wrong as rude. This shift of criteria raises the odd question of "good manners" in theology. There is a widely accepted etiquette to public discussion, one that demands a certain personal detachment from its participants. Anyone who openly demonstrates too much personal involvement in their inquiry implies that those who are not similarly involved are actually unable to understand the view of those who are. This is now considered a serious breach of etiquette. Such ill-mannered behavior can bring public discussion to a grinding halt. It is rude.

This etiquette is particularly demanding in the academy, where the demand for detachment is clearly articulated, and it is the task of this essay to explore what is at stake when theologians take it upon themselves to behave as well-mannered members of the academy. Even if theology is to be presented as, to use David Tracy's phrase, a "fully critical modern discipline," there remains the question of how theology plays that role. Is theology a full-fledged member of the social sciences, with all the academic acceptance that goes with it? If so, what is it that theology has to offer? If not, how does theology relate to the academy in general and to philosophy and the social sciences in particular?

In considering these questions, I will restrict myself to a brief engagement of the single significant attempt to provide a public model for theology in the academy: David Tracy's fundamental theology. In doing this, I hope to expose one of the inherent tensions that exists between the word "public" and the word "theology." I will first outline what is involved in Tracy's theological model, especially the fundamental specialty that outlines what is required for theology to be public. I will then turn to two remarkably similar criticisms that come from opposite directions. Jürgen Habermas, whose discourse ethics is appropriated by Tracy, criticizes Tracy from the side of the academic public that fundamental theology addresses. Stanley Hauerwas, sectarian extraordinaire and widely considered to be bad manners personified, criticizes Tracy's approach from the "theological" perspective that is to be modeled.[1] The fact that they reach the same negative conclusion from their radically different world-views suggests a crucial flaw in Tracy's model. This flaw will then be explored in terms of fundamental loyalties and good manners. The paper will conclude by offering suggestions as to how Tracy's "functional specialties" of theology could be reconfigured (e.g., widening the scope of the "systematic" specialty) to better maintain the integrity of theology in its conversations with other academic disciplines.

Tracy's Theological Model

Fundamental Theology

Tracy's correlationist model divides theology into three "functional disciplines," *fundamental, systematic*, and *practical* theology. These are held together by two hermeneutical constants: a theologian will always be involved in interpreting 1) a religious tradition; and 2) the "religious dimension" of a contemporary situation. Each specialty, however, is quite distinct within the constraints of those two constants. Each has its own reference group, mode of argument, ethical stance, faith-understanding, and formulation of meaning/truth. Here we are concerned primarily with the *fundamental* specialty, since this is the specialty whose primary reference group, its public, is the academy. The mode of discourse for fundamental theologians involves "arguments that all reasonable persons, whether 'religiously involved' or not, can recognize as reasonable." Their ethical stance is one of "honest, critical inquiry." Regarding their faith-understanding, fundamental theologians will, regardless of confessional stance:

> . . . in principle abstract themselves from all religious "faith commitments" for the legitimate purposes of critical analysis of all religious and theological claims. They will insist upon the need to articulate the arguments for theological discourse as openly public arguments in the obvious sense of argued, reasoned positions open to all intelligent, reasonable and responsible persons.[2]

Tracy portrays the fundamental theologian as a mediator. As a Christian, any theologian has a commitment to the texts and practices of Christianity. As a modern academic, the fundamental theologian also has a commitment to rational scientific inquiry. The task of the theologian is to correlate the two; to bring the Christian tradition to bear on an analysis of the "religious dimension" of human experience, and vice versa.[3] However, Tracy suggests that the particular publicness of fundamental theology requires that it submit itself to scientific scrutiny, and when the fundamental theologian is forced to choose between the two, it is tradition that comes out on the short end: "In principle, the fundamental loyalty of the theologian *qua* theologian is to that morality of scientific knowledge which he shares with his colleagues, the philosophers, historians, and social scientists. No more than they, can he allow his own—or his tradition's—beliefs to serve as warrants for his arguments."[4]

Theology, which stubbornly refuses to engage in correlating its positions to competing positions in the context of secular modernity, runs the risk of dying as a serious academic discipline, unable to meet the demystifying demands of the Enlightenment. Essential to the project is an optimism regarding the possibility of such a correlation, a belief that Christianity *can* ultimately be fused with secular reason and has little to fear from such a process. The ground for this optimism is that the secularist has a faith in "the ultimate significance and final worth of our lives," which is what Tracy means by "the morality of scientific knowledge" in the citation above. The secularist, however, lacks the "existentially appropriate symbolic representation" by which to express his faith, and the Christian tradition can provide this.[5]

The consequence of this is that when expressing truth claims, fundamental theologians must adapt to the general conversation structure of the academic community in which they operate. This involves tailoring their message to the restrictions regarding topic, warrants, and standards that are prevalent in the community. To ascertain what impact this might have on theological truth claims, we must consider these parameters in the concrete.

Public Discourse

Tracy's description of what constitutes public discourse in the academy is an appropriation of Jürgen Habermas's discourse ethics. This model divides possible modes of discussion into two major categories: the public realm and the life world.

The public realm is the arena of public discussion where "all participants, whatever their other particular differences, can meet to discuss any claim that is rationally redeemable."[6] There are no topics that are excluded *a priori* from such a discussion, though in practice many topics will not survive the criteria for discourse.[7] In this arena, the criterion for legitimate interaction is argumentation, where one must offer "good reasons" for the statements one makes. These reasons must appeal to publicly verifiable norms or scientific facts, not to traditional authorities recognized only by the speaker.

The life world is where we operate for the vast majority of our time. Religion, art, culture, and family are all elements of the life world. The formation of our opinions, the development of our tastes, the inculcation of our moral values, all of this happens in the life world. Communication in the life world is characterized by conversation, and this is the more encompassing of the two styles. The life world gives rise to all the topics that will be discussed in the world of public discourse.

No life world has *authority* in public discourse, however, which necessarily entails involving participants from different life worlds. I cannot appeal to my aesthetic preferences, you cannot appeal to your religious texts, and she cannot appeal to her family values. This is how discussion happens in the life world of friends, churches, and families. In argumentative discourse, on the other hand, "validity claims which previously remained implicit because they arose performatively are expressly thematized."[8] When one moves from the life world to the world of public discourse, the sources of one's claims must be identified and excised, leaving the opinion itself available for consideration. If good reasons cannot be offered for the claim, then it too will drop out of public discourse. This does not negate the claim, but merely excludes it from the public realm. For example, Christian commands such as "Thou shalt not steal" survive the process of public discussion, because good publicly accessible reasons can be offered for such a command. If challenged, however, fundamental theologians can refer neither to Scripture nor to tradition to justify their beliefs.[9]

Tracy is fundamentally in accord with Habermas on the distinction between "life world" and "public realm," but is less enthusiastic about the manner in which Habermas's model results in a *de facto* exclusion of religious claims in public discourse. Tracy allows that the "peculiar logic of religious claims" creates awkward issues for regulating argumentation, but these can be addressed "unless one assumes, rather than argues, that no religious or theological claims are argumentatively redeemable, a modern critical social theory should also account for and argue over just these claims."[10]

Tracy expresses dismay over Habermas's glib dismissal of theology as acceptable public discourse. Not only does he argue that theology should be given a chance to prove itself in the public arena, but he is also quite confident that theology is equal to the challenge: "Indeed, both the discipline of philosophy of religion . . . and the discipline of modern theology . . . are, at their best, fully modern critical disciplines. Both philosophy of religion and modern theology should be acknowledged as modern critical disciplines. . . ."[11]

This explicitly apologetic appeal affirms Habermas's notion that only good, publicly accessible reasons should be allowed into the public discussion, but argues that theology is up to the task of supplying them. It is crucial to note that Habermas's criteria are not being questioned by Tracy; the only objection is to Habermas's assessment of theology as failing to meet them. Also worth noting is that Tracy is defending both "modern theology" and "philosophy of religion" in the same breath.

Two Criticisms

Habermas Responds

There are two incisive criticisms that are leveled at Tracy's model, and the first comes from Habermas himself. In his only direct response to the theological appropriation of his critical theory, Habermas addresses Tracy's model specifically and raises several concerns as to its appropriateness for theology.

Habermas sketches a brief history of how religion and reason have interacted since the early modern period. The philosophical appropriation of religious content requires a "neutral" philosopher who does not bring her own self-understanding into the matter. Philosophy must content itself with a "methodical atheism in the manner of the philosophical reference to the contents of religious experience. Philosophy cannot appropriate what is talked about in religious experience as religious experiences."[12] Habermas recognizes that this "methodical atheism" presents a crucial obstacle for philosophy. There is a point at which philosophy must simply admit that it can go no further, and this is reached when there is no publicly accessible language by which a claim from a specific tradition can be redescribed.

Turning to the theologians directly, he confronts Tracy on the issue of validity claims and investigates what theologians are committing to when they present theology as a "fully modern critical discipline." The theologians seem willing to surrender theology's right to "privilege" so that theology, like every other discipline, will have to meet the demands for academic justification. Answering such demands successfully guarantees theology's position as a serious academic discipline, since it will be able to stand on the same critical ground. Habermas, however, sees it from a different angle: "If this is the *common ground* of theology, science, and philosophy, what then still constitutes the distinctiveness of theological discourse? What separates the internal perspective of theology from the external perspective of those who enter a dialogue with theology?"[13]

This is most incisive when it is recalled that Tracy consistently defends the philosophy of religion and modern theology in one breath. What does the theologian have to offer in a conversation with the philosopher of religion? What, if anything, separates their perspectives? If nothing, then what point is there in having a theologian in the conversation at all? Habermas sees this as a distinct possibility, and closes with a sobering prediction:

> . . . the more theology opens itself in general to the discourses of the human sciences, the greater is the danger that its own status will be lost in the network of alternating takeover attempts. . . .

> Theology also loses its identity if it only cites religious experiences, and under the descriptions of religious discourse no longer acknowledges them as its own basis.[14]

Habermas expresses concern on behalf of the secular discourse, which will lose a valued life-world perspective if theologians are willing to submit themselves without reservation to his criterion of argumentation. While the public theologians are busy attempting to demonstrate the *likeness* between theology and other disciplines (argumentative justification), Habermas points out that they have abandoned their claim to *distinctiveness*. He goes on to investigate the distinctiveness of theology on their behalf: If theology is not to be subsumed by other disciplines, what characterizes it? It is not distinctive simply by its reference to religious experience, for the retrieval of "religious experience" as phenomenon into the arena of argumentative discourse falls under the headings of anthropology, religious studies, sociology, and psychology. The distinctiveness of theology is in the manner in which it embraces religious experience. Theology, unlike philosophy and the social sciences, accepts religious experience as a basis or warrant for its discourse. Theology is not under the same constraints as public discourse. It seems to Habermas, however, that the public theologians are voluntarily constraining themselves in this manner. If they insist on doing so, they sacrifice their identity as theologians. In their eagerness to achieve full status as an "ology," they will have sacrificed the "theos," at least insofar as their method is concerned.

Stanley Hauerwas and the Postliberals

While Habermas criticizes public theology from a secular position, Hauerwas attacks from the perspective of the theologian. Postliberal theologians such as Hauerwas are deeply concerned with the integrity of theological identity and are strongly opposed to the imposition of any external criteria on theological discourse.

For postliberals, religious faith is a comprehensive totality that forms us, "a kind of cultural and/or linguistic framework or medium that shapes the entirety of life and thought," so it makes little sense to speak of "experience" to which it might be correlated.[15] Chief among their targets are those like Tracy who seem to assign "experience" a role independent of, and prior to, the Christian tradition. This approach, say the postliberals, gets it precisely backwards. The crucial decision is where to begin, and a postliberal points out that there is no definitively better place to begin than the gospel. For example, to take demythologizing criticisms regarding the "plausibility" of the resurrection, or the virgin birth, or the divinity of Jesus seriously on their own terms, and attempt to modify Christianity in light of these criticisms, is theologically unsound.[16] It offers a change that is discontinuous with the tradition that it proposes to change, with a corresponding fracture of *identity*.

The confusion arises from the fact that much of Christian morality is consistent with Enlightenment morality and that some Christian historical claims do satisfy the empiricists. But this is not always the case, and it is in just these cases that theologians find out where they stand. Hauerwas is cognizant of the quandary theologians face, given that "Christianity is at an awkwardly intermediate stage in Western culture where having once been culturally established it is still not clearly disestablished."[17] Thus, when other academics find the underlying reasons for theological claims (which they might otherwise find acceptable) offensive or implausible, the instinct is to correlate those underlying reasons with elements from the prevailing academic tradition (generally scientific naturalism), thus preventing further disestablishment. The fundamental theologians' commitment to the "methodical atheism" of scientific inquiry requires them to answer questions that are not proper to Christian self-understanding, and modify their positions if they cannot answer them to the satisfaction of their academic public. Hauerwas notes that this marks a significant shift in the way that theology has interacted with those outside the church: "The apologist of the past stood in the church and its tradition and sought relationship with those outside. Apologetic theology was a secondary endeavor because the apologist never assumed that one could let the questions of unbelief order the theological agenda."[18]

Hauerwas argues that the Christian contribution to any public discussion will have no power if the fact that such a contribution *is* Christian is hidden. If we prescind from our faith commitments for purposes of the argument, as Tracy says the fundamental theologian must do, our conclusions cannot help but be faithless. Hauerwas declares: "The first task is not . . . to write as though Christian commitments make no difference in the sense that they only underwrite what everyone in principle can already know, but rather to show the difference those commitments make."[19] What public theologians see as a threat to the viability of theology in the academy is what Hauerwas sees as making the conversation interesting in the first place. If the specifics of the Christian faith are to be omitted in an academic environment due to their distressing particularity, then theologians will finally self-censor themselves right out of theology.

Hauerwas and Habermas

The criticisms of both Hauerwas and Habermas are incisive, and even more so when considered together. Hauerwas argues that theologians may well have many things to add to the conversation, "but they will not say it significantly if they try to disguise the fact that they think, write and speak out of and to a distinctive community."[20] Freeing our religious convictions from their particularities is inherently self-defeating: "if what is said theologically is but a confirmation of what we can know on other grounds . . . then why bother saying it theologically at all?"[21] This is almost precisely what Habermas said to the theologians in Chicago: "If this is the *common ground* of theology, science, and philosophy, what then still constitutes the distinctiveness of theological discourse?"[22] Taken together, these two criticisms form a compelling indictment of Tracy's fundamental theology, at least in its present form. It voluntarily surrenders its distinctive identity.

We Christian theologians must have a coherent identity with which to engage the academy, or we as theologians will have nothing to offer. To refuse to bring our own specific Christian tradition into the discussion is to bring nothing worthwhile. This is most emphatically *not* advocating any kind of retreat from academic discussion. But neither does it allow the theological agenda to be set by external sources, which will invariably happen if Tracy's version of fundamental theology is practiced. Central Christian doctrines (e.g. Trinity, deity of Jesus) that cannot be conceptually redescribed in neutral language will not be so much abandoned as simply neglected.

Dealing faithfully and effectively with a pluralist culture does not entail becoming pluralist about our own religious identity. The well-being of the world is not our *primary* problem, although the well-being of the world will almost invariably be involved in living for

Christ. However, if a sound strategy were proposed that would ensure the indefinite continuation of a stable "civilization" that entailed sacrificing Christian identity, Christians should reject the proposal because the strategy negates why we were concerned about the problem in the first place. We are not trying to fix the world, but seeking to live the gospel faithfully as the body of Christ in the world. Indeed, it is a forceful proclamation that Christians have a unique gift to offer the entire world: a place where one can encounter Christ in a worshiping community. It goes without saying that this message will not always be welcome.

Hauerwas denies the very possibility of translating Christian insights into the framework of the public discourse in the academy, and Habermas is for the most part in agreement. But the issue can be framed even more concisely: the extent to which we are successful in such a translation is precisely the extent to which we have nothing to say.

Conclusion: Fundamental Loyalties

In this limited engagement of Tracy's approach to public theology we have begun to see the inherent tension that exists between "public" and "theology." As I mentioned in the introduction, it can be seen largely as a question of manners. If theology is to be successful in the academy, theologians must display good academic manners. How should we train our theologians to behave when out in public? It is clear that we should respect that our discussion partners may not share our beliefs, but what does this respect entail? Moreover, is there a time when we must reach the reasoned judgment that the discussion is not worth having?

Answers to these questions require a clear identification of our loyalties, and this is precisely where Tracy errs. The "fundamental loyalty" (Tracy's term) of the fundamental theologian is to a conversation that is methodologically atheistic in its form. It is *fides quaerens intellectum* without the *fides*, which is why Tracy can consistently use the terms "modern theology" and "philosophy of religion" interchangeably. He somehow manages to stay the course amidst these conflicting tensions in his own work, but only at the cost of ambiguity that borders on confusion. That he manages to hold the tensions at all is, I think, an act of theological and hermeneutical virtuosity. Lesser theologians have failed.[23]

Any correction here must first involve a re-assessment not of theology, but of the word "public," and it is here that we find the genuine confusion in Tracy's presentation. He asserts that the nature and reality of God "logically" demand publicness,[24] but as Owen C. Thomas notes, Tracy vacillates between two uses of the word public "without indicating the shift in meaning: 1) the nature of a claim, namely to universality or universal significance, and 2) the nature of the grounds offered for a claim, namely, evidence, warrants, and backing."[25]

Even the sectarian Hauerwas is significantly public in the first sense; namely that the Christian witness has universal significance. He speaks to anyone who wants to listen, and many who do not.[26] This is indeed logically demanded by our faith. What is *not* logically demanded is Tracy's Lonerganian criterion that demands that we speak in a certain manner "that any attentive, intelligent, reasonable and responsible person can understand and judge in keeping with fully public criteria for argumentation."[27] If the latter is to be the definition of "public," then Tracy's systematic specialty (the only of the three specialties whose "public" is the church) is not public at all, but rather takes place in the *privacy* of the Christian community.

If we are to keep the "functional specialties" framework at all, then a configuration that widens the scope and importance of systematic theology is required. The relationship between fundamental and systematic theology needs to be ordered, with fundamental theology accountable to systematic theology. *Every* theologian, regardless of specialty, needs to have a "fundamental loyalty" to the body of Christ, which will in turn order all other loyalties. Tracy is right in insisting that any theologian should be willing to discuss her position with anyone, that theology is directed outward by its very nature. But if our academic interlocutor is simply not willing to listen to what we have to say because it is explicitly theological, the last thing we should do is compromise the content of the message to improve its presentation. Theologians, when speaking *as* theologians, will at some point speak in theological language. An interlocutor who resolutely objects to the use of theological language is someone who does not want to talk to a theologian. And since the general plausibility structures are presently set by an academy that often reacts with confusion, indifference, or even hostility when faced with explicitly theological language, this will happen all too often.[28]

In order to keep our names on the invitation lists for future academy parties (i.e., continue to have a positive impact in the academic world), we must behave with the good manners appropriate to the occasion. The question is: how badly do we want to be at this party? When is it time to leave? Tracy's position requires him to answer the second question "never," for it would betray a fundamental loyalty. This is not to say that the appropriate answer is "now." But the fact is that theologians *are* radically different from other academics, in that we are not differentiated by our subject matter, but by our lived commitments. This will inevitably be unsettling in the present secular academic environment, where personally invested truth claims are looked upon with polite disdain. Theologians will assuredly be reproved for lacking the proper critical distance, or some variation on that theme, and perhaps not invited to the next gathering. But perhaps we will be invited regardless, and then we can make a genuine contribution. If we prescind from this personal investment in our theology, however, we become mere philosophers and sociologists of religion. We are still invited to the party, but at best only as those tiresome *poseurs* who have good manners, but nothing interesting to say. At worst, we blend in beautifully, having ceased to be theologians at all.

Notes

[1]For an example of Hauerwas's abrasive style, see his "The Importance of Being Catholic: A Protestant View," *First Things* (March 1990). For a heatedly sarcastic response to Hauerwas's "usual discernment and tact," see Dennis P. McCann, "Natural Law, Public Theology and the Legacy of John Courtney Murray," *Christian Century* 107 (S 5-12, 1990): 801-803.

[2]David Tracy, *The Analogical Imagination: Christian Theology and the Culture of Pluralism* (New York: Crossroad, 1981), 57-58.

[3]Ibid., 57. While *The Analogical Imagination* shies away from the catch-phrase "common human experience" that drew so much attention in *Blessed Rage for Order*, the second hermeneutical constant is strikingly close to the "phenomenology of the religious dimension" that typifies common human experience. See David Tracy, *Blessed Rage for Order: The New Pluralism in Theology* (New York: Seabury, 1975), 52.

[4]Tracy, *Blessed Rage for Order, 7.*

[5]Ibid., 8-9.

[6]David Tracy, "Theology, Critical Social Theory, and the Public Realm," in *Habermas, Modernity, and Public Theology*, ed. Don S. Browning and Francis Schüssler Fiorenza (New York: Crossroad, 1992), 19.

[7]This presents a problem, since the rules are to be purely formal; without any ethical content. However, since styles and topics of discourse are excluded *de facto*,

the rules themselves act as a negative ethic.

[8]Jürgen Habermas, "Transcendence from Within, Transcendence within This World," in *Habermas, Modernity, and Public Theology*, 240.

[9]Despite its centrality, it is difficult to see how a fundamental theologian could ever talk about the Trinity.

[10]Tracy, "Theology, Critical Social Theory, and the Public Realm," 35.

[11]Ibid., 36.

[12]Habermas, "Transcendence from Within," 233.

[13]Ibid., 230.

[14]Ibid., 230-31, 233.

[15]See George Lindbeck, *The Nature of Doctrine: Religion and Theology in a Postliberal Age* (Philadelphia: Westminster Press, 1984), 33.

[16]A concise, yet perhaps overstated, version of this attack can be found in Lindbeck: "Liberals start with experience, with an account of the present, and then adjust their vision of the kingdom of God accordingly, while postliberals are in principle committed to doing the reverse" (Lindbeck, *The Nature of Doctrine,*125-26). It should be noted that Tracy certainly does not fit this definition of liberal, as he is in principle committed to modifying each in terms of the other.

[17]Stanley Hauerwas, *Against the Nations* (Minneapolis: Winston, 1985), 8.

[18]Ibid., 24.

[19]Ibid., 44

[20]Ibid., 44.

[21]Ibid., 25.

[22]See n.14 above.

[23]Paul Knitter explicitly appeals to Tracy's fundamental theology to support a scientifically generated "cosmological faith" that serves as a "basic criterion for religion in general." See Paul Knitter, *Jesus and the Other Names: Christian Mission and Global Responsibility* (Maryknoll, NY: Orbis Books, 1996), 35. While this is a position that Tracy himself would never hold, the structure of fundamental theology is such that it will prescind from its own faith position in order to adapt to the demands of the discussion, so there is nothing *technically* wrong with Knitter's application.

[24]Tracy, *The Analogical Imagination*, 3, 63, 86.

[25]Owen C. Thomas, "Public Theology and Counter-Public Spheres," *Harvard Theological Review* 85:4 (1992): 456.

[26]It is unfortunate that Hauerwas's regrettable reputation for personal rudeness overshadows his more defensible lack of academic manners. The two are not logically interdependent.

[27]Tracy, *The Analogical Imagination*, 63.

[28]Tracy might correctly note that this is a "typically situational analysis," and use it as a defense against an anti-correlationist attack. This would fail, because the rejection of external plausibility structures is perennial. Only the particular application requires a situational analysis. See David Tracy, "The Uneasy Alliance Reconceived: Catholic Theological Method, Modernity, and Postmodernity," *Theological Studies* 50 (1989): 548-70.

Part II

SPECIAL THEORIES

Social Science and Ecclesiology

Cybernetics in Patrick Granfield's Theology of the Church

Peter C. Phan

> The church as a human society can of course be examined and described according to the categories used by the sciences with regard to any human society. But these categories are not enough. For the whole of the community of the People of God and for each member of it what is in question is not just a specific "social membership"; rather, for each and every one what is essential is a particular "vocation." Indeed, the church as the People of God is also "Christ's Mystical Body." Membership in that body has for its source a particular call, united with the saving action of grace. Therefore, if we wish to keep in mind this community of the People of God, which is so vast and so extremely differentiated, we must see first and foremost Christ saying in a way to each member of the community: "Follow me." It is the community of the disciples, each of whom in a different way is following Christ.[1]

These words of Pope John Paul II express in a nutshell the challenges encountered in bringing the social sciences to bear on ecclesiology. On the one hand, the use of the social sciences is possible and even necessary in ecclesiology because the church is a human society; on the other hand, it is not sufficient because the church is also a theological reality. The intent of this essay is precisely to examine how these two polarities can be reconciled by investigating the proper way in which the social sciences can be employed to enrich ecclesiology without renouncing its own methodology and at the same time preserving the nature of the church as the Mystical Body of Christ and a community of Christ's disciples. After a brief overview of the way in which the social sciences have been used in recent Catholic ecclesiology, the essay will examine an example of the use of the social sciences in ecclesiology by focusing on Patrick Granfield's use of cybernetics in his theology of the church. The essay will conclude with suggestions as to how theology and the social sciences can be brought together in such a way that each discipline retains its distinct nature and method.

The Use of the Social Sciences in Recent Catholic Ecclesiology

The Use of the Social Sciences in Ecclesiology

Until recent times not only fundamental ecclesiology but also dogmatic ecclesiology, while acknowledging the church as a human society, scarcely made any use of the social sciences to understand how the human element functions in the life of the church.[2] There was no attempt to study, by means of empirical methods, the concrete ways in which the church and its organizational structures should function so as to become a credible sign of God's presence. The method was strictly historical and theological.

It is only in the last three decades that Catholic theologians have turned to the social sciences to derive insights from them in order to help the church become an effective sign of the kingdom of God for the world. In her essay on the use of social science theories of organization in ecclesiology,[3] Clare Watkins examines the works of several theologians, in particular ecclesiologists, and sociologists who have contributed to what she terms "organizational ecclesiology." Among those studied are Dietrich Bonhoeffer, Patrick Granfield, Pieter De Looz, Peter Rudge, Gotthold Hasenhüttl, Pieter De Haas, and Mady Thung.[4] It is important to note that Watkins's essay does not deal with sociological studies of the church but with the application of social theories and, more specifically, theories of social organization, to the life of the church.

After her critical review of these authors, Watkins offers three conclusions regarding the contemporary use of the social sciences in ecclesiology. First, all these authors, both theologians and sociologists, have given theology short shrift: "A recurrent weakness in the studies considered here has been the simplicity and generality of the theological side of the conversation, compared with the concrete detail of the organization side; this lack of theological detail ultimately undermines the properly interdisciplinary nature of the endeavor and results in a dominance of the social sciences in the discussion."[5] Second, the way in which the social sciences are used in ecclesiology depends on the model of church adopted:

> If the Church institution is seen as a thoroughly human expression of a certain faith, then the organizational ecclesiologist may take a fairly adventurous approach to structural reform, in which, almost inevitably, the social science view will dominate in the actual conclusions drawn. A more sacramental ecclesiology, in which the relation of the divine or transcendent to the here-and-now Church is not so clear, will feel more restrained in its consideration of concrete change, and will tend to emphasize the theological in its conclusions.[6]

Third, organizational ecclesiology must retain its theological character in its conversation with the social sciences: "The theologian cannot stop being properly theological (talking of faith- and God-matters) but always needs to learn more about human realities, in which there are other experts, with whom she or he engages in conversation."[7]

Whatever the fairness of Watkins's evaluation of recent works in organizational ecclesiology, there is no doubt that she has raised one of the most important issues in the interdisciplinary dialogue between ecclesiology and the social sciences, indeed, between theology and any other academic discipline in general. That ecclesiology can and must make use of the social sciences has been convincingly argued by Gérard Wackenheim and Joseph Komonchak.[8] The question is how to use sociological insights to elaborate an ecclesiology, a "sociological ecclesiology" as it were,[9] in such a way that ecclesiology retains its epistemological status as theology and does not become a kind of religious or ecclesiological sociology.[10]

Before an answer can be suggested to this question in the course of the essay, two remarks may be in order. First, even though I have been using the terms "the social sciences" and "sociology" interchangeably to refer to an academic enterprise, it is important to remember that they do not represent a homogeneous and unified discipline. On the contrary, as Gregory Baum has lucidly explained, sociology is "a conflictual field of study" with a variety of interests. These interests include institution, organization, religion, knowledge, and culture, producing different "sociologies." More important, very different theoretical presuppositions, approaches, and research methods are used in these sociologies, resulting in different trends of sociology: classical, positivistic-empirical, functionalist, critical, and phenomenological.[11] Consequently, the relationship between sociology and theology in general and ecclesiology in particular is highly complex and very often is created ad hoc by the theologian who makes use of sociological theories with their very diverse, at times contradictory, approaches and methods.

Second, historically, the social sciences are a late comer to the dialogue between theology and the sciences, whether human or natural. The first serious and extensive use of the social sciences in theology was done by Latin American liberation theologians. Part of the novelty of the methodology of liberation theology lies in its conversational partners. As Gustavo Gutiérrez has argued, in contrast to theology as wisdom and theology as rational knowledge, liberation theology is "critical reflection on praxis" in the light of God's Word for the sake of social transformation.[12] Such reflection on historical praxis for liberation requires more than expertise in the Bible and philosophy. What is also needed is an accurate knowledge of the sociopolitical and economic conditions, as well as the causes of the oppression of the poor for whom the theologian has made the preferential option. Hence, the necessity of dialogue with and learning from the social sciences, or what Clodovis Boff calls the "socioanalytic mediation."[13] As Gutiérrez explains in an essay, the title of which is telling, liberation theology, which is concerned with the poor, must

> understand the situation of poverty, its causes, and the efforts of those suffering under it to escape from it. It is at this stage that recourse to the social sciences plays a significant part, for these sciences allow us to gain a more accurate knowledge of society as it really is and so to articulate with greater precision the challenge it poses for the proclamation of the gospel and thus for theological reflection as well.[14]

Ways of Relating the Social Sciences to Theology

With these two observations in mind, it would be useful to take a bird's eye view of how the social sciences have been used by theologians in recent times. Here, Clodovis Boff's typology is helpful. In his doctoral dissertation at the Catholic University of Louvain in 1976, Boff attempted to provide an epistemological basis for what he calls "the theology of the political" (rather than "political theology"), which is implicit in liberation theology.[15] There are three basic issues to be dealt with. First, how should the theology of the political make use of the results of the social sciences (or "the sciences *of* the social")? Second, how can the theology of the political retain its nature as theology in making use of the results of the social sciences? Third, how can praxis be brought into theological theory without jeopardizing the latter's theoretical character? At this point, only the first issue is of concern to us. Here, I will expound only Boff's view of how the social sciences and theology should not be related to each other, postponing to the last part of the essay his view of how they should be fruitfully related so as to preserve the theological character of the theology of the political and of theology in general. I will also bracket Boff's focus on liberation theology as such, and therefore his interest in praxis as the starting point of liberation theology, so as to highlight the methodological relationship between theology and the social sciences in general.[16]

For Boff, theology and the social sciences can be related to each other (what he calls the "social-analytic mediation" of the method of the theology of the political) in six ways, of which the first five are judged inadequate.[17] First, in "empiricism," theology does not even realize that social-analytic mediation is necessary, since according to empiricism, to know is just "to take a look," to use Bernard Lonergan's expression, without the need of any further conscious act, because the "facts speak for themselves." Of course, there is no such thing as an absolutely immediate reading of the real—here, of the social. All knowledge is necessarily mediated, so that a theology of the political is mediated either by a critical reading of the social or an uncritical reading of the same.

Second, in "methodological purism," theology claims that it has its proper object, namely faith, which furnishes its own principles for theorizing, and therefore rejects any extrinsic epistemology, be it that of the social sciences or any other discipline (this is the methodological equivalence of *sola fides*). While it is true that theology has faith as its basis and its own epistemology, its knowledge of faith is always mediated by human categories, those of philosophy in the past, as well as those of the social sciences today. As human discourse on God, theology is necessarily mediated.

Third, in "theologism," theology considers its reading of reality as the only one that is total and exhaustive and regards the knowledge of other sciences as partial and therefore replaceable by a more comprehensive theological knowledge. Such a theology, however, unavoidably becomes ideology since it eliminates other views and imposes itself as the only acceptable view. Incidentally, it is obvious that in the foregoing three positions, there is no dialogue at all between theology and the social sciences.

Fourth, in "semantic mix," theology makes use of the social sciences, but the two disciplines are not well integrated; rather they remain mixed, and very often the theological system dominates, so that sociological categories are emptied of their proper contents and given spiritual meaning.

Fifth, in "bilingualism," not unlike in "semantic mix," theology and the social sciences are juxtaposed, with one discipline dominating at one stage of the development of the theology of the political, and the other dominating at another, producing internal self-contradictions.

Lastly, the sixth way, which, according to Boff is the only adequate way to relate the social sciences to theology, is one in which the results of the sciences of the social enter into the theology of the political as a constitutive part. With regard to ecclesiology, the results or products of the social sciences will be taken up by the theology of the church as raw material, as something to be (re)worked by the ecclesiologist with procedures proper to theologizing, in such wise as to produce a theology of the church and not merely a religious sociology. Obviously, the scope of such a "sociological ecclesiology" is much broader than that of "organizational ecclesiology" that Clare Watkins envisages.[18] I will deal with this sixth way in detail in the last part of the essay.

In the meantime, I would like to turn to one attempt at organizational ecclesiology, Patrick Granfield's, that makes extensive use of one mode of social analysis, i.e., cybernetics, to understand and promote effective communication, participation in decision-making, and co-responsibility in the church. The choice of Granfield is amply justified by the fact that he was among the first North American theologians to make systematic use of the social sciences to resolve certain problems in the Roman Catholic Church, that he is the only ecclesiologist among the authors whose works were evaluated by Clare Watkins, and that he was awarded The John Courtney Murray Award in 1989 in recognition of the fact that, as the citation states, "his books, his articles, and his service to Catholic ecclesiology constitute truly distinguished achievement."[19]

Patrick Granfield's Use of Cybernetics in Ecclesiology

Patrick Granfield (b. 1930), a Benedictine, is the Shakespeare Caldwell-Duval Professor of Systematic Theology at the Catholic University, where he began his teaching career in 1962. For eight years he was associated in various capacities with *The American Ecclesiastical Review*, of which he was the editor-in-chief from 1968 to 1970. In addition to his own scholarly publications, Granfield also published a well-received book of interviews with influential theologians[20] and co-edited a mammoth two-volume *Festschrift* in honor of patristic scholar Johannes Quasten.[21]

Early Interest in Semiotics and the Right to Silence

Granfield's interest in cybernetics as the science of information and control was adumbrated in his doctoral dissertation in philosophy presented at the Anselmianum, Rome, in 1958.[22] The work deals with the behavioral semiotic as expounded by Charles W. Morris (1901-79), whose lifelong goal was to relate American pragmatism, especially the insights of Charles Peirce and George Herbert Mead, to logical positivism. Though subsequently Granfield did not take up semiotic as a scholarly specialization, his philosophical studies of the theories of signs had a lasting impact upon his theology. Even though he rejects Morris's account of human language as an intentional and interpretative act, Granfield commends him for having developed the three dimensions of semiotic; namely, semantics, syntactics, and pragmatics. In particular, he notes the importance of Morris's elaboration of pragmatics in which the social aspects of signs are attended to, that is, the origin, use, effect, and social environment of the signs.[23]

Granfield's interest in cybernetics was also foreshadowed in his doctoral dissertation in theology at the Catholic University of

America.[24] It deals with the right to silence or the privilege against self-incrimination ("pleading the fifth") and argues that this right is founded on the natural law but may be limited by the positive law for the sake of the common good. In his argument for the right to silence, Granfield already displays his overriding preference and profound respect for democracy, a theme he will develop at great length in his later work on ecclesial cybernetics. Furthermore, in his research on the development of the doctrine of the right to silence, Granfield points out the important role of non-ecclesial and non-theological factors (such as the change in civil law) in modifying the church's teaching. Here is an example of the "input" of the "environment" to the "output" of the church of which Granfield speaks in his ecclesial cybernetics.

Granfield elaborates his theory of ecclesial cybernetics at length in his first major book, *Ecclesial Cybernetics*.[25] The twofold inspiration underlying this work is: "first, the contemporary democratic experience with its stress on participation in decision-making and on the co-responsibility of all citizens for the common good; and second, the vision of the church suggested by Vatican II with its principles of liberty and collegiality and its recognition of the charismatic role of all members of the Body of Christ."[26] The book is divided into four parts: the first introduces cybernetics and presents a cybernetic analysis of the church; the second shows how cybernetics has functioned in the teaching of the church on issues such as slavery, birth control, the ecumenical movement, and priestly celibacy; the third argues for the application of democracy and cybernetics to the church; and the fourth highlights some of the problems in the practice of ecclesial cybernetics and suggests ways to foster this practice. Granfield's interest in the transmission of information for the purpose of communication and control is further developed in his two books on the papacy, namely, *The Papacy in Transition*[27] and *The Limits of the Papacy*[28] and in the volume he edited, *The Church and Communication*.[29] Here I will concentrate on Granfield's cybernetic analysis of the church, his theological justification for democracy in the church, and his application of cybernetics to some ecclesiological issues.

Cybernetics and the Organization of the Church

Granfield's first break away from the traditional mold of ecclesiology took the form of a thorough application of cybernetic theory to the understanding of the church by applying the communication model proposed by Norbert Wiener and others.[30] The science of cybernetics, Granfield notes, has been widely applied to electronics, neurology, engineering, telecommunications, political science, and economics. Its application to ecclesiology is now a necessity, because "an understanding of the problem of communication and control in the Church is basic to its future maintenance and development."[31]

Granfield begins with a brief explanation of cybernetics. He quotes Wiener's understanding of the purpose of cybernetics as "to develop a language and techniques that will enable us to attack the problem of control and communication in general, but also to find the proper repertory of ideas and techniques to classify their particular manifestations under certain concepts."[32] These concepts include the system, the environment, negative entropy, and the information-conversion process.

1. A "system" is the basic unit of control and communication in cybernetics. It is an undivided whole with a multiplicity of interdependent and interacting parts, bound together by communication, which organizes them into a unity. A system can be "closed," that is, static, because it is isolated from its environment and receiving no information from outside. Or it can be "open," that is, dynamic, because it is in constant interaction with its environment, receiving information from it for self-maintenance and self-development and thus avoiding entropy. Systems that are able to resolve to their advantage the tension between stability and change by adapting to their environment are called "ultrastable systems."

2. The "environment" is whatever is not part of the system and with which open systems interact. Interaction with the environment enables the open system to achieve two related goals: homeostasis (its ability to maintain steadiness) and evolution (its ability to improve itself). These two activities are anti-entropic, the former preserving the system, and the latter perfecting it. The environment can be internal (within the system, one part is related to and interacting with all the others) and external (the system as a whole is related to and interacting with all that is outside the system).

3. "Negative entropy" is the characteristic of open systems. Contrary to closed systems, which move inexorably to self-destruction, open systems avoid entropy or organizational dissolution by performing anti-entropic functions, that is, by interacting with the environ-

ment to achieve their goals in an orderly manner. "Positive entropy" is the tendency of systems, both closed and open, to move toward a totally undetermined and undifferentiated state, which is the antithesis of organization and order. In this process, there is a steady decrease of information from the environment and a consequent decrease of energy output, integration, and development. The only way to counteract entropy is to interact with the environment and receive input from it. This countervailing force is the "negative entropy" or anti-entropic functions that enable the system to regulate and renew itself through adaptation to the environment. In this way, the system is given a positive direction as order and information, rather than chaos and noise, are restored to it.

4. Anti-entropic functions are performed though an "information-conversion process."A cybernetic system is essentially an information-processing system. This information processing is composed of input, output, and feedback. An "input" is a unit of information that modifies the system in some way. Inputs flow within the system and act as determinants of behavior. There are two major kinds of input, namely, demands and supports. The former are stressful messages directed to authorities demanding positive or negative decisions and are usually communicated through research centers, publicity, protest, official conferences, and election. The latter are positive messages providing the system with continuity and enabling it to respond to the demands that are made to it. An "output" is a unit of information emanating from the system, normally from its authorities, and directed to the subordinate parts of the system or its environment in response to the "input," particularly to its demands, in light of the compatibility of the demands with the goals of the system, the availability of resources, and the feasibility of implementation.

The "feedback" is any unit of information that is returned to the system in reaction to antecedent output. It can be positive or negative, consisting again of demands and supports. This circular process of input and output, aptly described by the expression "feedback loop," functions in open systems continuously, repeating itself again and again.[33]

Can this system analysis be applied to the church so that the church itself may be understood as a cybernetic system? With repeated caveats that the church is a "mystery" and "a unique historical and sacramental manifestation of the Church of Christ on earth," Granfield nevertheless holds that "despite its uniqueness, it [the church] is an open system subject to cybernetic analysis."[34]

1. The first thing that strikes even a casual observer is that the church is a social institution, an "open system" that has a tight network of communication and control on both the natural and supernatural levels. Even as a spiritual organism, that is, as the Body of Christ, the church, Granfield argues, evidences all the cybernetic elements of an open system. It receives the input of supernatural grace from the "divine Ecosystem" whereby its members are bound together in the unity of creed, cult, and code. At the natural and organizational level, Granfield shows how the system of the Catholic Church consists of different layers of communication and control. At the universal level, there are the papacy, the college of cardinals, the Roman Curia, and the college of bishops; and at the local level, there are the bishop, the diocesan curia, the synods and councils, and the clergy and the laity. All these various organizations must be in communication with one another as parts of an open system, and this open system itself is in communication with the external environment.[35]

2. As an open system, Granfields points out, the church interacts with its environment to achieve homeostasis and evolution. Its environment is twofold: God and the world. As already noted, the church receives the "input" from God through word and sacrament by which its life is maintained and increased. But the church must also interact with the world, since its members are not only church people but also live their lives in cultural, social, political, economic, and ecological worlds with other human beings. In brief, says Granfield, "a cybernetic analysis of the church must give great importance to its environmental context, for the 'People of God,' as the church calls itself, are obviously and ineradicably part of the family of man."[36]

3. To survive and prosper, the church, as a cybernetic system, must resist entropy. The fact that Christ has promised that the church will endure till the end of time, Granfield notes, is no guarantee that it will not have to contend with the forces of entropy. As an incarnational church, it must achieve its ultrastability by adapting and responding to the signs of the time. Only in this way can the church fulfill what Vatican I has described of it, namely, "a great and perpetual motive of credibility and an irrefutable proof of its own divine mission."[37] Of course, the means the church has at its disposal, Granfield recalls, are not merely natural; rather, they include the Word of God, sacraments,

prayer, and good works. But, as any cybernetic system, it must make use of the various social techniques, such as recruitment of new members consisting of the offspring of the members or converts, education of the members, and reform of its structures.

Anti-entropic activities are performed by the church, of course, not for their own sake but in view of its goals and mission. Here, once again, Granfield shows a deep sensitivity to the theological side of ecclesial cybernetics. Unlike any other system, the church has as its ultimate goal "the glorification of God and the sanctification of man": "The Church, then, focuses on the permanent and eternal condition of man which can be fully realized only in the kingdom."[38] To arrive at this goal, the church has to perform its three main missions, which Granfield designates with three Greek words: the "kerygmatic mission" (the proclamation of the Word of God and the communication of the divine truth), the "diakonic mission" (service), and the "koinoniac mission" (forming and perfecting the community of believers). But these three supernatural missions, Granfield points out, are performed cybernetically, that is, through communication and control within an open system that is the church.

4. Finally, this communication and control within an open system is carried out by means of an information-conversion process consisting of input, output, and feedback. The input consists, as we have seen above, of demands and supports. In the church, there are, according to Granfield, four types of demands: demands for allocations of goods and services, demands for the regulation of behavior, demands for participation in ecclesial decision-making, and demands for information and communication. The church also makes use of the channels of organizing and communicating demands mentioned above: namely, research centers (to gather, correlate, and disseminate information; to undertake original data-gathering projects; and to make research data understandable to church policy-makers); publicity (through various media of communication, especially the Internet today); protest (demonstrations, confrontations, picketing, sit-ins, financial boycotts, and signed petitions); official conferences (episcopal conferences, both national and international, the synod of bishops, and the Pontifical Council for the Laity); and election (though not yet a widely used channel presently).

Besides demands, there are also supports in the church's input. These supports take four forms: contribution of material resources; obedience to doctrinal and moral teachings and disciplinary policies; participation in the liturgical services and community projects; and love and respect for authorities, rituals, traditions, symbols, and the institution itself.

As far as the output of the church is concerned, Granfield shows that the four main classes of the church's output correspond to those of a political system: extractions (ordinary financial support, tithing, special collections, and personal services); behavior regulations (laws, decrees, orders, and rules concerning both doctrinal and disciplinary matters); distributions (spiritual, educational, and social benefits as well as honors); and symbolic actions (communication of faith and morals, policies and values, and history and culture).

From this cybernetic analysis, it is clear that the church is an open system, an "information-processing unit," functioning through interaction with its environment by way of a continuous feedback loop of inputs and outputs. However, when this system is examined in its historical existence, Granfield notes that there is "an imbalance in its role structure. Authoritative outputs are almost solely within the exclusive competence of the hierarchy, with little significant participation by the lower clergy or the laity. Although inputs are received from the nonhierarchical members of the system, these channels are inefficient and in need of reorganization."[39] How to bring about this reform? Granfield's answer is: through the democratization of the church.

Democratization of the Church

Before explaining how the church should function as an open system, Granfield has to deal with the question of whether the church may function democratically. Is not democracy contrary to the church's hierarchical constitution? Has the church ever functioned democratically, at least in some instances, in the past? Is there any theological foundation for "democratization" in the church?

Before answering these questions Granfield makes some important observations about democracy and the nature of the church. As far as the church and the application of sociological theories to ecclesiology are concerned, Granfield makes three important points. First,

> any discussion of the Church's communication structure must take into consideration the unique nature of the Church. It is multidimensional, with paradoxes, conflicts, and tensions, but it

> is one. It is divine and human, invisible and visible, pneumatic and institutional. Although here we are concentrating on its human, visible, and institutional aspects, we are not prescinding from its spiritual side. . . . Although we focus to some extent on the organizational Church, we are also fully cognizant of the Church as the sacramental presence of Christ in the world, as the entire people moving as a pilgrim on the way to final glory. In a word, we view the Church as a mystery filled with the hidden presence of the divine.[40]

Second, Granfield highlights and accepts a critical difference between the church and human social systems, namely, the fact that the church owes its origin and existence to God's self-revelation in Christ: "Therefore, the validity of any ecclesiological conclusions about the nature of the Church is determined primarily by its fidelity to the kerygma. Unlike human societies with their man-made constitutions, the Church is founded on the communication of God to man."[41]

Third, another factor that distinguishes the church from purely human societies, Granfield points out, is "the Church's indefectibility": "This faith-affirmation means that the Church will remain in existence and will never be destroyed by the forces of evil and error. . . . This indefectibility of the Church is forged from that intimate union of Christ and the Church."[42]

With regard to democracy, Granfield recognizes that "direct democracy, with its rapid conversion of feedback, is no longer feasible on a large scale."[43] In its place, there is "indirect democracy" in which, instead of a continuous participation of the people in the direct exercise of power, there is a system of limitation and control of power.[44] For a democratic system to be established and flourish, two principles must be accepted by all its members: "that all members share a common human dignity and that the government exists for the people and not vice versa."[45] Granfield goes on to note three aspects of democracy: the principle of majority rule, the need for leadership, and the value of decentralization.

But may the church adopt even this indirect democracy in its structure? Are the democratic ideals of majoritarianism and decentralization, in particular, compatible with the hierarchical structure of the church? Granfield formulates his answer to these questions by looking back at church history, from the New Testament to the emergence of conciliarism. We do not need to tarry over his historical analysis. Suffice it to note his conclusion: "Ecclesial democracy is not a new thing. It has its deep roots in Christian tradition. Evidence of democratic elements in the open system which is the Church appears primarily in the selection of office holders."[46]

Following his historical investigation, Granfield builds the theological foundation for "ecclesial democracy" on the egalitarian aspect of the ecclesial system. This egalitarian character of the ecclesial community is elaborated in terms of Vatican II's teaching on the laity's participation in the threefold mission of Christ as priest, prophet, and king and on the principle of subsidiarity. Granfield is well aware that equality in the ecclesial system is not absolute since the church is established by Christ as a hierarchical structure. To show how ecclesial democracy is compatible with the hierarchical constitution of the church, Granfield distinguishes between the "vesting of ecclesial authority" and the "structure of ecclesial authority." With respect to the former, the official church has taught that bishops do not receive their authority from the community but from Christ and, ultimately, from God. In *this* sense, the church is not a democratic system, that is, it is not an organization in which the community itself possesses authority over its leaders and delegates its power to them. However, with regard to the structure of ecclesial authority, Granfield points out that the church need not and should not function as a monarchy, but in the model envisaged by the two teachings of Vatican II, that is, collegiality and the charismatic aspect of the church. Granfield concludes: "Theologically, power in the Church is held to come directly from God and not from the people. But nothing prevents the designation of the decision-makers by the members of the Church. Moreover, this same type of decision-making could function in other areas, excepting, of course, the special prerogatives of the Pope and the college of bishops."[47]

How, in practice, can the church be reformed cybernetically through democratization? Granfield is keenly aware of the difficulties facing the task of reform in the church, which can be miscarried by the immobility, ineffectuality (encouraged by inadequate selection process, ambition, and incompetence), and isolation of church leaders as well as by the lack of competence and control among the laity. To promote and facilitate such a cybernetic renewal, Granfield suggests several "techniques of ecclesial democracy," all the while conscious that because the church is a complex, "non-linear, multiple-loop-feedback system with variable elements,"[48] no single and simple solution is adequate to all the interconnected problems facing the church. Among these techniques, Granfield highlights commitment to community,[49] the exercise of minority power by means of protests and pressure groups,[50] the use of communication media,[51] the use of study commissions,[52] and the election of bishops either by a general plebiscite or by an elected committee.[53]

Cybernetics and Some Ecclesiological Issues

Granfield's conviction that some form of participatory democracy, cybernetically effective and theologically sound, is the most effective way for the church to achieve its mission in the modern world is put to the test by one of the most intractable and controverted ministries in the church: the papacy. His next two books are devoted to this issue. In Granfield's view, the basic difficulty with the papacy is its monarchianism, which reached its doctrinal apogee at Vatican I. While acknowledging the truth of Vatican I's definition of papal primacy and infallibility, Granfield draws a distinction between "the essence of the papacy" and "its exercise." For him, the most radical transformation of the papacy is its recent transition from the monarchic to the collegial model. Negatively, collegiality implies that there are limits to papal infallibility and primacy. Theologically, it is based on the concept of the church as *communio*, especially as it is applied to the relationship between the church of Rome and the local church. Organizationally, it calls for ecclesiastical structures to implement episcopal collegiality in an effective way.

With regard to the limits of the papacy, Granfield distinguishes four types: official, legal, dogmatic, and practical. Official limits emerge from the office of the papacy itself and are of two kinds: the first, flowing from the nature of the church as a mystery and a social institution, requires that the pope maintain and safeguard the visible unity of the church; the second, flowing from the way in which the papacy must be exercised, requires the pope to "build and not destroy the church." Legal limits are those connected with natural law, divine positive law, and, to a lesser extent, ecclesiastical law, all of which the pope is bound to obey. Dogmatic limits are those built into the way papal teaching authority must be exercised. The pope is limited by revelation, is bound to adhere to the dogmatic canons of earlier councils and all the dogmatic definitions of the faith, is limited by the stringent conditions for infallibility laid down by Vatican II, and is subject to removal for heresy and moral crimes. Last, practical limits are those derived from the personal qualities of the pope himself, the complexity of the papal office, and the social context within and outside the church that can limit the efficacy of the papacy.[54]

Concerning *communio* and the relationship between papal primacy and episcopal collegiality, Granfield stresses that the universal church is a *communio ecclesiarum*: The universal church comes to be out of the mutual reception and communion of the local churches united in faith and in the Holy Spirit. This communion is achieved at two levels: at the local level, between the bishop and the faithful of his church; and at the universal level, between the bishops and their local churches and the pope and the Church of Rome. Granfield focuses almost exclusively on episcopal collegiality—on the communion between the bishops and the pope. Episcopal collegiality is governed, Granfield points out, by three principles. First, it is rooted in *communio* and episcopal ordination and is therefore primarily a theological and not juridical reality. The diocesan bishops are not mere functionaries of the pope; they exercise their proper, ordinary, and immediate power in the name of Christ. Second, diocesan bishops are nonetheless dependent upon the pope as the head of the college of bishops. In this capacity, the pope is the "principle" (not source) of the unity of the universal church. Third, the principle of subsidiarity must be made to function effectively in episcopal collegiality. This principle rejects uniformity, resists centralization, and mandates legitimate diversity in the church.

Finally, with regard to ecclesiastical structures that can promote the democratization of the church, Granfield highlights the role of ecumenical councils, the synod of bishops, and episcopal conferences. To improve the efficacy of the synod of bishops, he makes a number of proposals: better process of consultation, relaxing the rule of secrecy, expansion of membership, conferral of a deliberative vote, clarification of its role vis-à-vis the Curia, and longer meetings.[55] Of episcopal conferences, despite several criticisms against this intermediate organization between the diocesan bishop and the Holy See, Granfield is persuaded of their theological foundations and their teaching authority, distinct from the papal and universal episcopal magisterium.[56]

Ecclesial Cybernetics: Ecclesiology or Religious Sociology?

In the first section of this essay I raised the question of how the social sciences can be used in ecclesiology in such a way that the nature and method of ecclesiology as a theological discipline is preserved. We have seen that this "socio-analytic mediation" can be performed in various ways, and that of these the only approach that is satisfactory is one in which the results of the social sciences are introduced into ecclesiology as its constitutive part.

With regard to Granfield's ecclesial cybernetics, I have noted that Clare Watkins's criticism that it lacks a theological perspective is unjustified. It cannot be said that Granfield has neglected the theological aspect of the church or that he has not taken into account the differences between the church and a purely secular society in developing his ecclesial cybernetics. On the contrary, Granfield has shown throughout his application of cybernetics and democratic principles to the church a deep sensitivity to the reality of the church as a supernatural mystery, as the Body of Christ, and as an eschatological community.[57]

Nevertheless, it is true that neither Granfield nor the other authors studied by Watkins have discussed explicitly the epistemological process involved in the application of the social sciences to ecclesiology. Their epistemological assumptions remain implicit in their theoretical practice. In what follows, I will draw on the works of French Marxist philosopher Louis Althusser and Clodovis Boff to explicate the epistemological process by which a scientific discipline and the knowledge proper to it are constituted.[58] In this way it will be made clear how the results of the social sciences can be introduced into ecclesiology as its constitutive part, so that ecclesial cybernetics is not merely religious sociology but theological ecclesiology.

The Process of Theoretical Practice as Production of Knowledge

In general, according to Althusser, every science is a work or labor, that is, a "production of cognition," an "operation of transformation," a "genuine practice," of course of a theoretical nature.[59] This process of theoretical practice is composed of three elements called "generality." The "first generality" consists of general and abstract notions that are found in a particular culture; these are not material, individual things themselves, but the universal concepts that represent them. These notions form the "raw material" or the "data" that a particular science deals with. The "second generality" is the "work" performed by the knower on these data to produce a determinate body of "theoretical concepts" that define the nature of the discipline, such as biology, sociology, or theology. The "third generality" is the "product" or "concrete thought" resulting from the process of working on the data received in the second generality. It is known as a "scientific theory" or the "empirical concepts" as distinguished from the "theoretical concepts" of the second generality. To summarize: "Theoretical practice produces third generalities by the operation of a second generality upon a first generality."[60]

Four observations are in order here. First, the theoretical practice truly transforms, of course, not the external things, except indirectly, but the data and the ideas or theoretical concepts; it produces something genuinely new, that is, the empirical concepts or scientific theory in the third generality. The third generality is truly different from the first generality, thanks to the "work" performed in the second generality. Second, what is important in the theoretical practice is not the generalities in themselves with their own independent contents, but the position they occupy in the process of producing cognition. For instance, the third generality of one discipline can be the first or even second generality of another discipline. Third, the most important element of a theoretical practice is the second generality. It is this "working" on the data under a particular point of view or perspective, or as Thomas Aquinas puts it, the "*ratio secundum quam considerantur*,"[61] that specifies the nature of that theoretical practice as a particular science. Fourth, this understanding of the theoretical practice is opposed to the view that knowing is simply a matter of relating the subject with the object, perhaps by means of a specific method, or by explicating the relationship between a theory and a thing, or even by the performance of a series of acts, namely observation, hypothesis, and verification. Rather, knowing is a "practice of the production of cognition."[62]

Theology, insofar as it is a "science" or theoretical practice, also follows this three-step production. As Boff puts it, "Theological practice comprises a first generality—its 'subject,' or material object—a second generality, which is the body of its asymptotic or analogical concepts, and finally a third generality, the theological theory produced."[63] Anything whatsoever can be theology's first generality; there is nothing that cannot be the raw material or subject matter of theology. But it becomes theology only if it is "worked on" in the second generality "in the light of revelation," what St. Thomas calls the "formal object" (the *objectum quo*, the *ratio secundum quam*, the *ratio qua*) of theology, that is, faith functioning here as the *principia* of theology or the *articuli fidei*, to produce a body of theological theory or science. In theology, no less than in any other scientific discipline, there is required a "working" by faith—the second generality—on the data made available by the first generality in order to transform them into a finished theological product of the third generality. Thus, insofar as it is a theoretical practice, theology is not different from any other scientific discipline; rather, it follows the same three-step process of the production of cognition.

In the past, theologians tended to derive the data of theology exclusively from the Bible and Christian tradition and from philosophy (the first generality), "worked on" them in the light of faith (the second generality), and produced a theological theory, e.g., church as the people of God or as the Body of Christ (the third generality). In this way, ecclesiology was developed. This kind of theology can be called "first theology."

In the theology of the political as a theoretical practice, the first generality is constituted by the theories of the social sciences (their third generality). In its second generality, the theology of the political "works" on this first generality by means of theological theories that are the third generality of "first theology." What results from this practice is the theology of the political of which liberation theology is a part. In this way, two things are achieved: first, the data of the social sciences are introduced into theology as a constitutive dimension of the theology of the political, since they are its first generality; and, second, the theology of the political retains its character as theology, since its theories are the outcome of the theologian's "working on" the data of the social sciences in the light of the theological theories of first theology. An example will make this clear. Suppose that the social sciences have shown that economic poverty in many parts of the so-called Third World is the result of the socio-political and economic structures adopted by foreign multi-national corporations (the third generality of economics). Suppose further that in the light of divine revelation, actions that inflict harm on other persons must be called sinful (the third generality of first theology). Suppose finally that a theologian wants to develop a theology of the political. She or he will take the social and economic theory and use it as the data of the new theology of the political (its first generality) and "work on" it by means of the teaching of first theology about sin (its second generality). The result of this theoretical practice (e.g., that there are "sinful structures") is the third generality of the theology of the political. Or again, suppose it is shown by the social studies that socio-political and economic liberation brings about the full dignity of the human person. Suppose that the first theology has shown that salvation by God makes the person whole and transformed. The theology of the political will make the concept of "liberation" its first generality, "works on" it by means of the theological concept of "salvation" in its second generality, and concludes that "liberation is salvation" (its third generality).

Cybernetic or Organizational Ecclesiology

Such a theoretical practice, I submit, occurs in what may be called cybernetic or organizational ecclesiology. In the case of Granfield, for instance, cybernetics as a science of communication and its concepts such as open system, environment, negative entropy, input, output, and feedback are used as the first generality of his cybernetic ecclesiology. Its second generality is constituted by the ecclesiology of first theology, which portrays the church as the communion of churches, as the Body of Christ, as the sacrament of the unity between God and humanity and the unity among humans themselves, and as the people of God. By "working on" the concepts of cybernetics in the light of this ecclesiology, Granfield is able to produce, in the third generality, a cybernetic ecclesiology in which, while the uniqueness of the church as mystery and the character of ecclesiology as a theological discipline are preserved, democracy, at least in its indirect form, can and should function in order to limit and control the exercise of power (in particular, papal power), to foster episcopal collegiality, to promote an effective and extensive participation of the laity in the life of the church, and to allow the use of certain democratic techniques (such as protest, pressure groups, communication media, study commissions, and election) to enhance effective communication, participation in decision-making and co-responsibility in the church.

Needless to say, since the publication of Granfield's *Ecclesial Cybernetics* in 1973, a plethora of works have been produced on organizational ecclesiology, not to mention writings on the organization of the church from the perspective of canon law.[64] In comparison with these, Granfield's cybernetic ecclesiology would need further development in at least three areas. First, as has been mentioned above, there are several often mutually antagonistic trends in contemporary sociology. Cybernetics is at home in functionalist sociology. The question arises as to what kind of sociological ecclesiology would emerge if the data of critical or phenomenological sociologies were used as its first generality.[65] No doubt Granfield's cybernetic ecclesiology would be enriched by ecclesiologies developed from other kinds of sociology.

Second, cybernetics as used in *Ecclesial Cybernetics* still remains at the general level in its description of an optimal way at achieving effective communication in an open system. There is no doubt that of the three schools of thought regarding organization, the organization as an open system proposed by cybernetics, as distinct from the organization as a machine or as an organism, is by far superior. As Joseph McCann puts it, "Of all the approaches to organizational analysis, the system approach offers the best hope of incorporating dynamism and energy, of explaining (and indeed, to some extent, predicting) change and transformation, and finally, of offering to the analyst a flexible model that can be applied satisfactorily to the phenomenon of the church and the churches."[66] However, this organization as an open system should be followed by a detailed study of different topologies of organizational structure and the kinds of regime under which the activities of the organization are performed. Only then can one judge how far these structures and regimes fit with those of the church.[67]

Third, Granfield's focus on how the papacy can be made effective by means of cybernetics should be enlarged to include especially the local church, both at the diocesan and the parish levels. It is of course at these levels that the lives of individual Catholics are most affected and therefore the need is all the greater to show how cybernetics can and should be applied.[68]

The dialogue between theology and, in particular, ecclesiology and the social sciences, though a recent enterprise, is vital both for the church and theology. The work of Patrick Granfield both serves as an inspiration for and is an important contribution to the interdisciplinary field of sociological ecclesiology.

Notes

[1]Pope John Paul II's March 4, 1979, encyclical *Redemptor Hominis*, no. 21.2. For the English text, see *The Encyclicals of John Paul II*, ed. Michael Miller (Huntington, Ind.: Our Sunday Visitor, 1996), 90.

[2]Among the earliest works by Catholic theologians that mentioned the need of making use of the social sciences in ecclesiology are Jérôme Hamer, "Ecclésiologie et Sociologie," *Social Compass* 7 (1960): 325-39; idem, *The Church Is a Communion* (London: Geoffrey Chapman, 1964), especially chapter XI, entitled "Psychological and Social Implications of Communion," and Yves Congar, *Lay People in the Church* (London: Geoffrey Chapman, 1957), at least indirectly, through his emphasis on the role of the laity. The first works that made a systematic use of the social sciences for ecclesiology are Jeremiah Newman, *Change and the Catholic Church: An Essay in Sociological Ecclesiology* (Baltimore: Helicon, 1965), and Mary Virginia Orna, *Cybernetics, Society and Church* (Dayton, Ohio: Pflaum Press, 1969).

[3]Clare Watkins, "Organizing the People of God: Social-Science Theories of Organization in Ecclesiology," *Theological Studies* 52 (1991): 689-711.

[4]The works reviewed by Watkins are these: Bonhoeffer, *Sanctorum Communio: A Dogmatic Enquiry into the Sociology of the Church* (1927, reprinted, London: Collins, 1963); Granfield, *Ecclesial Cybernetics: A Study of Democracy in the Church* (New York: Macmillan, 1973); De Looz, "Participation in the Catholic Church," *Pro Mundi Vita Bulletin* (Brussels, 1984); Rudge, *Ministry and Management: The Study of Ecclesiastical Administration* (London: Tavistock, 1968); Hasenhüttl, "Church and Institution," in *The Church as an Institution*, ed. Gregory Baum and Andrew Greeley (New York: Herder and Herder, 1974), 11-21; De Haas, *The Church as an Institution: Critical Studies in the Relationship between Theology and Sociology* (Jornker: Apeldoorn, 1972); and Thung, *The Precarious Organization: Sociological Explorations of the Church's Mission and Structure* (The Hague: Mouton, 1976).

[5]Watkins, "Organizing the People of God," 708. We will examine later whether this complaint regarding the lack of a theological perspective is justified, especially in the case of Patrick Granfield.

[6]Ibid., 709-710. There is some ambiguity in Watkins's distinction between an ecclesiology that views the church as "a thoroughly human expression of a certain faith" and what she terms "a more sacramental ecclesiology." In the sacramental model of the church (e.g., Avery Dulles's "church as sacrament" model), the external, visible, and institutional elements of the church are seen as efficacious signs of the internal, invisible, and transcendent elements of the church, namely, divine grace. While some of the external, visible and institutional elements are *de*

iure divino or established by divine law, others (perhaps the majority) are established by ecclesiastical law. Whereas the former may not be changed, the latter may and should be (and have been). But even in matters of divine law, church law defines and further specifies their actual implementation. In this sense, all external elements of the church are "a thoroughly human expression of a certain faith," that is, the Christian faith. At any rate, none of the theologians whose works are analyzed by Watkins considers the church as "a thoroughly human expression of a certain faith." The point of their "organizational ecclesiology" is to make sure that the visible elements of the church realize their full potential, that is, being truly efficacious signs ("sacraments") of divine grace.

[7]Ibid., 710. Watkins's suggestion of the model of "conversation" between theology and the social sciences is suggestive but remains abstract in the extreme. The last part of the essay will flesh out how this "conversation" should take place.

[8]Wackenheim argues that there must be a "sociology for ecclesiology" as well as an "ecclesiology for sociology." See his "Ecclesiology and Sociology," in *The Church as Institution*, ed. Gregory Baum and Andrew Greeley (New York: Herder and Herder, 1974), 32-41. Komonchak shows that as a systematic understanding of the church as a human and social reality, ecclesiology will have to look to the social sciences, both for a method to apply or adapt sociological insights and for assistance in working out its fundamental categories. See his "Ecclesiology and Social Theory: A Methodological Essay," *The Thomist* 45 (1981): 262-84, reprinted in Joseph Komonchak, *Foundations in Ecclesiology* (Boston: Boston College, 1995), 57-75.

[9]This term is taken from Jeremiah Newman, *Change and the Catholic Church: An Essay in Sociological Ecclesiology* (Baltimore: Helicon, 1965).

[10]For more recent studies on the relationship between the social sciences and ecclesiology, the following works should be noted: Severino Dianich, *La Chiesa mistero di comunione* (Torino: Marietti, 1977); idem, *Chiesa estroversa: Una ricerca sulla svolta dell'ecclesiologia contemporanea* (Milano: Ed. Paoline, 1987); idem, *Ecclesiologia: Questioni di metodo e una proposta* (Torino: Ed. Paoline, 1993); Bernard Donahue, "Political Ecclesiology," *Theological Studies* 33 (1972): 294-306; Roger Haight, "Historical Ecclesiology," *Science et Esprit* 39 (1987): 27-46, 345-74; idem, "On Systematic Ecclesiology," *Toronto Journal of Theology* 8 (1992): 220-38; idem, "Systematic Ecclesiology," *Science et Esprit* 45 (1993): 253-81; Franz-Xavier Kaufmann, *Kirche Begreifen. Analysen und Thesen zur gesellschaftlichen Verfassung des Christentums* (Freiburg: Herder, 1979); Joseph Komonchak, "History and Social Theory in Ecclesiology," *Lonergan Workshop* 2 (1981): 1-53; idem, "Lonergan and the Tasks of Ecclesiology," in *Creativity and Method: Essays in Honor of Bernard Lonergan, S.J.*, ed. Matthew Lamb (Milwaukee: Marquette University Press, 1981), 265-73; Joseph McCann, *Church and Organization: A Sociological and Theological Enquiry* (Scranton: Scranton University Press, 1993); and Johannes A. van der Ven, *Ecclesiology in Context* (Grand Rapids, Mich.: Eerdmans, 1996).

[11]See Gregory Baum, "Sociology and Theology," in *The Church as Institution*, ed. Gregory Baum and Andrew Greeley (New York: Herder and Herder, 1974), 22-

31. Briefly, classical sociology, founded by scholars such as de Tocqueville, Marx, Toennies, Durkheim, and Weber, is close to history and philosophy and analyzes society, culture, and religion as a human project. Positivistic-empirical sociology assimilates itself as much as possible to the natural sciences and privileges quantification and measurement of social action without presupposing overarching theories about society as such. Functionalist sociology presupposes that society is a system of social equilibrium and attempts to discover the meaning of social action, even conflict, by discovering its place and function within the total social system. Critical sociology, in opposition to functionalist sociology, does not regard society as a social equilibrium but as a conflictual system. Lastly, phenomenological sociology regards society not as an external object outside of humans but as an ongoing creation of people, and therefore claims society can be adequately studied only by examining the social process from within, that is, by studying people's interactions through words and gestures to symbolize their common purposes and intentions.

[12]Gustavo Gutiérrez, *A Theology of Liberation*, rev. ed., trans. Sister Caridad Inda and John Eagleson (Maryknoll, N.Y.: Orbis Books, 1988), 5.

[13]Clodovis Boff, *Theology and Praxis: Epistemological Foundations*, trans. Robert Barr (Maryknoll, N.Y.: Orbis, 1987), 1. The liberation theologian most insistent upon the need for theology to dialogue with the social sciences was Juan Luis Segundo, whose theological project was to dialogue with the social sciences in order to "de-ideologize" the customary interpretation of the Christian faith and its language that hide and legitimize oppression and social injustice. See especially his *Signs of the Times: Theological Reflections*, ed. Alfred Hennelly, trans. Robert Barr (Maryknoll, NY.: Orbis Books, 1993), especially two essays: "Theology and the Social Sciences" (7-17) and "The Shift Within Latin American Theology" (67-80). For a study of how the social sciences are used in liberation theologies, see Peter C. Phan, "Method in Liberation Theologies," *Theological Studies* 61 (2000): 42-46. It is well known that many Latin American theologians, at least in their early works, adopted the theory of dependence to explain the economic underdevelopment and exploitation in Latin America as the historical by-product of the development of other, mostly capitalist countries. The sociologists whose studies were relied on include Fernando Henrique Cardoso, Theotonio Dos Santos, and André Gunder Frank.

[14]Gustavo Gutiérrez, "Theology and the Sciences," in his *The Truth Shall Make You Free: Confrontations*, trans. Matthew O'Connell (Maryknoll, N.Y.: Orbis Books, 1990), 55. The essay was originally published in 1984. It is well known that liberation theology has been criticized for its use of the social sciences, especially of the Marxist type, in analyzing social conflicts. With regard to this criticism, Gutiérrez emphasizes the need for a critical use of social theories in general: "We need discernment, then, in dealing with the social theories, not only because of their inchoative character . . . but also because to say that these disciplines are scientific does not mean that their findings are apodictic and beyond discussion." See *The Truth Shall Make You Free*, 58.

[15]Clodovis Boff, *Theology and Praxis: Epistemological Foundations*.

[16]For Boff the theology of the political, which is rooted in Christian praxis, necessarily demands a dialogue with the social sciences. He carefully differentiates his own theological project from the approaches that he calls "unity of knowledge," social critique, pastoral, and sociology of knowledge. See *Theology and Praxis*, 3-8.

[17]For Boff's explanations of these ways, see *Theology and Praxis*, 20-34.

[18]The question may be raised here as to whether such a "sociological ecclesiology" necessarily takes on the contours of a liberation theology. In my judgment, not necessarily. It will be liberation theology only if the chosen sociology, the results of which are introduced into theology, is of the "critical" (or dialectical) type and not of the other four types (especially the functionalist type) described by Gregory Baum above. There is the further question of how a theologian should go about choosing one type of sociology rather than another. There are, according to Boff, both scientific and ethical criteria governing the choice. As to the scientific criteria, the theory that explains the most will have to be preferred. As to the ethical criteria, the preferred theory will be the one that is most helpful toward the realization of the values sought, e.g., freedom from economic exploitation and political oppression. See Boff, *Theology and Praxis*, 57-60.

[19]For a biography of Patrick Granfield, see David Granfield, "Patrick Granfield: A Biographical Essay," in *The Gift of the Church: A Textbook on Ecclesiology in Honor of Patrick Granfield, O.S.B.*, ed. Peter C. Phan (Collegeville, Minn.: Liturgical Press, 2000), 461-67.

[20]Patrick Granfield, *Theologians at Work* (New York: Macmillan, 1967). It was a "Book of the Month" selection by the Thomas More Association.

[21]Patrick Granfield and Josef Andreas Jungmann edited *Kyriakon* (Münster: Verlag Aschendorff, 1970).

[22]Patrick Granfield, "Behavioral Semiotic: A Critique" (Ph.D. dissertation, Pontifical Athenaeum of St. Anselm, Rome, 1958). An excerpt of the dissertation appeared as "Behavioral Semiotic: A Critique," *The Thomist* 24 (1962): 495-536. In this essay, references are made to this article, not to the dissertation.

[23]See Granfield, "Behavioral Semiotic," 534-35. One of the key elements in cybernetics is, as we will see shortly, the environment with which the system interacts.

[24]See Granfield, "The Theological Development of the Defendant's Obligation to Reply in a Civil Court" (S.T.D. dissertation, The Catholic University of America, 1962). The results of this research were published in two essays in *Theological Studies*: "The Right to Silence," *Theological Studies* 26 (1965): 280-98 and "The Right to Silence: Magisterial Development," *Theological Studies* 27 (1966): 401-20.

[25]Patrick Granfield, *Ecclesial Cybernetics: A Study of Democracy in the Church* (New York: Macmillan, 1973). Some of the ideas in this book were first presented in an essay entitled "Ecclesial Cybernetics: Communication in the Church," *Theological Studies* 29 (1968): 662-78.

[26]*Ecclesial Cybernetics*, xii.

[27]Patrick Granfield, *The Papacy in Transition* (Dublin: Gill & Macmillan, 1980).

[28]Patrick Granfield, *The Limits of the Papacy* (New York: Crossroad, 1987).

[29]*The Church and Communication*, ed. Patrick Granfield (Kansas City: Sheed & Ward, 1994).

[30]See Norbert Wiener, *Cybernetics: or Control and Communication in the Animal and the Machine* (New York: John Wiley, 1949), and idem, *The Human Use of Human Beings* (New York: Doubleday Anchor Books, 1954). Other scholars referred to by Granfield include: A. Rosenblueth, J. Bigelow, Claude E. Shannon, Warren Weaver, W. Ross Ashby, John von Neumann, David Easton, Karl W. Deutsch, and others. For the works of these authors, see *Ecclesial Cybernetics*, 2-3.

[31]*Ecclesial Cybernetics*, xii. It has been mentioned above that Granfield's earlier interest in the philosophy of sign finds further development in his study of the dynamics of communication elaborated in *Ecclesial Cybernetics.*

[32]*Ecclesial Cybernetics*, 2. Wiener's statement is taken from his *The Human Use of Human Beings*, 17.

[33]For Granfield's description of cybernetics, see "Ecclesial Cybernetics," 663-67, and *Ecclesial Cybernetics*, 5-33.

[34]*Ecclesial Cybernetics*, 8.

[35]For Granfield's detailed discussion of the organization of the Catholic Church, see *Ecclesial Cybernetics*, 34-58.

[36]*Ecclesial Cybernetics,* 14.

[37]*The Christian Faith in the Doctrinal Documents of the Catholic Church*, ed. Joseph Neuner and Jacques Dupuis (New York: Alba House, 1982), 43.

[38]*Ecclesial Cybernetics*, 19.

[39]Ibid. 58.

[40]"Ecclesial Cybernetics," 667-68.

[41]Ibid., 668.

[42]Ibid.

[43]*Ecclesial Cybernetics*, 131.

[44]The distinction between direct and indirect democracy is taken from Giovanni Sartori, *Democratic Theory* (New York: Praeger, 1965), 252.

[45]*Ecclesial Cybernetics*, 133.

[46]Ibid., 139. Granfield takes the practice of election of the bishop by the people as well as decision-making by consensus in the early church as the most convincing evidence of ecclesial democracy. See his "Episcopal Elections in Cyprian: Clerical and Lay Participation," *Theological Studies* 37:1 (1976): 41-52 and "Concilium and Consensus: Decision-Making in Cyprian," *The Jurist* 35 (1975): 397-408. For Granfield's discussion of papal election, see *The Papacy in Transition*, 124-50. In this context he proposes that there be a greater participation by a more representative electorate and that there be a fixed term of office or retirement at a fixed age.

[47]*Ecclesial Cybernetics*, 209.

[48]Ibid., 235.

[49]Granfield points out that intense commitment to large communities, such as parishes of several thousand people, is difficult if not impossible. He is therefore in favor of smaller communities.

[50]Granfield realizes that protests and pressure groups can be counterproductive, but says ". . . protests and pressure groups are valuable in the ecclesial community. Through their efforts, they bring to light sensitive issues and stimulate discussion about them. Important matters can move from a theoretical level to a practical one in a short time. Feedback, if adequately publicized, can at least force those in authority to listen. Well-organized and reasonably conducted protest has the best chances of success" (*Ecclesial Cybernetics*, 241). Granfield discusses the possibility of dissent from church teaching at length in *The Limits of the Papacy*, 158-62.

[51]Granfield makes three recommendations in the use of communication media: sound professional training, broadening of the horizon of the Catholic press, and institutional support. See *Ecclesial Cybernetics*, 144.

[52]Granfield supports the use of public opinion polls not "as an infallible index of public sentiment, but as one of the many ways for the Church to determine more accurately the *consensus fidelium*" (*Ecclesial Cybernetics*, 246).

[53]Granfield is inclined to the latter method, since "the election of bishops by general plebiscite does seem, on balance, to have so many disadvantages as to be prohibitive" (*Ecclesial Cybernetics*, 250).

[54]See Granfield, *The Limits of the Papacy*, 73-76.

[55]See Granfield, *The Papacy in Transition*, 85-88; *The Limits of the Papacy*, 92-97.

[56]See Granfield, *The Limits of the Papacy*, 97-104.

[57]Granfield writes later: "To focus solely on the human and social expects of the Church is to reduce the Church just to another social group. To focus solely on the divine and spiritual qualities of the Church is to exaggerate its supernatural aspects and overlook the crucial fact that its members are human beings living in the world. The Church is a human society, albeit unique because of its divine foundation, guidance, and goal." See *The Church and Communication,* 7.

[58]I have already referred to Clodovis Boff's work *Theology and Praxis*. Among Louis Althusser's works available in English, the following are to be noted: *Essays in Self-Criticism* (Atlantic Highlands, N.J.: Humanities, 1976); *Lenin and Philosophy and Other Essays* (New York: Monthly Review, 1971); *Politics and History: Montesquieu, Rousseau, Hegel, Marx* (New York: Schocken, 1978); *Reading Capital* (New York: Schocken, 1979); and *For Marx* (New York: Schocken, 1979). For Althusser's presentation of the process of theoretical practice, see especially *For Marx*, chapter 4, no. 3; *Reading Capital*, 40-43; and *Lenin and Philosophy*, 60-63.

[59]See Boff, *Theology and Praxis*, 71.

[60]Ibid., 72.

[61]Thomas Aquinas, *Summa Theologiae*, I, q. 1. a. 7. For Thomas, it is not the subject-matter studied—the *"ea quae in ista scientia tractantur"*—but the formal perspective under which the subject matter is treated that defines a science. For theology, it is faith that functions as this formal perspective.

[62]Boff, *Theology and Praxis*, 73.

[63]Ibid.

[64]For an extensive bibliography, see Johannes A. van der Ven, *Ecclesiology in Context*, 528-68.

[65]An example of sociological ecclesiology from the perspective of critical sociology might be Leonardo Boff, *The Church: Charism and Power: Liberation Theology and the Institutional Church*, trans. John W. Diercksmeier (New York: Crossroad, 1985).

[66]McCann, *Church and Organization*, 41.

[67]McCann distinguishes four different structures in terms of environment and membership (hierarchy, clan, collegium, and arena) and eight regimes (fief, bureaucracy, familia, guild, team, professional organization, coalition, and market).

[68]In this area, the work of Johannes A. van der Ven, *Ecclesiology in Context*, is most extensive and helpful. Van der Ven distinguishes four core functions of the church that he terms "identity," "integration," "policy," and "management." At the local level, he shows how these four core functions can be carried out in relation to the church as the Jesus movement (identity), as Body of Christ (integration), as building of the Holy Spirit (policy), and as church of the poor (management).

The Historical Fact of the Resurrection

Terrence W. Tilley

This essay about the relationship of theology to one of the social sciences, history, takes its departure from a particular claim made by Roger Haight in his recent magisterial Christology, *Jesus Symbol of God.* He wrote that it "is better to say that Jesus' resurrection is not an historical fact, because the idea of an historical fact suggests an empirical event which could have been witnessed and can now be imaginatively construed."[1] Although it might seem otherwise to some, Haight is *not* denying the reality of the Resurrection. Rather, he interprets Resurrection as Jesus' being "exalted and glorified" into the reality of God. "This occurred through and at the moment of Jesus' death, so that there was no time between his death and his resurrection and exaltation."[2] Haight finds misleading the "sensible representations" of the Resurrection, such as some found in the New Testament. He finds that these representations focus on (eminently dubitable) events, lead to embarrassing questions, and distract from faith in the transcendent, eschatological triumph of God symbolized in the Resurrection.[3]

Haight is opposing some Christians' obsession with proving "historically" that, at a certain place some thirty to forty hours after Jesus' death, Jesus' body was transformed in a manner akin to resuscitation. Haight suggests that such an obsession gets in the way of understanding, believing, and proclaiming the true significance of God's providential, salvific care symbolized in the Resurrection narratives. Moreover, it seems that such literalism leads to the confusion that the Resurrection is *the* epistemic foundation for Christian faith.[4] This sort of confusion leads one to think that winning or losing a debate about the crudely literal historicity of this event would verify or falsify Christian faith.[5]

One of Haight's main points seems indisputable, viz., that the *use* of "Resurrection" as if it were a fact that provided an epistemic foundation for faith is profoundly confused.[6] Another, that crude, imaginative reconstructions of the Resurrection are theologically unwarranted, is quite appealing. However, in skirting the Charybdis of literalism, Haight and others steer into the danger of the Scylla that makes the Resurrection just the opposite of a fact. The purpose of this paper is to find a way to understand the Resurrection as a historical fact without steering into literalist accounts or conceding that the Resurrection is mythical.

This paper recommends another tack. First, it makes some distinctions neglected by many theologians influenced by the discourse of European post-Kantian philosophy. Second, it argues that a set of theologians, inspired by Ernst Troeltsch and including Rudolf Bultmann, Jürgen Moltmann, and Roger Haight, work with a specific view of the relationship of history and theology that is unsustainable.[7] My claim herein is that history is best understood as a *discipline*, and that theologians and philosophers in this post-Kantian tradition have unwarrantedly construed the procedural *presumptions*, the "rules of thumb," proper to history in particular and to the social sciences in general, as if they were metaphysical *truths*. This confusion results from a failure to distinguish defeasible *methodological presumptions* of a discipline from indefeasible *substantive claims* of a metaphysics or ontology.[8] This misunderstanding has led to theological conundra and confusions that could be avoided. Third, the essay sketches an alternative account that allows us properly to continue to speak of the Resurrection as a historical fact.

Distinctions

Often overlooked in positions like the one under consideration is that a "fact" is not an "event."[9] One can *state* a fact; one cannot state an event. Events *happen* or *occur*. Facts do not "happen." In most circumstances, we take a statement as factual if it adequately and accurately represents an action, event, or state of affairs. We can challenge someone whose statement of "fact" we doubt to be true to "warrant the statement" or, more loosely, to "prove that fact." We cannot ask someone to "prove an event." We might want someone to prove "that an event occurred" or to warrant a statement "that an event occurred," but here we are dealing in the realm of facts, not in the realm of events. Remember, Sergeant Joe Friday in "Dragnet" did not say, "Just the events, ma'am, just the events," but "Just the facts, ma'am, just the facts." His witnesses could relate facts, not events.[10] My point is that linguistically and conceptually "facts" and "events" are not interchangeable; they are not the same thing.[11]

Generally speaking, then, a fact is a representation of a state of affairs. Some of those states of affairs are events. Some are actions. A "historical fact" is a representation of a state of affairs, an event, or an action that is in the past (not the present or the future) at the time the representation is made. We may accept some facts, reject others, be undecided about still others. But note that we don't (in the same sense) accept, reject, or be undecided about events, actions, or states of affairs. We evaluate the *way* events, actions, or states of affairs are *represented.* We evaluate *facts.*

Further, it is important to distinguish "events" from "actions."[12] In general, events *occur* while actions are *performed* by agents. Consider the following:

"Jamie, why did you hit your sister?"

"I didn't mean to, Dad. I was just swinging my arm and she ran into it."

What Jamie is doing here—whether telling the truth or not—is trying to deflect the question about an action Dad presumes she performed into a question about an event for which she is not responsible. Moreover, if we see someone engaging in behavior we don't understand, we ask what they are doing:

"Jean, why are you waving your arm like a fool at the traffic?"

"What? Why, I'm trying to catch Fred's attention; he's supposed to pick me up."

What Jean has done—whether truthfully or not—is to try to explain this behavior by telling her interlocutor the purpose or intention of the behavior, thereby letting him know that the behavior was not random or incidental, but was her *act.*

I do not want to argue here that we ought limit our understanding of agency to human agency or to intentional agency.[13] However, our ordinary "default" understanding of an action is that an action is intentional. If we don't understand why someone did something, we try to find out "why" or "to what purpose" he or she "did it." In doing so, we typically *presume* that her or his action was intentional, even if we are not clear on what the intentions were.[14] If someone tells us what the purpose of her or his action was, the response *ipso facto* validates our presumption that the act was intentional, even if we doubt the veracity of the report of the intention. If someone responds that he really didn't intend anything by the behavior in question, then he challenges our presumption that the occurrence was an action. He is claiming that what happened was an accident or an event or an occurrence; it was not a fully "human act," as some scholastics might put it.

The point of these distinctions is to get some clarity about the language we ought to use about the Resurrection. First and foremost, the Resurrection is *not* to be understood as merely an event. It is fundamentally, and more significantly, an action. The agent is God. The *result* of the action is that Jesus is exalted and glorified. If the Resurrection is a fact, that fact does *not* report or represent merely *an event that occurred*, but an *act of God*. The testimony at the root of the Christian tradition has not claimed that an event has occurred, but that God performed an action. Whether accurate or inaccurate, the putative fact is not that "the Resurrection occurred," but that God raised Jesus from the dead.[15] To construe the Resurrection as an "event," as theologians all too often do, is to construe it as behavior, the significance of which we do not understand. This is imprecise enough to be as misleading as Jamie might well be in the sample dialogue above.[16]

Second, the evidence for this action is the testimony of witnesses. Their testimony is clearly conditioned by factors too numerous to exhaust here. Some crucial ones include the "background beliefs" of the witnesses, for example, the religious context that leads them to expect the resurrection of the dead as God's eschatological act; the appearances to the disciples and to Paul; and the necessity for the body to be absent from the tomb. When one questions the "historicity of the Resurrection," one is questioning the veracity, accuracy, and adequacy of the witnesses, just as one might question whether Jamie was truthful, accurate, and adequate in her witness to her own intentions when she hit her sister. The testimony is *not* that an event occurred, analogous to Jamie's sister having a bruised shoulder. The testimony is that God has acted and that "we" have witnessed the results of that action. Questioning whether the Resurrection is a historical fact must be questioning the accuracy and adequacy of the testimony of the witnesses.[17]

Third, the witnesses never report directly on what that act of God looked like. While the Bible includes reports of "eye-witness" accounts of appearances and of the empty tomb, it does not include narratives that so graphically fill pious imaginations—flashes of light, stones exploding or majestically and magically moving away from the opening to the tomb, a talking cross, cowering soldiers, and so forth.[18] Even the accounts of the Ascension, so often imagined in literalistic terms, are rather cryptic at best (see Mark 16:19, Acts 1:9-11). In short, the "evidence" for the fact of the Resurrection, then, is a mass of testimony, not fully consistent and mostly hearsay, to an act of God (not an event) that led to Jesus' appearances (to many in various ways and places) and to a specific state of affairs (the empty tomb).[19]

Having made these distinctions, we can turn to what a line of theologians concerned with history and theology do when they question the historical fact of the Resurrection. My analysis is that the claims and counterclaims typical in this line of thinking, exemplified by Troeltsch, Bultmann, Moltmann, and Haight, are confused. I am not suggesting either that only these theologians take up this line of thinking or that this group constitutes a "type" or "school" in theological work, for they differ significantly in the methods and contents of their work. Rather, with regard only to the philosophical foundations of history and history's relationship to theology, these theologians (and others) share a specific angle of vision that accounts for their common reticence to acknowledge the Resurrection as a fact representing an act of God in history. Their other commonalities and differences are beyond the scope of this essay.

The Presumptions of Historical Investigation and the Claims of Metaphysicians

In an influential 1898 essay, Ernst Troeltsch developed three principles for critical history.[20] Jürgen Moltmann, who takes his own bearings on history from Troeltsch, presents these as axioms of probability, correlation, and analogy. I find problems with all these axioms.

The *axiom of probability* claims that historical knowledge is never "absolute" knowledge. Historical knowledge therefore cannot be the foundation of faith. While the antecedents of this claim in eighteenth-century philosopher G. E. Lessing's broad, ugly ditch divorcing the accidental truths of history from the absolute truths of faith are clear,[21] the logic of the claim is not. No knowledge, save (possibly) *a priori* knowledge, is "absolute" (and that only within a language game or discourse system). In a post-Cartesian era in which we find that the quest for absolute certainty has failed, the naive opposition between the absoluteness of faith and the conditionedness of historical knowledge is no longer an axiom we can accept.[22] All knowledge is conditioned, historical, and local, even if it is knowledge of what is unconditioned, beyond space, and beyond time. While there may be a distinction to be drawn between the gift of faith and the acquisition of knowledge, the *axiom of probability* does not capture such a distinction, but postulates a total separation.[23] For present purposes, we can simply set aside this axiom not only as dubious, but as no longer germane to the issues, if it ever was.

The *axiom of correlation* is that there are "interactions between all phenomena in historical life. *They are the ontological foundation* . . . for the connections between cause and effect which apply everywhere."[24] Another way of putting this is that historical events are caused by and only by other historical events. The *axiom of analogy* states that the ways events occurred in the past are analogous to the way they occur in the present. This axiom is based on the "homogeneity of all historical happening."[25] That is, an event that does not proceed according to the ordinary laws of cause and effect that we understand to be operative is not one that we can understand or accept on the basis of history.

The axioms of correlation and analogy are two sides of the same coin. The former is presented as an ontological foundation. The latter is an epistemological claim based on that foundation. To accept the axiom of analogy is to accept the axiom of correlation. Ontological correlation makes analogical thinking possible in historical analysis and social science investigations. Analogical thinking in history and the other social sciences makes ontological correlations visible. These linked axioms allegedly state the conditions that make possible historical investigations in particular, and social science analyses in general. It is only because of correlation and analogy, a thinker in this tradition would say, that we have any ability at all to understand the past and predict the future. For example, a thinker in this tradition would have to claim that a real, ontological correlation between an increase in unemployment and an increase in domestic violence and theft in a geographical region makes it possible to postulate that connection, to understand the effects of past or present social policies that increase unemployment, and to make actuarial calculations and set insurance rates.

Rudolf Bultmann accepted the linked Troeltschian principles of analogy and correlation. He writes that "modern science does not believe that the course of nature can be interrupted or, so to speak, perforated, by supernatural powers."[26] Bultmann simply rephrases the axiom of correlation; he proceeds in his own work by the axiom of analogy.

Roger Haight explicitly accepts the principle of analogy as intertwined with the axiom of correlation: "A positive statement of the principle [of analogy] is that one must understand historical events *within a unified ontological framework*."[27] Put negatively, it means that "one should ordinarily not expect to have happened in the past what is presumed or proven to be impossible today."[28] Haight thus accepts both the epistemic principle of analogy and its ontological foundation in the principle of correlation. This is the methodological basis for Haight's claim that it is better not to say that the Resurrection is a historical fact.

However, the question is whether this approach to the philosophical foundations of history and history's relationship to theology, exemplified in the "axioms" of correlation and analogy common to Troeltsch, Bultmann, Moltmann, and Haight, is sound. I will argue that it is not, as the postmodern suspicion of ontology undermines it, historical methodology does not support it, and analysis shows that it misplaces history as a practice and as a discipline in the humanistic social sciences.

First, if postmodern theory has taught us anything, it is that ontological foundations are profoundly suspect. Each of the theologians cited here—Troeltsch, Bultmann, Moltmann, Haight—accept the "ontological foundation" of the principle of analogy. But on what grounds can we warrant that ontological claim? Is this not merely a prejudice, as Wolfhart Pannenburg puts it, in favor of one specific metaphysics, a metaphysics based on a mechanistic world view that is clearly "obsolete"?[29] This axiom, in fact, gives this "ontological foundation" or the "prejudices" of modernity a veto over the results of historical inquiry. But this veto is suspiciously self-serving, for those who invoke it also accept the "modern world view" as the only possible or most reasonable one.

Second, historians have attacked this sort of principle. That most contemporary historians do not experience encounters with deities does not "alter the . . . fact that deities and salvations have been central to past actuality," as historian William A. Clebsch put it.[30] Clebsch goes on to note that no "available *historical* method can distinguish the way men and women personally and socially understood their universe from the way their universe actually was then and there."[31] Whatever people in other times and places experienced and gave witness to—unless they were deluded or lying—is the way things were for them then and there. "[A] license to rule out, as illusion or mere apprehension, everything testified to which lies outside the historians' own experience would collapse their narratives into little more than autobiography."[32] Clebsch concludes that "critical history issues no warrant for changing what happened into an apprehension of what happened."[33] *Mutatis mutandis*, "critical history" cannot warrant *on historical grounds* the redescription of the act of God to which the witnesses testify as "really" testimony to a non-historical (not locatable in time and space) fact, or to some other sort of event or state of affairs. The fact that their universe is not our universe does not license us to say that they were deluded and we have it straight. Clebsch shows that these are not *absolutes* for historical work, but defeasible *presumptions*.[34]

Third, these axioms misplace history as a practice and a discipline. Historian Carlo Ginzburg points out that history deals with individual "cases, situations, and documents, precisely *because they are individual*."[35] History is not a "Galileian science" because science deals with the repeatable and the quantifiable, while history, specifically as a humanistic social science, deals with unique, unquantifiable acts and events.[36] The Troeltschian axioms of correlation and analogy, in fact, treat history as if it were a Galileian science or a subsidiary of the hard sciences. But by its nature, history is not such a science.[37] Historical work does not presume an ontological foundation; its presumptions are like the presumption of innocence in U.S. law—procedural presumptions that may be overturned in specific investigations, but which are "rules of thumb" necessary for engaging in the practice of doing history. In the end these "axioms" are merely descriptions of the "common sense" of the disciplines of history and the other social sciences, not metaphysical necessities.

Moreover, social historians generally do not focus on whether specific events actually happened, just as intellectual historians do not focus on whether the ideas transmitted through time are true ideas.[38] What these historians find important and interesting are the ways in which practices and ideas have spread, affecting social, economic, and political constellations. For these historians, whether or not the Resurrection occurred or could be "validated" by historical work is irrelevant. The fact that people believed in the Resurrection, the analysis of the conditions under which that belief flourished among groups in the Greco-Roman world, the ways in which the notion of Resurrection was connected with the idea of the immortality of the soul, and the significance of all of these for the early Christian movements are the key items in their story.[39] Analogously, what is important for the social historian is not whether one man acting alone or with another or as part of a conspiracy killed John F. Kennedy in 1963, but on how that event and those hypotheses have affected the practices and people of the United States ever since. A factual answer to the question, "Who killed Kennedy?" may be unwarrantable on properly historical grounds—a claim that could be warranted by examining the various "historical" hypotheses advanced, mostly by non-historians.

Given these three points, then, we can say that the problem with this understanding of the philosophical foundations of history and the relationship of history to theology is that it raises the defeasible "rules of thumb" by which historians operate to indefeasible metaphysical principles. These metaphysical principles turn out to be nothing other than the "common sense" of modern scientific investigations. This "common sense" has no place for an act of God. When these practical principles of modern "common sense" or "the discipline of history" are raised to metaphysical principles, the consequences for faith and for theology are profoundly unsatisfactory.

Pannenberg highlights the results of such philosophical canonizations. He argues that a "negative judgment on the bodily resurrection of Jesus as having occurred in historical fact is *not a result* of the historical critical examination of the Biblical Easter tradition, *but a postulate* that precedes any such examination."[40] Methodologically, historians presume that "supernatural" entities do not act in history. However, this does not warrant the reductionist claim that actions attributed to supernatural entities must always and everywhere be reduced to historical claims about natural agents because of an indefeasible principle that "supernatural" agents cannot be said to act in history.

Like all presumptions of practices, such as the presumption of innocence in criminal trials in this country, the results of engaging in the practice can bear a burden of proof against the presumption. Despite the presumption of innocence, juries find defendants in criminal cases guilty. In the end, as historians, we may want to say that we have no acceptable natural explanation of some events, or that multiple explanations are available but not demonstrable in and of themselves. One may accept one of the explanations as more plausible, but that will depend on one's background beliefs: the testimony to the Resurrection may be a response to an act of God in history, or it may be the result of a widespread delusion, or a clever propaganda tactic by a desperate sect, or an expression of a Freudian illusion, and so on. It may be that the methodological presumption can be upset in some cases, as, for example, should there be an event for which there is no available natural explanation. A person working as a historian might remain agnostic about the causes of those events. That does not mean that that person, when she is not wearing the historian's mantle, must remain agnostic. Yet if the historians' rules of thumbs are raised to metaphysical principles, then historians would be inconsistent at least or irrational at worst to go beyond what their methodological presumptions allowed. William James wittily illustrated the problems attendant with allowing the principles of one practice to overflow into all of life:

> [J]ust as a man who in a company of gentlemen made no advances, asked a warrant for every concession, and believed no one's word without proof, would cut himself off by such churlishness from all the social rewards that a more trusting spirit would earn,—so here, one who should shut himself up in snarling logicality and try to make the gods extort his recognition willy-nilly, or not get it at all, might cut himself off forever from his only opportunity of making the gods' acquaintance.[41]

Besides having such potentially damning consequences, the naturalistic thesis that all events must have natural and only natural causes requires a metaphysical argument about the fictional status of all supernatural agents or a theological argument for the complete separation of historical from religious "facts." Even if such arguments could be successfully mounted, neither of these arguments are ones that historians can give *qua* historians; for the most part, they fail to focus on the sorts of questions that are amenable to answers developed by using historical methodologies.

In sum, the theologians considered here assume a connection between the axiom of correlation and the axiom of analogy. I maintain that that assumption is not warranted. Analogy is a procedural presumption of historical method, but one that does not require an ontological correlation as its basis. Moreover, that procedural presumption of analogy may be defeated—we may, upon investigation, find that the universe of the past is not ours, that it is a place stranger than we know.

The Troeltschian mutual implication of correlation and analogy implies that a procedural, defeasible methodological naturalism entails a substantial, indefeasible reductionist atheism (or deism) characteristic of modern science. But this implication is not necessary. That there is in some cases a profound disanalogy between the historical subjects' universe and the historical investigators' universe does not mean our ontology is correct and theirs wrong. Historically, all we can say is that this is the way the world was for them. The immediate move to reductionism—that they were deluded, lying, or inaccurate or inadequate in their reports—is another issue and requires a separate scientific or metaphysical or theological argument. While the "axiom" of analogy may be a good presumption of historical practice, especially of social and intellectual history, it can be defeated within the practice (as all good rules of thumb can be overturned occasionally) and its ontological foundation is at least superfluous, at most a canonized modern prejudice.

Given the problems with the first three axioms, Moltmann's fourth axiom fails.[42] The fourth axiom is that because of the principles of probability, correlation, and analogy, we cannot talk about the activity of a transcendent God in history. History is made by human beings, not by supernatural beings. Hence, the supernatural is precluded from inclusion in history. Moltmann here makes explicit the transubstantiation of procedural principles into metaphysical claims.

However, as the previous axioms are undermined, this one is as well. Historians and other social scientists may presume in their work that divine agents have not acted in history, but it is not proper for them to say that that presumption cannot be overturned in a particular investigation. While as a historian or social scientist, I may be able to say that an event, such as the curing of a withered hand or the remission of an intractable metastatic cancer, may be inexplicable given what we know presently, as a historian I can rule out neither a claim that a medical explanation might be available in the future nor a claim that this was an effect of an act of God.

If this analysis of Troeltsch's axioms as developed by Moltmann is correct, and if the axioms of correlation and analogy underlie the work of these theologians,[43] then we have an explanation of why these theologians are at least hesitant to construe the Resurrection of Jesus as a historical fact. They must say that since testimony to the Resurrection violates our understanding of the way the universe is, our ontology, we cannot accept it. Since we cannot accept the testimony, we cannot construe the Resurrection as a historical fact, but a symbol of another fact, a "transcendent" fact, i.e., a faith claim that Jesus' Resurrection is God's supernatural, non-historical (that is, not temporally or spatially locatable) act.

But who is this "we"? This "we" is a fiction covering over modern and postmodern diversity. It homogenizes "us" into a uniform "modern man"(*sic*). This "we" actually includes people of profoundly different metaphysical and religious belief. Rabbi Dan Cohn-Sherbok recognizes this diversity and gets the logic of the arguments laid out more accurately than the theologians discussed above.

In his essay, "The Resurrection of Jesus: A Jewish View," Cohn-Sherbok argues strongly against the "modernist" tendency to deny the historical fact of the Resurrection. He writes:

> Jesus was physically resurrected or he wasn't. It's as simple as that. The Gospel account of the empty tomb and the disciples' recognition of the risen Christ point to such a historical conception of the resurrection event. To them it would make no sense that in some spiritual—as opposed to physical—sense Jesus' body was revivified. And such an idea should make no sense to us either, because it is a muddle. As a Jew, I am not persuaded that Jesus was revived after death and that he sits at the right hand of the Father. But I am capable of being persuaded. I wait for the evidence.[44]

However, is it evidence that Cohn-Sherbok awaits? I think not. Earlier in his essay, he engages in an exercise in which he finds he can consent to about fifty percent of the Nicene Creed.[45] Those parts he rejects, of course, are those creedal items distinctive to Christian faith: the Trinity, the Incarnation, the Virgin Birth, the final judgment by Jesus, and the resurrection of the body. While Cohn-Sherbok demands "objective data"[46] as his evidence, what he demands is, finally, the

Second Coming, an objective proof not merely of the Resurrection, but of the whole of the Christian creed "televised on CNN and other forms of the world's media."[47] To convert him to Christianity, it would take indisputable evidence that this would be the Messiah's return engagement. Although it looks as though Cohn-Sherbok is treating the Resurrection as the *foundation* of faith, his standard of evidence shows that it is the whole system of religious practice and belief that would have to be warranted—including that key item of the Resurrection of Jesus.

What makes Cohn-Sherbok require such a heavy burden of proof is the fact that the Christian creed does not function as a component in his background belief structure. The evidence he requires would warrant the whole creed. But this leads us to another insight: The converse would also be true. That is, if one accepts the central and distinctive doctrines of Christianity, especially the Trinity and the Incarnation, then the burden of proof for the historical fact of the Resurrection should be rather light. Indeed, it can be met by brushing history against the grain, by reading the New Testament witnesses who were writing "propaganda" and finding what truths that propaganda proclaimed or presupposed.[48] In so doing, historians can discover that the witness contained in the New Testament is to a mighty act of God, not merely an event that occurred, and that this action was, for them, an act of God in history.

Roger Haight says that the Resurrection "is a transcendent reality which can only be appreciated by faith-hope."[49] One interpretation of this claim would make belief in the Resurrection a close analog of a Freudian illusion, a belief that one holds because one wishes it to be true. Another interpretation, which I would support, would be that the difference between those who accept the Resurrection as a historical fact and those who don't is a difference in the "background beliefs" they hold. As Dan Cohn-Sherbok does not accept the Christian belief and practice and Wolfhart Pannenberg does, their disagreement about the historicity of the Resurrection is best understood not as a foundation for, but as a constituent of their religious disagreement. If this latter interpretation is what Haight means by "faith-hope," then there is no good reason not to speak theologically of the Resurrection as a historical fact, properly understood. Reticence to do so is based on a philosophical account of the necessary foundations of history that supposedly make history and philosophy possible. This account is not sustainable, if the arguments here are sound.

I do not want to downplay the important contributions of those theologians who take the approach discussed in this essay. They have made some remarkably important points.

First, they have made it clear that the Resurrection is *not* warranted by "objective data" available to anyone of whatever metaphysical or religious persuasion. Because so many of "us" today blithely accept the universe of modern science as our own metaphysics, the "symbolist" accounts of the Resurrection appeal to many of "us." But even these do not warrant the fact of the resurrection to "all comers."

Second, they have clarified that there is no "event" that is somehow the "foundation" of faith. My point is that belief that God acted to raise Jesus from the dead is a constituent of Christian faith, a faith that makes the burden of proof of the Resurrection easy and light. If one can accept the camel of the Incarnation as in some sense true, then why draw the line at swallowing the gnat of God's raising Jesus from the dead?

Third, they remind us that there is no reason to think we can portray imaginatively the act of God represented by the historical fact of the Resurrection. Much Christian art has done so, but it needs to be interpreted as imaginative projection and propaganda, more like descriptions of the joys of heaven or drawings in American cartoons distributed during World War II caricaturing the Germans and the Japanese than like nuanced expressions of a philosophical or theological claims.

But what does this leave us in terms of a positive account?

The Historical Fact of the Resurrection: Toward an Account

A full-scale argument for the view implicit in the foregoing about the fact of the Resurrection is far beyond the scope of this paper. What we can do is to draw out those implications and in so doing sketch what I see as a warrantable view.

Negatively, historians and theologians have often sought to say far too much.[50] More positively, we can say, first, that sources in all major strata of tradition in the New Testament (save, possibly, "Q") testify to God's acting on Jesus to "raise" him.[51] Various sources offer different evidences for this act of God, and none of them portrays clearly just what that act was. The main strands in this testimony are the variety of "appearance" stories and the "discovery of the empty tomb" stories.[52] All of them, in different ways, presume or assert that God's act was "historical," that God acted to "raise" Jesus up at some time between Jesus' death and the time of the appearances or discoveries. This act of God brought about the effects of appearances and discoveries to which they testify.[53] For them, that God raised Jesus from the dead expressed an indubitable historical fact.[54] Moreover, it was a fact that was a major constituent in a religious tradition that became dominant in the Greco-Roman world in less than three hundred years.

Second, we can say that their testimony was conditioned by Jewish apocalyptic expectations in which the raising of the dead would be a sign of the day of God's triumph. To say, however, that such expectations *caused* rather than *conditioned* their belief that God raised Jesus from the dead is tantamount to saying that the witnesses were deluded. That they were indeed deluded is quite possible. Such a claim, however, is not new. As Acts 26 portrays the dispute between Paul and Festus, Festus yells that Paul has been made "mad" by his learning, while Paul asserts that he speaks "the sober truth." Alternatively, the witnesses might be seen as liars. However, if we reject the reliability of their testimony, we do so on the basis of other beliefs we hold, beliefs that make us find any sort of belief such as belief in the Resurrection to be self-deceptive or deceptive. We must say that their belief was caused or conditioned by expectations we do not have or beliefs we do not hold. Such rejections certainly do have some warrant, as the arguments of skeptics from Festus through Hume to Bertrand Russell and contemporary masters and mistresses of suspicion show. But these reasons to reject the Resurrection are not beliefs generated by historical investigations.

Third, as a principle of historiography, we can simply notice that the burden of proof is not merely "event-specific" and "context-specific," but "audience-specific."[55] For a person who believes in the Incarnation, roughly, that the Creator and Sanctifier of the universe was present in and through Jesus of Nazareth in a way that may be said to be "unique" and/or "definitive" and/or "final" and in so doing brought healing and/or atonement and/or reconciliation and/or redemption to us and/or this world and/or the universe, the burden of proof is rather light.[56] The burden of proof is substantially different for a person who does not participate in the practices that constitute the Christian tradition. Practically, to convince someone of the historical fact of the Resurrection is probably not to provide evidence or proof for that "event," but to bring that person to come to accept other beliefs that lighten the burden of proof of the Resurrection. Prescriptions for that apologetic task, however, are beyond the scope of this paper. In sum, the fact of the Resurrection is disputable *not* on the basis of the testimony of the witnesses, but on the basis of the explanations one gives of that testimony, explanations based on other beliefs a person holds.

Accepting the Resurrection as a fact, then, is not undermined by "the canons of historical method." Accepting the fact that God acted depends, rather, on whatever other beliefs one holds, especially one's beliefs about the possibility of God acting "immanently." To reduce the Resurrection to a symbolic representation of a transcendent fact is to concede far too much to the prejudices of modernity. These prejudices have been unwarrantedly elevated from rules of thumb into universal philosophical verities. This exaltation has led to a confused and confusing understanding of the relationship of theology and the social sciences, especially history. A different approach, one more nuanced in its appreciation of linguistic and conceptual distinctions, one that seeks to be both rhetorical and truthful, that acknowledges the limits of historians' interests and abilities *qua* historians, and that recognizes where the burden of proof actually lies in witnessing to the historical fact, including that of the Resurrection, provides an alternative way to carry out the revisionist task of contemporary theology without accepting this post-Kantian tradition's unfortunate construal of the foundations of history in particular and the social sciences in general.

As a Christian I claim that God acted to raise Jesus from the dead. I have shown, contra Moltmann, that his claim that we cannot say that God acts in history is incorrect. I have argued, contra Haight (with whom I agree on many more matters than I disagree in regard to Christology), that it is better to continue to speak of the Resurrection as a historical fact; his objections to this way of understanding the Resurrection are misplaced, especially if we construe "faith-hope" as providing the background beliefs that Christians (but not others) bring to the assessment of the historicity of the Resurrection.

Picturing that act of God adequately and accurately is, I believe, beyond human ability. Nor can I warrant the claim that God raised Jesus from the dead to all comers in all situations; hence, I cannot claim that this is an "undisputable" historical fact. But to claim that I have not stated, or ought not state, this fact, but made, or should make, some other sort of claim in some other sort of speech act, rather than to state a historical fact, as various theologians who accept the relationship of the social science of history and theology described herein, is simply unfair to the fact of the Resurrection.[57]

Notes

[1]Roger Haight, *Jesus Symbol of God* (Maryknoll, N.Y.: Orbis Books, 1999), 124.

[2]Ibid., 126.

[3]Haight is not alone in his position; Jürgen Moltmann, Hans Küng, and other theologians take similar positions. Moltmann, for instance, claims, "When we talk about Christ's resurrection from the dead we are not talking about a fact. We are talking about a process" ("The Resurrection of Christ: Hope for the World," in *Resurrection Reconsidered*, ed. Gavin D'Costa [Oxford: Oneworld, 1996], 80). Haight also acknowledges the arguments of others like Nicholas Lash and Wolfhart Pannenberg who take contrasting views, while also citing scholars like John Galvin and Gerald O'Collins whose views seem closer to his own.

[4]All too often, Paul's dictum that if Christ is not raised, our faith is in vain (1 Cor. 15:14) is read in our era as if Paul was an epistemological, evidential foundationalist. This retrojecting of contemporary philosophical approaches onto Paul's proclamation is anachronistic.

[5]See, for example, Gary R. Habermas and Antony Flew, *Did Jesus Rise from the Dead? The Resurrection Debate*, ed. Terry L. Miethe (San Francisco: Harper & Row, 1987).

[6]Belief in the Resurrection is better understood as a *constituent* of faith; I make an analogous argument with regard to revelation as a constituent, not a foundation, of faith in *Inventing Catholic Tradition* (Maryknoll, N.Y.: Orbis, 2000), 161-69.

[7]See Terrence W. Tilley, "Practicing History, Practicing Theology," *Horizons* 25/2 (Fall, 1998): 258-275, for a discussion of the relationship between the two disciplines.

[8]An analogous confusion occurs if one thinks that simply because a theologian uses sociological investigations that are methodologically "atheistic" to develop theologically relevant concepts, such use of sociology commits the theologian to substantive atheism. John Milbank, *Theology and Social Theory* (Oxford: Basil Blackwell, 1990), 101-140, makes this type of error in his critique of the use of sociology in theology.

[9]To surface these distinctions, I use an "ordinary language argument." This sort of argument notes the importance of what people ordinarily say when they are using their native language well. Such an argument is not necessarily decisive, a point recognized by its leading proponent, John L. Austin: "Certainly, then, ordinary language is *not* the last word: in principle it can everywhere be supplemented and improved upon and superseded. Only remember, it *is* the *first* word" ("A Plea for Excuses," *Philosophical Papers*, ed. J. O. Urmson and G. J. Warnock [Oxford: Clarendon Press, 1961], 133; emphasis in original). Failure to note that oftentimes

our "technical" vocabulary obscures important distinctions that can be teased out from ordinary language can result in philosophical (or other) obfuscations.

[10]I am not claiming that "events" occur independently of language and "facts" are linguistic entities; rather, I find that these two concepts have rather different uses in our language and different conceptual places in our discourses.

[11]For example, many in the United States think it a fact that O. J. Simpson killed Nicole Brown Simpson and Ron Goldman on the evening of 12 June 1994. That not *everyone* believes this claim does not make those who believe it think that it is a "symbolic representation" of some other action. In some circles, it is a "disputed" fact; in others, it is not disputed at all. Because no one could demonstrate at his criminal trial the (alleged) fact that Mr. Simpson killed those two people does not mean either that those events did not occur or that Mr. Simpson did not perform that act. Perhaps Mr. Simpson knows what events occurred and what actions he performed that morning. But whatever actions and events *actually were performed and occurred*, those actions and events alone are not sufficient to *warrant a claim* (to show a claim accurate and adequate enough in the context in which the claim was made) about the facts of the matter; an argument for this position is developed in Tilley, *Inventing Catholic Tradition*, 151-163.

[12]Even Van A. Harvey, *The Historian and the Believer* (New York: Macmillan, 1966), 229, fails to make this distinction.

[13]I am, however, persuaded by G. E. M. Anscombe that an "intentional action" is not a special kind of action, but rather that to say that some act is "unintentional" is simply to say that the question "why did you or she or he or they do that?" is not applicable to this action. See her *Intention* (Ithaca, N.Y.: Cornell University Press, 1957), 28. The argument here borrows heavily from her analysis.

[14]This "ordinary" presumption does not apply in the criminal justice system. That the courts have a different "standard of proof" from ordinary life is a construct that serves to protect the innocent in cases where there is reasonable doubt. Mr. Simpson, for instance, may have killed two people, but may be innocent of murder, perhaps by reason of temporary insanity.

[15]Haight, for example, highlights this point. See *Jesus Symbol of God*, 123.

[16]Another way of construing this is to say that in "inner history," the history of our life together as a community (which is primary), this fact represents an act of God, while from the perspective of "outer history," the fact portrays "events" significant in world history, even if God did not act. For the distinction, see H. Richard Niebuhr, *The Meaning of Revelation* (New York: Macmillan, 1960 [first edition, 1941]), especially 44-50; for criticism and use of this distinction see Harvey, *The Historian and the Believer*, 234-42, and Terrence W. Tilley, *Story Theology* (Wilmington, Del.: Michael Glazier, Inc., 1985), 148-50. A key problem with this typology of history is that there can be many external and internal histories, but that does not affect the point being made here. Another way of construing this distinction is to contrast the sorts of background beliefs one brings to analyzing historical claims, as discussed below.

[17]David Hume's chapter, "On Miracles," in *An Inquiry Concerning Human*

Understanding, ed. Charles W. Hendel (Indianapolis, Ind.: Bobbs-Merrill, 1955), gets the logic of this argument right. Miracle reports are based on testimony; no testimony amounts to a probability, much less a proof that a miracle occurred; one who believes in miracles believes "contrary to custom and experience" (141); that is, the consistent testimony to the law-like character of the patterns of events that the miracle story violates creates a burden of proof against which testimony for a miracle cannot bear. However, some reliable testimony to "events" contrary to custom and experience (e.g., to states of affairs "before and after" some alleged miracle cures occurred) might at least give some support to claims that miracle cures occurred. This seems not to have been a live option for Hume.

[18]One ancient text that does is the Gospel of Peter (8:28-13:55). See Edgar Hennecke, *New Testament Apocrypha*, ed. Wilhelm Scheemelcher, trans. R. McL. Wilson, 2 vols. (Philadelphia: Westminster Press, 1963), I:185-87. This is the only ancient text that relates the "events that occurred" in that fantastic manner so attractive to the popular and literalistic imagination Haight properly seeks to undermine. While historians working as historians should, as argued below, give some level of credence to appearance and empty tomb stories, accepting such as the Gospel of Peter as literally true or reliable testimony has far too heavy a burden of proof to bear against the presumptions of the practice of history to be a credible claim.

[19]Rowan Williams, "Between the Cherubim: The Empty Tomb and the Empty Throne," in Gavin D'Costa, ed., *Resurrection Reconsidered*, 87-101, notes the disagreements among historians about what strata in the New Testament are earliest, which most reliable, etc. But the disagreements are about the *events* and the *effects,* not about the key fact, that God has *acted* to raise Jesus.

[20]The discussion in this paragraph follows Jürgen Moltmann, "The Resurrection of Christ: Hope for the World," 77-78. Moltmann cites Ernst Troeltsch, "Über Historische and Dogmatische Methode in der Theologie" (1898), in *Gesammelte Schriften II* (Tübingen, 1913) 729-53; idem, "Historical and Dogmatic Method in Theology," in *Religion and History*, trans. J. L. Adams and W. F. Bense (Edinburgh: T&T Clark, 1991). Moltmann cites "four axioms," but the fourth is his own inference from Troeltsch's three principles.

[21]See Henry Chadwick, ed., *Lessing's Theological Writings: Selections in Translation* (Stanford: Stanford University Press, 1957), 53-55.

[22]Compare Harvey, *The Historian and the Believer*, 249: "The real issue, then, is not whether faith is independent of all historical criticism but whether Christian faith requires certain specific historical assertions that, in the nature of the case, are dubious or not justified. But if this is the issue, one must examine such assertions piecemeal."

[23]Harvey, *The Historian and the Believer*, 252, raises the issue well: "But . . . is this another of those false and artificial distinctions? What if symbol and event, timeless truth and history, are not strict alternatives?" Harvey's questioning of the dichotomy, like Ginzburg's rejection of the dichotomy between proof and rhetoric (see note 37, below), begins well. Unfortunately, his "perspectivist" approach

cannot be sustained on his terms, a point he recognized in his own later work.

[24]Moltmann, "The Resurrection of Christ," 78; emphasis added.

[25]Ibid.

[26]Rudolf Bultmann, *Jesus Christ and Mythology* (New York: Charles Scribner's Sons, 1958), 15.

[27]Haight, *Jesus Symbol of God*, 127; emphasis added. With regard to historical Jesus research, Haight earlier acknowledges the linkage: "The majority of the portraits of the historical Jesus in fact presuppose and are constructed on the basis of naturalist assumptions and the principle of analogy" (39).

[28]Ibid.

[29]Wolfhart Pannenberg, "History and the Reality of the Resurrection," in Gavin D'Costa, ed., *Resurrrection Reconsidered*, 64, 65.

[30]William A. Clebsch, *Christianity in European History* (New York: Oxford, 1979), 4.

[31]Ibid.; emphasis added. This should not be taken to deny a claim that we might have *scientific* evidence that historians can use to warrant a contemporary claim that people misapprehended their world. For example, if people really thought that the universe was 4000 years old in the same way we understand "universe," "4000," and "years," then we can warrant a claim that they were mistaken. It is not clear, however, that we have semantic constancy for all these terms.

[32]Ibid.

[33]Ibid., 5.

[34]Of course, we may make an *argument* for our ontology over that of our predecessors, for our symbolic approach as intrinsically philosophically superior to theirs, or for their being deluded or self-deluded; yet those are not properly *historical* arguments, but metaphysical or theological ones that go far beyond the discipline of history. Those who reduce, for example, the New Testament narratives of the Resurrection to code for something else or to illusions all too often presume modern ontology without argument.

[35]Carlo Ginzburg, "Clues: Roots of an Evidential Paradigm," in *Clues, Myths, and the Historical Method*, trans. John and Anne C. Tedeschi (Baltimore: Johns Hopkins University Press, 1989), 106; italics in original.

[36]This is not to deny the possibility of comparisons or generalizations, but only to assert that these are "ad hoc," and do not require "analogy" or "correlation" to be made.

[37]Ginzburg opposes the hard division between the "rational" and the "irrational." His basis for this is not a neo-Nietzschean denial of connections between historical constructions and what they represent (as some "deconstructionists" might maintain), but to question the division of understanding historical arguments as constituting real "proof" or mere neo-Nietzschean "rhetoric." For Ginzburg, what is *in* the text is also *outside* the text—but we need to "discover it, and make it talk." See Carlo Ginzburg, *History, Rhetoric, and Proof* (Hanover and London: University Press of New England, 1999), 23.

[38]I owe this point to Janet Bednarek. This is not to claim that historians do *not*

sometimes try to find out "what really happened," but for crucial events from Caesar's crossing the Rubicon, to the angel Gabriel's dictating to Mohammed the commands of God, to Truman's understanding of what he was doing when he authorized the use of atomic weapons in 1945, claims about the "facts" concerning "what actually happened" and what agents actually intended seem nearly impossible to warrant to a degree that can claim broad assent. Qualifying the claims (e.g., "Mohammed *said* he heard . . .") or stating them vaguely enough ("Truman ordered . . .") may lead to general assent, but one doesn't need the work of critical historians for that.

[39]Norman Perrin, *The Resurrection According to Matthew, Mark, and Luke* (Philadelphia: Fortress Press, 1977), 78-84, makes the point that the historicity of the Resurrection is a modern question, one that the biblical authors were not concerned with. Indeed, he finds the historically interesting factors similar to those of Clebsch and social historians in general. Focusing on the appearances to Jesus' followers, he writes: "In some way they were granted a vision of Jesus which convinced them that God had vindicated Jesus out of his death, and that therefore the death of Jesus was by no means the end of the impact of Jesus upon their lives and upon the world in which they lived. Very much to the contrary, since Jesus as risen commissioned them to new tasks and to new responsibilities, they found confidence in themselves and in the future of the world in which they lived precisely because they were responding to Jesus as risen, and because they were now living in a world in which Jesus was risen" (83). Whatever happened, it is the effect that is historically important, not "what happened."

[40]Pannenberg, "History and the Reality of the Resurrection," 64; italics in original.

[41]William James, "The Will to Believe," *The Will to Believe and Other Essays in Popular Philosophy* (New York: Longmans Green and Co., 1897; reprint edition, New York: Dover Publications, 1956), 28.

[42]Moltmann attributes this axiom to Troeltsch. However, Troeltsch does not make this "fourth axiom" explicit in the article Moltmann cites. Given that Troeltsch was distinguishing historical from theological methodologies, talk of God's act in history would be a theological claim, not a historical one. Moltmann seems, as does Bultmann, simply to rule out the possibility of such assertions on any grounds.

[43]I do not find either the first axiom or the last axiom operative in the work of Roger Haight. Haight does not rule out claims that God acts in history at all, but finds that they are not best understood as "factual" claims in a historical sense, but as claims rooted in "faith-hope," claims that have a historical *basis*, but for which historical *investigations* are not able to provide sustaining *warrant*.

[44]Dan Cohn-Sherbok, "The Resurrection of Jesus: A Jewish View," in Gavin D'Costa, ed., *Resurrection Reconsidered*, 200; Harvey, *The Historian and the Believer*, 227-30, also uses "we" as if it might be any rational human being whosoever.

[45]Ibid., 184-85.

[46]Ibid., 197.

[47]Ibid., 198.

[48]This alludes to Ginzburg's invocation of Walter Benjamin's "Theses on the Philosophy of History." See *History, Rhetoric, and Proof*, 24.

[49]Haight, *Jesus Symbol of God*, 126.

[50]For instance, some have asked, "What happened to Jesus' body? Did it go 'poof' and disappear, or was it lost, or was it transformed into some sort of body-shaped energy field (*soma pneumatikon*), or did the disciples steal it, or . . . ?" My answer is that we cannot know the answer to that question as a matter of historical fact. There is no clear testimony available about it. Perhaps someone knew what happened, so the "cannot" in the previous sentence is not a "logical" "cannot," but a practical one. The testimony we have is limited. It is not that the evidence can be taken multiple ways depending on one's background beliefs. (Even if some archaeologist claimed, "I found the Body," it is hard to imagine realistically how that claim might be warranted, as the "evidence" realistically discoverable now or in the future could be taken multiple ways.) Whatever evidence and testimony there may have been, if any, is no longer accessible to us as warrant; hence, we are not in position to be able to warrant any claim about "the Body" that goes beyond what remains of the scriptural testimony after passing it through the sieve of historical analysis.

[51]As many have pointed out, "raise" is not used literally. No one is claiming that God moved Jesus' body up a few feet to another part of the tomb or lifted it off the ground. To understand metaphorical usage, one does not try to reduce it to similes; one loses "the oak of metaphor in a forest of paraphrase." I have argued that metaphors are best understood as they are placed in stories (*Story Theology*, 4-6). The fact expressed using this metaphor of raising is best explicated in the story of Jesus as the Christ, a story told from the perspective of a member of Christ's body (1 Cor. 12).

[52]Clearly, "empty tomb" stories are not "proofs" of the Resurrection. Anthony Tambasco, *In the Days of Jesus: The Jewish Background and Unique Teaching of Jesus* (New York: Paulist, 1983), 111-12, has a concise and accurate account of the evidentiary value of the empty tomb texts. Tambasco (109) nonetheless seems to work under the problematic account of the relationship of history and theology criticized above.

[53]Gerald O'Collins, S.J., *Christology: A Biblical, Historical, and Systematic Study of Jesus* (Oxford: Oxford University Press, 1995) writes that "it is better not to speak of [God's act in raising Jesus from the dead] as a/the divine intervention" (111), although he does contrast the "extraordinary" and the "ordinary" acts of God in creation (106). John Shea, *Stories of God: An Unauthorized Biography* (Chicago: Thomas More, 1978), sharply contrasts an "interventionist" with an "intentionalist" approach to understanding God's acts (88-116), with a preference for the latter. How one understands how God brought about the Resurrection is a separate issue from the present discussion; what is being claimed here is that whatever theory of divine agency and causality one has, the agent is God.

[54]This description intentionally alludes to the epistemic concept of a "basic

belief," that is, a belief that is warranted not by other beliefs, but through some other cause. Such beliefs may be proper or improper, that is, warranted or unwarranted by our cognitive faculties working properly in a congenial environment. Basic beliefs are *not* unconditioned or uncaused, but those beliefs that are "foundational" (in a soft sense) in a person's structure of belief. Alvin Plantinga has explored this concept in great detail with regard to religious epistemology. His most recent major work in this area is *Warranted Christian Belief* (New York: Oxford University Press, 2000). For a discussion of the strengths and weaknesses of this approach in general, see Terrence W. Tilley, *The Wisdom of Religious Commitment* (Washington, D.C.: Georgetown University Press, 1995), 68-77, and the literature cited therein. My analysis and criticism of historico-critical scripture scholarship differs sharply from his (see *Warranted Christian Belief*, 386-399).

[55]In historiography, Carlo Ginzburg can be seen as applying "reception theory" or "reader-response criticism" to the discipline of history. His argument to keep both "truth" and "rhetoric" in play recognizes both the traditional historical criteria and the arguments of many postmodern theorists. See *History, Rhetoric, and Proof*, *passim*.

[56]Christian theologians continue to debate which of these options Christians ought adopt; the list is not meant to be exhaustive, but illustrative of the many options Christian theologians take.

[57]This final phrase alludes to the title of a paper by John L. Austin, "Unfair to Facts," in *Philosophical Papers*, 102-122. Thanks to Maureen Tilley, Dennis Doyle, Sandra Yocum Mize, Janet Bednarek, Jim Heft, Ann Riggs, Sue Perry, Roger Haight, and Dermot Lane, whose written comments and criticisms on an earlier draft have strengthened the argument of this paper; to the editor and anonymous referees for this volume who sought further clarifications; and to Gerry McCarthy, Bill Loewe, Michael Baxter, Tony Godzieba, and Bob Masson whose verbal interventions when I presented this paper and thereafter have been of great help. These colleagues, some of whom disagree sharply with significant parts of this paper, have nonetheless graciously helped me clarify and strengthen its argument.

Hans Urs von Balthasar on the Use of Social Sciences in Ecclesial Reflection

Exposition, Analysis, and Critique

James K. Voiss, S.J.

The years since the close of the Second Vatican Council have witnessed a veritable explosion of theological exploration and development at the intersection of theology and the social sciences.[1] The Council fathers themselves provided the impetus for this when they instructed that "sufficient use should be made, not only of theological principles, but also of the findings of secular sciences, especially psychology and sociology: in this way the faithful will be brought to a purer and more mature living of the faith."[2] The Council members therefore charged the church with incorporating the findings of the social sciences into the fabric of the church's reflections on its own nature and mission. After Vatican II, many Catholic theologians embraced the Council's mandate enthusiastically, often using their findings as a basis on which to advance the "continual reformation of which [the church] always has need."[3] But others have been less enthusiastic. While not denying the valuable insights to be gained by the social sciences, some theologians have emphasized the danger of theological distortion that can occur if the social sciences are not properly employed.

Hans Urs von Balthasar is among those expressing reservations about post-conciliar use of social sciences in ecclesial reflection. On the one hand, he recognized that the intersection of theology and social sciences is both necessary and inevitable. He observed,

> [B]ecause of the universal Christian sending into the world, [the theologian] will continually be in contact with non-theological

> sciences, whether these are carried on by Christians or non-Christians. Ecclesiology must accept the fact that its object is also handled by sociologists; catechists will be in contact with psychologists and demographers, and learn from them; the preacher and pastor will remain open to all forms of anthropology (to which medicine and psychiatry also belong). Christians do not thereby fundamentally step outside their domain, even though theology naturally cannot and should not absorb all these worldly sciences into itself. But the object of theology is so open that it must consider man, redeemed and claimed by God, in all his human relations, activities and destinies; it may not, for example, take him simply as an "immortal soul," for whose salvation in the beyond only the pastor and theologian should have to care.[4]

On the other hand, Balthasar was critical of both social scientists and other theologians for their efforts to integrate the social sciences into theology. He criticized the social sciences, for example, for their limited understanding of the human person, for their inadequacy to the task of addressing specifically theological questions, and for their failure to recognize the limitations of their own competencies.[5] He also criticized his contemporaries for their use of the social sciences. He feared that improper use of social sciences in theology had already led to theological distortions and was damaging the life of the church. For example, Balthasar critiqued the juxtaposition of the Christ of Faith with the Historical Jesus, a development in theology that he traced to a misappropriation of social scientific paradigms of truth into theological discourse.[6] He likewise criticized what he construed as false theological pluralism and the proliferation of what he termed "partial theologies" or "slogan theologies."[7] He held that these theological developments arose from the misappropriation of social sciences in theology and feared that they would undermine the unity of the church in its witness to Christ.[8]

The apparent tension in Balthasar's views raises important questions. First, if the use of the social sciences in theology is necessary and inevitable, and if the efforts of his contemporaries are so unsatisfactory, how does Balthasar think that the social sciences should be integrated into theology? To this question, Balthasar provides no direct, systematic answer. As will become apparent in what follows, neither the deeper concerns governing his theological project nor the implications of his theological method lend themselves to engaging the kind of constructive project which this first question demands.

Second, since he objects so strongly to the uses other theologians have made of social sciences, one must wonder, What are the theological bases of his reservations? Do they have any merit? Can Balthasar's perspective offer anything of value to current efforts to integrate social sciences into the church's reflections on itself and its relationship to the surrounding world? In order to critically evaluate the merits and limits of Balthasar's perspective, it will be necessary to examine its roots, first, by presenting the theological concerns that gave rise to his reservations and, second, by considering the theological foundations on which his assessment is based. We will then be able to sketch some observations on the merits and limits of Balthasar's contribution to the contemporary discussion of the use of social sciences in ecclesial reflection.

Balthasar's Concerns

The social sciences *per se* did not occupy Balthasar's scholarly attention to any great extent, yet he did express a very clear and consistent perspective on the relationship of the social sciences to theology and its tasks. His perspective emerges from his own theological synthesis and the concerns driving his larger theological project. While it is not possible in this short essay to do justice to the full depth and breadth of that larger project and its implication for Balthasar's views on any theological use of social sciences, three consistent themes in his work provide the necessary context for appreciating his position: 1) his critical appraisal of contemporary theology, 2) his concern for the fruitfulness of the church, and 3) his project of promoting a theological aesthetics.

First, Balthasar criticized much of contemporary theology because he believed that it had inverted the proper relationship between faith and reason.[9] Theology had begun to assimilate natural scientific methods based on Enlightenment epistemological premises, particularly as exemplified in the work of Immanuel Kant.[10] These premises define the knowable (and therefore truth) exclusively in terms of the processes and structures of human cognition. Balthasar rejected this foundation for theology because it intrinsically distorts theological reflection. It makes human critical reason the measure of all truth.[11] It leads theology to treat God as one object among others.[12] And it fractures theology into a multiplicity of competing theories based on human ingenuity and ideologies rather than on the wisdom of God.[13] According to Balthasar, Kantian assumptions have misled theologians into believing that they can conceptually control God's sovereign, self-revealing action under the rubrics of human systems of thought.[14] Proper theology, he argued, must be conducted entirely within a context of faith. For,

> . . . it belongs to the essence of this and only this science [theology] that its scientific objectivity rests on the decision to believe, and that there can be, therefore (theologically considered), no neutral objectivity, no consideration of the object of belief without belief, or apart from belief and unbelief. The theory which was favored at the beginning of our century—in which objective scientific method and subjective commitment were regarded as separable—even should it be applicable elsewhere, cannot be used here.[15]

Contemporary human sciences (social sciences and natural sciences) based on Kantian assumptions must eschew appeals to anything that cannot be verified empirically. Although they can provide useful information about the empirical realm, they are not adequate in themselves to address the concerns of theology. Balthasar perceived the uncritical appropriation of these scientific paradigms of thought into theology to be the cause of many post-conciliar theological distortions.

Second, Balthasar wanted to foster the fruitfulness of the church.[16] Fruitfulness shows itself in the visible holiness of the church. This holiness is visible through the church's unity in love[17] and in its willingness to follow the example of Christ's self-donation to the Father[18] by being poured out in loving obedience to the divine will. Thus, Balthasar maintains,

> It is only what is good and selfless that bears fruit; evil itself is unfruitfulness. And yet one knows that evil causes the good to suffer and that the suffering of the good is deepened fruitfulness. In his eucharist Jesus gained victory by anticipation over his enemies, even over his final enemy, death. And consequently the goal of the communion of saints is not properly the communal

> struggle against evil—as a corporation or club might set itself a common goal—but nothing other than the dissemination of the good; indeed not even that, for the good disseminates itself; the aim is quite simply to hold oneself ready, the aim is the abandonment of all aims of one's own, in order that God's aims may be fulfilled through his own people.[19]

This statement not only illustrates the intrinsic connection Balthasar draws between fruitfulness and self-donation. It also draws to the fore two characteristic elements of Balthasar's theology: first, that God is the primary agent in the drama of the world; human beings are supposed to be the receptive instruments of God's directing activity; and, second, that Balthasar assumes as axiomatic an opposition between divine and human will. This dialectical perspective shapes his understanding of the dynamics of revelation and leaves little room for the possibility that God's will might be expressed implicitly in and through human desires and choices independently of an explicitly recognized revelatory event. As will become clear shortly, both of these points bear significantly on Balthasar's conclusions regarding the relationship of theology to the social sciences.

In his writings, Balthasar confronted two temptations that he believed pose an on-going threat to the church's fruitfulness. The first is the temptation to preserve the church's holiness by a kind of isolationism. This would ultimately be a rejection of the church's mission to the world.[20] The second threat arises from a failure to distinguish between the world and the church. Balthasar saw this failure at work in post-conciliar theological efforts to treat the church as a merely human reality, to mold and reshape the church according to humanly conceived programs of reform.[21] He accused these efforts of fracturing the unity of the church, thereby undermining its witness to unity in love and diminishing its fruitfulness.

Third, Balthasar proposed a theological aesthetics as a corrective to contemporary theology and to the danger of ecclesial factionalism.[22] Since he traced these problems to the exaltation of critical reason over faith, he believed that restoring Christian faith as the primary stance of theological reflection would help correct these problems. His theological aesthetics operates from such a stance, employing a methodological shift from merely critical human reason in theology to aesthetic contemplation of Christian revelation. Balthasar believed this would correct the problems of contemporary theology, for, "true theology begins only at the point where 'exact historical science' passes over into the science of faith proper—a 'science' which presupposes the act of faith as its locus of understanding."[23]

Balthasar also believed that his theological aesthetics would foster the fruitfulness of the church. How so? Through contemplating the form of Christ. By this contemplation, the church (in its members) becomes stamped with (con-formed to) the image of Christ through obedient self-dispossession before God.[24] Self-dispossession before God unites the church and directs it outward on mission, making the form of Christ's own holiness visible to the world.[25] This kind of contemplation does not arise from critical reason. It grows out of the encounter in faith between the human person and the personal God who is ever-greater than human concepts of God and systems of human philosophical thought.[26]

These three themes in Balthasar's theology contextualize his fundamental discomfort with post-conciliar efforts to incorporate social sciences into ecclesial reflection. While many aspects of the ecclesial life can be examined and critiqued by the social sciences precisely because they are visible, one essential aspect of the church cannot be evaluated by empirical means: the living relationship between the church and God. This essential dimension of the church lies beyond the scope of the social sciences; it presupposes a stance of faith with respect to the church and to God's self-disclosure in history (revelation). Therefore, if theology is not to arrive at distorted conclusions, it must always privilege this posture of faith when examining ecclesial realities in the light of human sciences.

Balthasar's concerns make sense at first glance, but they also raise a question. If the essential aspect of the church is its relationship to God, and if this is not subject to empirical verification, what does aesthetic contemplation offer to theology that critical analysis does not? Balthasar's answer to this question lies in the foundations of his theological synthesis, particularly in his understanding of form, of revelation, and of the church.

Form, Revelation, and Church in Balthasar's Theological Aesthetics

Balthasar's theological aesthetics relies heavily on the metaphysical concept of form.[27] This concept grounds his insistence on contemplation in theological method, permeates his understanding of the church, and provides further theological justification for his critique of social sciences in ecclesial reflection. Form is a characteristic of all being; it is "an inner principle imposing a pattern."[28] This inner principle expresses itself in a way that can be apprehended by the senses through the finite existent.[29] As such, form has both an ontological and an ontic aspect. In its foundational ontological aspect, form is the unifying, identifying principle of the finite reality. In its ontic usage, form refers to the external appearance of that reality. The ontic is the external manifestation of the ontological. These two aspects stand in a dynamic tension. The inner form gives the manifestation its truth, goodness, unity, and beauty in its particular shape. The outer manifestation points behind itself to the source of that truth, goodness, unity, and beauty.[30]

In the realm of social scientific research, it is legitimate to examine only the external, perceptible expression. But for people of faith, particularly when dealing with the data of revelation, the outward form must be seen in its relationship to the transcendent inner form to which it points.[31] To arrive at a grasp of this inner form requires a contemplative "seeing," one that looks through the particularities of the external expression to the deeper unity, truth, goodness, and beauty behind it.[32] Balthasar's understanding of form is the metaphysical lynchpin to his theology of revelation, his Christology, and his theology of the church, all of which come into play in his assessment of the use of social sciences in ecclesial reflection.

Revelation, for Balthasar, is God's action in the world.[33] It expresses God's own self. God, therefore, is the inner form of God's external self-expression in the revelatory event. Revelatory events possess an objectivity rooted in God's own being.[34] Their external expressions, although finite, point back to the infinite reality of God.

What is true of revelation in general is preeminently true of Christ. Jesus Christ is the perfect expression of God's form in human history. For, "Jesus does not merely announce a true doctrine as prophets or wisdom teachers did. In his very existence he is Truth revealed by God."[35] In him there is a strict unity of inner and outer form (ontological and ontic). This is the presupposition of the claim that he is the revelation of God.[36] Balthasar's Christian theological aesthetics would therefore focus its contemplative gaze on the revelation of God in and through the form of Christ as the outer expression in history of God's own way of being. Balthasar names this form in terms of kenosis, for the dynamism that Christ reveals is self-bestowing, self-emptying love in obedience to God's will.[37] Self-donation in love marks the life of Jesus because it is the inner form of divine life.[38]

Balthasar's metaphysics of form permeates his discussion of the church. He sees the distinctive form of Christ as the inner principle giving unity, truth, goodness, and beauty to the church. The church expresses these qualities in and through its institutional structures and the dynamics of ecclesial life.[39] Its task is to conform itself to that form ever more fully. Jeffrey Kay captures this point when he observes,

> The church is transparent when it is composed of Christians who are willing with Christ and in Christ to love to the end. She shows this willingness by abandoning the pursuit of her own form and splendor. She must see that she has no figure, splendor, ideas or plans of her own but is called upon to become clay in which the Spirit can mold the form of Christ. By not resisting the guidance of the Spirit, the form and splendor of Christ can become visible in the structures of the institutional church.[40]

By conforming itself to this form of Christ, the church becomes an icon of Christ.[41] It displays his kenotic form so that the world may contemplate that form and be drawn to Christ by it. Thus, the church is a medium of revelation. But to be this medium, the church must keep its contemplative gaze fixed on the revelation of God in Christ, seeking continually to conform itself ever more fully to that form. To preserve that form, it must avoid accommodating itself to the canons of worldly wisdom. As Balthasar explains,

> The mystery of God cannot be manipulated. The visible contours of the Church's structure might perhaps be somewhat modified, provided we do so while obediently contemplating the mystery underlying the system, but only to bring out in bold relief the form that, from the very beginning, has been a stumbling block. We could even put it like this: our aim should be to remove the unreal stumbling blocks so that the Church's *real stumbling block* can become more evident to the whole world.[42]

Here we arrive at the intersection of Balthasar's theology and his position on the use of social sciences in ecclesial reflection. The church exists to sustain in time God's self-revelatory action in Christ for the contemplation of the world. It does so by holding fast to the form of Christ as the norm for ecclesial life, structure, and mission. Theological aesthetics preserves and intensifies the church's presentation of that form because it privileges revelation and faith over analysis and critical reason, thereby avoiding the pitfalls Balthasar perceived in the Kantian epistemological heritage. Since social sciences are limited to addressing what is observable, they are not adequate to the divine, revelatory, iconic nature of the church. Making decisions about ecclesial life based primarily on the findings of social scientific research would distort the church's essential nature and diminish its iconic-revelatory function.

Evaluating Balthasar's Perspective

The preceding exposition identifies the deeper theological issues underlying Balthasar's perspective on the uses of social sciences in ecclesial reflection. It explains his disaffection with the efforts of his contemporaries to use the social sciences in their theologies. It makes sense of his critique of ecclesial reform movements based on the findings of social scientific research. How are we now to evaluate Balthasar's perspective? Addressing three questions will bring us to a preliminary assessment: 1) What positive contribution, if any, can Balthasar make to the contemporary discussion of the use of social sciences in ecclesial reflection? In other words, what are the merits of his perspective? 2) What are the limits of his theological analysis of the relationship between theology and social sciences? Are his conclusions theologically sound? Necessary? 3) Might an alternative conception of that relationship have positive theological merit? Can theology gain anything (on its own terms) by conceiving of the relationship differently than Balthasar does?

First, Balthasar's appraisal of the social sciences in theology was not uniformly negative. He indicated their findings could and should be used by theology, but he devoted most of his attention to critiquing perceived abuses. One can see his concerns about the impact of social sciences on theology in his critique of contemporary theological pluralism,[43] in his appraisal of liberation theology,[44] and in his criticism of the effort to apply feminist social analysis to structures of ecclesial life.[45] In one way, this critical posture is a natural consequence of his emphasis on aesthetic contemplation. According to Balthasar, the contemplative posture requires that one be open and receptive to God's self-disclosure.[46] This receptivity is the contemplative expression of the obedience that he argues should characterize all human response to God. On the basis of this contemplative receptivity one can discern whether or not situations in the church accord with the form of Christ. His method, therefore, tends to be re-active rather than proactive.[47] It is ill suited to providing a "how to" analysis for properly integrating social sciences into theology. Consequently, although he affirms the theological use of the social sciences in principle, he devotes little (if any) energy to integrating them in any critical way into his own theological synthesis. Nor does he explain in detail how to go about effecting such an integration. Rather, he contents himself with critiquing the efforts of those who do.

Nevertheless, Balthasar did offer two principles of enduring value, even if he did not develop them adequately in relationship to our current question. Balthasar reminds us, in the first place, that the church is more than the sum of its visible elements. Social scientific analysis of those visible elements will never provide a complete basis on which to make decisions touching the life and mission of the church.[48] Second, if theology is not to confuse itself with religious studies (a legitimate discipline in its own right), then the theologian's faith commitment must play a role in shaping how the theologian uses the social sciences. Balthasar's proposal of a contemplative theological aesthetics offers a tantalizing hint at an approach to integrating social sciences into a fundamentally faith-based view of reality. Regrettably, despite the importance of the questions he raises, the creativity of his proposal, and the potential it appears to hold for bringing about such an integration, his comments do little more than hint. His perspective therefore merits closer examination in the ongoing discussion of social sciences in ecclesial reflection.

The second question concerns the limits of Balthasar's own analysis of and his response to current efforts. Can his theological perspective stand up to closer inspection? A complete answer to this question lies beyond the scope of this paper. However, two lines of thought will sketch some of the issues that a more complete treatment would need to address.

First, it appears that Balthasar is not consistent with his own stated position on the use of the social sciences in theology. Given his affirmation of their use in principle, one might reasonably expect to see evidence that Balthasar had engaged in serious theological reflection on the implications of the social sciences for his own work. Where would one find such evidence? How might Balthasar use the social sciences in his own theological project? One should expect to find such evidence in two places: in Balthasar's biblical hermeneutics and in social scientific critique of his own socially conditioned presuppositions. Yet in both of these areas, evidence that Balthasar has availed himself of social scientific research is lacking. One illustrative example will make the point.

Balthasar's biblical hermeneutics, with its emphasis on seeking the form of Christ, bypasses contemporary critical social scientific analysis of biblical texts, events, and figures. Particularly when dealing with the figures in the Christological Constellation of relations surrounding Jesus,[49] he abstracts from the very concrete particularity of the individual historical persons in favor of their "formal" defining characteristics (as Balthasar identifies them). Thus, for example, in his theological pursuit of the form of Mary, a first-century Jewish woman, the actual human person Mary recedes into the background to be replaced by "Mary, the ideal feminine," an image of the concrete, historical person that (more than coincidentally) neatly corresponds to representations of Mary in Renaissance and baroque (culturally European) art and imagination.[50]

The question arises: Can one really claim to have grasped the formal reality of who Mary was without first excavating the culturally conditioned assumptions one brings to the inquiry and then making strenuous use of social critical analysis and historical data to arrive at as much detailed information as possible about the actual conditions of her life? To answer in the affirmative would seem to render Mary, the historical person, virtually irrelevant to our theologizing about her (a charge that could be levelled against Balthasar). To answer in the negative would require that Balthasar show greater evidence of social scientific research in his theological reflections on this point than he does.

Second, if, as Balthasar contends, the appropriation of Kantian assumptions into theological reflection has reduced theology to a merely human "science of religion,"[51] then something like a theological aesthetics would seem to offer a viable approach to distinguishing theology from religious studies. But affirming the value of a theological aesthetics does not imply that Balthasar's theological aesthetics, as he delineates it, is the only or even the best possible response to his concerns. Balthasar's aesthetics reflects his explicit desire to preserve and promote the distinctively Christian form of revelation.[52] While this explicit preoccupation appears genuine, it does not seem to be a complete explanation of the motive forces behind Balthasar's theology. There appear to be other unarticulated, value-laden conceptual commitments shaping his distinctive approach to theological aesthetics. Two such commitments illustrate the point: 1) the choice of revelation as Balthasar's theological starting point; and 2) his distinctive understanding of revelation.

Balthasar has made revelation the primary theological category in his aesthetics. In the realm of theological knowledge, revelation may hold pride of place. In the realm of theological ontology, however, grace is prior; grace is the condition for the possibility of revelation. Balthasar does not examine the theological implications of this relationship in any detail. As a result, when he privileges revelation independently of a carefully articulated theology of grace, he opens the door to a kind of static revelational positivism, one that inevitably discredits extra-revelational insights in the realm of theological reflection.

Balthasar's choice of a theological starting-point tips the scales against the use of the social sciences from the outset, yet he has not justified this choice theologically.[53] Revelation is not the only theological resource on which to base a theological aesthetics. If, by contrast, one privileges grace in one's theological framework, the consequent assessment of so-called non-theological data and their relevance for theological reflection shifts. If grace operates even before it is known (a presupposition in the relationship of grace to revelation), then one may not assume at the outset that grace is inoperative in human scientific works—even in the social sciences. The social sciences may therefore have a positive theological value in themselves. Their findings regarding the church may be effects of grace and, therefore, have (at least *in potentia*) a quasi-revelational status. Thus, while Balthasar's choice of revelation rather than grace as a starting point for his project prejudices the case against a positive assessment of social sciences in theology, an alternative starting-point in grace opens the door to other possibilities.

But if we assume for the sake of argument that revelation should be privileged in theological aesthetics, this does not mean that one must accept Balthasar's understanding of revelation. For him, revelation is an irruption into human awareness of God's self-disclosing action. The experience of Paul on the road to Damascus is paradigmatic for Balthasar of revelatory events. In the dynamics of ecclesial life the Pauline paradigm achieves no institutionalized succession (in contrast to the Petrine paradigm). Balthasar sees the Pauline experience as a non-institutional charism, given for the sake of the community. Nevertheless, Paul's experience is merely a specification of the same revelatory irruption one finds in Balthasar's discussion of the call to office as "expropriation for appropriation" in service to the church. Humanity does not reach up to God and wrest revelation from God. God condescends to stoop down to the human condition to give Godself to us.[54] In the realm of ecclesial reflection Balhasar holds that this revelation—seen in terms of the form of Christ as he has defined it—will always be a stumbling block. Saint Paul, from whom he borrows this expression, saw that the gospel was a stumbling-block to Jews and Gentiles of his own day. But this does not mean that this "stumbling-block experience" can be taken as a normative or perpetual criterion for discerning what is essential to Christian ecclesial reflection. The use Balthasar makes of this principle rests on the assumption of a rupture and opposition between the divine and the human, a rupture that must be overcome by an unexpected divine initiative such as Paul experienced in his own call. The net result of this understanding of revelation is to conceive of the relationship between faith and reason and between theology and the social sciences as mono-directional. Faith and theology stand in judgment on reason and social science because faith and (derivatively) theology have access to a transcendent truth.

Balthasar's understanding of revelation is not the only one, however. One could account for revelation in ways that see greater continuity between the prompting of God's spirit and the reflective appropriation of those promptings in human consciousness.[55] Alternative understandings of revelation can be justified on the basis of scripture and have been embraced at different times in the unfolding of Christian history. This scriptural passage, therefore, cannot serve as a warrant for adopting Balthasar's understanding of the opposition between revelation and human reason. Nor can it justify his mono-directional approach to the uses of social sciences in ecclesial reflection.

These comments bring us to the final question of this paper: Might there be theological merit in conceiving of the relationship between theology and the social sciences differently than Balthasar has done? Specifically, might there be solid theological grounds for seeing the relationship as mutually correcting? Two lines of thought suggest an affirmative response.

First, it is clear that Balthasar's discussion of the social sciences in ecclesial reflection is limited. There are theologically defensible grounds for conceiving of the relationship between them differently than he has done. I have suggested that one approach might be to privilege grace as one's theological starting point. This could provide the basis for a properly theological aesthetics in which the social sciences and theology (reason and faith) are mutually correcting. Ironically, Balthasar's use of form in his theology of revelation opens the door to the affirmation of a mutually correcting relationship between ecclesial reflection and the social sciences. The external expression of the inner form, particularly when we are speaking of a revelatory event, never exhaustively expresses its ontological foundation. The outer expression is always couched in finite, human, culturally conditioned terms. A faith-based appropriation of the social sciences, particularly sociology and psychology, might well help to hone the external presentation of the inner form by calling to explicit awareness the limitations imposed on the external expression by those finite, human, culturally conditioned modes of expression. It could even serve to intensify the presentation of the form of Christ in the iconic church, although the characteristics of that form might prove to be different than Balthasar had envisioned.

Second, this examination of Balthasar's thought raises another important contribution that the social sciences could make to ecclesial reflection, one that arises implicitly from the deeper commitments shaping Balthasar's thought. Balthasar's commitments to revelation as his dominant theological category and to his understanding of the opposition between revelation and the wisdom of the world (especially as enshrined in Kantian epistemological assumptions) are integral to his appraisal of the use of social sciences in ecclesial reflection. Why does he align himself with these particular commitments when other theological resources are available? The reasons are not entirely clear, yet without those specific commitments, his conclusions do not necessarily follow. Such unexamined commitments may be the expression of genuinely Christian faith, but they may also reflect undisclosed, even un-Christian ideologies—a danger Balthasar himself named and condemned in the commitments of his contemporaries.[56] Judicious use of social sciences within a faith-grounded theological aesthetics could help to name non-theological agendas beneath theological formulations. It could help to excavate deeply embedded cultural assumptions that are not essential to the Christian message but that have become an unnecessary stumbling block to its acceptance in places that do not share those cultural assumptions. It could even help clarify the reasons why, of all the theological resources available in the Christian tradition, Balthasar chose to privilege revelation in his theological synthesis and why he arrived at the specific understanding of revelation he did.

Notes

[1]In the twentieth anniversary issue of *Concilium*, Gregory Baum observed, "The one important development to be recorded is that over the last ten years the dialogue of theology and the social sciences has come to be recognized in all the branches of theology and for that reason is being carried on today in all the sections of *Concilium*." See Gregory Baum, "Sociology of Religion 1973-1983," in *Twenty Years of Concilium—Retrospect and Prospect*, ed. Edward Schillebeeckx, Paul Brand, and Anton Weiler (New York: Seabury, 1983), 2. His affirmation is exemplified in Robert J. Schreiter, *Constructing Local Theologies* (Maryknoll, N.Y.: Orbis Books, 1985), and Robert J. Schreiter, *The New Catholicity: Theology Between the Global and the Local* (Maryknoll: Orbis Books, 1997), which both seek to integrate the insights of sociology and cultural analysis into discussion of local and contextual theologies.

[2]"*Gaudium et Spes*," in *Vatican Council II: Constitutions, Decrees, Declarations*, ed. Austin Flannery (1975; reprint, Northport, N.Y.: Costello, 1996), #62. The statement applies explicitly to the use of the social sciences in pastoral care, but implicitly extends to other dimensions of ecclesial reflection, as well.

[3]"*Unitatis Redintigratio*," in *Vatican Council II*, #6.

[4]Hans Urs von Balthasar, *Convergences to the Source of the Christian Mystery* (San Francisco: Ignatius Press, 1983), 71 (hereafter cited as *Convergences*). See also idem, "God Speaks as Man," in *Explorations in Theology 1* (San Francisco: Ignatius, 1989), 69 (hereafter cited as *ET*); idem, "Spirit and Institution," in *Spirit and Institution*, in *Explorations in Theology 4* (San Francisco: Ignatius, 1995), 211; and idem, *Love Alone: The Way of Revelation* (London: Sheed & Ward, 1968), 124 (hereafter cited as *LA*).

[5]For his critique of social scientific anthropologies, see Hans Urs von Balthasar, "Who Is Man?" in *Explorations in Theology 4*, 21-23. His views on the limitations of social sciences in their efforts to discuss religious themes appear in Hans Urs von

Balthasar, "Preliminary Remarks on the Discernment of Spirits," in *Explorations in Theology 4*, 338; idem, *Seeing the Form*, in *The Glory of the Lord: A Theological Aesthetics 1* (San Francisco: Ignatius Press, 1982), 167-68 (hereafter cited as *TA 1*); and idem, *The Christian State of Life* (San Francisco: Ignatius Press, 1983), 423 (hereafter cited as *CSL*). On the failure of social sciences to recognize their limitations and the consequent tendency to overreach their own competence, see Hans Urs von Balthasar, *Truth Is Symphonic: Aspects of Christian Pluralism* (San Francisco: Ignatius Press, 1987), 56 (hereafter cited as *TiS*).

[6]Balthasar, *TA 1*, 174.

[7]See, for example, Hans Urs von Balthasar, *Theo-Drama: Theological Dramatic Theory,* vol. 1, Prolegomena (San Francisco: Ignatius Press, 1988), 25 (hereafter cited as *TD* 1), and idem, *The Office of Peter and the Structure of the Church* (San Francisco: Ignatius Press, 1986), 25, 261 (hereafter cited as *OP*).

[8]On the question of theological relativism, see Hans Urs von Balthasar, *Elucidations* (London: SPCK, 1975), 234-35 (hereafter cited as *EL*); and idem, *A Theological Anthropology* (New York: Sheed & Ward, 1967), 256 (hereafter cited as *ThA*). For his views on partial theologies and their relationship to ecclesial factionalism, see Hans Urs von Balthasar, "The Claim to Catholicity," in *Explorations in Theology 4*.

[9]See the discussion of philosophy in Balthasar, *LA*, 11-42. On the proper relationship of faith to reason see Balthasar, *CSL*, 93; "The Characteristics of Christianity," in *Explorations in Theology 1*, 162; "Theology and Sanctity," in *Explorations in Theology 1*, 195, 206; "The Christian Form," in *Explorations in Theology 4*, 43; and *TA 1*, 113.

[10]For a discussion of von Balthasar's engagement with the Kantian heritage, see Louis Roberts, *The Theological Aesthetics of Hans Urs von Balthasar* (Washington, D.C.: Catholic University of America, 1987), 201-2, 210-14; and Edward T. Oakes, *Pattern of Redemption: The Theology of Hans Urs von Balthasar* (New York: Continuum, 1994), 72-73, 81-83, 88-89 (hereafter cited as *PoR*). For Balthasar's perspective on the Kantian distortion of personal relations and on the limitation of religion to what can be determined by reason alone, see Hans Urs von Balthasar, "Zum Begriff der Person," in *Skizzen Zur Theologie*, Bd. 5 (Einsiedeln: Johannes, 1986), 99.

[11]Oakes, *PoR*, 88.

[12]See Balthasar, *CSL*, 393; idem, *Does Jesus Know Us? Do We Know Him?* (San Francisco: Ignatius Press, 1983), 54-57 (hereafter cited as *DJK*); *TiS*, 74; and "Seeing, Hearing, and Reading within the Church," in *ET* 2, 477. See also Oakes, *PoR*, 225, for Balthasar's critique of efforts by reason to dissolve the necessary paradox of revelation.

[13]Balthasar, *TD* 1, 25-50.

[14]Balthasar's disaffection with the presuppositions of modern thought expressed itself in an anti-systematic bias. He was leery of attempts to control the contents of revelation conceptually by placing them under a system. He felt this distorted revelation by making God's transcendence subject to the dictates of human reason.

On his anti-systematic posture, see Manfred Lochbrunner, *Analogia Caritatis: Darstellung und Deutung der Theologie Hans Urs von Balthasar*, Freiburger Theologische Studien (Freiburg: Herder, 1981), 54; Georges de Schrijver, "Hans Urs von Balthasar's Christologie in der Theodramatik," *Bijdragen, tijdschrift voor filosofie en theologie* 59 (1998): 141-53. Balthasar expresses his anti-systematic perspective with respect to Karl Rahner's theology in Hans Urs von Balthasar, "Geist und Feuer: Ein Gespräch mit Hans Urs von Balthasar," *Herder Korrespondenz* 30:2 (1976): 72-82. Joseph Godenir draws a connection between systematization and ideological distortion in *Jésus, l'Unique: Introduction à la théologie de H.U. von Balthasar* (Paris: Éditions Lethielleux, 1984), 17-25. Despite his protestations against systematization, Balthasar has been seen as a systematic theologian, although his system(s) stand outside the mainstream of modern thought. See Thomas F. O'Meara, "Of Art and Theology: Hans Urs von Balthasar's Systems," *TS* 42:2 (June 1981): 276; and John R. Kevern, "Form in Tragedy: Balthasar as Correlational Theologian," *Communio* 21:2 (1994): 311-30.

[15]Balthasar, *Convergences*, 51.

[16]"Fruitfulness" is an imprecise concept. It does not admit of clear definition. His description of fruitfulness (as will become evident shortly) ties it to his understanding of the kenotic, obedient love of Christ that the church is to exhibit. However, von Balthasar's anti-modern stance does not allow him to adduce measurable criteria of fruitfulness. Consequently, the concept remains vague.

[17]Balthasar, *EL*, 174.

[18]See ibid., 13-14. See also the discussion of Christ's kenosis below.

[19]Balthasar, *EL*, 61.

[20]This is the basis of his critique of the church in Hans Urs von Balthasar, *Razing the Bastions*: *On the Church in This Age*, trans. Brian McNeil (San Francisco: Ignatius Press, 1993) (hereafter cited as *RB*). See also Balthasar, *EL*, 179; *New EL* (San Francisco: Ignatius Press, 1986), 72 (hereafter cited as *NE*); *ThA*, 70; and "Immediacy to God," in *ET* 3, 349-50.

[21]Balthasar wrote of plans of reform based on human wisdom as "reductionistic" and "ideological." See Balthasar, *NE*, 11, 172-73.

[22]One may find a general presentation of Balthasar's aesthetic theology in Lochbrunner, *Analogia Caritatis*, 150-65. Edward Oakes points out that Balthasar intended his theological aesthetics to emphasize the distinctively Christian. See Oakes, *PoR*, 151. For additional discussion of his aesthetics, see Angelo Scola, *Hans Urs von Balthasar: A Theological Style* (Grand Rapids: Eerdmans, 1995), 34-44; Noel O'Donaghue, "A Theology of Beauty," in *The Analogy of Beauty: The Theology of Hans Urs von Balthasar*, ed. John Riches (Edinburgh: T & T Clark, 1986).

[23]Balthasar, *TA 1*, 75.

[24]See Balthasar, *EL*, 134, 140. This is an unnuanced presentation of Balthasar's thought on this point. For a more detailed exposition and critique, see the discussion of "Theological Persons" in my dissertation, *A Comparison and Analysis of Karl Rahner and Hans Urs von Balthasar on Structural Change in the Church* (South

Bend: University of Notre Dame, 1999), 218-25. See also the section "The Christological Constellation and the Dynamics of Ecclesial Life," 261-69.

[25]Balthasar discusses this under the heading of "expropriation" and "appropriation." See Hans Urs von Balthasar, *Theology: The New Covenant*, in *The Glory of the Lord: A Theological Aesthetics 7* (San Francisco: Ignatius Press, 1989), 411 (hereafter cited as *TA 7*). See also Hans Urs von Balthasar, "Office in the Church," in *Explorations in Theology 2* (San Francisco: Ignatius, 1991), 118; and Hans Urs von Balthasar, "Eschatology in Outline," in *Explorations in Theology 4*, 465.

[26]In this connection Balthasar frequently drew on Anselm's dictum that God is "*id quod maius cogitari nequit.*" See the following works by Hans Urs von Balthasar: *The Moment of Christian Witness* (San Francisco: Ignatius Press, 1969), 95; *Convergences*, 67; "Movement Toward God," in *Explorations in Theology 3* (San Francisco: Ignatius, 1991), 32; "The Faith of the Simple Ones," in *Explorations in Theology 3*, 71; "Summa Summarum," in *Explorations in Theology 3*, 363; and "Homo Creatus Est," in *Skizzen Zur Theologie*, 332.

[27]Balthasar's discussion of form (*Gestalt*) receives a great deal of attention from the commentators on his theology. See, for example, John Milbank, *Theology and Social Theory: Beyond Secular Reason* (New York: Basil Blackwell, 1991), 220; Jörg Disse, *Metaphysik der Singularität: Eine Hinführung am Leitfaden der Philosophie Hans Urs von Balthasars* (Wien: Passaagen Verlag, 1996), 211-36; Peter Eicher, *Offenbarung: Prinzip neuzeitlicher Theologie* (Münich: Kösel Verlag, 1977), 293-346, esp. 330-35; Lochbrunner, *Analogia Caritatis*, 166-74. John Riches examines the importance of Balthasar's understanding of form for his exegetical method in John Riches, "Von Balthasar as Biblical Theologian and Exegete," *New Blackfriars* 79:923 (January 1998): 38-44. Edward Oakes compares the understanding of form in Balthasar with that of Barth in Oakes, *PoR*, 51-52.

[28]Balthasar, "Office in the Church," 106.

[29]Balthasar, *TA 1*, 152. For further discussion of Balthasar's understanding of form, see my dissertation, 187-99.

[30]Balthasar, *TA 1*, 118, 527.

[31]For this reason, Balthasar can observe that, viewed from a literary perspective, "Scripture does not possess a particular form of its own of any great theological relevance." However, because of this, "our attention is directed past this external form to the theological centres of gravity of its content" (Balthasar, *TA 1*, 550). See also Hans Urs von Balthasar, *Theo-Drama: Theological Dramatic Theory*, Vol. 3, Dramatis Personae: Persons in Christ (San Francisco: Ignatius Press, 1992), 59 (hereafter cited as *TD 3*).

[32]See Georges Chantraine, "Exegesis and Contemplation in the Work of Hans Urs von Balthasar," *Communio* 16 (1989): 366-83; Aidan Nichols, "An Introduction to Balthasar," *New Blackfriars* 79 (1998): 2-10; and Oakes, *PoR*, 225.

[33]See Balthasar, *LA*, 58. See also Oakes, *PoR*, 225.

[34]See Hans Urs von Balthasar, *A Short Primer for Unsettled Laymen* (San Francisco: Ignatius Press, 1985), 61 (hereafter cited as *ASP*). The form of revelation has its own objectivity—it is independent of the recipient. On this point, see Oakes,

PoR, 51. For further discussion of the ontological underpinnings of von Balthasar's theology of revelation, see Pascal Ide, *Être et Mystère: La philosophie de Hans Urs von Balthasar*, ch. 2 (Bruxelles: Culture et Vérité, 1995); and Eicher, *Offenbarung*, 324-30. For a critical appraisal of Balthasar's ontology, see Oliver Davies, "Von Balthasar and the Problem of Being," *New Blackfriars* 79:923 (January 1998): 11-17; and Riches, "Von Balthasar as Biblical Theologian and Exegete."

[35]Hans Urs von Balthasar, *OP*, 133. See also his "The Place of Theology," in *Explorations in Theology 1*, 150. Balthasar observes, "He [Christ] bears witness to himself in so far as every form, by revealing its content, also reveals itself as form. But he bears witness to himself only in so far as he bears witness to the Father (Jn. 17.6ff.), who in the Son bears witness to himself. Therefore, the truth is both the Father in himself and the expressive relationship between Father and Son as well as, finally, the Son in himself, in so far as he is the Word and the Expression of the Father" (*TA* 1, 615). See also *EL*, 161, and "Truth and Life," in *ET 3*, 269.

[36]For a detailed presentation and analysis of von Balthasar's trinitarian theology, see Karl-Josef Wallner, *Gott als Eschaton: Trinitarische Dramatik als Voraussetzung göttlicher Universalität bei Hans Urs von Balthasar*, Heiligenkreutzer Studienreihe 7 (Wien: Heiligenkreutzer, 1992). See also Godenir, *Jésus, L'Unique*, 151-58; Henriette Danet, *Gloire et croix de Jésus-Christ: L'analogie chez H. Urs von Balthasar comme introduction à sa Christologie* (Paris: Desclée, 1987), 83-104; Wolfgang Klaghofer-Treitler, *Gotteswort im Menschenwort: Inhalt und Form von Theologie nach Hans Urs von Balthasar* (Innsbruck: Tyrolia, 1992), 314-477. See also "The Word in History," in *ET 1*, 31-32.

[37]See Balthasar, *TD 3*, 189, 440. On the relationship of kenosis to love in Balthasar's theology, see Michael Albus, *Die Wahrheit ist Liebe: Zur Unterscheidung des Christlichen nach Hans Urs von Balthasar* (Freiburg: Herder, 1976). For an examination of his use of kenosis as an interpretive lens through which to view the passion, death, and resurrection, see Danet, *Gloire et Croix*, 137-308; and Brian J. Spence, "The Hegelian Element in Von Balthasar's and Moltmann's Understanding of the Suffering of God," *Toronto Journal of Theology* 14:1 (Spring 1998): 45-60.

[38]Wallner provides a detailed exposition and analysis of von Balthasar's trinitarian theology in Wallner, *Gott als Eschaton*. See also Godenir, *Jésus, L'Unique*, 151-58; and Klaghofer-Treitler, *Gotteswort im Menschenwort*, 314-477.

[39]Balthasar traces these institutional structures to a constellation of interpersonal relationships from the life of Jesus. These relationships are part of the enduring form of Christ's historical revelation of God. They attain a kind of succession in the church in and through the institutional structures and dynamics of which they are the archetypes. For a fuller treatment of this aspect of Balthasar's thought, see my dissertation, 213-87.

[40]Jeffrey Ames Kay, *Theological Aesthetics: The Role of Aesthetics in the Theological Method of Hans Urs von Balthasar*, Europaische Hochschulschriften. Reihe XXIII, Theologie, Bd. 60. (Bern: Herbert Lang, 1975), 82. See also 83, 86. Balthasar expresses the same idea when he states, "[L]est everything in the Church become superficial and insipid, the true, undiminished program for the Church

today must read: the greatest possible radiance in the world by virtue of the closest possible following of Christ." Hans Urs von Balthasar, *RB*, 11.

[41]Balthasar does not apply the designation "icon" to the church, as far as I know. At least two of his commentators, however, have used the notion of icon to describe aspects of his thought. Thomas O'Meara has indicated that Balthasar sees Christ at the "ikon" of God. See Thomas F. O'Meara, "Of Art and Theology: Hans Urs von Balthasar's Systems," *Theological Studies* 42:2 (June 1981): 273. Brian McNeil reads Balthasar's exegesis as an exercise in iconography. See Brian McNeil, "The Exegete as Iconographer: Balthasar and the Gospels," in *The Analogy of Beauty: The Theology of Hans Urs von Balthasar*, ed. John Riches (Edinburgh: T&T Clark, 1986). I apply the term "icon" to Balthasar's understanding of the church because it captures aspects of his understanding of ecclesial structures and dynamics and their relationship to revelation in a very succinct way.

[42]Balthasar, *OP*, 24-25 (Balthasar's emphasis).

[43]See, for example, Balthasar, *OP*, 43; and *TiS*, 56, where he specifically critiques the use of individual social sciences to justify theological pluralism. See also Hans Urs von Balthasar, "Der Friede der Theologie," in *Skizzen zur Theologie*, 312, where Balthasar argues that social sciences cannot be a basis for theological pluralism, since to allow them to function in this way would lead to distortion in the Christian message.

[44]In Hans Urs von Balthasar, *Test Everything: Hold Fast to What Is Good* (San Francisco: Ignatius Press, 1989), 41-42 (hereafter cited as *TE*), Balthasar expresses his concern that liberation theologies foster factionalism within the unity of the church. In Balthasar, *TD* 3, 45, he points to the Enlightenment and the materialist roots of liberation theology.

[45]In Balthasar, *ASP*, 88, 94, he argues against feminist critiques of the limitations constraining women in society because he sees them as based on a "masculine" functionalism. He makes a similar argument in Balthasar, *NE*, 187-91.

[46]For Balthasar's understanding of the role of receptivity in the contemplative method at the heart of his theological aesthetics, see Balthasar, *Convergences*, 91, 148; and *CSL*, 94, 218, 266, 399. For the role of obedience in theology generally, see Balthasar, "The Place of Theology," 155. For commentary on the role of obedience in Balthasar's thought, see Lochbrunner, *Analogia Caritatis*, 66 ff.; Antonio Sicari, "Hans Urs von Balthasar: Theology and Holiness," *Communio* 16 (Fall 1989): 551-66; and Davies, "Von Balthasar and the Problem of Being," 11-17.

[47]This is at the heart of his opposition to "programs" of reform based on human utopian schemes. See Balthasar, *OP*, 112; and *TD 1*, 42. I discuss this opposition to programs of reform in further detail in my dissertation, 304-10.

[48]Whether or not specific, individual, post-conciliar theologians can legitimately be accused of forgetting this in their efforts to make use of the social sciences does not affect the importance of the notion.

[49]The notion of the Christological Constellation is central to Balthasar's analysis of the church as institution. He presents this notion in *OP,* 131-82. See also his discussion, "Archetypal Experience," in *Seeing the Form*, in *TA 1*, 301-64. For a

focused exposition of the relationship of the Christological Constellation to the institutional church in Balthasar's thought, see my dissertation, 213-86.

[50]Elizabeth Johnson criticized efforts to portray Mary as the "ideal feminine" in her 2000 Aquinas Lecture entitled, "Mary: Friend of God and Prophet." The text of this lecture will appear in a forthcoming issue of *Theology Digest.* The analysis underlying her critique is part of her larger project, a book on Mary that is still in progress.

[51]Balthasar traces the emergence of contemporary approaches to a "science of religion" to the Kantian heritage in Hans Urs von Balthasar, "The Claim to Catholicity," in *Explorations in Theology 4*, 74. See also 72. For further aspects of his criticism of this approach to theology, see Hans Urs von Balthasar, "Understanding Christian Mysticism," in *Explorations in Theology 4*, 309, 324.

[52]Making revelation the controlling theological theme serves an important purpose when the purpose is to define the distinctively Christian. This is clearly one of Balthasar's concerns. See Balthasar, *EL*, 16; *ThA*, 230; "What Is Distinctively Christian in the Experience of God?" in *Explorations in Theology 4*; *OP*, 333; and *TA 1*, 246, 262.

[53]Balthasar does provide an *apologia* for starting with aesthetics at the beginning of *TA 1*, 17 ff. He argues that this starting point directs attention to neglected resources in the pursuit of God's truth. Although rhetorically engaging, this *apologia* leaves unaddressed the question of the theological propriety of this starting point in relationship to the question of the ontological priority of grace.

[54]See *TA 1*, 354; and *OP*, 143, for the irruptive character of the Pauline paradigm. See also Balthasar, "The Characteristics of Christianity," 178-80, for the basis of Balthasar's view. See also his discussion of "call" and the central role it plays in his understanding of the dynamics of faith as an interpersonal reality in his understanding of office and in his treatment of "theological persons" in Hans Urs von Balthasar, *Theo-Drama: Theological Dramatic Theory*, Vol. 3, Dramatis Personae: Persons in Christ (San Francisco: Ignatius Press, 1992), passim. For a concise exposition of this notion as it relates to Balthasar's discussion of ecclesial dynamics and structures, see my dissertation, 218-49.

[55]See, for example, Avery Dulles's discussion of history, inner experience, and new awareness as approaches to understanding revelation in Avery Dulles, *Models of Revelation* (1985; Maryknoll, N.Y.: Orbis Books, 1992), 53-85, 98-114.

[56]See, for example, his discussion of the danger of ideological impulses in theology in Hans Urs von Balthasar, *NE*, 11, 172-173; *TiS*, 77; and *OP*, 20, 35-36, 92. See also his critical comments on feminism and on liberation theology in *NE*, 187-90, 195-96; and *TE*, 41-43, 85.

Part III

CROSS-CULTURAL CONTEXTS

Sankara, Augustine, and *Rites de Passage*

Comparative Theology with Victor Turner

Reid B. Locklin

Religious transformation takes place in and through a social process.

This terse thesis might aptly summarize the contributions of the modern anthropologist Victor Turner to the social scientific study of religion. At the same time, it might just as aptly summarize the presuppositions of two ancient theological treatises: the *Upadesasahasri* of the Hindu teacher Adi Sankaracarya, and *De catechizandis rudibus* of the Christian bishop Saint Augustine of Hippo. In this paper I propose to read these two treatises in the light of Turner's work, to observe how his anthropological theory can illuminate, shape, and guide comparative theological inquiry. Such inquiry explicitly adopts an attitude of exchange, drawing upon multiple religious traditions in its theological reflection.[1] So comparative theology would seem to be a particularly fertile ground for dialogue with and appropriation of insights from anthropology.

Among anthropologists, on the other hand, Victor Turner (1920-83) stands out as a particularly suitable dialogue partner, not only because of his widespread influence across a variety of academic disciplines,[2] but also due to his own implicit sympathy with the aims and methods of comparative theology.[3] Turner is perhaps best well-known for his development of "liminality" and "communitas" as distinct categories for social analysis. As Turner reflected in the 1960s and 1970s upon various rites of change or reversal that he had previously observed among the Ndembu tribe of south central Africa, he came to identify what he believed to be a universal dynamic of human social and religious life.[4] The folklorist Arnold van Gennep had previously treated this dynamic under the rubric *rites de passage*, those rites in which ritual subjects are taken out of their established social positions, held in an isolated, "interstructural" condition for a period of time, and then subsequently reincorporated into new positions or roles in their society.[5] Turner extended and generalized van Gennep's insight through sustained attention to the interstructural or "liminal" period. Persons in a liminal state, Turner observed, experience a "generalized social bond" or a radical reversal of the more rigid and differentiated structures of their society. Turner named such an undifferentiated bond or social reversal "communitas."[6] He came to identify communitas and its opposite as universal generating principles of society: " 'Societas,' or 'society,' as we all experience it, is a process involving both social structure and communitas, separately and united in varying proportions."[7] Where formal *rites de passage* disappear—in complex, post-industrial cultures, for example—their "functional equivalents" inevitably arise in the more diffuse activities of religious pilgrims, mendicants, hippies, or even those artists, playwrights, and poets that Turner called "liminoid."[8] According to Turner's theory, liminality and communitas bubble to the surface in any functioning society—and this phenomenon is nowhere more evident than in religious practice.

While Turner has come under some criticism for generalizing too broadly in his treatments of liminality, communitas, and *rites de passage*, it is precisely these generalizations that make his work so fertile for appropriation by the comparativist. The indigenous African rites out of which his theory arose explicitly addressed moments of social transformation. Performances of these rites could be observed, their structures divided into discrete phases, and their social consequences measured in the community. Theologians, on the other hand, generally deal with texts and have no direct recourse to the communities in which those texts were produced. Turner's willingness to hypothesize universal social modes or patterns of experience allows us to inquire more deeply into the social function of these texts. His theory offers a lens through which we may take a fresh look at a familiar (or unfamiliar) text. And, where two texts are read together, his theory can serve a mediating role, lining up motifs that might not at first glance appear closely related. Under Turner's guidance, we will ask first whether two textual passages serve a comparable social function, and only then ask about doctrinal or philosophical content. Where disparate languages or inherited patterns of thought may divide two texts, Turner's theory, postulating as it does social processes that transcend both languages and thought patterns, may provide a much-needed bridge. It stands to reason that his theory would apply most readily to texts that themselves address social situations. Both Augustine's *De catechizandis rudibus* and Sankara's *Upadesasahasri* do just that.

Reading Sankara and Augustine with Victor Turner

Background

On or around the year 400 C.E., a deacon named Deogratias wrote to Augustine (354-430) for advice on instructing those who wished to enter the catechumenate as a first step to becoming full members of the Catholic Church.[9] Such initiates would receive a short evangelical address followed by four rites: the sign of the cross as a "shadow" of baptism, laying-on of hands as a "shadow" of confirmation, and handing over of bread and salt as "shadows" of Eucharist.[10] Augustine's response to Deogratias, entitled *De catechizandis rudibus* (hereafter *DCR*) or "On Catechizing the Uninstructed," however, focuses not on these sacraments but on the content and form of the evangelical address. He first discusses the methods and aims of this catechesis and then offers two sample addresses. The document stands apart in its simplicity both from the evangelical works of Augustine's predecessors and from other of his own writings on education. In it he endeavors to accomplish one task and one task alone: to demonstrate "how to present the 'good news' to one who now wishes to become a Christian."[11] True to his rhetorical training he adopts a classical framework for this task, comprising an introductory *exordium* to prepare the audience, a *narratio* to defend the faith, and a concluding *exhortatio* to encourage his listeners to live as true Christians in the face of adversity both within and without the church.[12] Augustine also took this text as an opportunity to consolidate many insights acquired from his early development and from his polemics against the Manichees—arriving, most importantly, at the "city of God" image that would appear so prominently in later writings. Located historically at a critical moment in Augustine's intellectual journey and rhetorically at a critical moment in the lives of its intended recipients, *DCR* thus offers a privileged glance into what this bishop considered essential for the initiation of new Christians.

A similar privileged glance can be found in the *Upadesasahasri*[13] (hereafter *US*), or "A Thousand Teachings," of Sri Sankaracarya (700-50?).[14] Although the *US* is the only non-commentarial text whose authorship by Sankara has been "conclusively demonstrated" by historical critics,[15] we know almost nothing of the circumstances surrounding its composition. Indeed, we know very little about Sankara as a historical figure, despite his vast importance for almost all subsequent Hindu schools of thought. Legendary biographies do exist, but they all post-date their subject by too great a distance to be used as reliable historical witnesses.[16] Most modern critical treatments of the great teacher simply define him as the author of the earliest extant commentary on the *Uttara-Mimamsa-Sutras* and then build all subsequent claims upon comparison to this foundational text.[17] From such philological study, the German scholar Paul Hacker tentatively attributed parts of the *US* to an early period of Sankara's intellectual development.[18] More certain is the evidence of the text itself. It consists of two major portions, a prose part (*USG*) offering a model for the Advaitin teacher and a metrical part (*USP*) that may be intended for direct study by students. In fact, if the teacher and students of the text are projected from Sankara's own experience—which we might reasonably hypothesize—then the *US* may well offer the most reliable historical information about Sankara's activity that we are ever likely to get. Indeed, the prose portion presents a third-person narrative portrait of the teaching process in three chapters, corresponding to the "triple method" of Advaita: "hearing" (*sravana*) of the non-dual unity of self, world, and God (*advaita*) as attested by the Vedas; well-reasoned "thinking" or "reflection" (*manana*) on this truth; and "meditation" or "concentration" (*nididhyasana*) to make one's conviction unshakable.[19] The metrical portion offers further detail to this portrait by addressing various disputed questions. Like Augustine's *DCR*, the *US* presents in a succinct form everything that Sankara deemed essential to a correct apprehension leading to final liberation.

If Sankara and Augustine occupy central places in their respective traditions, no less do *DCR* and the *US* reveal pivotal dimensions of their authors' shared task: namely, communication of salvific, liberating truth to those prepared to receive it.[20] In Turner's language, both Sankara and Augustine establish a "ritual field" for the reception of this truth in the performance of the teaching itself, wherein symbols—in this case, words—are employed to effect a transformation in the ritual subjects. Of course, these are not actual ritual performances. They do approximate such performances, however, by providing ideal models for them. Thus, the categories that Turner developed to analyze ritual performance seem uniquely well-suited to these particular texts. By reading the *US* and *DCR* with Victor Turner, we can discern at least three moments or motifs that govern both works, including separation from the dominant social system, an encounter with communitas as the culmination of the teaching process, and finally, in lieu of reaggregation back into the prevailing structure, a continuation of this liminal process through an alternate, enduring social system. I will treat each of these themes in turn.

Separation: Stripping Away the Non-Scriptural Self

In his treatment of *rites de passage*, Turner adopted from van Gennep three primary ritual moments: a "preliminal" phase, a marginal or "liminal" moment, and a final "postliminal" reaggregation into the dominant status system.[21] It is the first of these moments that will occupy us here. Of it Turner states: "The first phase, separation, comprises symbolic behavior signifying the detachment of the individual or the group from either an earlier fixed point in the social structure or from an established set of cultural conditions (a 'state')."[22] The subject must move from a position of relative security in the society to one of radical ambiguity or "sacred poverty."[23] This movement entails a "'leveling and stripping' of structural status."[24] Turner illustrates this point quite dramatically in his description of the installation of a Ndembu chieftain and his wife. In this rite, the selected couple is reduced symbolically to a "blank slate." Both lose their names and gender roles in favor of a single, generic name, they are stripped of their clothes and dressed in rags, and they sit, silent and submissive, in the face of insults by the "total community."[25] Like other neophytes in rites of transition, these individuals are "withdrawn from their structural positions. . . . They are also divested of their previous habits of thought, feeling, and action."[26] This process of withdrawal, the necessary precondition for liminal experience, is what we are treating here as "separation."

A similar process of stripping and withdrawal may be seen in the question posed by the teacher in the first prose chapter of the *US* (*USG* 1.9): "Who are you, my child?" In one sense the text itself has already provided a conventional answer: "That means of liberation . . . should be explained . . . to a pure Brahmin student who has adopted the life of a wandering *paramahamsa* ascetic . . . and who has approached the teacher in the prescribed manner and been examined in respect of his caste, profession, conduct, learning and parentage" (*USG* 1.2).

In light of these prerequisites it may come as a surprise that, when the disciple first answers by citing his caste, lineage, and renunciant status (*USG* 1.10), he receives a repudiation (*USG* 1.11): "My child, how do you desire to [achieve liberation] as your body will be eaten up by birds or will turn into earth even here when you die?" Rather, the disciple must see himself as different from the body, from lineage, and from state of life (*USG* 1.12-15). If the disciple, free now from this particular error, should say "I am in bondage, liable to transmigration, . . . and am entirely different from God. . . . [27] I want to worship Him through the actions pertaining to my caste and order of life by making presents and offerings to Him and also by making salutations and the like" (*USG* 1.25), he receives another reprimand, for "a doctrine of difference is forbidden" (*USG* 1.26). In fact, all actions directed toward God as somehow separate from the self, those rites and practices that have heretofore defined this brahmin disciple's life, are forbidden (*USG* 1.30-32, 44). Step by step, the teacher strips away the disciple's previous mistaken identification with his caste and obligatory duties to prepare him to realize his true identity as the self of all beings (cf. *USP* 1.1-7).[28]

One irony in Sankara's presentation stems from the fact that, in this first chapter, the teacher repeatedly shows how *sruti* (revealed scripture, primarily the Upanisads)[29] explicitly contradicts the disciple's false identification with the body, with caste, and even with those actions prescribed by *sruti* itself. First, *sruti* provides a model for the teaching situation in the form of *Mundaka Upanisad* 1.2.12-13, which describes the seeker's renunciation of Vedic obligations and decision to approach a teacher (*USG* 1.3). Second, the words of *sruti* point the way to the truth. Before questioning the disciple, the teacher offers a definition of the self as non-different from *brahman*, a definition supported by a multitude of proof texts drawn from the Upanisads (*USG* 1.6-8). As the disciple proceeds to make erroneous statements, the teacher turns him back to *sruti* again and again (e.g., *USG* 1.16-17;

1.27-28). "There are thousands of *sruti* texts," the teacher maintains, "conveying the same meaning [i.e., the truth of non-difference]" (*USG* 1.23). Third, *sruti* itself actively transforms the disciple: it is *sruti* alone that reveals what is really desirable (*USG* 1.42), *sruti* alone that uproots ignorance (*USG* 1.43), and finally *sruti* alone that provides a true means of knowledge (*pramana*) and the liberation that such knowledge brings (see *USP* 18.7-8; 18.220).[30] *Sruti* defines every step in the teaching process, providing a model, a content, and even its own agency to the event.[31] Under the guidance of the teacher, the disciple leaves behind his desire for reward, his body, his caste, his ignorance—in short, everything that is not *sruti*. Divested of his previous false identity by *sruti*, he stands ready to be inscribed anew.

At several points in *DCR* Augustine also employs scripture to remove candidates for the catechumenate from their previous identities. The main *narratio* of the address serves as the key element of the process:

> The narration is complete when the beginner is first instructed from the text: *In the beginning God created heaven and earth*, down to the present period of Church history. . . . [W]e ought by dwelling somewhat upon [the more remarkable events in this history] to untie, so to speak, and spread them out to view, and offer them to the minds of our hearers to examine and admire (*DCR* 3.5).

For Augustine this narration of sacred history represents a precious thread that, like the gold in a jeweled ornament, binds the "simple truth" of God to the hearers' own experience (*DCR* 6.10). The candidate must be, as it were, rolled into the scriptural account even as it is unrolled. But with whom does such a strategy hope to succeed? Prior to the narration, Augustine would have the catechist—like Sankara's teacher—question the candidates, not about their identities *per se* but rather about their motives for becoming Christians, hoping by this inquiry to remove misunderstandings and to purify the candidates' true intent (*DCR* 5.9). Similarly, Augustine offers advice for dealing with educated candidates. After ascertaining the breadth of their knowledge, the catechist weans them of any "heretical" notions that they may have encountered in their reading and sets before them "the authority of the universal Church" (*DCR* 8.12). To the rhetorician, he enjoins the virtue of "Christian humility" and warns that "there is no voice to reach the ears of God save the voice of the heart"[32] (*DCR* 9.13). To all, the catechist offers assurance in his *exordium* that rest, riches, and honors found in this life—any temporal security—will inevitably pass away. "Therefore he who desires true rest and true happiness must raise his hope from things that perish and place it in the Word of God;[33] so that, cleaving to that which abides forever, he may also together with it abide forever" (*DCR* 16.24). The hearers are thus enjoined to leave behind all obstacles to this Word.

For Augustine, moreover, there is an alternative to such eternal abiding with the Word of God. Indeed, if his catechist appears to assume a gentler disposition and to ask less penetrating questions than the teacher of the *US*, he also labors against the fear that the candidate may be or become a "child of hell" (*DCR* 14.21). Together, abiding with the Word and its opposite represent a dynamic that plays throughout history: "Thus there are two cities, one of the wicked, the other of the just, which endure from the beginning of the human race even to the end of time, which are now intermingled in body, but separated in will, and which, moreover, are to be separated in body also on the day of judgment" (*DCR* 19.31).

This division functions in at least two ways. First, it serves as a hermeneutical device to unite both Old and New Testaments into a single coherent account, joining contemporary Christians to the earliest patriarchs by means of their common membership in the "fellowship of the just," the true church (see *DCR* 3.6; 19.32-33). Second, it offers a warning. The candidates must separate themselves in will from the wicked city in the present time lest they find themselves joined to it in body on the day of judgment. In a world and even a temporal church comprising citizens of both cities, new Christians must exercise great prudence and self-discipline to wean themselves of false associations (*DCR* 7.11; 17.26). Thus Augustine urges candidates to "Associate with the good, whom you see loving your King with you" (*DCR* 25.49). Abide, in other words, with those who abide with the Word of God; and, by implication, separate yourself from those who do not. When Augustine lists in his *exordium* (and again in his *exhortatio*) those activities incompatible with the heavenly city—including heresy, gross immorality, attendance at the Roman theater, vanity, and any desire to gain prosperity or escape temporal loss (*DCR* 16.25; cf. 5.9; 17.26; 25.48; 27.55)—it becomes clear that he demands no less than a radical separation from the culture and concerns that have heretofore defined his hearers' lives. Barring such separation they will be members of the church "in a bodily sense only," ineligible for future reward (*DCR* 7.11).

In his call for radical separation from the wicked city and the culture that embodies it, Augustine's catechist echoes the teacher of Sankara's account. Certainly, the two calls differ from one another in the particular symbols that they employ. One uses the language of *false association*, while the other works to eradicate *false identification*. Sankara adopts a primarily *cognitive* model, Augustine a *communal* one. Yet both demand, at the inception of the ritualized teaching process, that the initiates divest themselves of their previous habits of thought and action. The candidates for the catechumenate—like the renunciant disciple—experience, in Turner's language, a "stripping and leveling" of their previous state. Moreover, in Augustine's demand that the citizen of heaven abide with the Word of God and in Sankara's description of *sruti* itself as the agent of true knowledge, we may see more than a shared high doctrine of scripture (although we must at least see that). We may also see scripture as providing a motive for such separation along with the unique means by which it takes place. Finally, it is the non-scriptural self *itself* that must be stripped away. Why? What is the goal of such separation? To explore this question we must return to Turner's social theory.

Culmination: Union with God and with One Another

In the introduction to this piece we noted that, as Turner explored the broader implications of *rites de passage*, he began to postulate two fundamental modes of human relatedness, labeled structure and communitas. In his words: "The first is of society as a structured, differentiated, and often hierarchical system. . . . The second, which emerges recognizably in the liminal period, is of society as an unstructured and relatively undifferentiated *comitatus*, community, or even communion of equal individuals. . . ."[34] In the elaborate circumcision rite of the Ndembu, communitas reveals itself in two important ways. First, having been stripped of their structural status in the preliminal phase of the ritual, the boys experience real equality with one another in the face of their instructors' absolute authority over all of them.[35] Second, they are at the same time exposed to stories, relics, and even grotesques that exhibit a "symbolic template of the whole system of beliefs and values in a given culture, its archetypal paradigm and ultimate measure."[36] These two primary aspects—the immediate encounter between equals and symbolic contact with the "archetypal" or ultimate reality—come to characterize liminality and communitas in Turner's later descriptions. Emotionally, communitas comprises "a strong sentiment of 'humankindness,' a sense of the generic bond between all members of society. . . ."[37] Historically, he sees it emerge not only in tribal rites of transition but also in "pioneering communities" of "prophets, saints, and gurus," as well as in the solitary "oneness" of mystical experience.[38] If, as we have already observed, Augustine and Sankara employ scripture to effect a ritual separation of their subjects from their previous social identities, it stands to reason that this would culminate in some expression of communitas. We can, in fact, find such a culmination described in both texts.

Augustine uses a communal image—the two cities—to lend coherence to the scriptural account and, through this account, to separate his hearers from their old selves. Distinct from this image but closely related to it stands a second hermeneutical key, the love[39] command. He writes:

> . . . it is evident that on these two commandments of the love of God and the love of our neighbor depend not merely the whole law and the Prophets . . . but also all the inspired books that have been written at a later period for our welfare and handed down to us. Therefore, in the Old Testament the New is concealed, and in the New the Old is revealed (*DCR* 4.8; cf. 23.4).

For Augustine sacred history, as well as its concrete performance by the catechist, works toward a common goal, "that end of love from which in all of our actions and words our eyes should never be turned away" (*DCR* 6.10). On the one hand, the climax of this history in the coming of Christ occurred for no other reason than to demonstrate God's love for humankind and, in this context, for the candidates in particular; on the other, this demonstration is intended to call forth a reciprocal, answering response (*DCR* 4.7). While Augustine readily praises intellectual acumen, he finds much greater delight in this love of God that, "the more graciously it descends to the lowliest station, irresistibly finds its way to the inmost recesses of the heart" (*DCR*

10.16). The candidates, having been symbolically lowered to such a station by the stern warnings of the *exordium*, may indeed be ready to accept this irresistible movement into their hearts.

One of the most striking features of Augustine's method resides in his insistence that the love enjoined by the scriptures also characterizes the teaching process itself. This insistence, embodied most concretely in his "chief concern" that the catechist experience "delight" (*delectatio*) in his ministry, possesses both practical and theological roots (*DCR* 2.4). Anyone who has ever been a student will readily concede the value of an environment and a teaching style conducive to learning. To this end, Augustine catalogues the various obstacles to the catechist's enjoyment as well as to the candidates' ability to receive his instruction (*DCR* 10.14; 13.18-19). Although the catechist should plan the teaching process carefully, he should also rejoice when these plans are ruined, "so that we may make our own the order which God has preferred to ours" (*DCR* 13.20). Indeed, Augustine enjoins the catechist to perform his work in God's love, and in so doing to "cheerfully permit *Him to speak through us* as best we can" (*DCR* 11.16 [emphasis mine]; cf. 7.11). In his description of the sympathy that should motivate the catechist he illustrates how this process joins catechist and candidates into one whole:

> For so great is the power of sympathy, that when people are affected by us as we speak and we by them as they learn, we dwell each in the other and thus both they, as it were, speak in us what they hear, while we, after a fashion, learn in them what we teach . . . for in proportion as we dwell in them through the bond of love, so do things that were old become new to us also (*DCR* 12.17).

Like the Old and New Testaments of the Catholic canon, catechist and candidates come to dwell in one another through their shared orientation toward love, a love that unites them to one another through their common bond with the one who first loved them in Christ.

Although Sankara does not speak so clearly as Augustine of the bond between "the teacher, the teaching, and the taught,"[40] he does illustrate, in the second prose chapter of the *US,* a process by which the disciple comes to understand their mutual coinherence. This is by no means obvious at the outset (*USG* 2.46), when the disciple, citing the pain of empirical experience, asks, "Is this my own nature, or is it causal, I being of a different nature?"As the following tightly reasoned account makes clear, it is causal (*USG* 2.49), caused by ignorance (*USG* 2.48-50) and by the "mutual superimposition" (*itara-itara-adhyaropana*) that ignorance produces between the body and the self (*USG* 2.51-64). Who makes this superimposition? Under the guidance of the teacher the disciple supplies his own answer: "So it is I, a conscious being, who makes that superimposition, the root of all evils, on the Self" (*USG* 2.64). The teacher replies, "Do not make any superimposition, if you know it to be the root of all evils" (*USG* 2.65). The disciple finds himself unable to comply (*USG* 2.66), and the argument proceeds apace (*USG* 2.67-108). An outside observer, confronted with the tangled mass of abstractions and distinctions that constitute the chapter, might deny any similarity of this process to the catechesis described by Augustine. But we can distinguish the content of the argument from the end to which it is directed. The central point emerges in the disciple's self-professed identity as a *conscious* being whose consciousness *per se* differs from the particular experiences of pain and pleasure illumined by it (*USG* 2.69-70). What then is this consciousness? Nothing other than the self-existent and eternal self of all beings. At the end of the debate the student announces:

> Just as a rope [mistaken for a snake], the water in a mirage and such other things are found to be non-existent . . . so, the duality experienced during waking and dream has reasonably no existence except the knowledge by which it is known. So, having a continuous existence, Pure Consciousness, the Self, is eternal and immutable and never ceasing to exist in any mental modification (*USG* 2.109).

The world of duality—including social differentiation—is ultimately unreal; the disciple now knows a deeper, more fundamental reality. The teacher boldly responds, "It is exactly so. . . . You are liberated from the misery of transmigratory existence" (*USG* 2.110).

Sankara further elucidates this undifferentiated reality by analogy to light. Just as a master and a servant each possess consciousness, so also two lamps both produce light (*USG* 2.71). Superficially, one lamp may well appear brighter than another, but the light remains the same by virtue of the common property—fire—from which it arises (*USG*

2.73). Hence also the master and the servant, possessed equally of consciousness, remain at base identical even though appearing superficially different (cf. *USP* 7.4). A typical progression of this theme takes place in the fourteenth metrical chapter. At *USP* 14.18 Sankara asks the rhetorical question, "Who . . . will attribute the ideas of 'me' and 'mine' to the Self as It is unborn . . . ?" The true self, free from such ignorant notions, is known to be one alone, without a second (*USP* 14.19). On the basis of this absolute oneness of the self, the individual of phenomenal experience can at its root only be "the seer, the hearer, the thinker and the knower that is *Brahman*, the imperishable One" (*USP* 14.20). Who else could it be? For, ultimately, there is nothing else. If this holds true for one conscious being, moreover, it necessarily holds for *all* such beings: "As all beings, moving and non-moving, are endowed with actions such as seeing, etc., they are *Brahman*, the imperishable One. Therefore I am the Self of all, the indestructible One" (*USP* 14.21). Recognition of this truth profoundly unites the disciple to all beings through their common identity with *brahman*—all-pervasive and free of attributes (see *USP* 8.3; 10.3; 17.76-77). Just as love joins catechist, candidates, and the God who first loved them in *DCR*, so also here disciple, teacher, and indeed all living beings stand united in the light of their shared consciousness, which is none other than the divine self.

At this point, it is important to recall what we are doing or, more importantly, what we are not doing. We cannot bluntly assert that Sankara's teaching of non-difference is simply identical to Augustine's interpretation of the love command; instead, by reading these texts through Turner's theory of communitas, we may see them as performing a comparable social function. As in the previous treatment of separation, so also with regard to this culmination the two figures differ significantly in their descriptions. One uses the language of *intellectual apprehension*, while the other extols *sympathetic understanding*. Augustine envisions an *affective* identity of hearts, Sankara a *metaphysical* identity of being. Yet both hold forth a vision of human persons that transcends all social barriers in favor of mutual indwelling or realized union with God and, consequently, with one another. Here we may see, in Turner's language, an "undifferentiated" bond that goes beyond even "humankindness" to the divine source of humankind and indeed of all living beings. At the same time, each author sees this bond arising in and through the ritualized teaching process, a process performed in time and hence bound by it. Augustine's catechist eventually concludes his evangelical address and, at some point, Sankara's disciple presumably ceases to receive instruction. What happens then? Does the communitas thus portrayed also come to a close? We turn now to these questions and to a broader issue opened by them, namely, the extension of the process beyond the boundaries of this teacher, this initiate, and this moment of ritual instruction. Here, as before, we will ask Turner to guide the inquiry.

Continuation: Reaching Beyond and Behind

Ordinarily *rites de passage*, as described by Turner, occur within and for the purposes of a social structure. As we saw in our treatment of "separation," however, the language employed by Sankara and Augustine to strip the ritual subjects of their previous, non-scriptural selves is uncompromising. Return in the form of a "postliminal" re-aggregation would constitute an abdication of heaven for one and a willful return to ignorance, the "root of all evil," for the other. Although communitas cannot replace structure as a permanent condition, Turner did hypothesize that attempts to do so could result in new institutions within the dominant structure, institutions intended to perpetuate a "founding experience" of communitas.[41] Such institutions he identified with "normative communitas," as distinct from the original, spontaneous "existential communitas." Providing an alternative to the outright yielding of communitas to structure, normative communitas organizes the original experience "into a perduring social system."[42] As a legitimate form of communitas it can foster the immediate and undifferentiated encounters typical of liminality, while as a "normative" structure it employs a social system or order to do so. It is a continuation of the same fundamental process, its translation onto a broader social canvas.

At the conclusion of the second prose chapter of the *US*, Sankara's disciple, pronounced free from transmigration, merely affirms this judgment with the sacred syllable "*Om*" (*USG* 2.111).[43] Yet the treatise continues into a third chapter, implying that more than the recognition already achieved may be required. Thus Sankara writes: "This method of repetition[44] is described [in the third prose chapter] for those who aspire after supreme tranquillity of the mind by destroying accumulated sins and virtues and refraining from accumulating new ones.

. . . This method is described here so that there may be a cessation of all these" (*USG* 3.112).

Here, we should note, the temporal sequence of the text breaks down: such repetition no doubt accompanies rather than follows the hearing and the reasoned reflection of the first and second chapters, respectively.[45] This observation notwithstanding, the method that Sankara prescribes does recapitulate the insights already gained. It begins with a summary of the teaching, reducing sound and the other senses to "brickbats" compared to that by which they are known: "The knower of sound and the like is of a nature different from theirs as It is the knower" (*USG* 3.113). The recitation that follows begins with the assertion, "I who am of the nature of Consciousness . . . cannot for the very fact of my being not attached, be made an object and touched by sound in general or its special forms . . . [I]t cannot do even the slightest good or evil to me who am a man of knowledge" (*USG* 3.115). Further stanzas proceed, one by one, to detach the one reciting from all of the senses (*USG* 3.115). Again and again the text states "I am," citing as true and complete the recognition that by implication has yet to be perfectly assimilated. The disciple concludes the repetition by pronouncing his freedom from pain, for "nothing really exists except the Self" (*USG* 3.116). Through such prescribed repetition seekers after liberation exert themselves to become in practice what they know from their hearing of *sruti* and from their reflection on Advaita that they already are.

Too narrow a focus upon repetition, however, might neglect the fact that for Sankara the premiere instrument for promoting this sustained recognition of non-difference is the teacher himself, who explains the means to liberation "again and again until it is grasped. . . ." (*USG* 1.2).[46] In the metrical portion of the *US*, for example, Sankara repeatedly turns the disciple back to the teacher, who shines light on the truth of *brahman* (*USP* 17.2), whose words destroy ignorance as the sun's rays destroy darkness (*USP* 17.3), who imparts a knowledge superior even to the kingdom of the god Indra (*USP* 16.74), and who offers refuge to all seekers of truth (*USP* 17.51-52). The disciple, besieged by the "hundreds and thousands" of errors of Buddhism and Hindu schools opposed to Advaita, is enjoined to abandon "all crookedness" in favor of the teacher who alone can communicate the "true import" of the Upanisads, namely, the Advaitin teacher (*USP* 16. 64-67).[47]

Elsewhere Sankara offers a more general description of the process: "[W]hen knowledge is firmly grasped, it conduces to one's own good and is capable of transmission. This transmission of knowledge is helpful to people, like a boat to one who wants to cross a river. . . . Otherwise there would be no attainment of knowledge" (*USG* 1.3; cf. *USP* 17.53). In seeking to grasp this knowledge, the disciple reaches behind to those who have grasped it before and reaches forward in anticipation to its further transmission once grasped. Indeed, this process, perpetuated by a lineage of qualified teachers, embodies true knowledge and ensures that it will always be available to those who seek it. It is within such a broader social dynamic, repeated across generations, that the disciple's own repetition assumes a small but significant role.

Augustine likewise identifies a structure that perpetuates the teaching and reception of truth from generation to generation: the church of God. This institution represents no less—but also no more— than the *raison d'être* of sacred history itself. Thus many Old Testament events symbolically reach beyond themselves toward Christ and, with him, toward the church. Thus Passover and the parting of the Red Sea refer to Christ's passion (*DCR* 17.34). Similarly, "by the symbol of the flood, wherein the just were saved by the wood (of the Ark), the Church to be was fore announced, which Christ, her King and God, by the mystery (of the wood) of His Cross, has buoyed up above the flood in which this world is submerged" (*DCR* 17.32).

The image of Jacob's birth also serves to illustrate the church's relation to those who prefigure it. Just as Jacob's hand, clasped around his brother's heel, emerged before his head while yet joined to his body, so too the patriarchs and prophets of the Old Testament arrived before their head, Christ, while joined to his body, the church (*DCR* 3.6; 17.33). Moreover, just as the patriarchs prefigure and symbolically represent the church, so too the carnal, mixed church of the present time represents the true spiritual citizens of the "heavenly Jerusalem" (*DCR* 17.36). These citizens, now in bondage to the world, will be delivered at the end of time (*DCR* 17.37). Until that deliverance comes, Augustine assures them, they can expect only to "taste" the comfort of the true rest and pure community that awaits them (*DCR* 16.25).

Such a "taste" of future rest finds apt symbolic expression in the "sacrament of salt," the "seasoning" that concludes the teaching ritual (*DCR* 26.50). This sacrament of course refers forward to the sacraments that the candidates will presumably receive in the future, above all that "foretaste of eternity," the Eucharist.[48] But it also refers back to the seasoning that the candidates have already received in the *exhortatio* of the evangelical address. Like Sankara's repetition, this final rhetorical flourish recapitulates many features of the *exordium* and the *narratio*, except now with the intent to render more permanent the separation tentatively achieved therein. Hence Augustine places special emphasis upon "the last judgment to come, with its goodness towards the good, its severity towards the wicked, its certainty in relation to all" (*DCR* 7.11). In the face of this judgment the catechist urges the candidates to cultivate the fire of love and "walk by faith" in God (*DCR* 25.47), remembering that God who created bodies can easily resurrect them on the last day (*DCR* 25.46). Such mindfulness and trust in God, along with good fellowship, will ultimately guide them on the right path toward their heavenly goal (*DCR* 25.48-49):

> The result will be what we must especially commend, namely, that when he who is listening to us, or rather listening to God through us, begins to make progress in morality and knowledge and to enter upon the way of Christ with eagerness, he will not venture to ascribe the change either to us or to himself, but will love both himself and us . . . in Him and for His sake, who loved him when he was yet an enemy, in order that by justifying him He might make him a friend (*DCR* 7.11).

Ultimately, the goal of the final *exhortatio* mirrors the goal of the entire teaching process and indeed of the church itself: to cultivate divine love in the heart of the one who receives it in faith. By calling to mind often the warnings and promises presented therein, the candidates may find themselves enabled to realize in their future lives of faith that love by which they have already been touched in the teaching itself.

In Turner's language, the mindfulness recommended to the candidates in *DCR*, along with the repetition prescribed in the *US* for the sincere disciple, builds upon an original experience of communitas, extending and organizing it into a "normative" social practice. Again, as in our previous comparisons, important differences emerge in the two accounts. One orients itself primarily toward *future* rest in God, while the other remains focused upon *present* identity with the divine.

Sankara emphasizes the *completion* of this goal in the realized teacher and even in the disciple who recites, whereas Augustine emphasizes its *incompleteness* even among the citizens of the heavenly city. Yet both the "seasoning" of Augustine's *exhortatio* and the "method for the cessation of results" prescribed by Sankara anticipate, continue, and recapitulate the intended goal of a much broader, perduring social system: the church and the lineage of teachers, respectively. Whether symbolized as a boat that carries its participants across the river of ignorance or as an ark buoyed by the wood of the cross above the flood of this world, these institutions represent the concrete possibility of religious transformation from one generation to another. Both are normative in the order that they prescribe for this transformation, but both aim through this order to foster that communion with God and with one another already treated as a form of communitas. Through their engagement in such a structure and in the teaching process that it perpetuates, initiates reach beyond themselves to others who have received or who will receive the truth, to all those—in Augustine's phrase—"who have been, who are, and who shall be" so transformed (*DCR* 17.36).

Final Reflections: Victor Turner and Comparative Theology

Religious transformation takes place in and through a social process.

This is where we began. Now, having read Sankara's *Upadesasahasri* and Augustine's *De catechizandis rudibus* with Victor Turner, we have seen how each in his own way affirms this basic idea. Turner's anthropological theory offers a way of drawing our attention to certain elements of both texts, places where Sankara and Augustine use analogous language to describe comparable social goals. Both employ scripture as a privileged means to separate their ritual subjects from the structures of the prevailing society, both describe a state of identification with God and with one another as consequence and culmination of the teaching, and both envision a continuation of this state through deliberate recollection on the part of the individual and through the perdurance of the teaching in a social institution. These elements we have already treated in some detail. Now we may ask: What has been gained by the comparison? What is the significance of this bridge now that it has been built?

One response is easy enough to formulate: no gain, no significance. It is possible that the very act of reading these ancient figures with a modern theorist like Turner—or comparing them at all, for that matter—inevitably introduces at least some distortion. Indeed, it seems very likely that neither Sankara nor Augustine would recognize themselves in these pages. Perhaps Augustine might say that the Christian scriptures make real separation from the world possible because the Christian scriptures—and *not* others—have been given by a God who is truly distinct from the world, not bound by it. Sankara's Upanisads are mere human speculation where human speculation cannot reach. Perhaps Sankara, on the other hand, might suggest that identifying *advaita* with an experience of any kind—including the experience of love—entirely misses the point. Experience presumes duality. *Advaita* is not a finite experience but an infinite reality to be known . . . and it cannot be so known through the faulty scriptures and even worse logic of someone like Augustine—who almost certainly could not escape the label "*dvaitin*," according to Sankara's rigorous standards. Finally, both Sankara and Augustine might together assert that a lineage of realized Advaitin teachers is just not the same as the Catholic Church. To place them in the same category only confuses the truth as it has been communicated to us by the divine.

We can and must recognize such outright rejection of the comparison as one legitimate response to this study, as well as guessing that both of our ancient writers would respond in precisely this way. But this doesn't mean that we have to follow them. Quite the opposite response is also possible. Indeed, we might assert that Augustine and Sankara do in fact describe an essentially identical process even if they wouldn't recognize it as such. The different symbols they use turn out to be merely accidental, the superficial trappings of one in the same human or divine reality. Turner himself espoused such a position, believing toward the end of his life that he had identified a "neurophysiological basis" for his theory of structure and communitas.[49] Just one step beyond this assertion is theologian Bernard Lonergan's hypothesis of a universal, infrastructural "religious experience" integral to every human person.[50] Vernon Gregson has extended Lonergan's theory to recommend cross-cultural and phenomenological accounts of spirituality as its next logical development.[51] Lonergan, according to this perspective, provides a fully adequate account of spirituality as such. The remaining task entails merely a close examination of the ways that various traditions symbolically mediate the experiential base that all of them share. This study of Sankara and Augustine might turn out to be one example of such examination.

Again, this is a completely legitimate response, made attractive by the fact that we get to keep the results of our study. Moreover, it seems to have the support of such scholars as Gregson, Lonergan, and even Turner himself. But here again we do not have to follow them. There is at least one other way. We can, instead of rushing to a theoretical conclusion, see the comparison as a practical opportunity. We might try to apply it directly to our own social context or contexts, conscious that the results of such an application defy clear prediction and will depend heavily upon the particularities of the comparison in question. I conclude by outlining one such application.

Throughout his career, Victor Turner insisted that the social world is "a world in becoming, not a world in being."[52] If "social world" refers only to the world of temporal experience, then both Augustine and Sankara substantively agree. Each, however, introduces a ritualized teaching process whereby this impermanent world gives way to a more or less permanent state of rest in God, a process of learning and transformation toward the truth of one's identity in scripture, in the proper institution, and finally in the divine self. We who have attempted to follow this process may now ask, "Who have we become and who are we becoming in the process of reading and comparison?" Our answer would have to include a candid recognition of our faith, identity, and commitments before the process, along with the changes that we perceive happening as we move forward in it. In his own study of Sankara, entitled *Theology after Vedanta*, Francis X. Clooney offers a description of this process:

> Theological comparison is therefore a practice in which one must purposefully and perseveringly engage. . . . its achievement of [a critical, intelligent relationship to the materials of the compared traditions] is a continually provisional and practical arrangement in which the comparativist engages in activities—theoretical, practical, interpretive, personal, communal—which are shaped in negotiation with the comparable activities of the communities which are being studied and compared.[53]

Clooney's description of comparative theology as a practical endeavor implicates the comparativist in a process that is simultaneously intellectual, social, and religious. Like the teaching described by Augustine and Sankara, the practice of comparative theology is a social process that aims for religious transformation.

Here is where Turner's theory may bear the most fruit for our further reflection. He builds a bridge not only between Sankara and Augustine, but also between their ancient texts and our contemporary practice. We can recognize the comparative theological endeavor as another such liminal phenomenon, "betwixt and between" the prevailing structures of the comparativists' home communities.[54] It is a *rite de passage* for the communities themselves. Turner's theory encourages us not to be naive about the radical implications of this process, as well as allowing us to appropriate Sankara and Augustine as our guides. Christian comparativists may begin to see how the self-conscious decision to "extend the Christian canon" by including other scriptures effects a kind of ritual separation from our native traditions of interpretation.[55] We may look for the culmination of our comparative work in a state of greater unity, not only with God and divine love, but also with others—other comparativists, other religious people, even others who oppose or refute our work. Finally, we may candidly see in the ongoing activities of dialogue and comparison—academic, pastoral, informal, accidental—a continual recollection of this goal, as well as a force that produces new communities, cultures, or alternative social structures. And we can speculate, based on this study, that an Advaitin comparativist might just recognize these same elements in her own work and opt to join us as we move forward in the process.

Religious transformation takes place in and through a social process. Turner has given us a theory. Sankara and Augustine have given us examples. Now we are enabled to enter the process, to make that transformation our own.[56]

Notes

[1]For an overview of the development of comparative theology as a subdiscipline, see Francis X. Clooney, S.J., "The Emerging Field of Comparative Theology: A Bibliographical Review (1989-95)," *Theological Studies* 56 (1995): 521-23; and James L. Fredericks, *Faith among Faiths: Christian Theology and Non-Christian Religions* (Mahwah, N.J.: Paulist Press, 1999), esp. 162-79.

[2]Beth Barrie attempts to assess Victor Turner's influence by surveying citations of his work in journals and books from 1985 to 1997. See Beth Barrie, "Victor Turner," *Theory in Anthropology*, <http://www.indiana.edu/~wanthro/turner.htm> (2 May 2000).

[3]In places Turner even engages explicitly in comparison across several religious and cultural traditions. See especially Victor Turner, *The Forest of Symbols: Aspects of Ndembu Ritual* (Ithaca: Cornell University Press, 1967), 59-92; and Victor Turner, *Dramas, Fields, and Metaphors: Symbolic Action in Human Society* (Ithaca and London: Cornell University Press, 1974), 231-71. For this account of Turner's theory and those that follow, I have drawn almost exclusively upon Turner's most influential works: *The Forest of Symbols, The Ritual Process: Structure and Anti-Structure* (Ithaca, N.Y.: Cornell University Press, 1969), and *Dramas, Fields, and Metaphors.*

[4]See Victor Turner, *The Ritual Process.*

[5]Turner, *Forest of Symbols*, 93-96, and *Ritual Process*, 166; cf. Turner, *Dramas, Fields, and Metaphors*, 52-53, 232-37; J. Randall Nichols, "Worship as Anti-Structure: The Contribution of Victor Turner," *Theology Today* 41 (1985): 401-9.

[6]Turner, *Ritual Process*, 96-97.

[7]Turner, *Dramas, Fields, and Metaphors*, 238; cf. *Ritual Process*, vii-viii.

[8]See Turner, *Ritual Process*, 107-8; *Dramas, Fields, and Metaphors*, 15-18, 65-66, 260ff.

[9]*De catechizandis rudibus* (*DCR*) 1.1, hereafter cited in the body of the text by chapter and section. I have used the English translation by Joseph P. Christopher: *St. Augustine: The First Catechetical Instruction [De Catechizandis Rudibus]*, Ancient Christian Writers, No. 2 (Westminster, Md.: Newman Press, 1962). I have also referred to the earlier translation by S. D. F. Salmond in *A Select Library of the Nicene and Post-Nicene Fathers of the Christian Church*, ed. Philip Schaff, vol. 3 (Grand Rapids: Wm. B. Eerdmans Publishing Co., 1956), 282-314; and to the Latin critical edition by I. B. Bauer in *Corpus Christianorum, Series Latina*, vol. 46 (Turnholt: Brepols, 1969), 115-78. My treatment of this text in its liturgical context depends heavily upon William Harmless, *Augustine and the Catechumenate* (Collegeville: Liturgical Press, 1995).

[10]F. van der Meer, *Augustine the Bishop: The Life and Work of a Father of the Church*, trans. Brian Battershaw and G. R. Lamb (London and New York: Sheed & Ward, 1961), 353-57.

[11]Harmless, 109. See ibid., 107-10, and Fannie LeMoine, "Augustine on Education and the Liberal Arts" in *Saint Augustine the Bishop: A Book of Essays*, ed. Fannie LeMoine and Christopher Kleinhenz (New York and London: Garland Publishing, 1994), 180-82.

[12]Harmless, 123-26; cf. 155.

[13]Hereafter cited in the body of the text by chapter and section or verse of each of its two major sections: the prose portion, or *Gadyabandha* (*USG*) and the verse portion, or *Padyabandha* (*USP*). I have used, with some alterations, the translation by Swami Jagadananda, *Upadesa Sahasri of Sri Sankaracarya* (Madras: Sri Ramakrishna Math, 1941). Although this translation does depend upon the commentary of Ramatirtha rather too heavily to fill in gaps and ambiguities in the original text, I do not think that this detracts significantly from its utility for the

purposes of this essay. See Sengaku Mayeda, review of Jagadananda, in *Philosophy East and West* 12, no. 3 (1962): 261-63. I have referred to two alternative translations: Sengaku Mayeda, trans., *A Thousand Teachings: The* Upadesasahasri *of Sankara* (Albany: State University of New York Press, 1992), and V. Narasimhan, trans. *Upadesa Sahasri: A Thousand Teachings of Adi Sankara* (Bombay: Bharatiya Vidya Bhavan, 1996), the latter of which also includes a translation of the commentary of Anandagiri. For convenience I have referred to the Sanskrit text printed alongside the translation in the Jagadanda volume, although Sengaku Mayeda has prepared a critical edition in Roman transliteration: *Sankara's Upadesasahasri, Critically Edited with Introduction and Indices* (Tokyo: The Hokuseido Press, 1973).

[14]These are the dates given by Mayeda, *A Thousand Teachings*, xv. Sankara's dates, however, are disputed. See discussion and references in ibid., 3; Karl H. Potter, ed., *Encyclopedia of Indian Philosophies: Advaita Vedanta up to Sankara and His Pupils* (Princeton: Princeton University Press, 1981), 14-15, 116; and Tilmann Vetter, *Studien zur Lehre und Entwicklung Sankaras* (Vienna: Institut für Indologie der Universität Wien, 1979), 11-12.

[15]Mayeda, *A Thousand Teachings*, 6. For the full argument, see Sengaku Mayeda, "The Authenticity of the *Upadesasahasri* Ascribed to Sankara," *Journal of the American Oriental Society* 85 (1965): 178-96.

[16]For some excellent attempts by scholars to sift through the legendary biographies and form a coherent narrative, see Jonathan Bader, *Conquest of the Four Quarters: Traditional Accounts of the Life of Sankara* (New Delhi: Aditya Prakashan, 2000); Mariasusai Dhavamony, "Sankara and Ramanuja as Hindu Reformers," *Studia Missionalia* 34 (1985): 119-30; Natalia Isayeva, *Shankara and Indian Philosophy* (Albany: State University of New York Press, 1993), 69-83; and S. Sankaranarayanan, *Sri Sankara: His Life, Philosophy and Relevance to Man in Modern Times*, Adyar Library General Series 14, ed. K. Kinjunni Raja (Madras: The Adyar Library and Research Centre, 1995). Mayeda, *A Thousand Teachings*, 3-10, and Potter, 15-18, 116-18, attempt more cautious reconstructions, reduced to the most probable events in Sankara's life, but even these minimalist interpretations rely heavily on the legendary biographies.

[17]See, for example, Paul Hacker, "Distinctive Features of the Doctrine and Terminology of Sankara: Avidya, Namarupa, Maya, Isvara," in *Philology and Confrontation: Paul Hacker on Traditional and Modern Vedanta*, ed. Wilhelm Halbfass (Albany: State University of New York Press, 1995), 57-100; and Potter, 115-16; cf. Francis X. Clooney, *Theology after Vedanta: An Experiment in Comparative Theology* (Albany: State University of New York Press, 1993), 31-34, 214-15 (n. 46).

[18]The essential elements of this argument are outlined in Hacker's 1968 article "*Sankara der Yogin und Sankara der Advaitin, einige Beobachtungen*," translated and reprinted as "Sankara the Yogin, Sankara the Advaitin: Some Observations," in Halbfass, *Philology and Confrontation*, 101-34.

[19]Mayeda, *A Thousand Teachings*, xiii; cf. William Cenkner, *A Tradition of*

Teachers: Sankara and the Jagadgurus Today (1983; Delhi: Motilal Banarsidass, 1995), 66-69; Yoshitsugu Sawai, "The Nature of Faith in the Sankaran Vedanta Tradition," *Numen* 34 (1987): 28-29.

[20]It should be noted, however, that while the *US* outlines a vision of the entire process of initiation into the Advaita tradition, *DCR* merely relates to the first phase of the ancient catechumenate, itself an extended ritual performance with several phases. In this sense, there is a critical lack of parity between the two texts. I maintain that the comparison is still viable, however, based on two considerations. First, with regard to *DCR*: due to the radical theology of baptism prevalent in Augustine's North Africa many people delayed their baptism until they were close to death—hence, the evangelical address and the "shadows" received thereafter might remain the primary ritual foundation for most of their lives as Christians (notwithstanding the sermons they would continue to hear on a regular basis). Second, with regard to the *US*: when we turn to Sankara's commentary on the *Uttara-Mimamsa-Sutras* we find an expansive treatment of Advaita pedagogy and practice. In the light of this massive commentary, the comparatively slim *US* appears somewhat preliminary, as an introduction to a life that would culminate in study, further commentary, and meditation in connection with these sutras.

[21]See Turner, *Ritual Process*, 166; *Dramas, Fields, and Metaphors*, 196-97.

[22]Turner, *Dramas, Fields, and Metaphors*, 232.

[23]Turner, *Forest of Symbols*, 98-99; *Dramas, Fields, and Metaphors*, 233-37.

[24]Turner, *Dramas, Fields, and Metaphors*, 252.

[25]Turner, *Ritual Process*, 97-106.

[26]Turner, *Forest of Symbols*, 105.

[27]Literally, "from that one, the shining one [*deva*], who is not liable to transmigration." Here, the God so described is personalistic, not the ultimate trans-personal *brahman* that will occupy most of Sankara's attention hereafter. In places, however, I will also use "God" as a generic term for both Sankara's impersonal *brahman* and Augustine's more personalistic *deus*. Although there are sharp distinctions between these two conceptions of the divine, there also seems to be sufficient common ground to warrant use of the term in both cases. In addition, the Advaitins with whom I have studied regularly use the term "God" for both personal and impersonal conceptions of the divine.

[28]Cenkner, *A Tradition of Teachers*, 61-64.

[29]In fact, in the *US* Sankara uses three terms to designate the scriptures: *sruti*, the revealed and eternal words of the Vedas, including the Upanisads; *smrti*, the traditional writings of epics, legal codes, and even the *sutras* and commentaries of the various orthodox schools of thought; and *sastra*, a generic term that includes both *sruti* and *smrti*. I have selected *sruti* for all of these terms, since it is the one most frequently used and, more importantly, since in Sankara's system the *smrtis* technically have only a supporting role to play. Hence, it would not be improper to say that the meaning of the *sastras* as a whole is theoretically governed and circumscribed by *sruti* alone.

[30]See K. N. Upadhyaya, "Sankara on Reason, Scriptural Authority and Self-Knowledge," *Journal of Indian Philosophy* 19 (1991): 121-32; Anantanand

Rambachan, "Where Words Can Set Free: The Liberating Potency of Vedic Words in the Hermeneutics of Sankara," in *Texts in Contexts: Traditional Hermeneutics in South Asia*, ed. Jeffrey R. Timm (Albany: State University of New York Press), 33-46; and Isayeva, *Shankara and Indian Philosophy*, 31-33.

[31]See J. G. Suthren Hirst, "The Place of Teaching Techniques in Samkara's Theology," *Journal of Indian Philosophy* 18 (1990): 113-50.

[32]Literally, "the devotion (*affectus*) of the 'seat of the feelings' (*animus*)." Of course, this is not a blithe truism. Just four years prior to the composition of *DCR*, in the *Ad Simplicianum*, Augustine had revolutionized his thinking on grace and free-will precisely through his analysis of human affections. See Peter Brown, *Augustine of Hippo* (Berkeley and Los Angeles: University of California Press, 1967), 153-56; and Paula Fredriksen, "Beyond the Body/Soul Dichotomy: Augustine on Paul against the Manichees and the Pelagians," *Recherches Augustiniennes* 23 (1988): 94-98, including the references in n. 45.

[33]Indicating, we may assume, primarily scripture (in the context of the *exordium* that sets a stage for the narration of sacred history) but also Christ himself, who exemplifies and produces sacred scripture through the inspiration of his Spirit (e.g. *DCR* 17.28).

[34]Turner, *Ritual Process*, 96.

[35]Turner, *Forest of Symbols*, 99-100.

[36]Ibid., 108; cf. 102-5.

[37]Turner, *Ritual Process*, 116.

[38]Turner, *Dramas, Fields, and Metaphors*, 203.

[39]In fact, in the selected passages Augustine uses several related terms for love: *dilectio*, *caritas*, and *amor*. While these terms differ somewhat in nuance, in *DCR* Augustine moves fluidly from one to the other without offering any technical distinctions between them. Hence, it seems appropriate to treat them all here under the generic term "love."

[40]Cenkner, *A Tradition of Teachers*, 57.

[41]Turner, *Dramas, Fields, and Metaphors*, 169-70.

[42]Turner, *Ritual Process*, 132-33 and passim.

[43]Jagadananda translates *om*, "Yes, sir." The term seems to be functioning here similarly to the Hebrew *amen*, indicating finality or completion.

[44]The translation of *parisamkhyana* is uncertain. Literally, it simply means the totality or total enumeration of something. In this context Mayeda, *A Thousand Teachings*, 251, uses "meditation"; Narasimhan, *Upadesa Sahasri*, 277, uses "recollection" and translates Anandagiri's interpretation as "contemplative repetition." Some form of meditation seems to be recommended, roughly corresponding to what came to be known as *nididhyasana* in Advaita tradition. See Mayeda, *A Thousand Teachings*, 254 (n. 1).

[45]The place of such meditation is disputed in Advaita tradition. The so-called *bhamati* schools tend to place a great deal of emphasis upon it, whereas the more conservative *vivarana* schools downplay its importance in preference to the self-sufficiency of the words of *sruti*. See Cenkner, *A Tradition of Teachers*, 96-103.

[46]See ibid., 32-38.

[47]On *sraddha* or faith in the authorized Advaitin teacher, see Sawai, "The Nature of Faith in the Sankaran Vedanta Tradition," 20-21, 27-28.

[48]See Gerald Bonner, "Augustine's Understanding of the Church as a Eucharistic Community," in LeMoine and Kleinhenz, *Saint Augustine the Bishop*, 50-55; cf. Harmless, *Augustine and the Catechumenate*, 150-51.

[49]See Mathieu Deflem, "Ritual, Anti-Structure, and Religion: A Discussion of Victor Turner's Processual Symbolic Analysis," *Journal for the Scientific Study of Religion* 30 (1991): 16. As early as 1969, Turner could write, "It [liminality] is not a matter of different cognitive structures, but of an identical cognitive structure articulating wide diversities of cultural experience" in *Ritual Process*, 3.

[50]For example, Bernard J. F. Lonergan, *Method in Theology* (1971; Toronto: University of Toronto Press, 1996), 105-9; cf. Frederick E. Crowe, "Lonergan's Universalist View of Religion," *Method: Journal of Lonergan Studies* 12 (1994): esp. 149-53.

[51]See Vernon Gregson, *Lonergan, Spirituality, and the Meeting of Religions*, College Theology Society Studies in Religion 2 (Lanham, Md.: University Press of America, 1985), esp. 80-91; also Vernon Gregson, "The Faces of Evil and Our Response: Ricoeur, Lonergan, Moore," in *Religion in Context: Recent Studies in Lonergan*, ed. Timothy P. Fallon, S.J., and Philip Boo Riley, College Theology Society Resources in Religion 4 (Lanham, Md.: University Press of America, 1988), 125-39.

[52]Turner, *Dramas, Fields, and Metaphors*, 24.

[53]Clooney, *Theology after Vedanta*, 9-10.

[54]On such liminal phenomena in the church, see especially Carl F. Starkloff, "The Church as Structure and Communitas," *Theological Studies* 58 (1997): 643-68.

[55]See Francis X. Clooney, "Extending the Canon: Some Implications of a Hindu Argument about Scripture," *Harvard Theological Review* 85 (1992): 209-15; and Francis X. Clooney, *Seeing through Texts: Doing Theology among the Srivaisnavas of South India* (Albany: State University of New York Press, 1996), 299-304.

[56]I gratefully acknowledge the assistance and support of my teachers, Bruce T. Morrill, Francis X. Clooney, Paula Fredriksen, and Swami Paramarthananda; in memoriam: Egerton Whittle and Jennifer Campbell Smith.

Ad Experimentum: The Paradoxes of Indian Catholic Inculturation

Mathew N. Schmalz

The Paradoxes of Inculturation

In the past two years, Catholicism in India has been the focus of international attention to the degree that it has never before received. Reports of violence against Catholic Christians in the Indian states of Gujarat and Madhya Pradesh were highlighted in *The New York Times* and in U.S. State Department reports on religious freedom.[1] Protests against the recent papal visit to India also seemed to underscore a rise in anti-Christian feeling, which the Western press has associated with resurgent Hindu nationalism.[2] The Indian press, for its part, has often viewed the Catholic Church with suspicion. During John Paul II's first visit to India in 1986, the Hindi periodical *Dinman* ran a story under the title "Is the Catholic Church Really a Time Bomb?"[3] *Dinman*'s answer to this question was "yes": the Catholic Church is a time bomb ticking away in Indian society since the Catholic Church's work with Untouchables and Tribals raises the specter of further unrest within an India still trying to define its nationhood.[4] The paradox of such attitudes is, of course, that Christianity has a long history on the Indian sub-continent. Christian communities identify their origins with the apostle Thomas and his legendary journey to India.[5] Historians would point to communities of Syrian Christians, with connections to the Nestorian Assyrian Church of the East, which had been established in South India from at least the year 600 C.E.[6] To describe Christianity as completely alien to South Asia thus ignores an indigenous Indian Christian tradition that extends over fourteen hundred years.

The suspicion and sporadic violence specifically surrounding Catholicism in India appears even more ironic given Catholic efforts to adapt to Indian culture. This process of "inculturation," begun in earnest after the Second Vatican Council, has sought to integrate various Indian cultural and religious symbols into the liturgical life of Indian Catholicism. Writing in 1981, the Indian scholar of Christianity K. N. Sahay predicted that Catholic inculturation would "gradually soften the attitude of Indian masses towards Christianity and in course of time Christianity will be treated by non-Christians on par with Hinduism."[7] The recent violence against Catholic Christians, however, emphasizes the failure of inculturation to achieve this rapprochement with Hinduism and Indian culture. But what is perhaps even more surprising is that inculturation has been resisted by Indian Catholics themselves. The paradox of Indian Catholic inculturation is that this effort to become more Indian has only elicited greater suspicion within Indian society as a whole.

While Indian Catholic architects of inculturation expected resistance, their theologies did not account for its depth. This inability to anticipate adverse reactions to inculturation was perhaps due to Indian Catholic theology's refusal to reach beyond its own boundaries to engage other disciplines that address the social and cultural components of religious expression. But anthropology, as the social science with the most dynamic tradition of cultural study, could make an oblique and revealing entry into the discourse surrounding inculturation, not only by suggesting an explanatory framework for understanding Catholicism's relationship to Indian culture, but also by charting a trajectory for dialogue between theology and the social sciences as both seek to probe the relationship between religion and culture. Accordingly, this essay will address the apparent paradox of Indian Catholic inculturation by examining its theology of liturgical adaptation within anthropological understandings of symbol and culture. Initially focusing upon the dialogical religious vision of D. S. Amalorpavadass, the leading proponent of Indian Catholic inculturation, we will see how the inculturation movement developed and later provoked controversy surrounding its use of symbols and its appropriation of Hindu religiosity. Turning then to contemporary anthropological discourse, we will consider how challenges to conventional understandings of symbol and Hinduism illuminate the tensions that have so shaped responses to Catholic adaptation to Indian culture. But anthropology does not simply provide an analytical apparatus for probing the social context of theological discourse. Instead, I will demonstrate that both theology and the social science of anthropology can find a common ground of concern underlying their seemingly conflicting reflections on symbolism and culture.

Ad Experimentum

Within South Asia, inculturation now refers to self-consciously theological efforts to integrate Indian forms of expression into the life of the Catholic Church. But before we discuss such attempts, it is important to realize that Christianity has long been "inculturated" within certain parts of Indian society. In South India, where the Apostle Thomas is reputed to have set ashore, Syrian Christians enjoyed the protection of local kings and practiced many customs that could also be said to characterize "Hindu" religiosity, such as the observance of Untouchability, the casting of horoscopes, and the ritual shaving of the head after important rites of passage.[8] But explicitly Catholic efforts to adapt to Indian culture were not as concerned with accommodating such practices as they were with appropriating them to articulate the message of the gospel. These efforts together form a narrative that extends from the work of Roberto de Nobili in the seventeenth century to the theology of D. S. Amalorpavadass following the Second Vatican Council. As we will see, the story of Indian Catholic inculturation is characterized by individual and institutional creativity as well as by bitter controversy.

From De Nobili to Amalorpavadass

Within the West, initial Catholic efforts at inculturation in India are usually associated with Roberto de Nobili, a Jesuit who founded a mission in the South Indian holy city of Madurai in 1606. De Nobili immersed himself in South Indian culture, studying both Sanskrit and Tamil. He wore the ochre robe of the renouncer or *samnyasi* and proclaimed the Bible as the completion of the four Vedas considered by many Hindus to be revealed texts central to their ritual practice.[9] De Nobili directed his efforts toward Brahmins, members of the highest caste within Indian society, and consecrated their sacred threads, the traditional emblems of Brahminical status, to the Father, Son, and Holy Spirit. This cultural accommodation went as far as the establishment of separate churches for high and low caste converts—a distinction that persists in parts of South India to this day. De Nobili argued that these practices were social customs with either coextensive or secondary religious meanings and thus were necessary adaptations if the truth of the gospel were ever to be fully proclaimed within Indian culture. While the forced Latinization of Christian communities by the Portuguese in the seventeenth century eradicated much of de Nobili's work, what emerged was a Catholic community in Southern India that developed its own distinct culture by blending both European and Indian elements.

De Nobili's seminal influence notwithstanding, perhaps the most creative Catholic proponent of inculturation was the Bengali nationalist Brahmabandhab Upadhyay. After his conversion to Catholicism in 1891, Upadhyay proclaimed himself a "Hindu Catholic." Writing in a dense literary Bengali, Upadhyay probed the relationship between Thomistic and Indian philosophical systems and maintained that the superstructure of Catholicism could be built upon a Hindu foundation.[10] In holding to this position, Upadhyay argued that Hinduism constitutes a complex of social practices in contrast to Catholicism's status as a preeminently supernatural construct concerning ultimate truth and salvation. Towards the end of his life, Upadhyay became vehemently anti-British and argued for a reassertion of traditional Hindu practices to protect India's purity. While still holding fast to his Catholic identity, Upadhyay advocated the veneration of Krishna as a moral exemplar and cultural symbol.[11] He also drew upon the Hindu text *The Laws of Manu* to assert the necessity of caste to preserve Indian society from the influence of half-breed Tribals and foreigners.[12] Upadhyay believed that this strengthening of Hindu identity meant the strengthening of Indian identity and would finally pave the way for Indian acceptance of a Christ and a Catholicism purged of its associations with colonial domination.

Brahmabandhab Upadhyay died in 1907 after being arrested by the British for sedition. Some sixty years later, the vision of a fully Indian Catholicism forcefully reemerged in the work and writings of D. S. Amalorpavadass. Born in Pondicherry in 1932 and ordained into the priesthood in 1959, Amalorpavadass pursued his doctoral studies at the Institut Catholique de Paris, completing his doctorate in 1964.[13] His dissertation, *Destinée de l'Église dans l'Inde d'aujourd'hui*, exerted a catalytic influence on Indian Catholicism well before its official publication in 1967. In his discussion of Indian Catholicism, Amalorpavadass diagrams an Indian society aching under the stresses of its relatively new nationhood and the concomitant pressures of modernization and Westernization.[14] This social crisis of identity then paved the way for Christ, who alone can fulfill the collective longings of humanity. But in order for this transformation to occur, Christ must come clothed in the garb of Indian culture. Given its general similarity to Upadhyay's own vision, it is curious that Amalorpavadass never mentions him or any other Indian Catholic theologian in his discussion of Catholicism's destiny on the Indian sub-continent. Instead, Amalorpavadass argues that the Catholic Church in India remains constricted by its Western customs and modes of worship. If India is ever to accept Christ, then Catholicism must first accept India and open itself to the wisdom of the Hindu tradition. Much of the story of inculturation in India over the last thirty years may be traced back to D. S. Amalorpavadass and his clarion call for a fully inculturated Indian Catholicism.

Indian Catholic Inculturation and Vatican II

The period immediately following the Second Vatican Council produced an intense environment of liturgical innovation in Indian Catholicism. At the direction of the Catholic Bishops' Conference of India, D. S. Amalorpavadass was appointed secretary of a new National Liturgical Center in the South Indian city of Bangalore that was to spearhead liturgical reforms. Empowered by a series of indults *ad experimentum*, the Center first sought to produce vernacular translations of the mass for the Syro-Malabar, Syro-Malankara, and Latin rites. Under Amalorpavadass's supervision, the Center held conferences and conducted surveys that addressed the issue of liturgical reform throughout the various regions of India. Some of the proposed changes reached a high degree of specificity, such as the rather trenchant suggestion that traditional penitential language if translated into the vernacular would needlessly frighten small children.[15] But beyond such liturgical minutiae, a consensus began to emerge at the Center that there should perhaps be a new rite for the entirety of India that would complement vernacular Eucharistic liturgies celebrated in the three rites of Indian Catholicism.

To this end of developing "A New Order of the Mass for India," the National Liturgical Center, with the approval of the Catholic Bishops' Conference of India, developed "12 Points of Adaptation" to be used as a framework for more extensive adaptation of Catholic liturgical life to Indian culture.[16] The "12 points of Adaptation" concerned what was called "indigenization in worship" and largely involved the adoption of characteristically Indian or Hindu postures during the Mass. These adaptations were approved by Rome in 1969 but were seen by Amalorpavadass and his colleagues as only an initial stage in liturgical renewal and inculturation. The second phase of reform proposed the development of an Indian Eucharistic prayer or anaphora while the third phase envisioned the use of non-Christian scriptures in worship.[17] Experimentation along these lines continued apace until 1975 when Cardinal Knox, the Prefect of the Sacred Congregation for Divine Worship, wrote to the Catholic Bishops' Conference of India to prohibit the use of the Indian anaphora and readings from non-biblical scriptures in the liturgy.[18] With this letter, the most radical forms of experimentation in the Eucharistic liturgy came to an end.

The legacy of the "12 Points of Adaptation" continues in the form of an experimental order of the Mass that is celebrated in what are called Christian ashrams—places of worship and meditation that are often described as Hindu monasteries. The Mass is held in a chapel that ideally is patterned after a Hindu temple. The priest dresses in an ochre-colored robe that within the Hindu tradition is associated with renunciation. Participants first remove their footwear, circumambulate the chapel, and then are welcomed by the priest who applies sandalwood paste to their foreheads. An oil lamp and sticks of incense are lit and rotated in a clockwise direction first toward the altar and then toward the participants. Often the lamp is moved in such a way that it traces the outlines of the sacred syllable *Om*, which in some Hindu theologies is considered to be the very embodiment of all that is real. Eight flowers are placed on the altar before the consecration and at the elevation of the Host all participants prostrate themselves before the altar. The Mass is usually in the vernacular of the particular location of the ashram although Sanskrit is employed in the form of litanies of praise such as "Hail Christ, Giver of Salvation" (*Jai Yesu Khrist Muktidata*) or "Hail Christ, Lord of the Universe" (*Jai Yesu Khrist Vishvanath*). The use of such phrases thus links Christian conceptions of Christ to well-known qualities that Hindus attribute to the Divine. The structure of this experimental Mass completely parallels the Latin Rite with the prohibited Indian Eucharistic prayer included in the accompanying missalette, its silent presence a reminder of the ever contentious debate over the extent and manner of Catholic adaptation to Indian culture.[19]

For D. S. Amalorpavadass, the experimental Indian Rite Mass was an exercise in both adaptation and dialogue. In his introductory remarks directed to the priests who would celebrate the Mass, he explains that:

> The project of adaptation might be briefly described as the expression of the same meaning in terms of new symbols belonging to a different cultural tradition. It can be compared to the project of translating a text from one language to another. To do a good translation, a capacity to rethink in another language is more necessary than a good dictionary.[20]

In order to facilitate this process of "rethinking," participants in the Mass often attend a retreat called the "Indian Christian Spiritual Experience," which includes an explication of the meanings of the symbols used in the experimental Mass.[21] Thus, *arati*, or the rotation of the oil lamp, is a sign of honor and is used to welcome participants as well as to acknowledge the presence of Christ in the host, or the Bible as the Word of God. Incense represents prayers rising toward heaven while the offering of eight flowers represents the submission to Christ of the four cardinal directions of the universe and the intermediate spaces between them. The various postures that participants assume during the Mass, such as the "bow of the five-limbs" (*panchanga pranam*) are glossed as signs of submission. These are all characteristic symbolic elements found in the diverse expressions of Hindu worship, but are not linked to any theological propositions that would challenge Catholic doctrinal claims. By integrating such symbols into the Mass, Amalorpavadass envisioned a reciprocal dialogue in which Hindus who witnessed the Mass would be able to understand Catholic religious expression, while Catholics who participated in it would be able not only to appreciate the aesthetics of Hindu religiosity but also to consider Hinduism itself a valid form of spiritual practice. Liturgy was then to be an initial meeting point for Hindus and Catholics, not as representatives of different religious traditions but as Indians who share a common spiritual and cultural heritage.

Theologies of Symbol and Culture

Amalorpavadass's writings on inculturation are voluminous and number well over one hundred books, pamphlets, and articles. Throughout his work, Amalorpavadass consistently places a Christian vision of creation and incarnation at the center of the process of inculturation. In *Gospel and Culture*, Amalorpavadass observes that just as Christ became incarnate within the specificity of human life, so too must Christianity assume the form of the culture of which it is a part. While the world still bears the imprint of sin, God's creation has become good again through Christ's work of reconciliation.[22] The Logos, however, has also been present in the whole of human history and has been revealed to all people under different external forms.[23] The enfleshment of God's self-gift in Christ is thus mirrored in the various manifestations of human community. Inculturation then is not a choice but an essential aspect of the church's mission to draw all to Christ:

> The Gospel lived by the Church in a living culture with all the transformations and realities it entails is what is called inculturation. . . . Hence there is no preaching of the Gospel without inculturation. There is no Church without being localised [and] concretised. . . . There is no salvation without the incarnation of the Word of God! [*sic*][24]

If culture is one of the primary forms of God's own self-expression, it also exists as an organic whole. The totality of Indian culture is suffused with an "ineffable Indianness" that, for Amalorpavadass, has continued to draw life from three thousand years of Hindu history. In his writings, however, Amalorpavadass focuses upon a very particular form of Hindu philosophy known as non-dualism or Advaita Vedanta.[25] Advaita Vedanta posits Brahman as the only source of reality, with the signs and symbols of the phenomenal world interpreted either as manifestations of Brahman or as Maya, illusion. In privileging this form of Hinduism, Amalorpavadass is able to understand specific forms of religious practice as symbols of a deeper reality, with Brahman seen as equivalent to Christian conceptions of Christ as Logos. What this does, of course, is to remove the problem of the worship of other gods in Catholic adaptations to Hindu culture. Indeed, the Hindu texts that Amalorpavadass argued should be integrated into the religious life of

Catholicism are not the mythological texts which Hindus so revere, but abstract philosophical works such as the Upanishads, which place Brahman at the center of their metaphysics. But in integrating non-Christian elements into the life of the church, Indian Christians are really not borrowing or appropriating anything. Amalorpavadass claims, citing the document *Ad Gentes*:

> "Particular traditions, together with the individual patrimony of each family, and of nations can be illuminated by the light of the Gospel, and then be taken up into Catholic unity." But in fact there is no borrowing, all that she appears to borrow is in fact what already belongs to Christ by creation and by resurrection and hence what the Church should claim and gather as her own. . . . As Indians we can claim all that is Hindu and Indian as our own; as Christians we can state that whatever belongs to Christ belongs to us. So we borrow nothing.[26]

Controversies

For many Hindu observers and cultural critics, this last statement by Amalorpavadass reveals a profoundly disturbing attitude toward Hinduism and Indian culture. For example, the radical Hindu critic Sita Ram Goel calls inculturation a swindle, designed to ape Hindu tradition in the hopes of winning converts.[27] Of course, what is at issue in much of what has been called anti-Christian violence revolves around charges of the forced conversion of Untouchables and Tribals to Catholicism. Inculturation then is seen as but another missionary tactic that illegitimately appropriates Hindu symbols with malign intent toward Indian society.

Many Indian Catholics were also suspicious of the changes proposed and enacted by the National Liturgical Center. Some even took Amalorpavadass to court in order to emphasize their resistance to new forms of the liturgy.[28] And for many Indian Catholics, the reforms envisioned by Amalorpavadass and the National Liturgical Center compromised Catholic truth claims by subordinating them either to Hinduism or to the secular goals of Indian nationalism.[29] Moreover, many Indian Catholics argued that inculturation failed to recognize that the distinctive identity of Indian Catholics was precious, and that while it was not Hindu, it had always been Indian. At issue then in discussions of inculturation are questions concerning the translation of symbols and how Hinduism itself is defined. We will now move to examine these issues through the lens of anthropological understandings of symbol and culture.

Understanding Symbols, Understanding Hinduism

One striking aspect of Amalorpavadass's writings, and indeed of nearly all Indian Catholic writings on inculturation, is the consistent refusal to engage any discipline beyond the confines of theology. The absence of any mention of anthropology is particularly surprising, since anthropology is one discipline that has a long tradition of probing the nature of symbolism and culture. While anthropologists initially envisioned a veritable science of culture, in recent decades anthropology as a whole has become less aggressively positivist and more concerned with the hermeneutics of cultural study. In its present interpretative and ever-contentious incarnation, anthropological theory would unpack the paradox of Indian Catholic inculturation precisely by challenging the assumptions that ground Amalorpavadass's belief in the communicative power of symbolism and his understanding of Hinduism as a coherent whole.

Of Symbols and Hinduism

As we have seen, Amalorpavadass relates inculturation to the process of translation. Indian or Hindu symbols are translated into a Christian context and held in place by the semantic whole of ritual. From this perspective, symbols become the crucial constitutive elements of culture itself. Although Amalorpavadass never mentions anthropology specifically, his view of symbolism would find support in the work of anthropological theorists such as Victor Turner and Clifford Geertz, who have likened culture to a fabric woven with symbolic threads that join together the disparate elements of human experience.[30] Within these perspectives, symbolism is "the semiotic minus the language" since the meaning of symbolism resides in the connection between explicit symbolic "signifiers" and "tacit signifieds" much in the way sound and meaning are joined in language.[31]

In his influential work *Rethinking Symbolism*, the anthropologist Dan Sperber observes that understanding symbolism as akin to language should come as no surprise since the study of symbolism has often been conflated with semiotics, the study of signs. To counter this theoretical confusion, Sperber catalogues the variety of ways that symbols differ from words in a language by demonstrating not only that symbolic meanings are radically underdetermined but also that symbols themselves, unlike words in a language, can neither be paraphrased nor confined to a single grammar.[32] Most crucially, culture in and of itself does not provide a coherent framework for interpreting symbolic materials. Accordingly, any attempt to decode symbols ignores the often fluid and shifting context that gives rise to symbolism in the first place. Yet Sperber is no cultural relativist since he diagrams a cognitive theory of symbolic processing that posits a "symbolic mechanism" as part of "the innate mental equipment that makes experience possible."[33] Within this framework, Sperber would have us understand symbols as evocative, providing access to the memory of words and things. Symbols are symbols precisely because they constitute data that do not conform to the conceptual categories available to us when we confront them. Our interpretations of them are not meanings but representations derived from the evocative field of memory that continue the symbolic process until conceptual conditions finally become satisfied.

Sperber's discussion of symbolism is complex and not well suited to concise explication. In contrast to many other philosophically inclined social scientists, Sperber looks not to Ludwig Wittgenstein but to Gottlob Frege and W. V. O. Quine for his theoretical bearings. Critics have challenged him not only for this reliance upon extensional semantics and its narrow conception of meaning but also for his dependence upon an apparently Cartesian division between conceptual and symbolic knowledge.[34] Yet even Sperber's sharpest critics would admit the compelling power of his argument against semiotic views of symbolism.[35] Sperber's crucial point is that in a strictly philosophical sense symbols do not mean. When we speak of the meaning of symbols, we are not talking about something that inheres in the symbol itself but are instead acknowledging the power of symbols to access memories of words and things. This distinction is crucial for understanding why the Indian Rite Mass and Catholic inculturation efforts have been interpreted in a manner wholly unintended by Catholic theologians such as D. S. Amalorpavadass. The Indian Rite Mass, as a signifying and meaningful whole, was intended to delimit or contain the symbols that it appropriated. Moreover, the inculturated symbols themselves were often understood to have a cultural and not religious meaning—largely so that the tender doctrinal sensibilities of the Catholic hierarchy would not be disturbed. But what Amalorpavadass did not envision was that the experimental Mass itself would become a symbol: not something that means, but instead something that would be interpreted fluidly and idiosyncratically by drawing upon the evocative field of memory.

Following Sperber's analysis of symbolic processing, any attempt to characterize the Indian field of memory would focus upon the mental imprints made by Christianity's colonial history and its exclusive claims to truth. To cite a recent example, the noted Indian journalist Arun Shourie argues that conversion to Christianity threatens the existence of the Indian nation.[36] In a public forum with the Catholic Bishops' Conference of India, Shourie pointed to the role of Baptist missionaries in promoting unrest in Northeast India as evidence of the political nature of supposedly religious activity.[37] Shourie has continued his attacks in a new book that details the flow of monies coming from abroad to fund missionary activities in violation of Indian law.[38] Within the field of Indian memory, Catholicism and Protestantism are often conflated and the apparent economic power of Catholicism is often seen as a pernicious source of influence. Within Indian society as a whole, the associations with Christianity derive from the experience and memory of British and Portuguese colonialism and the often aggressive denunciations of Hindu religiosity. While the hope behind Catholic inculturation was to counter such suspicions and associations, Sperber would remind us that there is no way to contain the evocative power of symbols because symbols, as symbols, can never be exclusively paired with a particular exegesis. From this theoretical perspective, it becomes clear why the Indian Rite Mass and other aspects of Catholic inculturation could never communicate the meanings necessary to serve the dialogical purpose for which they were intended.

Beyond questions concerning the nature of symbolism, the crucial issue within the controversy surrounding Indian Catholic inculturation remains how Hinduism is defined. As we have seen, Amalorpavadass often associates Hinduism with the non-dualist philosophical school called Advaita Vedanta. Nonetheless, he discerns three traditions within Hinduism as a whole—Vedic, Tantric, and Agamic. Without going into detail about what constitutes each tradition, Amalorpavadass argues that Hinduism has an overall coherence for it provides the very ground of Indian culture. Yet similar claims for a unified Hinduism have come under close scholarly scrutiny. Following Edward Said's seminal work *Orientalism*, scholars such as Ronald Inden and Richard King have observed that the Western world has understood Hinduism either as something mystically primal or as something very much like Christianity with a textual basis in the Vedas and Advaita Vedanta as its preeminent philosophical system.[39] In both cases, such interpretations of Hinduism have been designed to construct "an Other" that the West could control and dominate. While Amalorpavadass attempts to revalue the traditional dichotomy between East and West, his vision nonetheless has strong Orientalist resonances. The term "Hinduism" actually came into use in India with the writings of missionaries and colonial administrators.[40] Later, Indian leaders such as Ram Mohan Roy and Swami Vivekananda adopted the term in order to reimagine Indian identity.[41] The development of Indian self-understandings of Hinduism thus arose as a response to colonial rule and Christian evangelization. The bold move within Catholic inculturation to define Hinduism then necessarily becomes seen as another political intervention within the contested domain of national identity.

The Resonances of the Indian Rite Mass

The fundamental point about defining Hinduism that anthropologists and historians wish to make is that what is called Hinduism is so heterogeneous that it defies description under the Western rubric of religion. The category "religion" emerges from the Western experience and as such often emphasizes qualities that are associated with Christianity, such as a discrete set of central texts, emphasis upon public worship, and overall doctrinal coherence.[42] While a definition of religion may indeed be a necessary element in any specifically Christian theology of inculturation, religion is not necessarily helpful as a cross-cultural descriptive category. In the case of Hinduism, there has been what Romila Thapar has described as a progressive process of classificatory "syndication" in which "Hinduism's" obvious lack of ecclesiastic structure and doctrinal orthodoxy have been ignored in order to assert that Hinduism is a textually based and unified religion.[43] But those like D. S. Amalorpavadass, who see the essence of Hinduism reflected in the texts of the Vedas, Upanishads, or the philosophical works of Advaita Vedanta, often fail to acknowledge that Brahmins were the custodians of these texts. There are, of course, other textual and non-textual "Hindu" traditions that vary according to caste, class and linguistic group. What is conventionally called "Hinduism" is actually a diverse assemblage of traditions and practices, not all of which are doctrinally compatible or easily confined to a single descriptive rubric. The positing of an "essence" to Hinduism as a religion thus immediately elicits the rather vexing issue of which part of "Hinduism" is being privileged.

The issue of how "Hinduism" is defined and used within Catholic inculturation returns us to the question of anti-Christian violence that introduced our discussion. The primary targets of recent violence against Christians have been Untouchables, members of the lowest rung of the Hindu hierarchy who have converted to Catholicism. Untouchables are literally not to be touched by caste Hindus since they are considered to be inherently impure. The suspicion surrounding Catholicism stems from the fear that the adaptations of inculturation will be used for converting Untouchables, who would supposedly readily succumb to promises of economic and political power made even more pleasing in their suitably Indian disguise. But when we turn to how Catholic Untouchables understand inculturation, we find yet another paradox associated with the already perplexing question of Catholicism's adaptation to Indian culture.

On a morning in 1996, I was standing outside a chapel at a Christian ashram where the Indian Rite Mass was about to be celebrated. My companion was John Masih, a Catholic Untouchable who was working at the ashram. Before the Indian Rite Mass, the participants, who happened to be postulants for a women's religious order in South India, began to pray in Sanskrit and their voices echoed through the ashram: *Om Bhurbhurva Swah/Tat Savitur Varenyam/Bhargo Devasya Dhimahi/Dhiyo Yo Nah/Prachodayat*. This was a hymn from the Rig Veda that translated into English reads: "Om, may we meditate on the splendour of the vivifier divine, may he himself illumine our minds."[44] This is the *mantra*, or sacred phrase, that Brahmins are to repeat at key points in the day. Before the *mantra* was recited, the priest had admonished participants not to speak it aloud outside the ashram since Brahmins would surely understand it as an affront to their religious sensibilities.

When John Masih heard Sanskrit *mantras* issuing from the chapel, he was not concerned with the sensibilities of Brahmins. John Masih had been discouraged by the ashram's priest from participating because the priest feared that John Masih would be scandalized by the presence of such seemingly "Hindu" practices. In any case, the "Indian Christian Spiritual Experience" that preceded the Mass was entirely in English, a language that John Masih and most other converts from Untouchability do not know. John Masih was scandalized by the Mass but his reaction was more complex than the priest suspected. John Masih saw inculturation as an adaptation to Brahmin religiosity, something that he believed had oppressed his caste fellows for generations. Indeed, he converted to Catholicism precisely to resist caste distinctions and their legitimating Brahminical ideology. In John Masih's view, the recitation of Brahmin *mantras* in a Catholic church not only compromised Christian truth claims but also showed a callous disregard for the sensibilities of Untouchable converts. As a North Indian, John Masih would certainly not resist all forms of inculturation because for him the songs of the poet Kabir and the Untouchable Saint Ravidas have a deep and affecting resonance in their denial of caste and hierarchy.[45] But as a Catholic Untouchable, it was a bitter irony indeed to be excluded from a Mass because Catholics who knew no Hindi wished to lay claim to the religious practices of Brahmins.

The experience of John Masih adds to the litany of paradoxes and ironies of Indian Catholic inculturation: what is presented as Indian is resisted by Indians themselves; what is portrayed as a dialogical opening to Hinduism is seen as plot to undermine it; and what is perceived to be a tool of conversion has failed to win any converts at all. Amalorpavadass and others who extolled the virtues of inculturation claimed they were borrowing nothing because all belongs to Christ and there are no other Gods before Him. But within the contested religious landscape of India, what Catholic inculturation emphasizes most clearly is that appearances can easily deceive.

Theology and Anthropology

The application of anthropology to the paradox of Indian inculturation initially reveals the potential for using social scientific reflection on symbol and culture as an analytical tool. While Sperber and other theorists we have discussed would resist the label "postmodern," their work is part of an intellectual movement in anthropology to reclaim the heterogeneity of human experience from broadly romantic or colonialist generalizations about culture and static understandings of the nature of symbolism. While understanding human culture as fissured and human identity as fluid might seem a fragile basis for theological reflection, such indeterminacy lies at the heart of the paradox of Indian Catholic inculturation. Following theorists who would question any coherence to Hinduism as a religion, one might envision an Indian Catholic inculturation that turns its gaze more sensitively to the concerns of Untouchable converts such as John Masih who desire an inculturation that embraces indigenous traditions explicitly opposed to dominant cultural forms. Following Dan Sperber, one might envision a theology of the symbol that focuses not upon symbols themselves but instead upon the conditions under which symbols become symbols. Such an epistemological turn to the subject, certainly not unknown to Catholic theology, might even allow for understanding inculturation as part of symbolic processing itself. To say that Hinduism is not a religion is not to dismiss Indian traditions but to refuse to impose categories from the Western experience upon them. To question whether symbols mean, is not to deny any possibility of meaning but is instead to recognize that concepts such as "communication" or "dialogue" cannot fully account for the idiosyncratic interplay that characterizes cultural symbolism. It is perhaps precisely by raising such challenges that anthropology can contribute most to theological reflection.

The idea that anthropology could contribute to theology is, of course, hardly novel. Recently, both Kathryn Tanner and Michael Barnes have probed the different ways anthropology can inform the work of theologians.[46] Within liturgical theology in particular, there has been great interest in how anthropological understandings of ritual can deepen pastoral and constructive theological reflection on worship.[47] Rarely, however, has anthropology reciprocally turned to theology as a source for reflection upon itself. In his last major address before his sudden death in 1990, D. S. Amalorpavadass remarked that one's view of inculturation would depend upon the theological questions one asks.[48] For anthropologists, perhaps, what might be most valuable is reflection on the very fact that theologians ask provocatively broad questions that concern the relationship among culture, religion, and practice.

When one looks at the expanse of contemporary anthropological theorizing about culture, one finds incessant questioning concerning the ultimate horizon of value for cultural research. In his introductory chapter for the collection of essays aptly titled *In Near Ruins*, Nicholas Dirks reflects upon the agony of contemporary anthropology and cultural theory struggling to come to terms with their own past within an academic context rent by post-modern suspicions.[49] Indeed, the most recent joining of cultural studies to cultural politics is informed by a desire to redeem a discipline that too often has used the pretense of social scientific objectivity to conceal its complicity in the project of Western colonialism.[50] Theologians of inculturation, like D. S. Amalorpavadass, have encountered similar issues in their effort to articulate a renewed Christianity that is fully at home in the cultures of which it is a part. But in doing so, theologians of inculturation have dared to presume that the context for such an encounter lies not only within but beyond the confines of human society and culture. Perhaps the final paradox of inculturation is that it continues to raise questions of ultimate meaning in the face of social scientific doubt and suspicion.

Notes

[1]Celia W. Dugger, "Attacks on Christians Unsettle Rural India," *New York Times* (January 23, 1999); "47 Suspected Militants in India Charged with Missionary's Death," *New York Times* (January 25, 1999); and "India's Christians: A Double Standard," *New York Times* (February 19, 1999). Also U.S. State Department, *U.S. Department of State Annual Report on International Religious Freedom for 1999: India* (http://www.state.gov/www/global/human_rights/irf_rpt/199/irf_india99.html).

[2]Robert Marquand, "In India, a Pattern of Attacks on Christians," *Christian Science Monitor* (June 29, 2000).

[3]Ramesvak Srivastav, "Kya Katholik Charch Sachmooch Ek Taim Bam Hai" [Is the Catholic Church Really a Time Bomb?] *Dinman* (February 2-8, 1986).

[4]Untouchables are members of endogamous groups, often sharing the same occupation, called castes; within traditional forms of Hinduism, they are considered to be so impure that touching them would bring defilement. Within Indian society, Untouchables are often considered to be prime targets of Christian conversion efforts and Untouchables who do convert are denied affirmative action benefits entitled to lower castes under Indian law. Tribals are considered to be the indigenous inhabitants of India and are defined by Tribal social organization and their non-Indo-European languages. Christian groups have recorded their greatest gains in conversion among Tribal communities in northeast India.

[5]This tale can be found in the *Acts of Thomas*; see M. R. James, *The Apocryphal New Testament* (Oxford: Oxford University Press, 1926), 364.

[6]F. E. Keay, *A History of the Syrian Church in India* (Delhi: ISPCK, 1960), 19.

[7]K. N. Sahay, "Indigenization of Christianity in India," *Man in India* 61 (1981): 3.

[8]Leslie Brown, *The Syrian Christians of St. Thomas* (Cambridge: Cambridge University Press, 1982), 168-169.

[9]For a discussion of de Nobili along with translations of his writings see Roberto De Nobili, S.J., *Preaching Wisdom to the Wise: Three Treatises*, trans. and ed. Anand Amaladass and Francis X. Clooney (St. Louis: Institute of Jesuit Sources, 2000)

[10]Julius Lipner, *Brahmabandhab Upadhyay: The Life and Thought of a Revolutionary* (New Delhi: Oxford University Press, 1999), 111-118, 191-196.

[11]Ibid., 330.

[12]Brahmabandhab Upadhyay, *Samaj* [Society] (Calcutta: Birman Publishing House, n.d.), 32.

[13]For a biography of D. S. Amalorpavadass, see John Berchmans Barla, *Christian Theological Understanding of Other Religions According to D. S. Amalorpavadass* (Roma: Editrice Pontifica Universita Gregoriana, 1999), 25-28.

[14]D. S. Amalorpavadass, *Destinée de l'Église dans l'Inde d'aujourd'hui* [The Destiny of the Church in Contemporary India] (Paris: Fayard-Mame, 1967), 33-92. See also Amalorpavadass's master's thesis, *L'Inde à la recontre du Seigneur* (Paris: Éd. Spes, 1964).

[15]D. S. Amalorpavadass, ed., *Post-Vatican Liturgical Renewal in India* (Bangalore: National Catechetical and Liturgical Center, 1968), 9.

[16]D. S. Amalorpavadass, *Towards Indigenisation in the Liturgy: Theological Reflection, Policy, Programme, and Texts* (Bangalore: National Biblical, Catechetical and Liturgical Centre, n.d.), 31-32.

[17]Ibid., 26-53.

[18]The text of Cardinal Knox's letter may be found in the Indian lay periodical, *The Laity* (January 1976): 12-14.

[19]Matri Dham Ashram, *Prarthana Manjari* (Varanasi: Divine Printers, 1993), 28.

[20]D. S. Amalorpavadass, *New Orders of the Mass for India* (Bangalore: National Biblical, Catechetical and Liturgical Centre, 1974), 11.

[21]The following is based upon my participation in the Indian Christian Spiritual Experience at Matri Dham Ashram in Varanasi, India, in February, 1996.

[22]D. S. Amalorpavadass, *Gospel and Culture: Evangelisation, Inculturation, and "Hinduisation"* (Bangalore: National Biblical, Catechetical and Liturgical Centre, 1978), 17.

[23]Ibid., 18.

[24]Ibid., 20.

[25]Amalorpavadass's use of non-dualist philosophical terms and concepts is especially evident in his address to the Societas Liturgica in York, England, in 1989. See D. S. Amalorpavadass, "Theological Reflections on Inculturation," *Studia*

Liturgica 20 (1990): 116-29.

[26]Amalorpavadass, *Gospel and Culture*, 40-41.

[27]Sita Ram Goel, *Catholic Ashrams* (New Delhi: Voice of India, 1988).

[28]Barla, *Christian Theological Understanding of Other Religions*, 425.

[29]Paul Hacker, *Theological Foundations of Evangelization* (Cologne: Steyler Verlag, 1980), 93-94.

[30]See Victor Turner, *The Forest of Symbols* (Ithaca: Cornell University Press, 1967) and Clifford Geertz, *The Interpretation of Cultures* (New York: Basic Books, 1973).

[31]Here I am drawing explicitly on the characterization of such views of symbolism in Dan Sperber, *Rethinking Symbolism* (Cambridge: Cambridge University Press, 1975), xi.

[32]Ibid., 1-16, 85-114.

[33]Ibid., xii.

[34]In extensional semantics, meaning and truth are understood as functions of the relationship between words or linguistic terms and "their extensions" or, more simply, what they contain or denote. Extensionalists often limit the properties of extensions to include existent objects or entities and emphasize the importance of substitution or paraphrasibility in determining whether or not a particular linguistic context is extensional. Although influential in analytic philosophy, extensionalism has been challenged for excluding imaginary entities from its theoretical framework, as Sperber has done in arguing that symbolism does not mean.

[35]For such a critique, see E. Thomas Lawson and Robert N. McCauley, *Rethinking Religion: Connecting Cognition and Culture* (Cambridge: Cambridge University Press, 1993), 68-77.

[36]Arun Shourie, *Christian Missionaries* (New Delhi: ASA Publications, 1994).

[37]Ibid., 234-35.

[38]Arun Shourie, *Harvesting Our Souls—Missionaries, Their Designs, Their Claims* (New Delhi: ASA Publications, 2000).

[39]Ronald B. Inden, *Imagining India* (Oxford: Oxford University Press, 1990) and Richard King, *Orientalism and Religion: Postcolonial Theory, India and "the Mystic East"* (London: Routledge Press, 1999).

[40]King, *Orientalism and Religion*, 98-101.

[41]Paul Hacker, "Aspects of Neo-Hinduism as Contrasted with Surviving Traditional Hinduism," in *Philology and Confrontation: Paul Hacker on Traditional and Modern Vedanta*, ed. Wilhelm Halbfass (Albany: SUNY Press, 1995), 229-56.

[42]For a helpful recent discussion of the genealogy of the term "religion" and its relationship to theology and religious studies, see Paul J. Griffiths, "The Very Idea of Religion," *First Things* 103 (May 2000): 30-35.

[43]Romila Thapar, "Syndicated Moksha," *Seminar* 313 (1985): 21; King, *Orientalism and Religion*, 104-8.

[44]Matri Dham Ashram, *Prarthana Manjari*, 31.

[45]For a discussion of this aspect of Catholic Untouchable religiosity, as well as for more on John Masih, see Mathew N. Schmalz, "Images of the Body in the Life

and Death of a North Indian Catholic Catechist," *History of Religions* 39 (1999): 178-201.

[46]Kathryn Tanner, *Theories of Culture: A New Agenda for Theology* (Minneapolis: Fortress Press, 1997), and Michael Horace Barnes, "Universalist Pluralism and the New Histories," in *Theology and the New Histories*, ed. Gary Macy (Maryknoll NY: Orbis Books, 1999).

[47]See Theodore Jennings, "Ritual Studies and Liturgical Theology: An Invitation to Dialogue," *Journal of Ritual Studies* 1 (1987): 35-56; John D. Witvliet, "For Our Own Purposes: The Appropriation of the Social Sciences in Liturgical Studies," *Liturgy Digest* 2 (1995): 6-35; Nathan D. Mitchel, *Liturgy and the Social Sciences* (Collegeville: The Liturgical Press, 1999).

[48]Amalorpavadass, "Theological Reflections on Inculturation," 36. D. S. Amalorpavadass died in a car accident in South India.

[49]Nicholas B. Dirks, "In Near Ruins: Cultural Theory at the End of the Century," in *In Near Ruins: Cultural Theory at the End of the Century*, ed. Nicholas B. Dirks (Minneapolis: University of Minnesota Press, 1998), 1-18.

[50]For an excellent discussion of this connection, see Adam Kuper, *Culture: The Anthropologists' Account* (Cambridge: Harvard University Press, 1999), 209-48.

Karl Rahner's Principles of Ecumenism and Contemporary Religious Pluralism

Jeannine Hill Fletcher

Current projects in Christian theology rely on the social sciences to provide empirical data for theological reflection. In no area are the implications of this more important than in considerations of the diversity of religions. Here, descriptions of the world's religions make evident that our global space is shared among a wide variety of religious paths, practices, and traditions. From even the briefest glance at the demographics, the Christian theologian must recognize that the majority of the world's population claims religious identities different from his or her own.[1] As persons constructing theological visions of the world that include those with whom we share the context of our existence, this sociological data, or more accurately, those 3.7 billion persons must be taken into account. A realistic discourse on religious pluralism must take a theologically wide scope and explain how the diversity of religions can fit conceptually within a Christian theological framework of God, Christ, and humanity.

In the discourse on religious pluralism, the work of Karl Rahner figures prominently. Writing in the 1960s and 1970s, Rahner aimed to explain the diversity of religions with his concept of the "anonymous Christian." In contemporary discussions, two very different receptions of this concept are evident: it is either strongly criticized for its colonizing language, or retrieved and adapted into a variety of forms of "Spirit-Christologies" (albeit while dropping the particular language of "anonymity"). In both cases, Rahner's work is a touchstone for discussion, yet it is only one aspect of Rahner's work relevant to religious pluralism. The concept of the "anonymous Christian" is not Rahner's only reflection on the experience of religious diversity. He also wrote on a different sort of religious diversity—diversity *among*

Christians both within Catholicism and in the ecumenical movement. In this essay, I will argue that these two sites of reflection produce two competing models for understanding religious pluralism. I will suggest that among Rahner's reflections on intra-Christian diversity we might find principles to be applied for contemporary theological reconstructions that move beyond Rahner's concept of the "anonymous Christian."

Rahner's discussion of the "anonymous Christian" is based on a transcendental deduction of God's presence and a doctrine of universal grace. Endowed with grace in creation, the human person longs for the infinite source of this grace and moves toward it through the process of transcendence. Each and every time the human person goes outside him- or herself in growth or love, or extends into the unknown in the process of knowing, or embraces a trust or faith not bound by what is presented in the material world, that individual extends beyond the limits of what he or she presently is and creates something new. The realization that the self's extension is limitless and that the ultimate term toward which we reach can never be grasped or understood places the individual in the context of an infinite horizon. This ever-receding horizon of transcendence is what Rahner names God. He writes that we know God from our experience *a posteriori*, "only as the term of transcendence."[2] In the very structure of human knowing, willing, and loving, God is present to all persons who remain open to the grace-filled movement into ever-greater becoming.[3]

The grace of creation possesses a dynamism toward its fullest expression in incarnation when God expresses Godself "in the region of the extra-divine" and the human person comes into existence.[4] For Rahner, both modes of God's self-communication—grace and incarnation—find their most complete and "historically tangible" expression in Jesus Christ.[5] Through the perfect acceptance of God's self-communication of grace, Jesus Christ fully extends the process of transcendence into the fullness of union with God, making God's gift of grace irreversible.[6] Perfecting the structure of human being in the world, Christ *becomes* "the very thing towards which [hu]mankind is moving."[7] This intimate connection of creation and incarnation is key to safeguarding the universal presence of grace and God's "direct proximity" to humanity.[8] For Rahner, all of creation is graced and all of humanity participates in God's incarnation. All persons who participate in transcendence are participating—whether they know it or not—

in a process made possible by Christ. Here is Rahner's greatest contribution against theological constructions that might limit God's grace or deny the inherent goodness of the human person. Yet, it is precisely this intimate connection between grace and incarnation, between anthropology and Christology, that forms a problematic backdrop for considerations of religious pluralism. When Rahner uses the idea of the "anonymous Christian" to describe persons who participate in grace and transcendence but who do not recognize Christ as the source, he leaves little room for valuing religions in their diverse particularity.

Critiques of Rahner's "Anonymous Christian"

Critiques of Rahner's concept of the "anonymous Christian" traditionally come from two locations within Christian theology: those concerned with safeguarding Christ's particularity, and those wishing to uphold the dignity of the diversity of religions.[9] From the first side, for example, the liberationist perspective of Johann Baptist Metz is concerned that the idea of "anonymous Christian" does not fully provide a dangerous historical memory for a praxis of following Christ.[10] George Lindbeck similarly argues that it is not "human nature" generally, but precisely and uniquely the categories made available in Christian scripture that shape persons for an encounter with the God whom Christ reveals.[11] William Thompson summarizes this first set of critiques: "If there is an 'anonymous Christianity' where the Christ is genuinely encountered in an 'anonymous' way, this would seem to departicularize and deincarnationalize the Christ, ending up with a sort of '*Logos*-idea,' rather than the concretely universal God-Man Jesus."[12]

These critiques, while important to take into account, too easily overlook the incarnational Christology that always accompanies Rahner's transcendental anthropology. Even if not explicitly rearticulated in each instance, whenever Rahner speaks of Christ, the Logos, the second person of the Trinity who makes possible the human process of transcendence, he is at the same time referring to the "human reality" visible in Jesus of Nazareth, whose witness is contained in the New Testament.[13] While not limited to the historical individual, the particularity and specificity of the incarnation in Jesus Christ now has positive content, which functions for Rahner as the criterion for distinguishing appropriate and inappropriate relationships to God.

He writes, "In Jesus Christ, the crucified and risen one, then, we have a criterion for distinguishing in the concrete history of religion between what is a human misunderstanding of the transcendental experience of God, and what is the legitimate interpretation of this experience."[14] The crux of the problematic is in how this criterion will function. Either Jesus Christ is a specific criterion connected to the life and practice of Jesus of Nazareth in some critical way, or Jesus Christ is in some sense an "anonymous criterion" to be filled with whatever Christians determine is "of God." If the former is the case, we should expect to use the life and practice of Jesus as the lens through which to assess the practices of the diversity of religions. If the latter is the case, the permeability of the Christ criterion means that nothing in the various religious traditions is "of God" unless it is determined to be *a priori* of Christ. This raising of the problematic of the "Christ criterion" is not simply a rhetorical device to undermine the currency of "anonymous Christian," but rather derives directly from Rahner's own project of encouraging the historian of religion to seek Christ present in the non-Christian traditions. The dogmatic theologian may establish Christ's presence as an *a priori* possibility, but it is the role of the historian of religion to assess this presence *a posteriori* or in actuality.[15] It would appear that Rahner is suggesting that through the tools of social science, historians of religion can identify Christ's presence in the outward expressions of religious persons.

And yet, when historians and anthropologists use the tools of social science, they describe for us a world of stunning religious variety, each form with a particularity that is, perhaps, not measurable with the Christ criterion. Historians of religion tell us of how in Sri Lanka and Southeast Asia Buddhist monks broadcast daily, chanting texts that remind and instruct in the four noble truths, the constituents of grasping, the abodes of being, and the eightfold path.[16] Anthropologists describe the ritual drawings made each day on the floors of Hindu homes to welcome the family's chosen deity,[17] and the more elaborate *puja* that pays homage to God resident in the temple, with a ritual washing and dressing of the images of the god and goddess, a food sacrifice, and vedic hymn.[18] Or historians of religion might describe a less elaborate but no less sincere offering made to the newly incarnated goddess of AIDS at a roadside stone in rural India,[19] or a gathering outside of London invoking Agni (God represented in fire) and worshiping Lord Krisna fully manifest in the sacrificial *soma*.[20] In addition to observance of the five pillars of Islam (which include testimony to the oneness of God [*shahada*], ritual prayer [*salat*], almsgiving [*zakat*], fasting during Ramadan, and performing pilgrimage to the holy city of Mecca [*hajj*]), sociologists can describe how Shiite Muslims demonstrate their love for the prophet Muhammad, his family, and their descendants through cries of grief and mourning performed on their feast days.[21] Through the sociological lens we see Jews commemorating God's presence in the desert by gathering, rain or shine, for the celebration of Sukkot in outdoor booths of their own making,[22] and Jain mendicants refusing to go outdoors on days when it rains so as not to risk harming one of the sentient insects who may have been driven from their homes by the water.[23] My point here is to underscore how anthropological and sociological research presents us with very distinct practices that are promoted by diverse beliefs regarding the aim and process of human becoming. Seeing these diverse forms in their particularity, we have to ask, according to Rahner, how are we to understand this diversity? Are these teachings legitimate or illegitimate understandings of the transcendental experience? Are the practices described by anthropologists comparable to the criterion of "Jesus Christ" or are they not?

Regardless of the specific answers to these questions individually, the Christ criterion devalues diversity. If other pursuits and practices of the world's religions are found not to meet the Christ criterion, they are devalued. If they do meet the Christ criterion, these diverse religious ways of being in the world are valued insofar as they are demonstrations of Christ's presence, not for the particularity of the tradition itself. While the experiences of "anonymous Christians" are valued because they reveal Christ, they are simultaneously devalued as incomplete (because implicit) expressions. Because proper relation to God in transcendence is made possible by Christ, and all expressions of right relation with God are understood as "anonymously Christian," Rahner argues that implicit forms of being a Christian (meaning, the anonymous Christian in another tradition) have as their goal an explicit form of Christianity. In describing how the term "anonymous Christian" implies this dynamism, Rahner writes,

> This name implicitly signifies that this fundamental actuation of a man, like all actuations, cannot and does not want to stop in its anonymous state but strives towards an explicit expression,

> towards its full name. An unfavorable historical environment may impose limitations on the explicitness of this expression so that this actuation may not exceed the explicit appearance of a loving humaneness, but it will not act against this tendency whenever a new and higher stage of explicitness is presented to it right up to the ultimate perfection of a consciously accepted profession of Church membership.[24]

Here, and in many places in Rahner's writing, we see that the dynamism of the "anonymous Christian" devalues the variety of religious forms by suggesting that the fullness of transcendence and grace is the possession of only one religious community. The concept of the "anonymous Christian" understands only one way of being in relation to God—a way predetermined by the person of Jesus Christ. Such a construction of the religiously other is based on sameness and a singular vision of human fulfillment and relation to God. The religiously other is described with reference to oneself and one's own vision of fulfillment. From this starting point, all people are judged insofar as they are "like" Christ; and in turn, all religions are judged insofar as they are "like" Christianity. Taking Christ as the norm, all persons, paths, and ways of being in relation to God are judged on the basis of their similarity or difference from this norm: difference denotes a deviance from the norm.

Even if judged to be "like us" and therefore "same," the other is seen as a deficient model of the singular norm because, unlike Christians, the other lacks the self-awareness to realize that it is the grace of God made available through Christ that makes possible and propels their quest for human becoming; the other does not realize that it is Christ who anonymously makes possible their transcendence. Such a stance is demeaning toward persons of various faiths. In this self-referential construction, the other is not perceived as other, but rather a deficient example of the "same."[25]

To interpret the diversity of religions through self-referential constructions of otherness eliminates both the distinctiveness of Christian witness, practice, and aim, and the distinctiveness of the witness, practices, and aims of diverse religious communities. To judge another as "good" insofar as "same" does not let the other be other in him/her own particularity. Seeing difference as a problem, we are encouraged to retreat to the security of sameness.

Unfortunately, the construction of the other based on an underlying sameness can be found in many positions within the discourse on religious pluralism. Spirit Christologies that follow Rahner's lead (while leaving behind the term "anonymous Christian") seek sameness and see Christ as the singular norm. However, many so-called pluralist positions also seek sameness. For example, when Paul Knitter employs John Hick's idea that a turn from self-centeredness to Reality-centeredness is shared among all major religions, he too chooses a singular norm for all humanity and seeks a sameness in the religions.[26]

Thus the search for sameness is a common strategy employed within Christian theology as a way of understanding the sociological data of religious pluralism. But if the search for sameness leads to the dissolution of particular identities, we might instead (or also) seek a construction of religious pluralism that honors differences and values them theologically. Perhaps surprisingly, Rahner offers us some resources for such a theological reflection.

Principles of Pluralism from Rahner's Ecumenical Writings

The starting point of our reconstruction returns us to Rahner's concept of God as the context of our existence and the horizon of transcendence. As the term of transcendence, God is not known as one object within our experience, but as "precisely that mystery of the incomprehensible, the inexpressible, toward which at every moment of my life I am always tending."[27] That the term of transcendence and horizon of existence (which Christians name God) is ultimately incomprehensible, holy mystery, is not the cause for disappointment on our part, but is instead understood as a positive characteristic of God. Incomprehensibility follows from "the infinity of [God's] unlimited and pure being" in the contemplation of which the human mind *overflows*.[28] Using these terms to describe God, Rahner enables us to read incomprehensibility as complexity, whereby God contains within Godself the boundless range of infinite possibility for human becoming. Rahner maintains the Thomistic claim of God's simplicity to ensure God's unity of Being, but this does not rule out the idea that from the human perspective this infinite simplicity contains all that we see as endless complexity. Read as the inexhaustible source of complexity, God's incomprehensibility encountered in transcendence opens one up to the unlimited expanse of all possible reality.

When Rahner describes mystery or the infinite unknown as the prerequisite for all knowing, and the limitless horizon outside the self as a necessary condition for becoming, he is describing difference as *the* constitutive element for human participation in the inexhaustible source of complexity that is God. That which we are not—God—is the necessary condition for our becoming. Similarly, that which we are not—in the world around us and others we encounter—allows us opportunities to grow beyond our present selves. Difference serves the essential function of opening us up to the vast possibilities for growth and encounter with God in a concrete way. Here we see that transcendence into the incomprehensibility of God is not a vague, disembodied concept for Rahner. Rather, the recognition of God is present to us precisely in the context of our world. Rahner writes,

> It is only in terms of this personal, social environment that man can be brought to a realization of himself as subject, and it is only in terms of this that those transcendental experiences of freedom, responsibility, absolute truth, love and personal trust are borne in upon man in which alone it can be made intelligible to him what is meant by God. For this God is not any kind of particular object side by side with many others (albeit of a peculiar excellence) which impinge upon him, but rather is present to him as the ground, the horizon, and the ultimate goal of man's own personal movement outwards towards his social environment in all its complexity.[29]

The encounter with the other, with her or him who is different, brings the human person both to a realization of him/herself as subject and to a realization of all that lies outside him/herself that extends to the infinite context of existence. Difference opens a person up to ever more possibilities for transcendence into the incomprehensible mystery of God.

In the context of Christian diversity, Rahner recognized this important function of difference for opening up new ways of being in the world. Without the ongoing exchange of different perspectives within Catholic theology and the church, for example, the Catholic community could get stuck in static understandings that would block the transformation necessary for a historical institution to grow toward God.[30] Difference is a necessary element in the ongoing process of transcendence.

Similarly, in the ecumenical process, Rahner saw difference as a valuable quality reflecting the diverse receptions of God's presence in Christ. Here "the treasure of all the churches together is not only quantitatively but qualitatively greater than the actual treasure that can be found in a single church."[31] The particularities engendered by different sociological configurations of Christianity are to be preserved as valuable in their distinctiveness. This principle of ecumenism is a theological principle born of a sociological reality. Sociologically, Rahner recognized that much of ecumenical diversity is the result of social tradition rather than persons consciously determining the denomination with which to identify. He argues that "the vast majority of the members of all Christian Churches are, from the point of view of the sociology of religion, members each of one such Church on specifically historical and psychological grounds, but not properly on theological grounds."[32] Yet while the differences do not arise on properly theological grounds, they serve an important theological function, namely that these differences can open Christians up to growth toward God. In the ecumenical discussion, difference is a treasure revealing ever greater understandings of the Christian relationship to God.

In addition to valuing the other for how their differences might transform us and open us up to the source of complexity that is God, Rahner suggests that the other brings us closer to that source of complexity in an even more intimate way—by participating in it. He explains that, "all beings, and above all the created spirit in its transcendence towards absolute being, partake of the mysterious character of God."[33] By virtue of the grace of creation and participation in transcendence, the human person participates in the mysterious complexity that is God. Self-reflectively, we recognize our own complexity as related to God's own being; reflecting on the other, we must recognize the demands of their complexity as well. Rahner continues by explaining, "all beings are inscrutable and unfathomable, because they are creatures. Since they are the *result* of the creative knowledge of God their reality and objective truth has such infinite ramifications, essential to an adequate knowledge of them, that comprehensive knowledge of even the tiniest of them is possible only to God. . . .[34] Here we recognize the real presence of God within each individual. This recognition demands that we approach the other in ways that do not intend to master or control their complexity but rather suggest an attitude more like the loving contemplation and awe we feel for God's own incomprehensibility.

For Rahner, recognizing the incomprehensibility of the other has two consequences. On the one hand, it means that we "can learn an infinite amount from each other."[35] On the other hand, it also means that we can never fully know the other. Since the perspective of the other is ultimately not our own, and his or her presuppositions might be distinct from ours, we must admit that we do not know another's perspective comprehensively. Recognizing this, Rahner understood that in the context of ecumenical discussions, this means that we are often in a position where we are not competent to pass judgment and must therefore allow for "epistemological tolerance."[36] Such tolerance is necessary in order to safeguard the other's freedom, which is at the heart of transcendence and human becoming. In Rahner's words,

> Intolerance cannot be practiced, even when we are absolutely convinced that we are speaking for the truth and for the greater good of our opponents, because intolerance would eliminate or unduly restrict the freedom of others, without which they cannot be what they want to be or ought to be, namely, free persons, whose reality, as far as possible, is of their own making.[37]

Here, we see Rahner's characteristic optimism that grace-filled existence allows individuals to freely choose among the possibilities for growth toward God.

Rahner was not naive about the problems of tolerance in a world where freedom also allows for the destruction of God's grace-filled creation. The promotion of freedom always has its limits in certain restrictions on tolerance, but the careful balance between freedom and the limits of tolerance cannot be decided once and for all. As Rahner recognizes, even definitions of the "common good" as the deciding factor between freedom and its limits vary across location and historical situation. This variability is, for Rahner, not the relinquishing of responsibility in relativism; rather it necessitates an ongoing commitment to reconstructing the balance of freedom and its limits within the human community. "We cannot escape history, in which the concrete coexistence of freedom and necessity must always be determined ever anew and always in a different way."[38] With respect to religious pluralism, the promotion of freedom and tolerance also has limits, but those limits cannot be determined *a priori* as only those ways of being in the world that are designated as Christian—anonymous or otherwise. As the horrors of the Crusades and Nazism have shown, limits of freedom and tolerance must be drawn, and the designation "Christian" does not guarantee right relation with God and others. In determining the limits of tolerance, Rahner insists that freedom must have priority: "There can exist unavoidable necessities, coercions, and restrictions of freedom. But in the final analysis they have to justify themselves before the bench of freedom, and not the other way around."[39] It is incumbent upon the Christian, and the theologian, to place freedom and tolerance as important features as far as possible, so that none may be restricted in their growth toward the mysterious horizon that Christians name God.

The ultimate context of existence that Christians name God and that they encounter through Christ is infinitely more than what we can comprehend. God is incomprehensible mystery. Rahner helps us to conceive of this theologically when we read incomprehensibility as the source of endlessly rich complexity and as the overflowingness of God, containing within Godself ever greater possibility for the human person. This complexity is mirrored in humanity. To this theological reflection, we can bring the resources of social scientific research. We can recognize the life-giving pursuits of the diversity of religions. We can see men and women devoting their lives to the specific religious goals and pursuits of their distinct traditions, and witness the real depth of their traditions for providing the means and practices for human becoming, even forms of human becoming that might be different from our own. We need to take care, therefore, that our need to see sameness and that which we *can* understand does not block the growth and transcendence made possible by difference.

In Rahner's work we thus have two competing models for understanding religious diversity. If we follow the model of the "anonymous Christian" we run the risk of limiting the transcendence of ourselves and others by eliminating the distinctiveness of differences that lead to growth. If, however, we reclaim the principles of pluralism from Rahner's discussions of ecumenical diversity, we might apply them to establish a new model for understanding interreligious diversity. Not only epistemological tolerance, but the positive valuation of diversity and the recognition of distinct ways of relating to the complexity that is God, provide potent tools for a reconstruction of religious pluralism that values religious diversity as human participation in the God who surpasses all that we can understand.

Notes

[1]According to the United Nations *World Population Prospects: The 1994 Revision*, Christians make up approximately 33% of the world's population. Other affiliations include: Islam-20%, Hinduism-15%, no affiliation-15%, Buddhism-6%, Chinese traditional religions-4%, indigenous traditions-4%, Judaism-1%, Yoruba-1%, and others. While global populations are extremely difficult to assess, this report estimates the total population mid-1995 to be approximately 5,716,425,000, including 1,927,953,000 Christians. Figures taken from *1996 Britannica Book of the Year*, ed. Glenn M. Edwards (Chicago: Encyclopedia Britannica, Inc., 1996), 298.

[2]Karl Rahner, *Foundations of Christian Faith: An Introduction to the Idea of Christianity* (New York: Crossroad, 1994), 64.

[3]For a description of transcendence as a process of grace, see Rahner's "Reflections on the Experience of Grace," *Theological Investigations,* vol. 3 (Baltimore: Helicon Press, 1967), 86-90. For Rahner's transcendental anthropology, see "Theology and Anthropology," *Theological Investigations,* vol. 9 (New York: Herder & Herder, 1972), 28-45.

[4]Rahner, "Anonymous Christians," *Theological Investigations,* vol. 6 (New York: Seabury, 1974), 393.

[5]Rahner, "The One Christ and the Universality of Salvation," *Theological Investigations,* vol. 16 (New York: Seabury, 1979), 221.

[6]Rahner describes Jesus as a sacramental sign and final cause of salvation. For his discussion of how Jesus is a real symbol wherein grace achieves fullness and forms an irreversible gift, see "The One Christ and the Universality of Salvation," *Theological Investigations*, vol. 16, 213-14. Or see *Foundations of Christian Faith,* 193-95.

[7]Rahner, *Foundations of Christian Faith,* 170.

[8]Rahner, "Anonymous Christians," 394.

[9]For an overview of the critiques of Rahner, see Janice Poorman, *The Critics of Karl Rahner's Theology of the Universal Offer of Salvific Grace Through Jesus Christ* (Ph.D. dissertation, University of Notre Dame, 1996).

[10]Johann Baptist Metz, *Faith in History and Society: Toward a Practical Fundamental Theology* (New York: Crossroad, 1980), 165.

[11]George Lindbeck, *The Nature of Doctrine: Religion and Theology in a Postliberal Age* (Philadelphia: Westminster, 1984), 34, 52-63.

[12]William M. Thompson, "Word & Spirit, Hermeneutics & Transcendental Method: Exploring Their Connections in Karl Rahner," *Philosophy & Theology* 7, no. 2 (1992): 207. For further analysis of these critiques see Mary Maher, "Rahner on the Human Experience of God: Idealist Tautology or Christian Theology," *Philosophy & Theology* 7, no. 2 (1992): 127-164. Also J. A. Colombo, "Rahner and

His Critics: Lindbeck and Metz," *The Thomist* 56, no. 1 (1992): 71-96.

[13]Rahner, *The Trinity*, trans. Joseph Donceel (New York: Herder & Herder, 1970), 28. See also *Foundations of Christian Faith,* 228-264.

[14]Rahner, *Foundations of Christian Faith,* 157.

[15]Rahner makes this assertion in his essay, "Jesus Christ in the Non-Christian Religions," *Theological Investigations,* vol. 17 (London: Darton, Longman & Todd, 1981), 40.

[16]See, for example, Anne M. Blackburn, "Magic in the Monastery: Textual Practice and Monastic Identity in Sri Lanka," *History of Religions* 38, no. 4 (1999): 354.

[17]See, for example, Helene Stork, "Mothering Rituals in Tamilnadu: Some Magico-Religious Beliefs," in *Roles and Rituals for Hindu Women*, ed. Julia Leslie (Delhi: Motilal Banarsidass Publishers, 1992), 101.

[18]See, for example, G. Saraswathi, "Agamic Way of Worshipping God and Priesthood in Three Different Temples of Mysore District," *Man in India* 79, nos. 1 & 2 (1999): 94-95.

[19]See Anna Portnoy, "There in the Making: In Search of an AIDS Goddess." (A thesis presented to the Committee on the Study of Religion, Harvard College, March 2000).

[20]See Frederick M. Smith, "Indra Goes West: Report on a Vedic Soma Sacrifice in London in July 1996," *History of Religions* 39, no. 3 (2000): 247-267.

[21]See, for example, David Pinault, "Shia Lamentation Rituals and Reinterpretations of the Doctrine of Intercession: Two Cases from Modern India," *History of Religions* 38, no. 3 (1999): 291.

[22]See, for example, Irving Greenberg, *The Jewish Way: Living The Holidays* (New York: Touchstone, 1988), 94-118.

[23]See, for example, John E. Cort, "The Gift of Good to a Wandering Cow: Lay-Mendicant Interaction Among the Jains," *Journal of Asian and African Studies* 34, no. 1 (1999): 92.

[24]Rahner, "Anonymous Christians," 395.

[25]For this phrasing, I am indebted to Lynda Lange's description of the self-referential construction of the other in "Burnt Offerings to Rationality: A Feminist Reading of the Peoples in Enrique Dussel's Theory of Modernity," *Hypatia* 13, no. 3 (1998): 132-145.

[26]See, for example, Paul Knitter, *One Earth, Many Religions: Multifaith Dialogue & Global Responsibility* (Maryknoll, N.Y.: Orbis Books, 1995), 106-9. See also John Hick, *A Christian Theology of Religions: The Rainbow of Faiths* (Louisville, Ky.: Westminster John Knox Press, 1995), 18.

[27]*Karl Rahner in Dialogue: Conversations and Interviews, 1965-1982*, ed. Paul Imhof and Hubert Biallowons (New York: Crossroad, 1986), 217.

[28]Rahner, "An Investigation of the Incomprehensibility of God in St. Thomas Aquinas," *Theological Investigations*, vol. 16, 247.

[29]Rahner, "The Church's Commission to Bring Salvation and the Humanization of the World," *Theological Investigations,* vol. 14 (New York: Seabury, 1976), 304.

[30]Rahner, "Schism in the Catholic Church?" *Theological Investigations,* vol. 12 (New York: Seabury, 1974), 108-111.

[31]Rahner and Heinrich Fries, *Unity of the Churches: An Actual Possibility,* trans. Ruth C. L. Gritsch and Eric W. Gritsch (Philadelphia: Fortress Press, 1985), 48.

[32]Rahner, "Ecumenical Theology in the Future," in *Theological Investigations,* vol. 14, 266.

[33]Rahner, "The Concept of Mystery in Catholic Theology," *Theological Investigations*, vol. 4 (Baltimore: Helicon Press, 1966), 62.

[34]Ibid.

[35]Rahner, "Reflections on Dialogue Within a Pluralistic Society," *Theological Investigations*, vol. 6, 40.

[36]In Rahner's collaborative text with Heinrich Fries, *Unity of the Churches: An Actual Possibility*, the two theologians outlined six theses envisioning practical steps to ecumenical progress. The commentary on thesis two was authored by Rahner and presents the idea of epistemological tolerance. For a study of the thesis itself, see Myroslaw Tataryn, "Epistemological Tolerance: A Step Toward Christian Unity," *Journal of Ecumenical Studies* 27, no. 4 (1990): 753-766. As Tataryn outlines, this principle was pinpointed for critique, even from within the Roman Catholic Church; notable opposition comes from Joseph Cardinal Ratzinger.

[37]Rahner, "Dialogue and Tolerance as the Foundation of a Humane Society," *Theological Investigations,* vol. 22 (New York: Crossroad, 1991), 22. For a discussion of the theological dimension of freedom, see "The Dignity and Freedom of Man," *Theological Investigations,* vol. 2 (Baltimore: Helicon Press, 1963), 235-255; and "Theology of Freedom," *Theological Investigations*, vol. 6, 178-196.

[38]Rahner, "Dialogue and Tolerance as the Foundation of a Humane Society," 24.

[39]Ibid.

Part IV

THE SOCIAL SCIENCES AS RESOURCES

Religion and Society—
Two Sides of the Same Coin

Part I

James D. Davidson

As the title, "Religion and Society: Two Sides of the Same Coin," suggests, we[1] believe there is a close relationship between religion and society. To understand society, social groups, and human behavior, sociologists need to understand the effects that religion has on people's behavior. Likewise, theologians cannot fully understand the supernatural without understanding the way social conditions affect people's religious beliefs and practices. If theologians were addressing a convention of sociologists, their charge would be to show social theorists and social researchers that they cannot understand society without fully understanding the role that faith plays in people's lives. As sociologists addressing a meeting of theologians, our task is to show theologians that they cannot understand faith without understanding its social foundations. I will focus on the way that "generation" affects individuals' religious beliefs and practices, and Patricia Wittberg will focus on the interaction between society and Catholic institutions, especially religious communities.

Generation

Sociologists often examine the effects that factors such as race, ethnicity, gender, and age have on the way people think and act. For example, social researchers have learned that there is a U-shaped relationship between age and religious commitment.[2] While in the care of parents, children tend to be religiously active. As youngsters reach their teenage years, begin to take on their own personalities, and become independent of their parents, their religious practices tend to decline. When they get married, and especially when they have children of their own, they tend to become more active in devotional and parish activities. While the relationship between age and religiosity is not be denied, the U-shaped scenario overlooks the social context into which people are born and the long-term effects that birth cohort—or generation—has on people's attitudes and actions. Three national surveys of American Catholics have shown that generation's impact on religious belief and practice is at least as great as, and probably greater than, the effects of race, ethnicity, gender, and age.[3] This fact has generated considerable interest in church circles.

A generation is defined by four characteristics.[4] First, its members grow up in a relatively specific social context; for example, they might all share the experience of being American. Second, they are born during a specific period of time. A generation usually spans a period of about twenty years. Third, members of a generation have a set of distinctive experiences during their formative years. The term formative years describes the years when young people wean themselves from their parents and make important personal decisions, such as whether to go on to college or work, what kind of job to accept or career to follow, whom to marry, where to live, when to have children, and how many to have. In our society, these formative years occur roughly between the ages of 11 and 21. During these years, members of a generation have experiences that set them apart from other generations. Finally, Mannheim calls these experiences "traumatic" because they leave imprints that affect the rest of people's lives.[5] They don't determine everything that happens later in life, but they set parameters within which people live out the rest of their lives. Whether they are fully conscious of it or not, 57-year-olds interpret current events in relation to things that happened in their seventeenth year.

Three Generations of Catholics

Today there are three generations of American Catholics: pre-Vatican II, Vatican II, and post-Vatican II. Pre-Vatican II Catholics were born in the 1920s and '30s and their formative years were the 1930s and '40s. They are products of the "roaring twenties," economic depression of the '30s, and World War II. Tom Brokaw calls them "the greatest generation."[6] Now 60 years of age and older, members of this generation now comprise about 20 percent of the adult Catholic population. Religiously, they are products of the "old church." They, or their parents, were products of nineteenth- and early-twentieth-century European immigration to this country. They had limited education, low-status jobs, and modest family incomes. In addition to ranking low in socio-economic status, they also experienced religious prejudice and discrimination. Partly as a result of being excluded from other neighborhoods and partly by choice, they lived in so-called "Catholic ghettos," ethnic enclaves where they had their own parishes, parochial schools, convents, Catholic hospitals, Catholic newspapers, Catholic Boy Scouts, and Catholic Girl Scouts. While the Irish belonged to the Hibernian Society and went to the Irish parish and the Italians belonged to the Sons of Italy Lodge and attended the Italian church, they all learned that the Roman Catholic Church is the "one true church." They were raised in the "old church," long before the time of Vatican II.

Vatican II Catholics, who were born between 1941 and 1960, comprise one-third of all adult Catholics. With their formative years in the 1950s and '60s, they are today's baby boomers and are now 40 to 59 years of age. What makes them interesting are the reversals they experienced during their formative years. They grew up in the cultural conservatism of the 1950s and political tranquility of the Eisenhower years. Then, right in the middle of their formative years, they experienced a 180-degree turn into the cultural liberalism and political turmoil of the 1960s. The Birmingham bus boycott triggered the civil rights movement and, later, the black power movement. Betty Friedan's 1963 book, *The Feminine Mystique*, launched the modern-day women's movement. As college students, they led the anti-war and the counter-culture movements. They experienced the same kind of 180-degree turn in the church. They grew up in the "old church," but right in the middle of their formative years Vatican II ushered in the "new church." Having been taught that the church was apart from the world, suddenly they were hearing that they were to be fully involved in the world. Instead of the church's more parochial view of itself as the "one true church," they were now urged to have a more ecumenical attitude toward other religious faiths. They started out singing "Tantum Ergo" and ended up singing "Kumbaya." At Mass, the priest, who used to have his back to the people, now faced the people. They had learned that eating meat on Friday was a sin, but all of a sudden the church said this was no longer so.

Post-Vatican II Catholics were born after 1961. Those born between 1961 and 1981 are often known as "Generation X." Now between 19 and 38 years of age, they represent 46 percent of all adult American Catholics. Those born since 1982 are known as the "Millennial Generation." Now in grade school and high school, their generation is still in the process of being formed.

I will focus on Generation X, the people who are in our classrooms today and the young adults about whom church leaders are so concerned. These post-Vatican II Catholics have grown up in a period of political conservatism, economic segmentation, cultural liberalism and relativism, technological innovation, and destructive behavior. Their presidents have tended to be Republicans. They have experienced great prosperity, but the benefits have gone to the top 20 percent of Americans, while the economic resources of the bottom 80 percent have stagnated or declined. While they have seen the creation of more millionaires and billionaires, they have also seen an increase in the percentage of Americans who are poor. They have witnessed increased police surveillance of poor neighborhoods and use of the death penalty. They have also experienced revolutionary changes in the roles of women in society, especially in the workforce. They have been part of the liberation of gays and lesbians. Theirs is a post-modern world in which they have been taught to be tolerant, to accept everyone, not to judge people's different values and different ways of life. They have experienced the "highs" of personal computers and the Internet and the "lows" of drug-related suicides and random acts of violence.

"Gen Xers" have also lived through two decades of post-Vatican II religious experimentation. In terms of faith and religious formation, they are the first generation not to use the Baltimore Catechism. Unlike previous generations, they have been taught to take personal responsibility for their own faith. Also, unlike previous generations, they have been taught that they are on their own personal faith journey, and they have been taught that Catholics have a lot in common with other Christians. Unlike previous generations, when religion teachers paid more attention to content than process, this generation's religion teachers have probably paid more attention to process than content. When asked to recall their CCD experiences, they are more likely to talk about balloons, banners, collages, and leaf collections than what they learned. But all these generations of American Catholics share the experience of being American and they share the experience of being Catholic. Thus, in addition to their differences, they also have some things in common.

Similarities

I conducted three national surveys of the religious beliefs and practices of these three generations in 1993, 1995, and 1999.[7] The results point to five areas where the generations are more similar than different, and five where there are important generational differences. First, the areas where there are very few differences. One area of agreement includes issues on which there is cultural consensus in American society. The first of these issues is the desire for democratic decision-making. Because they are Americans, Catholics of all generations want more democratic decision-making in their parishes, in their dioceses, and even in the Vatican. A second area of cultural consensus concerns the importance of the individual. This is evident in Catholics' belief in the importance of spirituality and personal growth and their belief that the way one lives one's life is more important than whether one is Catholic. A third area of cultural consensus involves the use of the death penalty (with which 70 percent of Americans and American Catholics agree).

A second area of agreement includes core beliefs that are grounded in documents such as the Nicene Creed. These core beliefs include the Real Presence, Mary as the Mother of God, the Resurrection, Incarnation, and the Trinity. Post-Vatican II Catholics are as likely to agree with these teachings as pre-Vatican II Catholics.

A third area of agreement is the social teachings of the church. Regardless of generation, Catholics believe in the importance of helping the poor and building a just world. Though most Catholics have not read the social encyclicals or the bishops' pastoral letters on peace and economic justice, they have heard about the arguments presented in these documents and they tend to agree with them. For example, they agree that Catholics have a special duty to close the gap between the rich and the poor and they agree that political and economic decisions that hurt the poor are morally wrong.

Fourth, there is agreement on the importance of the sacraments and the presence of priests to administer the sacraments. This area includes specific findings about the consequences of the so-called priest shortage. All three generations of Catholics do not want the number of masses reduced. They believe that priests should be available to visit the sick and administer last rites. They have mixed feelings about having a lay administrator and no resident priest. They believe that occasionally it is all right to have communion services instead of mass, but they would rather have masses said by priests. That is why they approve of the ordination of married men and are willing to welcome back priests who have married.

The final area of similarity concerns the relatively new, scripture-oriented forms of devotional activity that the church emphasized in the post-Vatican II years. Very few Catholics in any of the generations read the Bible on a regular basis or are actively involved in Bible study or prayer groups. When Catholics of all generations think about being a "practicing Catholic," they are still more likely to think of mass attendance and reception of Holy Communion than they are to think about practices such as reading the Bible, participating in Bible study groups, or belonging to prayer groups.

Differences

There also are five areas where the generations are quite different. The first is participation in sacraments. While Catholics believe in the importance of the sacraments, all of our surveys point to declining rates of mass attendance, declining reception of Holy Communion, declining participation in the sacrament of reconciliation, increasing interfaith marriage, and an increasing tendency to marry outside the Roman Catholic Church. Second, there is declining participation in traditional devotional activities. As one goes from the pre-Vatican II generation to the post-Vatican II generation, one sees a declining frequency in private prayer, declining devotions to Mary and other saints, and declining use of the rosary.

A third area of difference involves declining commitment to the institutional church. This is evident in declining belief that the Roman Catholic Church is the one true church, declining belief in the teaching authority of the Vatican, and declining financial contributions to the church. It also appears in Catholics' increasing doubt that racism or sexism are any less present in the church than in society as a whole.

There is also an increasing belief that one can be a good Catholic without going to mass every Sunday, without obeying the church's teaching on birth control, without obeying its teaching on divorce and remarriage, and without obeying its teaching on abortion.

Fourth, Catholic identity is declining. As one goes from pre-Vatican II Catholics to post-Vatican II Catholics, one sees declining belief that being Catholic is an important part of who one is, a declining sense that others know you are Catholic, a decline in the importance of having younger generations of your family grow up Catholic, the declining importance of the church in people's personal lives, an increasing ability to imagine circumstances under which one might leave the church, and increasing uncertainty about what is special about being Catholic.

The fifth area of difference concerns the individual's right to make decisions on faith and morals (especially sexual and reproductive ethics). All of our surveys point to an increasing tendency to say that individuals, not church leaders, have the final say on issues such as divorce and remarriage without an annulment, birth control, abortion, homosexual behavior, and sexual relations outside of marriage. They also point to increasing disagreement with the church's teaching on birth control, abortion, non-marital sexuality and homosexual behavior. Finally, they all point to an increasing willingness to ordain women.

Let me offer two concluding comments. The generations tend to agree on many of the church's core values and beliefs. They also hold similar beliefs in a number of areas where there is cultural consensus in the society as a whole. We should not overlook these areas of common ground. However, generation also is one of the most important sources of diversity in today's church. Its effects are at least as large as the effects of race, ethnicity, class, and gender. Given the generational differences we have reviewed today, church leaders should not assume that religiously inactive post-Vatican II Catholics will automatically return to the church when they get married and have children of their own: some will, but many will not. Nor should church leaders assume that members of this generation will think and act like their parents when they do rebound. If and when they do return, they will bring with them the beliefs and behaviors that are indigenous to the post-Vatican II generation—not the ones that pre-Vatican II and Vatican II Catholics learned during their formative years.

Notes

[1]See also Part II by Patricia Wittberg, s.c., pages 205-13.

[2]See, for example, Charles Y. Glock, Benjamin B. Ringer, and Earl R. Babbie, *To Comfort and to Challenge: A Dilemma of the Contemporary Church* (Berkeley: University of California Press, 1967).

[3]James D. Davidson, "Generations Have Different Views of the Church," "Increasing Indifference to Church Is Concern," and "Marriage Trends Signal Declining Role of Church," *National Catholic Reporter* (October 29, 1999): 15, 18, 20; idem, "The Post-Vatican II Generation of 'Christian Catholics,' " *New Theology Review* (February 1998): 12-22; James D. Davidson, Andrea S. Williams, and Richard A. Lamanna, *The Search for Common Ground: What Unites and Divides Catholic Americans* (Huntington, Ind.: Our Sunday Visitor, 1997); William V. D'Antonio et al., *Laity: American and Catholic* (Kansas City: Sheed & Ward, 1996); and Andrea Williams and James D. Davidson, "Catholic Conceptions of Faith: A Generational Analysis," *Sociology of Religion* 57 (1995): 273-289.

[4]Karl Mannheim, *Essays on the Sociology of Knowledge* (New York: Oxford University Press, 1952); Douglas Alan Walrath, *Frameworks: Patterns of Living and Believing Today* (New York: Pilgrim Press, 1987); Wade Clark Roof, *A Generation of Seekers: The Spiritual Journeys of the Baby Boom Generation* (San Francisco: Harper, 1993); and James D. Davidson, Andrea S. Williams, and Richard A. Lamanna, *The Search for Common Ground.*

[5]Karl Mannheim, *Essays on the Sociology of Knowledge.*

[6]Tom Brokaw, *The Greatest Generation* (New York: Random House, 1998).

[7]See references in note 3, above.

Religion and Society—Two Sides of the Same Coin

Part II

Patricia Wittberg, S.C.

The previous essay by James D. Davidson outlines some sociological research on U.S. Catholic generations. His focus is on the beliefs and behaviors of individual Catholics—what we in sociology call "microsociology." My research focuses on a somewhat different topic—that of religious *organizations*, such as new and established religious orders,[1] Catholic schools and hospitals, and denominations. This brief overview is intended to highlight some of the ways the two disciplines of sociology and theology can enrich each other. In other words, how do social conditions affect religious organizations, and how do religious organizations affect society? And what contributions can the two disciplines make in studying these mutual effects?

First of all, how do social conditions affect religious organizations? The most obvious answer—and the one that has already been researched for decades by entire professional associations of sociological practitioners—is the impact that changing demographics have had on the membership of religious groups. The Religious Research Association, for example, was originally established for denominational officials who wanted to discover nodes of population growth that would be the most propitious for the "planting" of new churches. But the simple availability of large numbers of potential recruits is not, of course, sufficient. If it were, Catholic religious orders would be filled with Baby Boomer and Generation X religious. Thus, it is not surprising that a second societal condition affecting recruitment to a denomination, a local church, or a religious order is the implicit theology, the particular variant of religious searching, that is prevalent among these potential recruits and how well the target denomination or religious order is able to fulfill it. Davidson has already pointed out how different generations of American Catholics differ and how they do *not* differ in what they seek from the church. Sociologists of religious organizations look at how the churches can meet these differing expectations.

In the past decade a new paradigm in the sociology of religion has arisen that describes how denominations compete for adherents in the pluralistic marketplace of the American religious scene. This "rational choice theory" gives insights into the reasons why religious denominations grow and decline and why "high demand" faiths may attract more members than less rigorous ones.[2] My own research, in conjunction with the Center for Applied Research on the Apostolate (CARA) at Georgetown University, has focused on the growth and decline of Catholic religious orders. Last year, CARA published a directory of some 160 emerging religious communities and lay movements that have been established in the United States since Vatican II.[3] In contrast to the last major foundation period of religious orders in the nineteenth century, only about one-third of these new communities listed some apostolic work in their mission statements. A larger number are contemplative in focus or concentrate on evangelization, and it is these evangelizing and contemplative groups, on the average, that are attracting new entrants. This finding mirrors several CARA surveys of established religious orders, as well as studies by other researchers, all of whom find that more new members are attracted to religious life today because of its opportunities for common life and common prayer.[4] In a forthcoming article, Roger Finke and I argue that religious life has long been the vehicle by which those Catholics who are the most troubled by the unique strains and hungers of a given society can devise innovative ways for the church to address these strains and hungers.[5] Without the creative impulse of religious orders, Catholicism would be subject to the same pressures for sectarian fission that have bedeviled our Protestant brothers and sisters.[6]

Sociological research, therefore, would urge denominations, religious orders, and other religious organizations[7] to look at the specific spiritual hungers that exist today among various groups of people. Is this or that group's spiritual quest something which the denomination or religious order can meet without sacrificing its own core mission?

And what, exactly, *is* the order's or denomination's core mission and what is simply the mental "rut" that a given generation has become too comfortable with? Here sociological research, such as Davidson's, for example, on the desires of today's spiritual seekers, as well as studies like my own of other religious denominations or congregations that have or have not succeeded in meeting these seekers' quests, can fruitfully dialogue with theologians specializing in ecclesiology, spirituality, and the theology of religious life.

In addition to the many ways a church's or a religious order's surrounding social milieu may influence the number and the expectations of religious seekers who might be exploring membership, other aspects of culture and society also affect these organizations' implicit theology. By taking for granted the cultural values of bureaucratic credentialism, efficiency, and power, for example, a church may forget its commitment to a more consensual or servant form of leadership. A classic study of this process is Paul Harrison's *Authority and Power in the Free Church Tradition,*[8] which chronicles how the American Baptist Church developed a centralized bureaucratic structure that wielded significant power—in spite of the denomination's official theology of "soul competency" and its deep suspicion of hierarchy. More recently, several sociological studies have examined a similar process in the Southern Baptist Convention.[9]

Again, in recent years an entire sociological literature known as neo-institutionalism has emerged to describe how these larger societal expectations and values can worm their way into the operations of various nonprofit organizations.[10] As a colleague of mine has recently written, "We live in a society in which all organizations tend to take similar forms—thanks to tax laws, accounting practices, and the standard corporate model of governance by boards of directors."[11] In order to be taken seriously and to attract government funds, for example, a local church's program for at-risk youth may have to juggle complex reporting forms, hire a credentialed Master of Social Work to supervise its volunteer staff, draw up measurable outcome criteria, and so on. These environmental expectations tend to "institutionalize"—to crystallize in professional accreditation standards and governmental regulations—until it becomes increasingly impossible for the administrators and staff to envision any other way of operating. Gradually, the "mission effectiveness" office is isolated in a little ghetto off to the side, honored by lip-service, to be sure, but otherwise ignored.[12] To the patient in the hospital bed, the nurse or orderly on the floor, or the student in the college classroom, there may be little or no evident difference between a Catholic or Baptist hospital or university and a secular one.[13]

A question raised by my current research is whether there is any interaction between the two influences I have described. That is, does the increasing "institutional isomorphism"—the tendency of religious hospitals, colleges, and social welfare agencies to resemble their secular counterparts—make them less likely to be seen as a "holy work for God" that is suitable for a denomination or a religious order? A century ago, church people considered the building and running of these institutions to be an essential part of building the Kingdom of God. Catholics and Protestants alike saw the creation of hospitals, colleges, orphanages, and other social services as their religious duty: "These associations were designed to offer moral individuals the appropriate vehicles with which to engage in social activism; they were non-coercive associations of the like-minded moral elect, entitled to exclude and reform the unregenerate for their own good."[14] The most important duty of nineteenth-century Catholic hospitals was *not* to cure patients; it was to assist the dying poor in setting their spiritual houses in order. The most important duty of Catholic schools—explicitly articulated as late as the 1940s—was not to impart secular knowledge, but rather to save their students' souls.[15] It was immediately evident to men and women in nineteenth-century religious orders how working in such schools and hospitals was intimately connected to their religious vocation. By contrast, recent survey evidence shows that persons now entering religious orders are *not* attracted by the opportunity to work in modern hospitals, colleges, and Catholic social agencies.[16] Many are troubled by the moral compromises that must be made in such institutions as they juggle the exigencies of government regulations, bottom lines, and professional standards.[17] Others note that they can teach, nurse, or administer in Catholic institutions without entering a religious community. This "desacralization" of the health care, educational, and social service institutions run by religious sponsors may be a fundamental reason behind the comparative attractiveness of monastic and contemplative variants of religious life over the apostolic models.

Again, looking at these questions through the dual lenses of sociology and theology could be much more profitable than using either perspective by itself. As several of my interview respondents have plaintively informed me, we have long lacked a theology of institutional administration.

> We have, and religious across the country have, created a dichotomy between sacred and profane ministries. Futurists predict that, in ten years, the majority of all college degrees will come out of business/entrepreneur/service majors. We have declared these profane and less acceptable. Say three women enter a religious congregation. One is a lawyer, one is a stockbroker, and one is CEO of a small business. And we feel we have seven years to change their minds and move them into some "religious" ministry like Director of Religious Education. What would happen if we really considered the *ministry* potential of business occupations? (Interview with the CEO of a health care system, 1997)

As one historian has pointed out, this lack has perplexed sisters as far back as the 1940s: "As the ratio of sisters to lay staff declined, the orders had to re-examine their basic assumptions: were their members primarily labor or management? And, if the latter, how did their management functions relate to their traditional ministry of providing personal care to the sick and dying?"[18] In other words, a fruitful area for the collaboration of sociology and theology may be in looking critically at the religious mission of the institutions we have inherited. Is it possible to run a hospital or a college in a distinctively Baptist or Catholic way? What would that entail? In the past thirty or forty years, we have developed many theologies of systemic change —liberation theology, the option for the poor, social analysis. What we may now need are theologies of system *sacralization.*[19] While sociology is not equipped to provide such theologies, those of you who are equipped and interested in doing so would benefit from a dialogue with sociology on how organizations really work.

These are some of the topics that could be considered under the question of how social conditions affect religious organizations, with an expansion into how sociology and theology might collaborate to address them. There is the additional question of how religious organizations affect societal conditions. I will simply note that there is extensive sociological literature on the social movements that have been sparked and sustained by churches, from the Civil Rights Movement to the Sanctuary Movement.[20] On a practical level, Saul Alinsky's Industrial Areas Foundation has amassed a large repertoire of strategies whereby church groups can use the power of their members to attack and change unjust social structures.[21] I am sure theology has also looked at the role of churches in these struggles. A dialogue between these two disciplines would be fruitful.

The title for this presentation came from an image I have held from childhood. In those pre-historic times, my family did not have a television set, and I remember listening to children's programs on the radio. One such program re-told a Paul Bunyan story of a hard winter in the logging camp when the food was so scarce that "even the pancakes had only one side." I can still remember puzzling my 5-year-old brain with trying to imagine how a pancake could have only one side. In the same way, religion and society are two sides of the same coin—or pancake! Neither can exist without the other; the imperatives of each infuse and shape the other. The disciplines that study religion and society must likewise be intertwined. Sociology can offer a valuable reality-check on the writings and speculations of theologians. John Coleman quoted Robin Gill in his paper printed in this volume. This quotation bears repeating: "Theologians tend to make claims about the society or culture within which they operate and then incorporate these claims into their theology. Sociological analysis could provide incisive and rigorous tools for the theologian to understand better the social context within which he operates."[22] In other words, are the claims these theologians make about society grounded empirically or not?

I firmly believe that just as there is no contradiction between theology and the findings of the *physical* sciences—whenever seeming contradictions have appeared, either the theology or the science is faulty—in the same way there is no contradiction between social scientific findings and theology. When sociological research finds that conservative denominations or religious orders are growing more rapidly than liberal ones, or that religious hospitals do not differ from secular ones in the amount of labor strife they experience or in the amount of charitable care they deliver, theology will have to deal with such findings in its analysis of the option for the poor, the prescriptions of Vatican II, and so forth, just as it had ultimately to deal with the findings of Galileo and Darwin. Not only does the "lava of the Holy Spirit flow through existing societal fault lines," the mustard seed of ecclesial structures subsequently sprouts and grows in the same volcanic soil. As a sociologist, I have sometimes tended to be impatient with what I viewed as some popular theologians' blithe willingness to make statements and predictions in ignorance of the way societal "fault lines" affect the phenomena they are describing.

On the other hand, theology can offer much to sociology as well. The famous sociologist Max Weber held that sociologists must *understand* (*verstehen*) the motivations and values of those they study. Religion is among the most profound and basic of these motivations, and sociologists have too often been guilty of ignoring it in the past. Sociologists who study the family or social movements or political sociology or criminology or, of course, religion itself *must* take the religious motivations of their subjects seriously. Theology is an essential aid in doing theory, forcing us, as John Coleman stated, to clarify our too-often implicit and unexamined assumptions about the image of human nature we employ, our accounts of the sources of primary evil, and our projected future trajectories of societal change. Theologians have just as much justification to be impatient with my unexamined theological assumptions as I do with their sociological ones.

To remedy this, however, we must talk to each other, to a much greater extent than we currently do, and we must listen to each other as well. In my own personal experience, when sociologists and theologians get together, we often end up talking past each other. We need to be willing to stop and question each other as to exactly what our words mean, what we think is important, and why. If we take the time and energy to do this, such conversations will prove to be valuable precursors to a future flowering of both our disciplines.

Notes

[1]Strictly speaking, of course, I am referring primarily to diocesan and pontifical religious *congregations*. However, to avoid confusion with local Protestant church congregations, which I will also be mentioning later on, I am using "order" to refer to all varieties of Catholic religious life.

[2]Roger Finke and Rodney Stark, *The Churching of America, 1776-1990: Winners and Losers in Our Religious Economy* (New Brunswick, N.J.: Rutgers University Press, 1992); R. Steven Warner, "Work in Progress toward a New Paradigm for the Sociological Study of Religion in the United States," *American*

Journal of Sociology 98, no.5 (1993): 1044-1093; Lawrence Iannacone, "Why Strict Churches Are Strong," *American Journal of Sociology* 99, no.5 (1994): 1180-1211.

[3]Center for Applied Research on the Apostolate, "Emerging Religious Communities in the United States, 1999" (Washington, D.C.: Georgetown University Press, 1999); Patricia Wittberg, S.C., and Mary E. Bendyna, R.S.M., "Portrait of Emerging Religious Communities in the United States," *Horizon, Journal of the National Religious Vocation Conference* 25, no.2 (2000): 15-21.

[4]Patricia Wittberg, S.C. and Bryan Froehle, "Generation X and Religious Life: New Findings from the CARA Studies," *Horizon, Journal of the National Religious Vocation Conference* 23, no.3 (1998): 3-8; Helen Rose Ebaugh, *Women and the Vanishing Cloister: Organizational Decline in Catholic Religious Orders in the United States* (New Brunswick, N.J.: Rutgers University Press, 1993).

[5]Roger Finke and Patricia Wittberg, "Revival from Within: Religious Orders as Sectarian Movements," *Journal for the Scientific Study of Religion*, forthcoming.

[6]Patricia Wittberg, S.C., *Pathways for Recreating Religious Communities* (New York: Paulist Press, 1996), 79-85.

[7]I am presently studying the United Methodist Women and United Methodist deaconesses and have found some fascinating parallels with communities of sisters.

[8]Paul Harrison, *Authority and Power in the Free Church Tradition: A Social Case Study of the American Baptist Convention* (Princeton University Press, 1959).

[9]Nancy Ammerman, *Baptist Battles: Social Change and Religious Conflict in the Southern Baptist Convention* (New Brunswick, N.J.: Rutgers University Press, 1990); Arthur E. Farnsley, II, *Southern Baptist Politics* (University Park, Penn.: Pennsylvania State University Press, 1994).

[10]Walter W. Powell and Paul J. DiMaggio, eds., *The New Institutionalism in Organizational Analysis* (Chicago: University of Chicago Press, 1991).

[11]Rhys H. Williams, "Social Movements and Religion in Contemporary American Politics," in *Religion and American Politics: The 2000 Election in Context*, Mark Silk, ed. (Hartford, Conn.: Trinity College, Pew Program on Religion and the News Media), 58.

[12]John Meyer and Brian Rowan describe just such a process in their "Institutionalized Organizations: Formal Organizations as Myth and Ceremony," *American Journal of Sociology* 83, no. 2 (1987): 340-363.

[13]This process has been described by George Marsden in *The Soul of the American University: From Protestant Establishment to Established Nonbelief* (New York: Oxford University Press, 1994); James T. Burtchaell in "The Decline and Fall of the Christian College," *First Things* (April/May, 1991) for religious universities; and by Christopher J. Kauffman in *Ministry and Meaning: A Religious History of Catholic Health Care in the United States* (New York: Crossroad, 1995) for Catholic hospitals.

[14]Rhys Williams, "Visions of the Good Society and the Religious Roots of American Political Culture," *Sociology of Religion* 60 (1999): 29.

[15]Patricia Wittberg, "Called to Service: The Changing Institutional Identities of

American Denominations," *Nonprofit and Voluntary Sector Quarterly*, forthcoming.

[16]David Nygren and Miriam D. Ukeritis, *The Future of Religious Orders in the United States: Transformation and Commitment* (Westport, Conn:. Praeger, 1993). See also Wittberg and Froehle, "Generation X and Religious Life."

[17]See Robert Jackall, *Moral Mazes: The World of Corporate Managers* (New York: Oxford University Press, 1988); and D. F. Chambliss, *Beyond Caring: Hospitals, Nurses, and the Social Organization of Ethics* (Chicago: University of Chicago Press, 1991).

[18]Mary Carol Conroy, "The Transition Years," in *Pioneer Healers: The History of Women Religious in American Health Care*, ed. Ursula Stepsis and Dolores Liptak (New York: Crossroad, 1989), 153.

[19]There is already one such theology, of course: the traditional Catholic teaching on the supreme authority of the magisterium. This particular theology is not attractive to many Catholics, including myself. It would be helpful to have others.

[20]Doug McAdam, *The Political Process and the Development of Black Insurgency, 1930-1970* (Chicago: University of Chicago Press, 1982); and Christian Smith, *Resisting Reagan: The U.S. Central American Peace Movement* (Chicago: University of Chicago Press, 1996).

[21]Mark R. Warren, "Community Building and Political Power: A Community Organizing Approach to Democratic Renewal," *American Behavioral Scientist* 41 (September, 1998): 78-92.

[22]Robin Gill, "Sociology Assessing Theology," in *Theology and Sociology: A Reader*, ed. Robin Gill (London: Cassell, 1996), 147.

Traversing the Social Landscape

The Value of the Social Scientific Approach to the Bible

Victor H. Matthews

Since the advent of historical-critical studies of the Bible, new approaches have been introduced reflecting changes in literary analysis, archaeological techniques and, recently, the introduction of social-scientific methods and theories. The aim of social scientific criticism as a sub-field of biblical exegesis is to study the biblical materials as a reflection of their cultural setting. The meaning and/or the social background of the text are thus more fully illuminated by the exercise of sociological and anthropological methods and theories.

The era of modern social-scientific research began in the late nineteenth century with the work of Karl Marx, Auguste Comte, and Herbert Spencer.[1] Their social theories created an atmosphere of curiosity about the human condition and advanced the evolutionary perspective that had taken hold with the writing of Charles Darwin. As sociology and anthropology emerged as separate sciences, scholars like W. Robertson Smith and Louis Wallis adapted their methods (at least comparative and functionalist perspectives) to Israelite history and culture. Despite this early start, there was a hiatus in the use of the social sciences (especially psychology, sociology, and anthropology) in the study of the Bible during the period between 1930 and 1960 as literary and archaeological approaches (W. F. Albright School) predominated. However, in the last several decades, building on the work of Max Weber and continuing with the study of Israelite origins by George Mendenhall and Norman Gottwald, they have had a revival and have burgeoned into a major sub-field.

Early Approaches

In the earliest works that employ social sciences methods, the emphasis is on collecting data from biblical narrative and laws, from archaeological excavations, and from ancient Near Eastern texts. In addition, a few comparative studies were done with modern "primitive cultures," such as the Bedouins of the Middle East and African tribal groups. Very often, however, assumptions of the evolutionary character of cultures and the "survival" of ancient societal forms hampered the usefulness of these studies and in some cases discredited their findings.

Among the most influential of the nineteenth-century scholars employing social scientific methods was W. Robertson Smith, considered by some as the founder of social anthropology. In his extensive writings on Semitic life and culture (especially kinship, marriage, and sacrificial practices), he posited an evolutionary process of ancient Israelite culture from a primitive, to a matrilineal, and a totemistic phase.[2] Sacrifice, he suggested, was designed to create within the tribal group a sense of social unity and to tie the members to their patron god.[3] Using this model, he then asserted that as society became more complex, sacrifice became more ritualized and subsidiary to the growing influence of state development. In fact his interest in ritual ran counter to the comparative myth models of many of his contemporaries.[4]

While many of Robertson Smith's views have been disputed, the questions he asked have continued to hold a central place in reconstructing the social world of ancient Israel. For example, in his examination of the role of ritual in Semitic culture, he strongly emphasized the materialistic origins for the development of social ideas and practices. This in turn became central to the development of the theories of the sociology of religion by Emile Durkheim and to the comparative folklore studies of James G. Frazer. In addition, Robertson Smith's careful examination of Arab culture created a model for the careful field studies that characterize modern social and cultural anthropology today.

Another early pioneer in the social scientific study of ancient Israel was Louis Wallis. He suggested that people's social development was the direct result of cultural and class struggle. This clash of ideas was caused by the conflict between rural and urban societies, first Canaanite urban culture versus Israelite village culture and then a struggle for supremacy between the local and regional Israelite village establishment (championing the covenant with Yahweh) and the growing urban elite of the monarchic period.[5] It is this conflict model as well as Wallis's insistence on separating theological from sociological studies of the biblical world that helped spark the work of George Mendenhall, Norman Gottwald, and Frank Frick since the 1960s.

A third major influence on modern critical study is the work of Max Weber. As a sociologist, he brought an outsider's expertise on social organization and the relationship between religion and society to biblical studies. His work on ancient Judaism analyzed the elements of Israel's cult, including the role of the Levites within the priestly hierarchy. He also examined the manner in which Hebrew prophecy served as a focal point of conflict in the struggle between Israelite religious ideals and the growing socioeconomic forces of the emerging Israelite state.[6] Weber developed an "ideal type" model categorizing the social structure and the levels of social authority in ancient Israel.[7] For example, in his definition of priests as cultic specialists, he set them apart from the normal categories of human enterprise. He further magnified this perception by including "charisma" as a personality trait that distanced those in leadership roles from the masses.[8]

Weber's work on the forces within organizational structures and the transformation of a culture as it shifts from a collective mentality in the village setting to a more individualistic and competitive pattern in the urban setting was also taken up by the French sociologist Antonin Causse. This transition, according to Causse, eventually led in the post-exilic and Hellenistic periods to a further reinterpretation of social symbols. When political autonomy ended,[9] social identity became more individualistic. As a result, community values came to be centered more on individual faithfulness to the religious tradition rather than to a political entity.

During the 1930s to the 1950s, however, these early efforts introducing anthropological and sociological methods into biblical interpretation ceased to advance as quickly. For instance, the very useful and influential study of Israelite religious and cultural institutions by Roland de Vaux[10] provided a form of encyclopedic register, but was not tied to specific social theories. The very dominant American scholar/archaeologist, W. F. Albright, turned his students and their research to comparative studies of the ancient Near Eastern context of the biblical world.[11] Their emphasis on linguistic analysis, archaeological investigations, and historical reconstruction added to the store of available data, but did not effectively explore the social prospects of cultural development. In fact, his insistence on using archaeological materials to prove the accuracy of the portrayal of the Israelites in the biblical account placed a barrier on broader and more objective approaches.[12]

Recent Developments

Since the 1970s the emphasis of social scientific critics has been on the application of a variety of sociological and anthropological methods in conjunction with the emerging field of ethnoarchaeology. The delineation of social models allows researchers in both Hebrew Bible[13] and New Testament studies to identify both common and apparently unique cultural elements and behaviors.[14] While some studies do choose to look at isolated cultural phenomena, it is more common to find comparative studies.[15] These investigations can then be designed to examine cultural units over long or short periods of time,[16] as well as within particular regions or in comparison with culture areas in widely dispersed locations. The structures that make up society, from the family unit to the ruling elites, can be studied in the light of both historical data as well as a macroorganizational perspective.[17]

Since there are multiple perspectives from which a culture may be examined, it is not surprising to find that social theorists disagree on which method is most effective.[18] The principal methods that have been employed center on structural-functional traditions, conflict theories of social development, and cultural materialist perspectives that examine subsistence strategies or economic patterns. It is also quite common for scholars to employ multiple methods that complement each other.

Structural-Functionalist Methods

The structural-functionalist approach takes the position that all aspects of a culture interrelate and therefore cannot be understood except as components of the overall structure of that society.[19] Each cultural facet, such as religious or legal systems, contributes to the advancement and the stability of the society as a whole and thus works toward equilibrium through consensus building. When conflict occurs within society, the forces calling for change would either be absorbed into acceptable and recognizable social structure (understood as necessary adjustments to established procedures) or denounced and outlawed as a danger to society.

The chief value in examining a culture from a functionalist viewpoint is found in its emphasis on analyzing a culture as an interrelated whole, categorizing its structure, and establishing the relationships between these various facets of the society, such as kinship patterns or the economic system, and actual behaviors of the inhabitants.[20] However, there is also a tendency in such studies to limit the perspective and the study of a culture to a particular period. This does not allow sufficient latitude to deal with a culture with a long history and multiple social transitions.

Conflict Theory

As originally formulated by Karl Marx and adapted by Max Weber, conflict theory examines forces within a society that either contribute to or promote conflict between the classes or structures of a society.[21] At work are ideological differences on how to control the means of power and the modes of production. It is therefore necessary to first identify competing groups within the society. The task is then to analyze their methods for either protecting their own interests or supplanting the assets of other groups. The assumption is that the potential for social change and social conflict is endemic within society. The only way that this potential for flux or open conflict can be avoided is through methods of constraint. An ordered society is one, therefore, that has achieved control over the forces of conflict by coming to know and understand their potential for violence.[22] Their energies are channeled into less revolutionary pursuits and the society achieves equilibrium without totally suppressing the possibility for change.

Cultural Materialist Theories

Cultural materialist theories attempt to classify societies based on their modes of subsistence (hunting and gathering, pastoral nomadism, agriculture), and on the technologies they develop to better take advantage of the natural resources of the area they inhabit.[23] In this way, cultural evolution and the likelihood of the survival of a particular culture can be determined as new technologies or subsistence strategies are introduced. There is also a sense of environmental determinism inherent in this position since it bases cultural development on the opportunities and limitations of the topography of the culture zone.[24] The danger with this type of classification, however, is found in a too rigid approach that does not always allow for multiple economic endeavors.[25] For instance, few farmers live exclusively off of their crops. They realize it is necessary to balance the risk of below-normal rainfall or flood by keeping a few sheep and goats or engaging in small cottage industries (pottery, weaving, metal work). Similarly, pastoralists often engage in seasonal agriculture or the care of fruit trees (olives and dates in the Middle East).[26]

These theorists also study the organizational aspects of subsistence strategies. It is understood that an economy is based on resources, labor, and leadership. An evolutionary process is posited in which society shifts from classless, egalitarian societies that share resources and combine their labor to rigidly stratified societies dominated by those who control the modes of production. According to this position (based on Marx and employed by Norman Gottwald),[27] the cultural transformation of ancient Israel from a village-based society to an urban-based society, dominated by a centralized authority, is explained by the imposition of taxation and the means to enforce discipline by the monarchy. The later transition to vassal status under the domination of the Mesopotamian empires simply added an even more authoritarian level of control, depriving the Israelites of political and economic autonomy and draining them of their resources.

The materialist approach is sometimes in conflict with those scholars who choose to emphasize cultural origins and evolution based on ideological development. It is possible to see a particular cultural attribute, such as conducting legal and economic transactions on the threshing floor, simply as a result of farmers regularly coming together at the harvest to a communal agricultural installation to process their grain. Gathered together, they see the advantages of also doing business and conducting legal proceedings. On the other hand these activities could be seen as a part of a larger picture in which the egalitarian ideal of the village culture finds its voice in collective understandings of justice and fair dealing.

In sum, it is apparent that no one social science model can be touted as the most reliable or most useful for the reconstruction of the ancient world. Instead, while scholars may favor a particular method or theory, most choose a more eclectic approach, applying a variety of social theories to what is revealed by the ancient textual material and the exposed archaeological data. Most also recognize that building a social model of an ancient culture based on information drawn from the study of modern cultures has its dangers. Presuppositions or the desire to make the data fit the chosen model simply discredit the process.[28] However, critical use of models can be useful in tying data together. This more objective stance allows for self-evaluation and restructuring of the analytical approach when too many factors indicate the need to refine or recalibrate the model.

Application of Social Science Methods in Biblical Research

One of the difficulties that biblical scholars have had in adopting social science methods to their study of ancient Israel has been in mastering an additional scholarly field. This has limited the number of scholars applying these methods to their interpretations of the biblical text. There has also been some difficulty in gaining acceptability for their findings by the academic community as a whole. However, the growth of interest in the reconstruction of the social world of the ancient Near East within its cultural milieu has created a better climate for new theoretical orientations. This has already had an effect on archaeological investigations, drawing them away from the functionalist approach of the 1960s as the so-called "New Archaeology" emerged,[29] and reinvigorating the movement to tie artifactual remains to historical reconstruction.[30]

Modern Interpreters

With the publication in 1962 of his essay, "The Hebrew Conquest of Palestine," George Mendenhall set the stage for the reintroduction of social scientific criticism into biblical studies.[31] By questioning the existence of the amphictyonic tribal league posited by Martin Noth[32] and the assumption that Israel was an ethnic group separate from the Canaanites, having originated as pastoral nomadic tribes (Albrecht Alt),[33] Mendenhall shattered a scholarly paradigm and left the issue open for new interpretations.[34] He called for a reexamination of the very limiting notions of tribe and posited a conflict theory that placed the rural peasant classes at odds with urban elites. The struggle for the emergence of Israel, out of a "peasant revolt," was strengthened, in his opinion, by the unifying character of the covenant with Yahweh.[35]

Norman Gottwald then took Mendenhall's model a step further by applying in a more systematic way the principles of the structural-functionalist and cultural materialist approaches. Using an interdisciplinary model, he diminished the importance of Yahwism as the driving force behind Israel's emergence. Instead he pointed to a disaffection by the lower classes in Canaanite society that chose to revolt with their feet, withdrawing from the urban centers, "retribalizing" in a village setting, and eventually reemerging as a rival political entity.[36] Although Gottwald's economic determinist model has been strenuously critiqued,[37] his careful delineation of the social facets of ancient Israel (from its tribal structure patterns to its modes of subsistence management) has guided many scholars over the last three decades. His study has reinforced the fact that while biblical scholars need to be familiar with the theories of Marx, Durkheim, and Weber, they must also be cautious in making broad assertions about the sociology of religion of an ancient culture such as Israel.

Methods for Political Development

Ongoing studies of Israel's origins and its eventual political evolution into a chiefdom and then a monarchy have built upon or responded to the work of Mendenhall and Gottwald. For instance, Gerhard Lenski traces the pattern of Israel's political development from a "frontier society" existing on the margins of Canaanite control that naturally returns to monarchic and bureaucratic structures once it has grown in size and social complexity.[38] Frank Frick points to better management of natural resources, improvements in technology, and the resulting economic surpluses attendant with population growth as a combination of factors leading to the development of a chiefdom and eventual political stability under the leadership of a single family.[39] The numerous archaeological surveys and excavations by Israel Finkelstein,[40] L. E. Stager,[41] and others in Israel and Jordan over the last two decades have helped to support this widening social perspective and have pointed to the necessity for a multi-faceted approach to the reconstruction of cultural and political development. Plus David Hopkins's effective use of geomorphology, climatic studies, and agricultural economic principles in his study of the Central Hill Country settlements of the Iron I period has added a further dimension to social world studies.[42]

Investigation of Social Institutions

The other major interest area in social scientific criticism is the investigation of social institutions in ancient Israel, which include kinship patterns, concepts of honor and shame, gender roles, and prophetic activity. At the heart of these studies is a blending of the older comparative methods of ethnographic analogy with materialist and ideological analysis. There is also a strong emphasis placed on human experience as a generator of cultural patterns and customs.

Kinship studies take into account the work of cultural anthropologists like Claude Lévi-Strauss.[43] They include the examination of marriage patterns (endogamy, exogamy, incest taboos, and divorce), inheritance customs (primogeniture, patrilineal and matrilineal), and rules of association (patron/client relations, class distinctions, and economic strictures such as usury). Among the recent studies of kinship in the Bible,[44] there is a clear realization that while ideal patterns existed, they had to give way to the realities of childlessness, political dislocation due to immigration, and shifts in available or eligible marriage partners.

Since the ancient Near East is not a living culture, much of the data for this type of analysis has to come from textual and artifactual evidence. However, careful use of analogous data from the study of preindustrial cultures in the Middle East as well as modern tribal groups has proven useful. For instance, obligations placed upon daughters to remain virginal prior to marriage and chaste after marriage as well as the obvious social and legal concerns over adultery are found in both the biblical and the ancient Near Eastern law codes, and in the customary practices of Middle Eastern cultures.[45]

The models employed by cultural anthropology also demonstrate that reciprocity appears to be one of the major social forces at work in the ancient and modern Middle East.[46] This social principle appears in the *lex talionis* ("eye for an eye") clauses in ancient law and is a central feature of the determination of personal and household concepts of honor and shame. Thus an honorable household was one in "good standing" with its community, contributing to the economy, arranging marriages, functioning as civic leaders or elders, and providing warriors to defend the village or town. Honor is therefore defined in this model by the wise person (both male and female),[47] who recognizes proper behavior and understands the implications of every social action. For example, the offering of hospitality does two important things. First, it transforms a potential enemy from a stranger into a guest and therefore nullifies, temporarily, any threat to the safety of the household. Second, playing the host garners honor for the household because it contributes to the welfare of the entire community and places an obligation on the guest to reciprocate when the opportunity arises. This sense of mutual obligation is also found in the laws providing for the "protected classes" (widows, orphans, strangers), and in the conventions of political patronage and clientage.[48]

With regard to gender studies approaches to the biblical text, among the most influential have been by Carol Meyers and Phyllis Trible. Meyers, a field archaeologist, applies the principles of ethnoarchaeology as well as economic models to demonstrate that in the labor-intensive village culture, the small population relied upon the contributions of every person, male or female.[49] She notes that women worked hard, both in the fields as well as child-bearers and managers of the household's resources. They might not have the right to own land or serve in the assembly of elders, but their control over the domestic economy would have given them status within the household. Meyers has also studied female participation in the cult, especially their role in musical performance and celebratory activities.[50]

As a literary critic and feminist scholar, Trible has attempted to break down stereotypical images of women in the ancient world and provide a more realistic evaluation of Israelite restrictions on their behavior. This ideological approach, coupled with the methods of rhetorical criticism, examines dialogue, social status, social identity, as well as the creating of a set of social categories for the characters in the biblical text.[51] In her study of metaphors, she elicits the connotations attached to God as "father," "mother," "king," and "warrior." In this way, the theological dimensions of the text are coupled with its social context through the telling of stories.[52] Her approach has sparked many recent studies that attempt to draw out the importance of both gender roles and the social status of the female in ancient Israel.[53]

Prophetic figures and prophetic activity comprise yet another major area of study of Israelite social institutions. Building on the "ideal type" described by Weber, Robert R. Wilson described prophets as "intermediary figures" and discussed the social forces that required their intermediation.[54] He pointed to central or establishment prophets, who relied upon the cultic community and the monarchy for support or recognition (Isaiah, for example), and to "peripheral" prophets such as Elijah and Elisha whose "support group" was drawn from the marginalized classes of society.[55] While, on the whole, this has been a useful foundation for the study of prophetic activity,[56] Herion has criticized Wilson's over-emphasis on the group orientation of prophetic figures as too limiting. He notes that Wilson starts with the assumption "that there are no socially isolated intermediaries" and then concludes his reconstruction by stating that "there indeed were no socially isolated prophets."[57] This approach forces the prophet into the ideological mold of his/her interest group without allowing for any autonomous expression of viewpoint or social context.[58]

Building upon Wilson's use of comparative materials,[59] Thomas Overholt has employed Native American religious traditions to create a social psychological approach to the biblical prophets. He has done comparative research using historical and ethnographic studies of the "Ghost Dance of 1890" and of shamanism among various tribal groups.[60] In his study of shamans, "spirit mediums," and diviners, he points to community belief systems in the supernatural as the key to understanding prophetic authority and power. These practitioners take their cue from crisis within the community and shape their message based, at least in part, on feedback from the community they serve.[61] This may include trance-state or ecstatic performance, acting out traditional gestures or pantomime, or reciting sections of sacred writ or story as forms of social reassurance or direction. Realizing the dangers inherent to the comparative approach, Overholt emphasizes that "the most successful cross-cultural comparisons will likely be those couched in terms of social patterns or structures."[62] This more concrete set of data provides a necessary check on interpretation and also requires the investigator to very carefully examine the validity of comparisons being made between ancient and modern cultures.

The Layering of the Text

Since I have been involved with archaeological investigations over the last several years, I have become more acquainted with the concept of thinking in terms of stratification of artifactual remains within a tell or settlement. With this in mind, I would suggest that we, as biblical scholars, need to acknowledge that the Bible is a cultural artifact and that it must be analyzed within its social context. What I would advocate is the development of a form of cultural consciousness by biblical scholars. This would sensitize them to the layers of cultural meaning, understanding, and intent that are embedded in every text. This layering effect has a dual character. First, the repeated editing of the material over centuries as the canonical text was developed determined the way in which stories were told and how information was eventually shaped to fit the political and religious agendas of editors from different eras.

Literary critics from J. Wellhausen onward have provided maps, guidebooks, and charts that attempt to identify these layers. This is an important task, but it is one that cannot be complete until the other form of layering is identified and taken into account. What I am referring to is the cultural layering that provides social signposts in the text. These layers are reflections of how the original audience identified with and reacted to the narrative based on culturally defined norms, values, and language. In this way, the researcher can attempt to reconstruct the emic or "insider" viewpoint.[63] Of course, ancient Israelite culture no longer exists and its members cannot be observed or interviewed to obtain first-hand information. As a result, reconstruction of the emic viewpoint becomes a matter of interpretation (in fact, an etic = "outsider" or observer process) and is subject to the degree of objectivity that the researcher can apply to the text and to archaeological data.

In order for the outsider to reproduce an emic perspective from the artifactual remains of an extinct culture, a very careful examination and description of social signifiers is necessary. The etic interpreter may attempt to make comparative claims about apparent cultural acts and "redescribe" them based on a sort of universal cultural scale. What I hope to demonstrate is that even though we cannot fully understand the ancient Israelite emic perspective on beliefs and actions, there is still a possibility of deriving insights into what the "insiders" can tell us about their world. However, we must be careful in this process not to fall into the trap of simply becoming "passive documenters of indigenous claims."[64] In fact, the biblical writers seldom explain everyday acts or behaviors. These are so much a part of who they are that to explain them would be redundant to their audience. By "unpacking" the text and trying to discover the emic meaning behind what the writer considered "common knowledge," the modern researcher may be able to recreate the emic perspective implicit in the text.

However, it must be recognized that social signifiers change over time and it is only through the identification of these changes that the social scientist can trace the cultural evolution evident in the text. It will be the task of the remainder of this paper to provide a preliminary model for identifying the cultural layering of the biblical text, and to present one means of reconstructing emic structures embedded in the received text.

Spatiality

In a recent article,[65] Jon Berquist presented a case for the use of spatiality theory as one basis for understanding not only how space is utilized in the ancient world, but also how it is defined, recognized, and how it relates to other space(s). It is his contention, and I would agree, that space, once it has become culturally defined, further defines those who utilize or interact with it. Thus, for example, the entrance to a temple marks the transition point in space between the sacred and secular world. Someone who stands in that strategic space and gives a speech (such as Jeremiah in chapter 7 and 26) obtains an enhanced social definition in distinction to that same person standing in the middle of an empty field and making the same speech. The cultural ambiance of the temple threshold, while neither fully sacred nor fully secular—and thus a liminal or culturally ambivalent location— transforms the person who stands there and his or her words into someone and something of heightened importance. In the case of Jeremiah, it increased the extent to which he was perceived to be a threat to the temple authorities and required them to take drastic action in order to silence him. His use or usurpation of what they considered to be their "private space" or "sphere of authority" threatened them.[66]

Drawing on this concept, let us now consider the city gate of a walled settlement. Here are some of the ways in which it can be defined as space:

- A city gate is an opening in a uniformly closed space.
- The gate is a line of demarcation between the "safe" or "familiar" world and the "dangerous" or "foreign" outside world (Judg 9:35-40; Prov 18:10).

• It functions as an element in the city's defense system (Josh 2:5; 2 Sam 11:23).

• It is a social determinant of free citizen status (those who may go in and out).[67]

• It provides a setting for business and legal transactions derived from its function as a main thoroughfare and its social definition as an assembly point for the elders.[68]

• Having the right to "sit in the gate" provides social layering: a nondescript human is augmented to the status of a free citizen or resident alien, leading to an established identity as an elder or respected businessman.

The social function of this defined space can then be determined by the way in which the city gate is embedded into the biblical narrative:

• Lot sits in the gate at Sodom (Gen 19:1). In this way the biblical writer indicates Lot's social status and thus identifies him as an accepted member of the community/a resident alien, who has been granted the right to conduct business in a space recognized by the community as suitable for business transaction. The heavy traffic pattern, visibility of either personal presence or wares, and ancillary activities (military presence and legal activities) further defines this space as desirable to the businessman.

• Boaz calls on village elders to gather at the city gate to witness the testimony of Naomi's levir (Ruth 4:1-2). Boaz had come to the gate because it was a space recognized and accepted by the people as a meeting place. His chances of catching the levir as he went out to the fields is increased and there does not seem to be any problem in pulling together a group of ten elders to hear the case (see Prov 31:23). The subsequent drama illustrates the symbolic power attached to the gate area and the manner in which it contributes to the solemnity of the proceedings.

• The rebellious son is brought before the elders at the city gate. His parents testify against him and the citizens stone him (Deut 21:18-21). Legal procedures require a defined space that the community has identified as being communal, thus symbolic of their collective presence and authority to act in the protection of their lives in that place. Just as the gate area has advantages for businessmen, it literally provides the space necessary for a public gathering. However, for it to function as a place of justice, it must become socially acceptable. The convenience of a high traffic area to gather witnesses and elders may serve as a factor in this identification, but this is coupled with the security function of the gate as a defensive installation, and with its association with freedom and citizenship.

• Jeremiah stages an execration ritual at the "entry of the Potsherd Gate" in Jerusalem (Jer 19). Like the episode of the rebellious son mentioned above and the story of the suspected virgin in Deuteronomy 22:13-22, Jeremiah casts judgment in a place most intimately associated with the crime committed. The rebellious son had harmed the entire community by his refusal to obey the command to "honor your father and your mother" (Ex 20:12). Thus his execution in the space identified by the people as symbolic of their unity, strength, and prosperity was appropriate since his actions jeopardized all of these qualities. The young woman whose virginity was proven to be a fraud is stoned to death in her father's doorway. His household had been shamed by her actions and by the actions of her father who allowed the marriage contract to be concluded. His doorway symbolized the integrity and the fertility of his household and her execution publicly demonstrates the failure of that household to manage its affairs and uphold the honor of the entire community. Jeremiah's condemnation of the people of Jerusalem is made in a place associated with their idolatrous practices.[69] The blood of sacrificed children and the devotion of the people of Jerusalem to Baal worship was most evident in this place.[70] Thus their inappropriate use of space given to the Israelites by Yahweh required a gesture that both signaled an end to divine patience and was recognizable as a form of cursing in the ancient Near East.[71]

Future Directions for Social Science Criticism

As is clear from the foregoing review, the field of social scientific criticism does not rely on a single approach or method. Like cultural anthropology, from which it draws many of its theories and much of its comparative data, the social scientific approach to the biblical text is eclectic. It includes an understanding and appreciation for the various theoretical approaches that have been formulated since the mid-nineteenth century, but it also has a healthy recognition of the contradictions that are apparent between the ideals that societies put forward as their norms and the realities of individual variations. Humans may be governed or shaped by their social environment, but that does not mean that they always follow the rules or are never working to effect social change through nontraditional means.

Having said this, it must also be understood that biblical scholars are not anthropologists. They may use the tools of other academic fields, but they must also recognize that they are generally a step removed from the cutting edge of critical inquiry in those fields. This can be the basis for discrediting the social science approach by some biblical scholars who are either unfamiliar with the theoretical underpinning being used or who feel their belief in the uniqueness of Israelite culture is being threatened or "deconstructed." As a result, it is imperative that biblical scholars who choose to use social science approaches carefully define their approach and explain what they hope to achieve with their chosen theories and models.[72] A discipline that hides behind jargon or becomes a form of academic "gnosticism" will never attract general recognition or acceptance of these interpretations.

It seems likely that future efforts in reconstructing the social world of ancient Israel will continue to apply a variety of methods. Structural-functional approaches will continue to be coupled with ideological and ethnoarchaeological data. However, an over-emphasis on any one approach, whether it is determinative, relativistic, reductionistic, or positivistic, will be subject to criticism and reexamination. Without careful self-examination and a willingness to rethink what has been previously assumed to be paradigms of interpretation, the field cannot change as new data or theories emerge.

What may insure the continuation and the growing acceptance of this approach will be closer cooperation between scholarly communities. It is clear from the paper titles at the annual meetings of the Society of Biblical Literature and the American Schools of Oriental Research that a growing synthesis is occurring. Instead of "dig reports," scholars are speculating on the anthropological implications of the social horizon of the ancient Near East as represented by artifactual discoveries. Any vision of ancient settlements or demographics thus becomes a part of a larger social milieu. Biblical texts are being reinterpreted based on sociological principles that add new dimensions to our understanding of the world in which the stories were composed and edited. This greater sensitivity to the "cultural grid," a holistic understanding of symbol, ritual, custom, expectation, and behavior as related in the text and evidenced by artifactual remains, holds great promise for future biblical study.

Notes

[1]See Charles E. Carter, "A Discipline in Transition: The Contributions of the Social Sciences to the Study of the Hebrew Bible," in *Community, Identity, and Ideology: Social Science Approaches to the Hebrew Bible*, ed. C. E. Carter and Carol L. Meyers (Winona Lake, Ind: Eisenbrauns, 1996), 5-8.

[2]See W. Robertson Smith, *Kinship and Marriage in Early Arabia* (Cambridge: Cambridge University Press, 1885), and *Lectures on the Religion of the Semites: First Series, the Fundamental Institutions*, 2nd ed. (London: Black, 1894).

[3]See Smith's article on sacrifice reprinted in C. E. Carter and Carol L. Meyers, eds., *Community, Identity, and Ideology*, 43-64.

[4]See the analysis of Smith's theories in Thomas Beidelman, *W. Robertson Smith and the Sociological Study of Religion* (Chicago: University of Chicago Press, 1974).

[5]See Louis Wallis, "Sociological Significance of the Bible," *American Journal of Sociology* (1907): 532-52, and *Sociological Study of the Bible* (Chicago: University of Chicago Press, 1912).

[6]Andrew D. H. Mayes, "Sociology and the Old Testament," in *The World of Ancient Israel: Sociological, Anthropological and Political Perspectives*, ed. Ronald E. Clements (Cambridge: Cambridge University Press, 1989), 43-46.

[7]See Andrew D. H. Mayes, *The Old Testament in Sociological Perspective* (London: Marshall Pickering, 1989), 36-43.

[8]Max Weber, *Ancient Judaism* (Glencoe, Ill.: Free Press, 1952). For helpful excerpts of this volume, see C. E. Carter and Carol L. Meyers, eds., *Community, Identity, and Ideology*, 65-94, esp. 70-72, 80.

[9]Antonin Causse, "Du groupe ethnique à la communauté religieuse. Le problème sociologique du judaïsme," *Revue d'histoire et de philosophie religieuses* 14 (1934): 285-335, and *Du groupe ethnique à la communauté religieuse: Le problème sociologique de la religion d'Israël* (Etudes d'histoire et de philosophie religieuses 33; Paris: Alcan, 1937).

[10]Roland de Vaux, *Ancient Israel, Volume 1: Social Institutions. Volume 2: Religious Institutions* (New York: McGraw Hill, 1965).

[11]Among his influential works are *Archaeology and the Religion of Israel*, 2nd ed. (Baltimore: Johns Hopkins University Press, 1946), and *From the Stone Age to Christianity: Monotheism and the Historical Process* (Garden City, N.Y.: Doubleday, 1957).

[12]Paula McNutt, *Reconstructing the Society of Ancient Israel* (Louisville: Westminster/John Knox, 1999), 11-14.

[13]It is impossible to mention all of the groups that have chosen to systematically employ social science methods in biblical research. Among the most influential, however, are the "Constructs of the Social and Cultural World of Antiquity Group," headed by James Flanagan, and the "Social World of Ancient Israel Consultation" (later known as the "Social Science and the Interpretation of the Hebrew Scriptures"

section), both of which met annually at the Society of Biblical Literature convention. The latter group, originally founded by Norman Gottwald and Frank Frick in 1975, was complemented by the "Sociology of Monarchy Seminar." This program unit was co-chaired by James Flanagan and Frank Frick, and produced most of the volumes in the Almond Social World of Ancient History Series. Each of these sections have provided a forum for social scientific research and have featured presentations by most of the scholars who work in that area of biblical studies.

[14]Since I am concentrating primarily on Hebrew Bible in this survey, I will only mention here the contributions of Bruce Malina, Jerome Neyrey, and the New Testament Context Group that has met at the Westar Institute, Catholic Biblical Association, and Society of Biblical Literature annual meetings for the last decade. Among the contributions they have made is a collected volume, *The Social World of Luke-Acts: Models for Interpretation*, ed. J. H. Neyrey (Peabody, Mass.: Hendrickson Publishers, 1991).

[15]See the cautionary article on this approach by Shemaryahu Talmon, "The Comparative Method in Biblical Interpretation: Principles and Problems," *SuppVT* 29 (1978): 320-56. For an example of the comparative approach, see David Fiensy, "Using the Nuer Culture of Africa in Understanding the Old Testament: An Evaluation," *JSOT* 38 (1987): 73-83.

[16]See Mary Douglas's study of defilement in the Levitical law as chronicled in *Purity and Danger: An Analysis of the Concepts of Pollution and Taboo* (London: Routledge & Kegan Paul, 1966), 41-57.

[17]For a general discussion of this method, see Gerhard Lenski and Jean Lenski, *Human Societies: An Introduction to Macrosociology*, 5th ed. (New York: McGraw Hill, 1987), 27-51.

[18]See the survey of methods in Cyril S. Rodd, "On Applying a Sociological Theory to Biblical Studies," *JSOT* 19 (1981): 95-106.

[19]Functionalist theory has its foundations in the work of Emile Durkheim and Alfred R. Radcliffe-Brown. Among their studies are Durkheim's *The Elementary Forms of Religious Life* (New York: Free Press, 1954 [1915 reprint and translation]), and Radcliffe-Brown's *Structure and Function in Primitive Society* (New York: Free Press, 1952). See also Paula McNutt, *Reconstructing the Society of Ancient Israel*, 20-21, for a recent synthesis of these approaches.

[20]Steven T. Kimbrough, *Israelite Religion in Sociological Perspective: The Work of Antonin Causse* (Wiesbaden: Harrassowitz, 1978). See also A. D. H. Mayes, *Old Testament in Sociological Perspective*, 105-13, for a summary of the literature.

[21]A. D. H. Mayes, *The Old Testament in Sociological Perspective*, 18-23. See also Randall Collins, *Three Sociological Traditions* (New York: Oxford University Press, 1985), 47.

[22]Bruce Malina, "The Social Sciences and Biblical Interpretation," *Interpretation* 37 (1982): 233-35.

[23]Gerhard Lenski and Jean Lenski, *Human Societies*, 78-82.

[24]See Marvin Harris, *Cultural Materialism: The Struggle for a Science of*

Culture (New York: Random House, 1979), 56-58, for a discussion of "infrastructual determinism." Harris notes that "the need to eat is constant, but the quantities and kinds of foods that can be eaten vary in conformity with technology and habitat" (p. 58).

[25]See the argument made by David Hopkins that a mixed economy is necessary for the cultures in the environmentally marginal regions of the Near East in "Life on the Land: The Subsistence Struggles of Early Israel," *BA* 50 (1987): 178-91.

[26]See Victor H. Matthews, *Pastoral Nomadism in the Mari Kingdom ca. 1830-1760 B.C.* (Cambridge, Mass.: ASOR, 1978), 85-86, and Philip C. Salzman, "Multi-Resource Nomadism in Iranian Baluchistan," in *Perspectives on Nomadism*, ed. William Irons and Neville Dyson-Hudson (Leiden: Brill, 1972), 63-66.

[27]Gottwald traced the use to sociological models in "Sociological Method in the Study of Ancient Israel," in *Encounter with the Text: Form and History in the Hebrew Bible*, ed. Martin J. Buss (Missoula, Mont.: Scholars Press, 1979), 69-81. In "Sociology (Ancient Israel)," *Anchor Bible Dictionary*, VI, ed. David N. Freedman (New York: Doubleday, 1992), 82-87, he lays out his cultural materialist view on the development of Israel from the "tribal" period to what he calls "colonial Israel: a slave-based mode of production" during the Roman occupation.

[28]See the very helpful article by Gary Herion, cautioning biblical scholars about the dangers of limiting themselves to either a determinist, reductionist, relativist, or positivist approach to the text, "The Impact of Modern and Social Science Assumptions on the Reconstruction of Israelite History," *JSOT* 34 (1986): 3-33.

[29]William G. Dever, "Impact of the 'New Archaeology,'" in *Benchmarks in Time and Culture: An Introduction to Palestinian Archeology*, ed. Joel F. Drinkard et al. (Atlanta: Scholars Press, 1988), 337-52. Dever sees this as a major paradigm shift, moving away from the Albrightian emphasis on proving the authenticity of the biblical account and attempting to take a broader view of the evidence by "employing models drawn from anthropology, sociology, and the history of religions" (p. 345).

[30]An excellent example of this trend is Lawrence E. Stager, "The Archaeology of the Family," *BASOR* 260 (1985): 1-35.

[31]George E. Mendenhall, "The Hebrew Conquest of Palestine," *Biblical Archeology* 25 (1962): 66-87.

[32]Martin Noth, *The History of Israel*, 2nd ed (New York: Harper & Row, 1960), 88-97.

[33]Albrecht Alt, *Der Gott der Vater: Ein Beitrag zur Vorgeschichte der israelitischen Religion* (Stuttgart: Kohlhammer, 1929).

[34]Marvin L. Chaney provides an excellent overview of the literature and the assumptions of the three models of the settlement and conquest period that emerged from Mendenhall's and Gottwald's works. See "Ancient Palestinian Peasant Movements and the Formation of Premonarchic Israel," in *Palestine in Transition: The Emergence of Ancient Israel*, ed. David N. Freedman and David F. Graf (Sheffield: Almond Press, 1983), 39-90.

[35]G. E. Mendenhall, *The Tenth Generation: The Origins of Biblical Tradition* (Baltimore: Johns Hopkins University Press, 1973).

[36]Norman K. Gottwald, *The Tribes of Yahweh: A Sociology of the Religion of Liberated Israel, 1250-1050 B.C.E.* (Maryknoll, N.Y.: Orbis Books, 1979), 210-33, and n. 148, 736-37.

[37]Gary Herion, "The Impact of Modern and Social Science Assumptions on the Reconstruction of Israelite History," *JSOT* 34 (1986): 3-33, and Jack Sasson, "On Choosing Models for Recreating Israelite Pre-Monarchic History," *JSOT* 21 (1981): 3-24.

[38]Gerhard Lenski, "Review: N. K. Gottwald, *The Tribes of Yahweh*," *Religious Studies Review* 6, no. 4 (1980): 275-78. This criticism of Gottwald's reconstruction is also leveled by Marvin Chaney, "Ancient Palestinian Peasant Movements and the Formation of Pre-monarchic Israel," in *Palestine in Transition: The Emergence of Ancient Israel*, ed. D. N. Freedman and D. F. Graf (Sheffield: Almond Press, 1983), 39-90.

[39]Frank S. Frick, *The Formation of the State in Ancient Israel* (Sheffield: Almond Press, 1985), 71-97.

[40]For a summary of some of the most recent finds, see Israel Finkelstein, *The Archaeology of the Israelite Settlement* (Jerusalem: Israel Exploration Society, 1988), and I. Finkelstein and Nadav Na'aman, eds., *From Nomadism to Monarchy: Archaeological and Historical Aspects of Early Israel* (Jerusalem: Israel Exploration Society, 1994). There have been a large number of studies published within the last few years arguing over the historicity of the biblical materials and the relevance of archaeological data to a reconstruction of Israel's history. Those taking a minimalist view include Philip Davies, *In Search of "Ancient Israel"* (JSOTSup 148; Sheffield: Sheffield Academic Press, 1995); Keith Whitelam, *The Invention of Ancient Israel: The Silencing of Palestinian History* (New York: Routledge & Kegan Paul, 1996); and Niels P. Lemche, *Ancient Israel: A New History of Israelite Society* (Sheffield: JSOT Press, 1988). William G. Dever has published a series of articles refuting this position, including: "Unresolved Issues in the Early History of Israel: Toward a Synthesis of Archaeological and Textual Reconstruction," in *The Bible and the Politics of Exegesis*, ed. David Jobling et al. (Cleveland: Pilgrim Press, 1991), 195-208, and "Revisionist Israel Revisited: A Rejoinder to Niels Peter Lemche," *Currents in Research: Biblical Studies* 4 (1996): 35-50.

[41]Lawrence E. Stager, "The Archaeology of the Family," *BASOR* 260 (1985): 1-35. See also I. Finkelstein, "The Emergence of the Monarchy in Israel: The Environmental and Socio-Economic Aspects," *JSOT* 44 (1989): 43-74.

[42]David C. Hopkins, *The Highlands of Canaan: Agricultural Life in the Early Iron Age* (Sheffield: Almond Press, 1985).

[43]Claude Lévi-Strauss, *The Elementary Structures of Kinship* (Boston: Beacon Press, 1969). For a more recent treatment of kinship in the Middle East, see Ladislav Holy, *Kinship, Honour and Solidarity: Cousin Marriage in the Middle East* (Manchester: Manchester University Press, 1989).

[44]See, for example, Abraham Malamat, "Tribal Societies: Biblical Genealogies and African Lineage Systems," *Archives européens de sociologie* 14 (1973): 126-36; Martha E. Donalson, "Kinship Theory in the Patriarchal Narratives: The Case of the Barren Wife," *JAAR* 49 (1981): 77-87; and Naomi Steinberg, *Kinship and*

Marriage in Genesis: A Household Economics Perspective (Minneapolis: Fortress Press, 1993).

[45]See Victor H. Matthews, "Honor and Shame in Gender-Related Legal Situations in the Hebrew Bible," in *Gender and Law in the Hebrew Bible and the Ancient Near East*, ed. V.H. Matthews et al. (JSOTSup 262; Sheffield: Sheffield Academic Press, 1998), 97-112.

[46]Victor H. Matthews and Don C. Benjamin, *The Social World of Ancient Israel* (Peabody, Mass.: Hendrickson, 1993), 121-22. See also V. H. Matthews, "The Unwanted Gift," *Semeia* 87 (2001): 91-104.

[47]V. H. Matthews, "Female Voices: Upholding the Honor of the Household," *BTB* 24 (1994): 8-15.

[48]See V. H. Matthews and D. C. Benjamin, *The Social World of Ancient Israel*, 82-87, and V. H. Matthews, "Hospitality and Hostility in Judges 4," *BTB* 21 (1991): 13-21.

[49]Carol L. Meyers, "Procreation, Production, and Protection: Male-Female Balance in Early Israel," *JAAR* 51 (1983): 570-74. Also see her monograph *Discovering Eve: Ancient Israelite Women in Context* (New York: Oxford University Press, 1988), 37-45.

[50]C. L. Meyers, "Of Drums and Damsels: Women's Performance in Ancient Israel," *BA* 54 (1991): 16-27. She has also explored aspects of women and sacrifice in "The Hannah Narrative in Feminist Perspective," in *Go to the Land I Will Show You: Studies in Honor of Dwight W. Young*, ed. Joseph Coleson and V. H. Matthews (Winona Lake, Ind.: Eisenbrauns, 1996), 117-26. Phyllis Bird also employs modern ethnographic studies in her influential essay on "The Place of Women in the Israelite Cultus," in *Ancient Israelite Religion: Essays in Honor of Frank Moore Cross*, ed. Patrick D. Miller et al. (Philadelphia: Fortress Press, 1987), 397-419.

[51]Phyllis Trible, *God and the Rhetoric of Sexuality* (Philadelphia: Fortress Press, 1978).

[52]Phyllis Trible, *Texts of Terror: Literary-Feminist Readings of Biblical Narratives* (Philadelphia: Fortress Press, 1984).

[53]See the series of volumes edited by Athalya Brenner as "Feminist Companions to the Bible" (Sheffield Academic Press), as well as the collection of articles in Alice Bach, ed., *Women in the Hebrew Bible: A Reader* (New York: Routledge, 1999) and Carol L. Meyers, ed., *Women in Scripture:A Dictionary of Named and Unnamed Women in the Hebrew Bible, the Apocryphal/Deuterocanonical Books, and the New Testament* (Boston: Houghton Mifflin, 2000).

[54]Robert R. Wilson, *Prophecy and Society in Ancient Israel* (Philadelphia: Fortress Press, 1980), 27-88. Wilson is influenced by the central and peripheral intermediation models found in Ioan M. Lewis, *Ecstatic Religion: An Anthropological Study of Spirit Possession and Shamanism* (Baltimore: Penguin Books, 1971). See A. D. H. Mayes, *The Old Testament in Sociological Perspective* (1989), 116-17, for an examination of Wilson's view as a functionalist approach.

[55]Robert R. Wilson, *Prophecy and Society in Ancient Israel*, 38-39, 72-73. See Thomas Overholt, *Prophecy in Cross-Cultural Perspective: A Sourcebook for*

Biblical Researchers (Atlanta: Scholars Press, 1986), 12-19, for a discussion of the "support group" as both an "enabling" and "constraining . . . force in the intermediary's performance level."

[56]See David L. Petersen, *The Roles of Israel's Prophets* (JSOTSup 17; Sheffield: Sheffield Academic Press, 1981), 51-60, for a discussion of the forces leading to the emergence of central and peripheral prophetic figures. In a more recent study, Tamis H. Renteria, "The Elijah/Elisha Stories: A Socio-cultural Analysis of Prophets and People in Ninth-Century B.C.E. Israel," in *Elijah and Elisha in Socioliterary Perspective*, ed. Robert B. Coote (Atlanta: Scholars Press, 1992), 75-126, also draws on Wilson's approach.

[57]G. Herion, "The Impact of Modern and Social Science Assumptions," (1986), 11.

[58]Ibid., 10-14.

[59]Robert R. Wilson, "Prophecy and Ecstasy: A Reexamination," *JBL* 98 (1979): 321-37. Overholt's summary of Wilson's arguments and his own justification for using anthropological studies as a means of adding precision to the use of terminology and fuller understanding of trance state is found in *Prophecy in Cross-Cultural Perspective*, 333-40. See also Overholt's *Cultural Anthropology and the Old Testament* (Minneapolis: Fortress Press, 1996), 13-17.

[60]T. W. Overholt, *Channels of Prophecy: The Social Dynamics of Prophetic Activity* (Minneapolis: Fortress Press, 1989), 27-51, 102-109.

[61]T. W. Overholt, *Cultural Anthropology and the Old Testament*, 34-36. See also I. M. Lewis, *Religion in Context: Cults and Charisma* (Cambridge: Cambridge University Press, 1986), 88, for the use of "out of body" experiences and other means of controlling the spirits by shamans.

[62]T. W. Overholt. *Prophecy in Cross-Cultural Perspective*, 5.

[63]Kenneth L. Pike first formulated the emic/etic viewpoints in *Language in Relation to a Unified Theory of the Structure of Human Behavior*, 2nd ed. (The Hague: Mouton, 1967). See the re-examination of emic (insider) and etic (outsider) analysis in Marvin Harris, *Cultural Materialism*, 32-41, and his contention that etic structures cannot, as Pike asserts, provide "steppingstones" to emic structures. Instead the researcher should "describe both [emics and etics] and, if possible, explain one in terms of the other" (p. 36).

[64]Russell T. McCutcheon, "Introduction," *The Insider/Outsider Problem in the Study of Religion: A Reader* (London: Cassell, 1999), 17-18. See also Marvin Harris's warning about collecting emic data in *Cultural Materialism*, 37.

[65]Jon Berquist, "Theories of Space and Construction of the Ancient World," presented to the Constructs of the Social and Cultural Worlds of Antiquity Group, AAR/SBL Annual Meeting, November 20, 1999, and on the web at http://www.cwru.edu/affil/GAIR/papers/99papers/jberquist.html. Berquist's model draws on the work of James Flanagan, including a forthcoming article in *Semeia*, "Ancient Perceptions of Space/ Perceptions of Ancient Space."

[66]This situation fits Bruce Lincoln's discussion of instances in which "authority" is caught "in moments of revealing disarray, where one can see how it responds to

challenge," *Authority: Construction and Corrosion* (Chicago: University of Chicago Press, 1994), 74-89.

[67]Ephraim A. Speiser, " 'Coming' and 'Going' at the City Gate," *BASOR* 144 (1956): 20-23. See the amplification of this article in Geoffrey Evans, " 'Coming' and 'Going' at the City Gate—a Discussion of Professor Speiser's Paper," *BASOR* 150 (1958): 33.

[68]V. H. Matthews, "Entrance Ways and Threshing Floors: Legally Significant Sites in the Ancient Near East," *Fides et Historia* 19 (1987): 25-29. See also Donald A. McKenzie, "Judicial Procedure at the Town Gate," *VT* 14 (1964): 100-104, and Georg P. F. Van Den Boorn, "*Wd'-ryt* and Justice in the Gate," *JNES* 44 (1985): 10.

[69]See 2 Chronicles 28:3 and 33:6 and Jeremiah 32:45 for other examples of idol worship and the sacrifice to Baal in the Valley of Hinnom.

[70]Compare this to Moses' smashing of the tablets of the law at the foot of the golden calf in Exodus 32:19.

[71]See the similar expression in Psalm 2:9. The Egyptian execration texts, while dating to the early second millennium B.C.E., may be part of a more general method of cursing one's enemies through a symbolic act. On this, see William L. Holladay, *Jeremiah 1-25: A Commentary on the Book of the Prophet Jeremiah* (Philadelphia: Fortress, 1986), 541, and James M. Weinstein, "Egyptian Relations with Palestine in the Middle Kingdom," *BASOR* 217 (1975): 12-13.

[72]See Bruce Malina, "The Social Sciences and Biblical Interpretation," *Interpretation* 37 (1982): 229-42.

The Value of the Social Scientific Approach to the Bible

A Response to Victor H. Matthews

Carol J. Dempsey, O.P.

The social scientific approach to the Bible has indeed made a significant contribution to the field of biblical studies as outlined by Victor Matthews in his article "Traversing the Social Landscape: The Value of the Social Scientific Approach to the Bible." Hermeneutically, though, this approach, like others, needs to be held up for further scrutiny. As a response to Matthews's presentation, my comments focus on three areas: (1) the development of social scientific criticism and its contributions to the biblical enterprise; (2) the topic of spatiality; and (3) future directions for social scientific criticism.

In the opening sections of his essay, Matthews clearly states the aim of social scientific criticism, namely, "to study the biblical materials as a reflection of their cultural setting." As a colleague of Matthews in the area of biblical studies, I would argue that the information gleaned from social scientific research is necessary if one wishes to understand something of the attitudes, mindsets, and cultural mores that were part of the shaping of the biblical text as we have it today in its received canonical form. Furthermore, I would agree with the comment that "such information more fully illumines the text," but I would disagree with such information as helping to establish "the meaning of the text," because, in my opinion, one can never establish the meaning of the text once and for all. The biblical text flows from a living tradition and takes on a life of its own in relation to the various communities that hear it, read it, and re-read it. I agree with Matthews's assertions that biblical scholars need to acknowledge that the Bible is a cultural artifact and needs to be understood within its social context. I also agree with Matthews that biblical scholars do need a form of "cultural consciousness" when dealing with the biblical text. However, I would argue that the Bible must never become merely a cultural or historical artifact or a window into the past whose cultural, social, and religious ideologies and attitudes become authoritatively normative for today, without ongoing reflection and critique. As I stressed previously, the biblical text is organic, and the biblical tradition is a living tradition. Culture has shaped the text and the text has the potential for informing and shaping culture today. There needs to be a healthy tension in the midst of the dialectic, and ongoing honest critiques of the Bible and culture and tradition, both past and present. Social scientific criticism helps to lay part of a foundation for such a critique and, when viewed as one method of inquiry among many, as Matthews states so cogently at the end of his paper, social scientific criticism opens the door for further conversation.

As Matthews points out, the development of social scientific criticism has been a long and rich evolutionary process that has by no means reached its end or climax. With new technologies and new data come new information, new insights, and new understandings of both past and present cultural situations and realities. Thus, I would agree with Matthews that social scientific methods pose a challenge to biblical scholars, first, because of the sheer wealth of material being unearthed; second, because of the different approaches to social scientific criticism as one of several biblical methods of inquiry; and third, because of the many other biblical methods and hermeneutical approaches to the biblical text that both affirm and challenge the work of social scientific critics or, in some instances, dismiss it altogether for one reason or another.

Perhaps the most intriguing section of Matthews's article is the discussion on spatiality in which he makes three points: 1) culture defines space; 2) space then defines how people use that space; and 3) people further define space, and space then has the potential for transforming people and redefining them. Take the city gate, for example. Matthews clearly points out that while the city gate is nothing more than "an opening in a uniformly closed space," it becomes a symbol and soon begins to provide a variety of functions on the militaristic, social, economic, and judicial levels. Most important, as Matthews so accurately observes, "the right to 'sit in the gate' provides a social layering: a nondescript human is augmented to the status of a free citizen or resident alien, leading to an established identity as an elder or respected businessman." A contemporary example could be the New York Stock Exchange. It is a place of trade and commerce where an ordinary nondescript human could change from a stock clerk to a powerful stock broker by purchasing a seat on the exchange. For the one who acquires a "seat," whether at the city gate or at the Stock Exchange, there is a certain rise to power, and usually the one who sits in the gate or at the Stock Exchange has been male, both in biblical times and in the business world.

Thus, space that can transform and redefine a person becomes associated with power, authority, class, status, and gender. In the ancient world, the elders who were all male sat at the city gate. A classic example is Proverbs 31:10-31, which describes a multi-talented, astute woman who hustles and bustles around the house, is adept at buying a field and planting a vineyard, and who has great skills at weaving and sewing, cooking and organizing. And where is the husband? Off taking his "seat" among the elders at the city gate. She has the talent, brawn, ingenuity, skill, and creativity, and yet he has the position of power, authority, and status. Thus, space that transforms and redefines people can lead to exclusivity, inequality, and discrimination, and can foster the reinforcement and proliferation of certain cultural and social attitudes that place power and authority in the hands of a select few who happen to be the right gender, the right class, the right status, and so forth.

Additionally, court cases were tried at the city gates. Legal power, then, rested in those who sat at the city gates, and those who sat at the city gates were, for the most part, males. Thus, legal power rested with the male gender. Today in our social location in the United States, legal power, for the most part, also rests in the hands of males, although culture and opportunities are changing. What Matthews's social scientific study points out is that what existed socially and culturally in biblical times continues to exist and oftentimes dominates contemporary times. Thus, one clearly sees that the biblical text reflects its cultural times, is conditioned by culture, but also has the potential for reinforcing certain social attitudes today that are non-inclusive, discriminatory, and ultimately, unjust.

In Matthews's last section of the paper where he offers future directions for social scientific criticism, his caution against an over-emphasis on any one approach is a wise one, and his call to "rethink what has been previously assumed to be paradigms of interpretation" is laudable. Furthermore, his concluding remark that "greater sensitivity to the 'cultural grid,' a holistic understanding of symbol, ritual, custom, expectation, and behavior as related in text and evidenced by artifactual remains, holds great promise for future biblical study" needs to be taken seriously if biblical scholars and theologians are to grapple with the biblical text in its historical, social, cultural, literary, and religious contexts, past and present, so that it can be used as a touching point for informed theological reflection. Matthews's discussion and use of social scientific criticism as he understands it, and as he employs it as a method among other methods, opens the door to help us see that: 1) the Bible and the biblical tradition reflect ancient social and cultural mores, attitudes, and mindsets, many of which are still operative today, and in need of further dialogue, discernment, and critique especially from an ethical and theological perspective; and 2) though separated by centuries and now another millennium, we as a human community are still grappling with some of the same struggles that involve power, gender, class, and justice, as were our ancient ancestors. What has become "socially," "culturally," "politically," and "religiously" correct and acceptable over time has indeed defined space and people to the point where re-visioning has, at times, become impossible. When we speak of paradigm shifts, we are speaking about major shifts that will alter that which has been deeply embedded in culture.

Finally, Matthews's presentation and his use of social scientific criticism points us to the realization that embedded in the biblical text and tradition and in culture itself are visions and values worth retrieving for the ongoing liberation, redemption, and restoration of all creation. If compassion and reconciliation are to become benchmarks of holiness and signs that the year of the Lord's favor—the jubilee year—has indeed dawned, then all creation needs to be liberated from whatever is oppressive and sinful. Furthermore, culture, space, and people are all in need of transformation if the first earth and the former things are to pass away and the new heavens and the new earth are to blossom forth. This new vision is in our midst and within our grasp. Are we embracing it, and if so, how? And if not, why not?

From Catholic Social Teaching to Catholic Social Tradition

Judith A. Merkle

What is social teaching? The first part of this paper will investigate four partially overlapping views to see what each brings to the identity of social teaching. Some view social teaching as social policy, others as prophecy. A third group emphasizes social teaching as moral doctrine. A fourth refers to social teaching as perennial moral principles to be applied in specific societal situations. Each view brings to social teaching a set of expectations. Each also struggles with attendant disappointments when social teaching does not measure up to the expected task.

The first group views social teaching as the church's social policy suggestions for the modern world. The social policies found in the social encyclicals of the popes from Leo XIII's *Rerum Novarum* to John Paul II's *Centesimus annus* comprise the corpus of what is usually called Catholic social teaching.[1] The encyclicals are seen as "Vatican social theory," providing a "comprehensive program for the Roman Catholic Church concerning the economic and social problems of the modern era."[2]

Critics of this first view charge that social teaching does not reflect a distinctive church social theory but often simply affirms mainstream progressive political platforms. Rather than providing a distinctive church social theory, often social teaching either lacks an adequate social theory or relies on a premodern concept of society for its analysis.[3]

A second view sees social teaching as the prophetic action of the church. The role and task of social teaching is not to provide solutions to global issues of poverty, the environment, and warfare, but to be a voice of criticism calling humankind to the "tranquillity of order" upheld in the church from ancient times.[4] While the prophetic role of the social encyclicals is assumed, this school of thought includes a broader range of literature in prophetic social teaching. The work of Catholic Worker movements, Pax Christi, liberation and political theologians and the like are seen as links to the economic, political, and social specifics necessary for the church's prophetic task. Those who view social teaching as prophetic expect the church as institution to affirm these voices of protest. We hear an echo of this prophetic expectation in the words of Bishop Thomas Gumbleton, who laments its absence in official church proclamation.

> In an age when "crimes against humanity" became almost commonplace, the church seemed strangely silent. The prophetic word was not spoken in Nazi Germany or Hiroshima. At a historic moment when the world needed the clear call of denunciation against horrendous crimes and when individual Christians needed the strong, clear guidance of the teaching church, it was not there.[5]

Critics of this second view doubt the capacity of an institution to adopt a single prophetic stance. When the Bishops' Pastoral on the Economy called for a reform of capitalism, some desired a full condemnation of international capitalism, while others saw this as too simplistic for a global church. Critics of the second view also charge that social teaching must be more than an institutional action. When linked so closely to the institution, social teaching can be mistakenly viewed as mainly an action of the magisterium and less connected to the life of the church as a whole.

A third view emphasizes social teaching as moral doctrine. Social teaching enunciates the social implications of Christian faith in secular society. In this sense, social teaching teases out the implications of faith for social living. It obliges the conscience of the Christian across the same spectrum of obligation as other moral teachings.[6] Social teaching in this sense is not the revealed word of God, such as the Ten Commandments. It is simply the application of Christian teachings and natural ethics to society at a particular moment in history. In this view, social teaching contains both solemn doctrinal teachings, as well as advice, exhortation, and prudential guidance. As historical responses, the social teaching of one period can become outdated.

Usually those who see social teaching as moral doctrine limit their view of social teaching to the social encyclical tradition. However, they are attuned to the variety of language within the encyclicals, distinguishing broad biblical themes from focused reflections of societal analysis, and their subsequent claims on conscience. For example, in its encyclical tradition of the last one hundred years, the church has offered a third way between socialism and capitalism, a way that allows the church to critique the excesses of both systems. While the Christian is left to judge the best means to arrive at the goals of social teaching, the specific ends stated in social teaching oblige in conscience. A Catholic would be obliged to be concerned whether a just wage is given. Whether a minimum wage law is the best means to this goal would be left to individual conscience.

Critics claim that because social teaching encompasses such a broad range of moral language and analysis, it needs to be too generic to be obligatory. It can only exhort and raise social consciousness. It does not offer a parallel sense of obligation to moral teaching in the other areas of Catholic moral thought, such as sexuality and medicine. In this sense, social teaching comes in as a soft second to moral teaching that defines Catholic identity.

So the fourth approach presents social teaching as more general moral principles to be applied in specific societal situations. Social teaching, in this sense, is a guideline for social action. A specific action can be discerned by reliance on the Catholic tradition's view of a just society, which is implicit in social teaching.

Those who share this approach to social teaching take one of two approaches. They either draw on key themes of social teaching, or enunciate social "principles." The American bishops leaned to the first approach in their 1998 pastoral letter on social teaching: "In these brief reflections, we wish to highlight several of the key themes that are at the heart of our Catholic social tradition."[7] The bishops view social teaching as a treasure of wisdom about building a just society and living holy lives in modern society. Social teaching offers both moral principles and coherent values, according to the bishops. However, their use of the term "principle" is general. A principle is a product that emerges as a result of pastoral action for justice.[8]

A second approach to social teaching as moral principle derives these principles from the church's classical definition of a just society as a well-ordered society governed by law.[9] Natural law is the participation of the rational creature in the eternal law. Human reason is capable of reflecting on human nature and arriving at ethical wisdom and knowledge. In this classical approach to ethical wisdom in the Catholic tradition, civil authority has a major role in seeing that society is just. Because of its power, civil authority has the attendant responsibility to see that civil institutions reflect an order of reason for the common good. Civil authority creates human laws, which apply the natural law in changing circumstances.

For those using this approach, social teaching is the enunciation of the principles of natural law for the whole society by the magisterium of the church. Social teaching can be offered to all in society, since it appeals to principles binding on the conscience of all men and women. While the best source of the church's understanding of a just society is in the social encyclical tradition, this teaching goes beyond church boundaries in its import. Those who approach social teaching as perennial moral principles, either in a thematic or classical way, assume that these principles aid consistency in commitment and coherency between belief and practice. Critics of the social principle model would charge that the principle approach, abstracted from the social movements necessary to make values politically effective, ends up as good moral rhetoric but not capable of transforming society.

All except the first view (those interpreting social teaching as social policy) regard social teaching as moral teaching. Each perspective might arrive at this teaching by different means. Some use the inductive strategies of an action-reflection-action theological method and others more classical deductive strategies. Those taking a more inductive approach ground the obligation contained in social teaching in scripture, the tradition of the church, images of the Kingdom of God, and reading the signs of the times. The latter three models also have different interpretations of the level at which social teaching binds on conscience. In due course I will suggest instances where these views relate differently to the social sciences.

Social Teaching and the Life of the Church

No one model of social teaching is sufficient. Social teaching is not simply a listing of principles for social action or strategies for solving policy questions of poverty, discrimination, warfare, and the like across the globe. Social teaching is also more than an action arising from the institutional church. When it is primarily the action of the magisterium or the teaching church, it can be poorly connected to the life of the church as a whole. Lastly, social teaching is not merely the social implications of the faith. Brian Hehir suggests that in the twentieth century the church's social teaching was an effort to provide a systematic, normative theory relating the social vision of the faith to the concrete conditions of the century.[10] Social teaching then is a hybrid of moral doctrine, societal criticism, and social vision. It is a complex act of the church in context.

Because social teaching is an act of the church in context, it carries with it the ambiguities of historical knowledge. Social teaching involves ethical problems whose solutions require information beyond the scope of revelation; thus other forms of knowledge are required, especially the social sciences. The social sciences need not secularize social teaching. The social sciences can serve instead to aid social teaching to assume its place not simply as one social theory among others in the world, but as teaching that comes directly from the heart of ecclesial life.

We do not understand what social teaching is unless we recognize the essential link of social teaching to the life of the church. Social teaching flows from and requires the broader life of the church for its understanding and implementation. Even though social teaching is addressed to the world, many aspects of the church's life are implicit for its full functioning. There has been little serious study of how social teaching is linked to other areas of Catholic belief and practice. For this reason, it is easy for the casual student of social teaching to overlook this essential connection.

There are three ways the connection between social teaching and the life of the church is evidenced. First, social teaching, in the church's social encyclical tradition, has in the last one hundred years changed the image of the public church. Over the years, attention to Catholic social teaching has shifted the image of the church from an institution without a sufficiently explicit social expression of its faith to one that in its pastoral practices, institutions, and programs shows more attention to the social impact of Christianity. While today there is more consensus that the church *has* a public role in social policy formation, there is less on the nature of how social activism is related to the nature of the church and its role in personal faith formation.

Hehir comments on problems associated with this lack. While religion is a strong and growing force in the way Americans think about politics, religious activists are often not noticeably influenced by the positions church leadership takes. This raises the question of what ideas undergird a conception of the public role of the church and how they shape personal conceptions of faith in practice. Implicit in Hehir's comment is a call to make these ties more explicit.[11]

Second, in public policy debates we also meet the limits of the ethical and purely moral argument to address underlying dimensions of public policy disputes and decisions. These debates involve deep issues that are often not pressed or pursued. Questions such as to whom we are responsible and for what we are responsible frame the extent to which a group pursues a solution to a social problem. This type of question relies on pre-moral values formed or not formed in church community. These pre-moral values influence the extent that social teaching is even "heard" or received. The link between social teaching and Christian life is real and needs to be made more immediately conscious to the Catholic community.

A third ramification of the gap between social teaching and its link to other areas of church life is the relationship between social teaching and evangelization. This connection between social involvement and church life is often overlooked in the first-world countries. Paul VI, in his exhortation on evangelization, *Evangelii Nuntiandi* (1975), stresses that evangelization has a social dimension.[12] Human rights, family life, peace, justice, development, and liberation involve social conditions "without which personal growth or development is hardly possible."[13] The person "who is to be evangelized is not an abstract being but is the subject of social and economic questions."[14]

Evangelization in *Evangelii Nuntiandi* refers to the proclamation of Christ to those who do not know him, which involves preaching, catechesis, and conferring baptism and other sacraments.[15] Yet the church seeks to convert both the personal and the communal.[16] In other words, evangelization involves action by the church to upset the criteria of judgement used in a society. In its evangelizing efforts, the church must touch culture and measure whether its points of interest, lines of thought, sources of inspiration, and models of life are in line with the gospel. A culture, however, cannot be penetrated with the gospel without a visible witness of how adherence to Jesus Christ influences how one lives in community.[17] This witness must be grounded in church life: acceptance of the church, participation in the sacraments, and continual investment in the "new state of things" inaugurated by faith in Christ.[18]

Evangelii Nuntiandi depicts the church's work of evangelization as more than social reform. Evangelization involves yet transcends the social, political, economic, and cultural changes stirred by the gospel. Changed structures are not enough; individuals within the structures are to undergo a change of heart. The document also argues that this evangelization, which involves the realm addressed by social teaching, cannot be done without the action of the Holy Spirit.[19] The social transformation the church envisions is grounded in its doctrine of grace. Without the Spirit the most convincing social theory has no power over the heart. Implicit in social teaching is the message that its social mission involves the continued conversion of the church.

From Catholic Social Teaching to Catholic Social Tradition

All four models of social teaching—social policy, prophecy, moral doctrine, and social principles—reflect real functions of social teaching. However, none of these retrieve the ecclesial identity of social teaching. To locate social teaching in its proper center of ecclesial life and practice, it is more accurate to see it as an expression of the Catholic social tradition. This more comprehensive term implies a wider framework of belief and practice that grounds it. According to John Paul II, the core of Catholic social teaching is what it means to be human at the beginning of a new millennium. He asserts, "the complete truth about the human being constitutes the foundation of the church's social teaching and the basis also of true liberation."[20]

The human person is understood in social teaching not just in himself or herself, but vis-à-vis the social systems and processes of the day. These processes are to be directed to the good of the human person, and their utility is measured by how they build community. The human person is the fundamental "way" for the church, a way that is grounded in the paschal mystery and that leads the church to the cross of Jesus Christ, its share in the redemptive mystery. The defense of human dignity taken up by the church in social teaching is more than a moral endeavor, an effort to frame social policy, or even to give prophetic witness.[21] It is for the Catholic Church an ecclesiological imperative.[22] The church, by its nature, must engage in the defense of human dignity. The defense of the dignity of the person specifies the challenges confronting the church in its mission at any particular period of history. The church must engage in all four responses as represented by the various models. It must contribute social vision, prophetic challenge, moral language, and general principles to the complexities of a global society.

But the ground of the church's response transcends even social policy, prophetic witness, and engagement in moral discourse. It is inseparably linked to the inculturation of the gospel, an endeavor that finds its roots in the incarnation of Jesus Christ. John Paul II, more than any of his predecessors, translates this challenge into a radical confrontation with culture itself, a response by the church to the cultural pluralism of global culture.[23]

Social Teaching, the Social Sciences, and the Church

We have suggested that a full understanding of Catholic social teaching involves recognition of both its ecclesial foundations and its essential link to the social sciences. This section explores some broad paradigms of this relationship, suggesting that the three elements in this triad—social teaching, the church, and the social sciences—must be related in order to understand social teaching. A shift in one influences the other. This short presentation can only indicate highlights of their relationship.

The social sciences to which we refer today were rather inchoate when social teaching first appeared in Leo XIII's encyclical *Rerum Novarum*. In the 1880s the academy was still discussing just what the social sciences were going to be. Nonetheless, Protestant social gospel writers as well as Catholics like John A. Ryan began to bring information from the social sciences into theology. Social ethics, with its attempt to use the social sciences in ethical reflection, had to emerge as a discipline.[24] The changed social conditions of the Industrial Revolution, the problems of new immigrants to the United States, and the social ills caused by laissez-faire capitalism challenged ethicists both within and without the church to develop new methods. Even as the church struggled to move from a philosophical and theological ethical model designed for individual guidance in the past rather than to shape social policy, social reality itself was changing significantly.

The "social question" was a collective term used by the popes and the social gospel movement to refer to the problems related to the growth of industrialization. The complexity of new issues was enormous. Beneath the growing anxiety that these problems would remain unsolved was the fear that class conflict would be exacerbated and ultimately cause the decay of Western civilization. This new situation required theological renewal. Efforts were made to retrieve the importance of the "Kingdom of God" in moral theology and to explore the social dimension of salvation in systematic theology.

The church also engaged in the social science debate on the nature and function of society. Early understandings of such social questions in the United States were a European creation, even though attempts at application to the American scene were made.[25] Catholic thought rejected the Marxist claim that people would create in an unspecified future a majority secular society that would voluntarily agree to establish an intimate, organic set of social institutions.[26] Early Catholic social teaching also distanced itself from the "survival of the fittest" picture of social evolution; and it rejected theories of any "already established harmony of natural forces" inherent in laissez-faire economic theory. But its own scholastic concept of society was not up to the task of the social question.[27] Scholastic theology was not capable of articulating a vision of society adequate to both criticize and meet the problems of modern secular and democratic social reality.[28]

In fact, neither religious nor secular efforts at social ethics were very well developed. For instance, Preston Williams comments that neither Catholic nor Protestant forms of early social reform did or said much about racism. In fact, either through racist concepts of human nature or through an implicit social Darwinism, theories of white superiority remained untouched in reform movements sponsored by social teaching or social gospel influences. Even those who used class analysis ignored race. Early class analysis focused the churches on industrial problems, yet overlooked race as integrally linked to class in new industrial situations.[29]

Catholic social teaching was often criticized for attempting to apply old scholastic concepts to a modern secular and democratic society. Gregory Baum notes, however, that even when social reflection in the church became more sensitive to its context, reading the "signs of the times" could lead to acquiescence to evil rather than to social transformation.[30] Many German theologians embraced an interpretation of Christian faith that endorsed Nazi ideology. Baum highlights a passing comment by Victor Consemius that theologians who sought to be open to new ideas might thereby be open also to the new Nazi ideology.[31]

Despite the struggles and sometimes failures to integrate theology and the social sciences in social teaching, the church continued its efforts to bring the values that grew out of the richness of its internal life to the problems of the modern world.

Social Teaching and Ecclesiology

Outmoded understandings of the relation of the church to society both impeded social action and hampered the efficacy of social teaching. The relation between ecclesiology and social teaching can be seen in three ways. First, excessive claims for the role of the church in social reform constituted a serious obstacle to formulating a realistic vision of social mission in the church. Leo XIII, as a teacher of natural law, maintained that the Roman Catholic Church alone could solve social problems. The term "alone" suggested that the moral task of social reform be reserved in some unique manner to the church. This implied that no one else but the church could do it or that only with the church would a solution be possible; in other words, without the contribution of the church no adequate solution would be found.[32] Oswald von Nell-Breeding found the first position "exceedingly arrogant." The second position reflected the belief that disorder in society was not just social but also moral. The church had a unique role in the formation of conscience; thus the church was required as an agent of change. Today this role would be attributed more generally to religion as a whole, in its capacity to call men and women to a sense of transcendence.[33]

A second connection between ecclesiology and social teaching was the relationship between early social teaching and ultramontanism, which had the aim of establishing a systematic set of authoritative instructions binding for all the faithful as a Catholic response to social problems.[34] This self-understanding of the church gave rise to a sense of social "doctrine" that could be applied universally, regardless of context. High centralization, a focus on doctrine, a strong desire, through the church, to "restore all things in Christ" in modern society and the creation of a parallel Catholic society with large Catholic social organizations and a strong Catholic subculture to do this was the ecclesial context of early social teaching. This church climate was more conducive to the control and assessment of personal moral responsibility than it was to social responsibility. The latter requires, among other factors, a new capacity to include the conditions of the social context into the assessment of moral obligation and to work with those outside the church in carrying out social goals.

In the 1930s Pius XI had introduced a new concept that transcended the tradition of the seminary manuals, that of social justice. Social justice involves the embedding of moral ideals in the laws, customs, institutions, and structures of society in order to promote the common good. It involves a moral call to transform a social situation, to change a context, a call that often goes beyond the decisions of one individual. But in the 1930s in the United States, Catholic priests were educated in the Thomistic system and subsequent manual tradition of general, legal, distributive, and commutative justice. The manner in which social and cultural conditions had to be factored into the understanding of moral obligation of social teaching was not prominent in its methodology. Clergy tended to interpret Pius XI's encyclical *Quadragesimo Anno* like biblical fundamentalists. For example, confessors interpreted literally the teaching of Pius XI that a living wage was due in strict justice. Clergy considered it a duty of the individual employer, and approached employers with this obligation, without consideration of the complexity of wage creation in the economic market or of the meaning of the term "social justice" introduced by Pius XI.

Given this understanding of social justice, a just wage cannot be given apart from the transformation of the system that produced the wage. The obligation in the encyclical for a just wage was not on the employer alone, as interpreted by the confessors of the 1930s. The obligation for a living wage was part of a larger notion of social justice. This new category of moral thought in the church took into consideration the role of context in moral obligation. It called for the reorganization of the economic society so that a worker could in fact produce the economic equivalent of such a wage.[35] The obligation on the employer was understood within a context. An accurate understanding of the teaching regarding a just wage required a grasp of the "sciences" of wage creation.[36]

There was a tension between Pius XI's call for a just wage in social justice and the ultramontane notion of church that was still prevalent at that time. On the one hand, the moral obligation on the employer was part of social justice, involving societal change. On the other hand, the ideal of the ultramontane church was a church set apart from the world. Its moral categories were still more suited to personal conversion of the Catholic in the protective church-world environment of the ultramontane church. The church could not influence the factors necessary in the science of wage creation through individuals alone. It needed to be more open to the world, and engaged in it.

At the time of Pius XI, the church's suggestion of a corporatist model of society was consistent with its own ecclesiological ideal. A highly centralized church could more easily influence a highly centralized economy. Cronin remarks that the failure of pastors to interpret the meaning of *Quadragesimo Anno* more accurately in the U.S. context arose from the "difficulties faced by those who were advanced and liberal in their economic views, yet limited and fundamentalist in their ecclesiology."[37] History reminds us, however, that modern society failed to receive corporatism, except when imposed by fascism.

It was not until Vatican II that the church opened to the world and accepted a spirituality of engagement in society, and espoused political action as a form of Christian discipleship. Paul VI corrected the ultramontane vision of the church in its desire to offer a "social doctrine" that could be universally applied when he stated that Rome could no longer hand down solutions to world-wide social problems, and called for more regional discernment.[38] John Paul II more comprehensively laid out the moral obligation of wage creation in a free market with the concept of the "indirect employer." He acknowledged the power of structures beyond the employer's control that influence the payment of a just wage.[39] As the church shifted in its ecclesiology, it also became more nuanced in determining moral responsibility in the social realm.

This leads us to a third connection between ecclesiology and ethics in social teaching—the change that engagement in social action created in the church. In the beginning, social action was often viewed as a highly specialized apostolate reserved for the few. Later, however, Catholic Action, a wide-ranging network of Catholic social organizations directed toward change in society, provided many Catholics with the experience of social involvement under the auspices of the church. Some studied the encyclicals in workers' groups and unions, others engaged in the "think, judge, act" methods of sodalities. Many adopted the militant "army of youth" ideals of mid-twentieth-century Catholicism, gaining impetus for Catholic action from the vision of the "mystical body of Christ" promoted by Pius XII.

Interest in the encyclical tradition and social action began to wane after WW II, as the new economic development suggested that major social problems could be solved through economic growth.[40] Secular writers like Michael Harrington, however, began to point anew to the great poverty that still existed in an affluent nation. The civil rights movement blossomed. The feminist movement took on new life. The church in Latin America made the pastoral decision to join efforts for national development. Instead of the church changing society, the society began radically to change the church, and its self-understanding.

While the church often sees itself as a forerunner in social reform, the fact is that the church is often transformed by changes in the social arena and becomes a "better" church as it learns from society. Struggles over race, arms control, war and peace, poverty, women's issues, and ecology have engaged the church from without. As the church interacts in social issues, which are not ecclesial issues per se, this interaction becomes part of the spiritual and moral formation of the church itself as mediated by others in God's world.[41] The church also borrows social theories, such as theories of progress, development, human rights, and ecological sustainability, to express itself and its theology. It makes clear its inner life either by resistance or acceptance of these social maps.

The Message from the Social Sciences

As the social sciences enter into dialogue with social teaching, their impact on the church and its teaching and the church's identity before the sciences comes to the fore. First, the sciences raise questions of the function and social location of theology. Social science reminds the church that in its effort to transform society it cannot simply apply principles ahistorically to contemporary situations. Rather, the church itself is a subject, and does not simply look at the world from the outside as an object to be understood. The church views the world from within and is already impacted by the world it seeks to transform.[42] The social sciences have challenged the church, not to betray the proper character of theology but to acknowledge the necessary connection of thought with reality.[43]

Second, the social sciences consistently remind the church that she is more than a mystical union. One cannot find an invisible church on a sociological map. Lewis Mudge claims that the church must always be ready to answer the question, how would one know it if one saw it in this society?[44] This raises issues for the church internally and externally. The church needs boundaries to distinguish it from non-church, yet those boundaries must communicate the essence and spirit of the church in the socio-cultural situation. This is commonly called inculturation. The social sciences serve the church in this essential task.

The church also exercises its role in service to the Kingdom of God in the conditions of a given society. This role engages it not only in proclamation but also, as a visible church, in ethical behavior. Since the testimony of the church's own inner life is of the essence of its witness, it must be self-critical about the kind of social reality it constructs in its own living, and the type to which it contributes in its communal and public practice. This means that the church has to be a critic of society, as well as self-critical. Both require data about social reality that only the sciences can provide. The sciences can provide the church with more than tools of reflection; they can also challenge. They can request that the church manifest distinguishing marks of its core identity, through its corporate behavior and standards. They can ask for a translation of "see how they love one another" in any social situation.

In response, the church can both question and affirm the sciences as it engages with various social theories and ideologies in their task of criticism. Different theories of society provide different social maps and offer different analyses of what is going on in the world. The church can approach these theories critically, with awareness that a social theory is like a grid placed over the reality of common human life. As a map of this reality, what the theory names is not absolute. Through the centuries, the church has formed its identity by how it concurs or not with the position given to it or to its people by a social map. Liberalism relegated the church to the home, communism to obscurity. Social Darwinism explained away those who were at the bottom of society. More recently, the ideology of the arms race has undermined social investments needed by the poor. In all these cases, the church begged to differ.

The church's social teaching has sometimes suffered because it has ignored the social sciences or distorted their methods, partly because it did not agree with the current forms of social analysis or theory. Paul Lakeland criticizes the church's social teaching because it does not always respect the type of social analysis needed to talk coherently about society. He charges that church teaching offers a "piecemeal approach to social problems" because of the absence of a developed social theory.[45] Yet religious traditions themselves do not have the resources for the construction of a social theory; hence interactions are always hybrid and dependent on the sciences for its own forms of truth.

A third connection between social sciences, the church, and social teaching is the capacity of the social sciences to remind the church of its own internal diversity. Social issues can actually be more divisive and more of a challenge to the unity of the church than familiar kinds of confessional diversity. James Fowler remarks, "For at least a decade and a half broad coalitions of religious and political groups in the United States have polarized into moral and value stances that reveal deep and seemingly irreconcilable differences."[46] Fowler uses the term "temper" to describe the combination of emotional, moral, and ideological dispositions that constitute the unifying characteristics of opposing "orthodox" and "progressive" orientations. Tempers, or mindsets, influence both content and process in opposing movements in national values, lifestyle options, and public policy to be determined in the country. Alignments of opposing views cut across the lines of traditional religious and political boundaries. Pluralism in the United States is no longer defined only in terms of the differences between Protestants, Catholics, and Jews. Even racial or ethnic divisions do not always capture the pattern of conflict often popularly called "culture wars." In other words, differences can be stronger within a church, such as among Catholics, than among some churches.

The presence of internal criticism and conflict stands deep in the church's history and identity. Yet the church is also a people called to greater unity among its members. While the social sciences indicate the tension between progressives and conservatives in all major religions, the church's tradition contains the call to move beyond these divisions. By offering the church a mirror in which to look at itself, the social sciences offer the church a choice. Will it embrace its true identity and move toward unity or will it simply sink into the polarities of its social location? The church defines itself not just in the tempers that divide it, or in its ideas for society, but by the ability to love and move toward unity amid huge problems and diversities.

Often when we think of the relation of the church to society, the desire to be prophetic comes to the forefront. The prophetic element of the Christian life needs to be not just social criticism but also by an appreciation of the value of the "other" and his or her needs. David Tracy remarks that we can be deceived in thinking that if we have better special teachings than others we are actually more prophetic than others, thus more Christian. He warns that no one can be sure that their social criticism alone will lead them to an effective care for a true "other." Such musings can lead them only to themselves and not to the other who is suffering.[47] Even as the church seeks to provide responsible social teaching, it should never take pride in that teaching unless it also engages in effective social practice.

Today we know that ideas by themselves lack moral power. In our postmodern age, only spirituality centered on rather than detached from community can transform society.[48] This mark distinguishes the church from the spectrum of groups seeking social reform. The church is not just a "prophetic" social group or a "teacher" of moral ideals, but a community formed in discipleship of Jesus Christ. It gains its identity not just from social criticism, whether progressive or conservative, but from the paschal mystery that forms the heart of its life. The life of the Eucharist at its center is fully expressed only in the development of a community that is in service to the other in the conditions of our global society.

Notes

[1]For a distinction between social teaching as "merely encyclicals" and wider traditions of social thinking that develop and specify themes expressed in the encyclicals, see the work of European scholars of Catholic social thinking: *Catholic Social Thought: Twilight or Renaissance?*, ed. Jonathan S. Boswell, Francis P. McHugh, and Johan Verstraeten (Louvain: Peters: 2001, forthcoming).

[2]Richard L. Camp, *The Papal Ideology of Social Reform: A Study in Historical Development 1878-1967* (Leiden: E. J. Brill, 1969), 1.

[3]Paul F. Lakeland, "Ethics and Communicative Action: The Need for Critical Theory in Catholic Social Teaching," *Thought* 62, no. 244 (March, 1987): 60.

[4]Carlo Maria Martini, *The Dove at Rest: Contributions for a Possible Peace* (Middlegreen Slogh, England: St. Pauls, 1995), 20.

[5]Thomas J. Gumbleton, "Peacemaking as a Way of Life," in *One Hundred Years of Catholic Social Thought,* ed. John A. Coleman, S.J. (Maryknoll, N.Y.: Orbis Books, 1991), 304.

[6]John F. Cronin, *Christianity and Social Progress: A Commentary on Mater et Magistra* (Baltimore & Dublin: Helicon, 1965), 7.

[7]United States Catholic Conference, *Sharing Catholic Social Teaching: Challenges and Directions. Reflections on the U.S. Catholic Bishops* (Washington, D.C.: United States Catholic Conference, 1998), 4.

[8]See also Donal Dorr, *The Social Justice Agenda: Justice, Ecology, Power and the Church* (Maryknoll, N.Y.: Orbis Books, 1991), 83.

[9]Charles Curran, "What Catholic Ecclesiology Can Learn from Official Catholic Social Teachings," in *A Democratic Catholic Church: The Reconstruction of Roman Catholicism,* ed. Eugene C. Bianchi and Rosemary Radford Ruether (New York: Crossroad, 1992), 102.

[10]J. Brian Hehir, "Personal Faith, the Public Church, and the Role of Theology," *Harvard Divinity Bulletin* 26, no.1 (1996).

[11]Ibid.

[12]Thomas R. Rausch, *Catholicism at the Dawn of the Third Millennium* (Collegeville, Minn.: Liturgical Press, 1996), 154.

[13]Paul VI, *Evangelii Nuntiandi,* 29.

[14]Ibid., 31.

[15]Ibid., 17.

[16]Ibid., 18.

[17]Ibid., 22.1.

[18]Ibid., 23.

[19]Ibid., 75.

[20]John Paul II, Puebla Address, *Origins* 8 (Feb. 8, 1979): 535.

[21]John Paul II, *Redemptor Hominis,* 14.

[22]J. Brian Hehir, "John Paul II: Continuity and Change in Social Teaching of the Church," in *Readings in Moral Theology No. 5: Official Catholic Social Teaching,* ed. Charles E. Curran and Richard A. McCormick, S.J. (New York: Paulist Press, 1986), 255.

[23]Michael Paul Gallagher, S.J., *Clashing Symbols: An Introduction to Faith and Culture* (London: DLT, 1997).

[24]Paul Deats, Jr., "The Quest for a Social Ethic," in *Toward a Discipline of Social Ethics: Essays in Honor of Walter G. Muelder*, ed. Paul Deats, Jr. (Boston: Boston University Press, 1972), 235.

[25]Marvin L. Mich, *Catholic Social Teaching and Movements* (Mystic, Conn.: Twenty-Third Publications, 1998), 59.

[26]Preston N. Williams, "The Social Gospel and Race Relations," in *Toward a Discipline of Social Ethics.*

[27]Lakeland, "Ethics and Communicative Action," 60.

[28]Jean-Yves Calvez, S.J., and Jacques Perrin, S.J., *The Church and Social Justice: The Social Teachings of the Popes from Leo XIII to Pius XII (1878-1958)* (Chicago: Henry Regnery Company, 1961), 124-132.

[29]This weakness persisted through Vatican II. See Mich, *Catholic Social Teaching and Movements*, 132-133.

[30]Gregory Baum, "Concluding Reflections: Looking Back over the Century," in

The Twentieth Century: A Theological Overview, ed. Gregory Baum (Maryknoll, N.Y.: Orbis Books, 1999), 239.

[31]Ibid. For Consemius's comment, see 22-23.

[32]Mich, *Catholic Social Teaching and Movements*, 23.

[33]Secular writers and Christian social ethicists echo this view. See for example: Richard Falk, "Satisfying Human Needs in a World of Sovereign States: Rhetoric, Reality and Vision," in *World Faiths and the New World Order,* ed. Joseph Gremillion and William Ryan (Lisbon: The Interreligious Peace Colloquium, 1997), 136ff; Larry L. Rasmussen, *Earth Community, Earth Ethics* (Maryknoll, N.Y.: Orbis Books, 1966), 177.

[34]Staf Hellemans, "Is There a Future for Catholic Social Teaching after the Waning of the Ultramontane Mass Catholicism?" in Boswell et al., *Catholic Social Thought: Twilight or Renaissance?,* 11.

[35]John F. Cronin, S.S., "Forty Years Later: Reflections and Reminiscences," in *Readings in Moral Theology, No. 5: Official Catholic Social Teaching,* ed. Charles E. Curran and Richard A. McCormick, S.J. (New York: Paulist Press, 1986).

[36]Albino Barrera, "The Evolution of Social Ethics: Using Economic History to Understand Economic Ethics," *Journal of Religious Ethics* 27, no. 2 (Summer 1999): 285-305.

[37]Cronin, "Forty Years Later," 73.

[38]Paul VI, *Octogesima Adveniens,* 4.

[39]Donal Dorr, *Option for the Poor: A Hundred Years of Catholic Social Teaching* (Maryknoll, N.Y.: Orbis Books, 1992), 290-294.

[40]Cronin, "Forty Years Later," 73.

[41]Lewis S. Mudge, *The Church as Moral Community: Ecclesiology and Ethics in Ecumenical Debate* (New York: Continuum, 1996), 95.

[42]Ibid., 63.

[43]Ricardo Antoncich raises the question of the power of social teaching as "ideology": "Social teaching has the power as thought to both transform reality and immobilize it" *(Christians in the Face of Injustice: A Latin American Reading of Catholic Social Teaching,* trans. Matthew J. O'Connell [Maryknoll, N.Y.: Orbis Books, 1987], 68).

[44]Mudge, *The Church as Moral Community*, 92.

[45]Lakeland, "Ethics and Communicative Action," 61.

[46]James Fowler, *Faithful Change: The Personal and Public Challenges of Postmodern Life* (Nashville: Abingdon Press, 1996), 161.

[47]David Tracy, "Theology and the Many Faces of Postmodernity," *Theology Today* 51 (1994): 107.

[48]Gallagher, *Clashing Symbols*, 135.

Domestic Churches

Sociological Challenge and Theological Imperative

Florence Caffrey Bourg

Students in my "Theology of Human Sexuality and Marriage" course have a semester project that entails interviewing two individuals or couples who consider themselves Christian and who are engaged or have some experience with marriage. Students devise their own questions, but they are instructed to discuss a variety of information from the course with the interview subjects. In the end, the students write a synopsis that treats the following items:

- Is it relatively easy or relatively hard for your subjects to see these two parts of their lives—Christian faith and marriage/sexuality—as complementary?
- Do your subjects consciously rely upon the Bible, or some other part of Christian tradition, to guide them in their marriage and sexual lives?
- Is there any consensus among your subjects as to the relationship (if any) between Christian faith and marriage/sexuality?

One item I ask students to include in their synopsis for my own assessment purposes is, "What information from this course was most interesting to the persons you interviewed?" *Domestic church* has been by far the most frequently cited response—beating out such juicy topics as gender roles, birth control, infertility therapies, interfaith marriage, divorce, and homosexuality. I have not kept a count of how often domestic church has been cited, but I have had about 125 students complete the exercise thus far, each conducting two interviews, and the interest in domestic church has been consistent. The idea seems of interest as much to those interview subjects who consider themselves actively practicing churchgoers as to those who consider themselves believers but find the institutional church boring, unwelcoming, or out of touch with real life. Because students devise their own interview questions, the fact that they are introducing the topic of domestic church to their subjects seems to indicate some level of interest in the topic among the students. (Students are split about equally between traditional age students and adult students.) I should also note that in polling students informally, via class discussion, I have found only two or three who were familiar with the expression "domestic church" before this course.

Now, it seems to me that if my students and their interview subjects are fairly representative of the general population, at least the general population of Catholic liberal arts colleges, then this pattern of interest is worthy of our attention, whether we are theologians or sociologists. Perhaps active churchgoers and "non-practicing" believers are attracted to the idea of domestic church for different reasons; perhaps not. We will never know without further investigation. Scholars who are weary of writing on birth control, divorce, and so on, take note!

Knowledge about domestic churches—and, perhaps more importantly, knowledge about God to be articulated by believers as members of domestic churches—is an area in which theology can clearly benefit from the tools of the social sciences. Social scientists who document religious experiences of typical Christian families might identify:

- events these families consider most sacred,
- forces that appear to assist or inhibit families who seek to maintain a spiritual relationship with the being they call "God," and
- characteristics of the God whom Christians attest to encountering through sacred experiences.

In so doing, scientists might assist theologians in their understanding of God, whose work in the ordinary lives of domestic churches throughout Christian history has been attended to only recently and who therefore (we may presume) is far from being fully understood.

This essay will attempt the following tasks. First, it will recap recent revival of the expression, "domestic church," with attention to patterns of use or neglect. Second, it will examine established concepts of Catholic theology and doctrine that, brought to bear on the emerging idea of domestic church, provide the rationale for use of social science tools to probe the religious knowledge of Christian families. Third, it will reveal the current lack of such knowledge and suggest underlying causes. Finally, it will suggest ways our theological knowledge might continue to grow if social and behavioral sciences assist in accessing the knowledge of God to be gained from domestic churches.

Revival of the Notion of Domestic Church

The concept of "domestic church" directs attention to Christian families as ecclesial entities and to humans as "God's family." Though the expression has precedent in scripture[1] and the patristic[2] authors, it was neglected by Catholicism until the Second Vatican Council.[3] Even after Vatican II, the notion of domestic church (sometimes called "little church" or "church of the home") remained relatively uncommon until publication of John Paul II's *Familiaris Consortio* in 1981. Since then, this new way of talking and thinking about Christian families has enjoyed a slow but steady revival.

Christian families are nothing new, of course; what is new is the way this term has come to be used to stress that the Christian family is the smallest community or manifestation of church. Given Catholicism's history of separation (both real and perceived) between religious leaders and laity—focused largely around familial status—recognition of Christian families with this title is a truly significant event, with implications still to be uncovered.

If the idea of domestic church were something imposed from the top down, rather than an expression that captured the wisdom emerging from grassroots experience, it would have no enduring value. It would likely be rejected by the average believer, minister, and theologian as a form of hierarchical intrusion.[4] This being the case, it is noteworthy that this new way of thinking and talking about Christian families is not confined to official church documents, or to academic theology, or to resources for pastoral ministers, or to popular reading for average believers. References to domestic church are found in all these genres. Moreover, authors who invoke the idea of domestic church come from many countries and continents,[5] and from everywhere on the ideological spectrum. The concept has ecumenical appeal—it has a place in Orthodox Christian theology of marriage,[6] and parallels in Protestant authors, especially from the American Puritan and Pietist traditions.[7]

It is true that many authors who allude to the idea of domestic church don't make it the central focus of their writing or agree on exactly what it implies for church institutions, but this need not reflect poorly on the idea itself. Indeed, the idea gains credibility or significance when we consider the range of authors and writings that have used the expression, however briefly. Their fields of interest include biblical studies, ecumenism, religious education, the magisterium and canon law, spirituality, ecclesiology and inculturation of the church, the trinity, sacramental theology, feminist theology, and social justice.

Judging by their citations, it seems most of these authors are largely unaware of each other's writings on the theme of domestic church. While this is unfortunate, at the same time it reveals something very positive about the concept. The fact that so many authors have "discovered" and embraced the idea of domestic church—relatively independently of each other—shows that the expression captures a significant, widely shared religious experience. The results of my marriage course's interview project appear as corroborating evidence. Perhaps this shared experience, described through the concept of domestic church, represents an opportunity for repairing some of the divisions within the church, and between the church and those who consider themselves alienated from her. Such opportunities for building consensus cannot be taken for granted, and should not be wasted.

Theological and Doctrinal Considerations

Writing in 1995, Michael Fahey provided this progress report on theological exploration of families as domestic churches:

> Despite the theological correctness of Catholicism's reappropriation of the family as "domestic church," the teaching is formulated in a doctrinal vacuum that fails to address serious issues that need to be articulated in dialogue with sociologists, psychologists, and demographers, to name only a few. As the

> Catholic Church approaches the new millennium, its teachers will need to listen attentively and painstakingly to the signs of the times.[8]

Why does Fahey call for dialogue with the social sciences? Do these fields of study have any common ground for dialogue? Given the frequency with which Catholicism surfaces as a critical voice in many of the debated scientific and social issues of our day, some explanation is in order. Though its spokespersons have undoubtedly been critical of certain scientific opinions, and in hindsight it can be said that Catholic leaders have made mistakes in reacting negatively to scientific development, Catholicism has traditionally posited an affirmative relationship between faith and reason, and therefore between theology and science.[9] Science is understood as concerning itself with knowledge of human beings and their world that is demonstrable; theology explains demonstrable elements of humans and the natural world in light of something not scientifically demonstrable, namely, their relationship with God. The two disciplines observe and interpret the same phenomena from different points of view, but both include among their ends a more complete understanding and advancement of humanity.[10] The scientist does not claim, as a result of his or her scientific investigation, the authority to speak directly about an unseen God; at most he or she may aim to observe and clarify the religious experiences of humans. However, products of scientific inquiry should interest the Catholic theologian, who bases her investigations upon the premise that the unseen God can be known, at least in part, through the created world, most notably through humans made in God's image.

Having established the premise of a positive relationship between theology and the sciences, we can now consider theological precedents that support collaboration between theologians and social scientists specifically. Four established concepts of Catholic theology and doctrine that appear significant in interpreting the emerging idea of domestic church are: the "people of God," the local church, the *sensus fidelium*, and "reading the signs of the times."

These closely related ideas were important to the deliberations of the Second Vatican Council, and it is fair to say that they represent neglected components of Catholic Christianity, the rediscovery of which poses theoretical and pastoral complexities still being worked out by the church as a whole.

The People of God

Vatican II's *Constitution on the Church* speaks of the "people of God" as follows: "At all times and in every race, anyone who fears God and does what is right has been acceptable to him."[11] The document explains that God desires these people, *as a community*, come to acknowledge and serve God by leading holy lives. To that end, God has revealed himself historically, culminating in the incarnation of Christ, and the church has been established by Christ "in order to shepherd the People of God and to increase its numbers without cease."[12] Though *Lumen Gentium* affirms the indispensable nature of the institutional elements of the church, it also clarifies that *God's spirit works in many ways that are not institutionalized*, and that the capacity to truly know God is possessed not simply by the ordained, but by countless ordinary God-fearing people.

Vatican II's statements on the "people of God" have resulted not only in changed attitudes among Catholics toward persons of other faith traditions, but also in changed attitudes toward their identity as Catholics. The idea that the church is first and foremost the people of God is generally understood as a corrective to a viewpoint that sees the church's institutional aspect as its most indispensable quality. The church is first and foremost the community of believers, not the buildings, and not the clergy in isolation. By extension, a new appreciation of the workings of God in the ordinary lives of average believers—as indicated in the notion of domestic church—is beginning to emerge among clergy and laity alike. But the emphasis here is on *beginning*. Old habits are hard to break, as Bernard Boelen explains:

> The shift from preconciliar understanding of the Christian family in terms of "functions" and "subjects" to the renewed understanding in terms of the "domestic church" is so profound, so overwhelming and far-reaching, that its full realization will be long in coming. . . . It goes without saying that the Christian family encounters many obstacles to its attempt to renew itself. The habit of looking upon itself as "laity" in the preconciliar sense is hard to break. . . . Many laypersons and their families still want to be told what to do. . . . The habit on the part of some Church officials of looking upon themselves as "hierarchy" in the preconciliar sense is understandably hard to break too.[13]

Local Church

A second important principle of the Second Vatican Council was an affirmation of "the patristic ecclesiology according to which each local church is the Catholic Church. The universal church is the communion of all these local churches, the *koinonia* of all the Catholic Churches."[14] In Catholicism the term "local church" is equivalent to "diocese." It refers to a "community celebrating an authentic eucharist," headed by a bishop.[15] Loosely speaking, it refers to smaller worshiping communities—usually geographically defined parishes. Sometimes there are also communities of vowed religious or other groups who may or may not have an ordained pastor-in-residence, but who are recognized by a bishop and submit to his leadership. Vatican II clarified that bishops are not vicars of the pope, but true vicars and legates of Christ.[16] By extension, local churches are not incomplete or subordinate pieces of the church; each represents the fullness of church in a particular locale.[17] For our purposes, the important point to draw from the concept of local church is that it is a true church and thus in some way an authoritative source of knowledge of God.

The ecclesial status of domestic churches is, in my assessment, an important matter of unfinished business in the church's ongoing discernment. John Paul II has stated repeatedly that Christian families should view themselves as "living images" and "historical representations" of the church, or "churches in miniature."[18] The U.S. bishops have written, "The point of the teaching is simple, yet profound. As Christian families, you not only belong to the Church, but your daily life is a true expression of the Church."[19] Though specifics remain to be worked out, it is hard not to assume that much of what the magisterium has said about local churches could in some manner be extended to domestic churches, to the extent that they are recognized by, and are in communion with, their local bishops (or their delegates).[20] This conclusion is plausible if one considers that households were the building blocks of early Christian local churches, as well as the fact that geographic or juridical connotations of domestic church appear to have been in the forefront of the minds of the bishops who included the expression in *Lumen Gentium*.[21]

And yet, articulating the ecclesial significance of domestic churches remains a project on the "back burner," because despite the provocative language just cited, most ecclesiologists seem oblivious to the concept, or mention it only in passing.[22] Compared to a wealth of research on similar ecclesiological concepts retrieved at Vatican II (*sensus fidelium*, local church, collegiality), the neglect of domestic church is curious. Why the blind spot among some of the best and brightest theological minds? Perhaps behavioral scientists could help us discover the reason. In the meantime, most Christian families have never heard the expression, "domestic church"; they do not instinctively recognize themselves as ecclesial entities or their ordinary family activities as having religious significance. Is there a causal link here? For instance, if theologians were more conscious of the idea of domestic church, would this be reflected in the courses they teach and the books they publish for future parish priests, deacons, directors of religious education, Catholic school teachers, marriage preparation leaders—as well as the catechical materials written by these folks, which are all that filter down to average believers?

Sensus Fidelium

Admittedly, Vatican II's teachings on the status of local churches are focused on the authority of bishops, but they are complemented by its statements regarding the *sensus fidelium*, which pertains to clergy and laity alike.[23] The supernatural "sense of the faith" is a gift of the Holy Spirit given to all the faithful by baptism and confirmation for the purpose of understanding revealed truth. It is synonymous with the charism of infallibility granted to the church as a whole: "The whole body of the faithful who have an anointing that comes from the Holy One cannot err in matters of belief. This characteristic is shown in the supernatural appreciation of the faith (*sensus fidei*) of the whole people, when, 'from the bishops to the last of the faithful' they manifest a universal consent in matters of faith and morals."[24]

Belief in the existence of such a charism, and the possibility of exercising it to attain such a degree of certainty concerning God and God's will for humans, would seem to make it incumbent upon the church as a whole, especially its leadership, to ensure that all means available be used to access this communal knowledge and articulate it as clearly as possible. If the tools of the social sciences can help us in this regard, we are foolish not to use them for matters of such importance.[25] As Bernard Boelen aptly remarks, "When Church officials fail to listen to what the Holy Spirit is revealing to the domestic church, *they fail to listen to the Church itself.*"[26]

Reading the Signs of the Times

Catholicism is committed to the principle that infallible truth about God is knowable, but since Vatican II it has also been (more or less) committed to the belief that human formulations and applications of revealed truth must be open to revision. "The substance of doctrine is one thing, and the way it is expressed is another."[27] This is true partly because linguistic forms and concepts that were intelligible in one era as a means for conveying the truths of revelation often become obsolete. It is also true because God continues to intervene in history in new ways, and this forces us to rethink our understanding of the once-and-for-all Gospel. Vatican II expressed this latter conviction in *Gaudium et Spes* as follows: "At all times the Church carries the responsibility of reading the signs of the times and interpreting them in light of the Gospel. . . ." (4). Elsewhere this document comments that it is often the laity who will face the most rigorous work of ongoing discernment:

> It is their task to cultivate a properly informed conscience and to impress the divine law on the affairs of the earthly city. For guidance and spiritual strength let them turn to the clergy; but let them realize that their pastors will not always be so expert as to have a ready answer to every problem (even every grave problem) that arises; this is not the role of the clergy: it is rather up to the laymen to shoulder their responsibilities under the guidance of Christian wisdom and with eager attention to the teaching authority of the Church. (43)

My teaching experience, especially the interview exercise discussed earlier, tells me that many sincere believers and their families are *already* doing this rigorous work of "reading the signs of the times and interpreting them in light of the Gospel," but usually *not* in conversation with their pastors or other church leaders. Chances are that domestic churches, parishes, and higher level manifestations of church are all impoverished by this lack of conversation. What one individual or group learns through this rigorous process remains private knowledge, not shared knowledge. When similar occasions of discernment are faced again, each party is left to "reinvent the wheel," rather than learn from others' successes and failures.

What are the barriers to such conversation? Is it lack of desire, lack of available time, lack of faciliating structures, lack of shared language of discourse due to different catechetical training, fear of the unknown, fear of rejection, or something else? Could the social sciences help us identify barriers and suggest remedies?

The Task at Hand and Obstacles to It

If these four theological concepts are brought to bear on the emerging idea of domestic church, two conclusions appear indisputable: first, the domestic church appears as a crucial setting where God is known on an ongoing basis, and second, the domestic church is therefore a voice (or rather, a countless number of voices) who must be heard if God's working in the world is to be accurately understood. Surely there is much untapped religious wisdom still to be gained from Christians immersed in family life, a population whose contributions to both local level and high-level religious discourse appear to be limited by their own lack of self-appreciation as religious and ecclesial communities, neglect on the part of religious authorities, and logistical difficulties in locating, accessing, and organizing the knowledge of this population.[28]

Catholicism at both the institutional and grassroots levels has come a long way since Vatican II in redressing disjointedness between sacred and secular life, and separation between lay and clerical constituencies, which presumably has impeded a full appreciation of the domestic church as a resource for knowledge of God. Nevertheless, the work of accessing domestic churches' religious knowledge has barely begun. Sacred/secular and lay/clerical dichotomies historically associated with Christianity, especially Catholicism, are entrenched emotionally, supported by centuries of theoretical argument, and embodied in institutional structures and symbols. These dichotomies may be exacerbated by Western culture's current tendency to restrict religious discourse in the public sphere by attempting to confine it to specifically religious settings. Perhaps when religious discourse is culturally confined to institutional religious settings, it becomes more difficult to use in connection with everyday family life. (My students' interview projects, as well as classroom discussion, seem to reveal this in many cases.) And so, whatever knowledge of God is gained in the home setting becomes difficult to put into words, and what is difficult to put into words eventually becomes difficult to experience.

However, despite the fact that the concept of domestic church is practically unknown at the grassroots level, many spiritual authors attest that the family life of average Christians is indeed an important arena for experience of God. A good number of my students' interviews found the same phenomenon. It appears quite significant from theological, sociological, and psychological points of view that numerous Catholics (and probably persons of other faiths) find family life an important experiential link to God, often without much support from religious leaders or cultural customs/symbols, and sometimes despite institutional discouragement. Wendy Wright cites results of a survey conducted by the National Association of Lay Ministry:

> Laypersons involved in a variety of ministries were questioned about their prayer, their spiritual disciplines, and the resources for professional ministerial and personal growth they most favored. One of the questions asked was: What is the most important experience of God you have had? To my surprise, a full ninety percent of the respondents answered in ways that would have bewildered our forefathers and mothers in prayer. No one listed a solitary encounter with God: reading scripture, alone in the desert, in silent prayer. Instead, most gave relational responses: they had met God in the context of a faith-sharing group, in the crisis of a failing marriage, in the long patient work of parenting, in difficulties with a co-worker or boss. The answers were extremely varied but they had little in common with more traditional experiences associated with interiority, withdrawal, silence or solitude. God certainly acts and speaks in all our lives. What is needed now is a more public, shared enunciation of the texture and distinct sound of the sacred as it is refracted in the lives of familied Catholics.[29]

On the other hand, the long-standing assumption that God is to be encountered through specifically religious activities—especially those sponsored by the "official" church—apparently remains in the psyche of many Catholics, Vatican II reforms notwithstanding. Because their religious formation has not sufficiently alerted them to the possibility of doing so, many persons appear compromised in their ability to perceive God at work in everyday life. Wright elsewhere contends,

> The faithful, after all, *are* the Church. My impression, however, is that families do not often think of themselves as Church. At best, families either simply claim agreement with official church doctrine or import "churchy" rituals or prayers into their homes hoping this will impart religious meaning to their shared life. Most Christian families seem not to feel their very family-ness as sacred. They fail to name their most profound moments of shared memory—birth, death, sexual intimacy, estrangement, forgiveness, gathering, the daily struggles to be with and for each other—with words associated with religion or the spiritual life.[30]

Joann Heaney-Hunter, who uses principles of institutional culture studies to assess the impact of official teachings concerning the domestic church, comments:

> I have had conversations with many people who consider themselves knowledgeable about the theology of marriage (from graduate students to priests to marriage preparation leaders) and many say that they have never read about or even heard of the concept. For various reasons, this appears to be a case of a good idea that never found its way out of the documents. To return to the language of scholars of institutional culture, there appears to be a sharp discontinuity between the guiding beliefs about domestic church articulated in the documents and theological writings, and daily practice or understanding of it in the church community itself.[31]

Why does a good idea like the rediscovery of the domestic church remain largely hidden in unfamiliar documents, unable to impact persons who stand to be most affected? This is the sort of question the social and behavioral sciences are designed to answer. I expect that if scientists collaborated with religious leaders to investigate the current state of affairs, they would find that contributions of Catholic domestic churches to religious discourse continue to be limited by unintended neglect on the part of religious authorities, as well as families' own lack of self-appreciation as religious communities and logistical difficulties in documenting their religious knowledge—and that these difficulties increase as discourse proceeds to higher institutional levels. My hypothesis, of course, remains to be verified.

What Would Theology with Input from Domestic Churches Look Like?

After pinpointing reasons why official teachings concerning the domestic church have had little impact thus far, the social and behavioral sciences might be able to suggest methods to improve families' self-awareness as religious and ecclesial communities. Presumably these strategies would incorporate the inductive and empirically based style of investigation and reasoning, which is the hallmark of the sciences, generally speaking, but less influential in the science of theology.[32]

The results of such collaboration could influence popular and academic understanding of God in many ways. For example, in my ongoing research on family as domestic church, I have found several authors whose experience of God's presence in the midst of family crisis and breakdown has led them to re-read romanticized, antiseptic accounts of the Holy Family with a renewed appreciation for the belief that in Jesus God became fully human, "like us in all things but sin."[33]

Some theologians have rethought the traditional precept of humans being made in God's image with human families, rather than individuals, as their point of departure. The result is a deeper understanding of the centrality of the doctrine of the Trinity.[34] Many authors have tied the concept of domestic church with contemporary theologies of church as the basic sacrament, namely, a visible sign of God's invisible grace.[35] With this starting point, what once appeared as "merely human" family experiences of unconditional love, forgiveness, sacrifice, patience, joy in creation, and so forth are now recognized as lenses that focus and, indeed, instruments that mediate, the love and forgiveness of God. A few authors take this reasoning a step further and apply it to contentious issues of ecumenism and shared communion. Based on the traditional Catholic premise that any marriage of two baptized Christians is sacramental and an image of Christ and the church, as well as the testimony of actual families, Timothy Lincoln, among others, contends that interdenominational families are domestic churches with ecclesial standing no less significant than those founded upon the marriage of two Catholics. He concludes, "[B]ecause of the existence of interdenominational families, the Catholic Church and various Protestant Churches are already in a closer degree of communion with one another than official documents on both sides indicate."[36] Rethinking of Christian traditions on vocation, ascetical discipline, death and resurrection, and being a "child of God" appear more often in these writings. We have probably only begun to scratch the surface.

If taken seriously at a grassroots and institutional level, the concept of domestic church would undoubtedly change Christianity as we know it. The God in whom many of us already believe might be encountered, interpreted, and worshiped in new ways. Persons who have been able to locate God primarily in traditional institutional structures may more easily find God in the context of family life, understood as domestic church. As I see it, the potential significance of domestic churches will remain untapped unless and until theologians and other religious leaders incorporate the tools of the behavioral and social sciences to access the religious knowledge gained through family life.

Notes

[1]See Vincent Branick, *The House Church in the Writings of Paul* (Wilmington, Del.: Michael Glazier, 1989); Robert Banks, *Paul's Idea of Community: The Early House Churches in their Historical Setting* (Grand Rapids: Eerdmans, 1980); J. H. Elliott, "Philemon and House-Churches," *Bible Today* 22 (1984): 145-150; Hans-Josef Klauck, "Die Hausgemeinde als Lebensform im Urchristentum," *Münchener Theologische Zietschrift* 32, no. 1 (1981): 1-15; Normand Provencher, O.M.I., "Vers une Théologie de la Famille: L'Église Domestique," *Église et Théologie* 12 (1981): 15ff.; Carolyn Osiek and David Balch, *Families in the New Testament World: Households and House Churches* (Louisville: Westminster/John Knox Press, 1997).

[2]For sources, see Provencer, "Vers une Théologie de la Famille," 19ff.; Vigen Guroian, "Family and Christian Virtue: Reflections on the Ecclesial Vision of John Chrysostom," in *Ethics after Christendom: Toward an Ecclesial Ethic* (Grand Rapids: Eerdmans, 1994), 133-154; Michael Lawler and Gail Risch, "Covenant Generativity: Toward a Theology of Christian Family," *Horizons* 26, no. 1 (Spring 1999): 25; Joann Heaney-Hunter, "Domestic Church: Guiding Beliefs and Daily Practices," in *Christian Marriage and Family: Contemporary Theological and Pastoral Perspectives*, ed. Michael Lawler and William Roberts (Collegeville, Minn.: Liturgical Press, 1996), 62ff.; Paul Evdokimov, *The Sacrament of Love: The Nuptial Mystery in the Light of the Orthodox Tradition* (Crestwood, N.Y.: St. Vladimir's Seminary Press, 1985), 121-123; idem, *Marriage and Christian Tradition* (Chicago: Divine Word Publications, 1966), 85-87.

[3]*Lumen Gentium* 11; see also *Apostolicam Actuositatem* 11 and *Gaudium et Spes* 48. A record of conciliar interventions that led to inclusion of the concept is provided by Michael Fahey, "The Christian Family as Domestic Church at Vatican

II," in *The Family*, ed. Lisa Sowle Cahill and Dietmar Mieth, *Concilium* 4 (1995): 85-92.

[4]This concern was voiced in summary documents of an NCCB consultation on domestic church hosted at Notre Dame University, June 15, 1992. Some participants "question the value of the concept because they suspect it might be a means of the official church extending its control into family life" ("A Theological and Pastoral Colloquium: The Christian Family, A Domestic Church," 9).

[5]I have collected texts from North and South America, Europe, Africa, and Australia that include the concept of domestic church; they are written in English, Spanish, Italian, French, and German.

[6]See Guroian, "Family and Christian Values," and also Paul Evdokimov, "Ecclesia Domestica," *L'Anneau d'Or: Cahiers de Spiritualité Conjugale et Familiale* no. 107 (1962), 353-362.

[7]See Max Stackhouse, *Covenant and Commitments: Faith, Family, and Economic Life* (Louisville: Westminster/John Knox Press, 1997); John Witte, *From Sacrament to Contract: Marriage, Religion, and Law in the Western Tradition* (Louisville: Westminster/John Knox Press, 1997).

[8]Fahey, "The Christian Family as Domestic Church at Vatican II," 91.

[9]See *Gaudium et Spes* 36: "[M]ethodical research in all branches of knowledge, provided it is carried out in a truly scientific manner and does not override moral laws, can never conflict with the faith, because the things of the world and the things of faith derive from the same God. . . . We cannot but deplore certain attitudes (not unknown among Christians) deriving from a shortsighted view of the rightful autonomy of science; they have occasioned conflict and controversy and have misled many into opposing faith and science" (Austin Flannery, ed., *Documents of Vatican II*, [Grand Rapids: Eerdmans, 1975]. All citations of Council documents will be to this edition).

[10]*Familiaris Consortio* 8: "Science and its technical applications offer new and immense possibilities in the construction of such a humanism. Still, as a consequence of political choices that decide the direction of research and its applications, science is often used against its original purpose, which is the advancement of the human person."

[11]*Lumen Gentium* 9.

[12]*Lumen Gentium* 18.

[13]Bernard Boelen, "Church Renewal and the Christian Family," *Studies in Formative Spirituality* 2, no. 3 (November 1981): 367, 369; see also David Thomas, "Family Comes of Age in the Catholic Church," *Journal of Family Ministry* 12, no. 2 (Summer 1998): 38-51.

[14]J. M. R. Tillard, "Bishop," in *New Dictionary of Theology*, ed. Joseph A. Komonchak et al. (Wilmington, Del.: Michael Glazier, 1987), 132.

[15]Ibid. The authentic nature of a community and its eucharist derives from its bond to the pastoral and governing authority of an authentic bishop, meaning the one whose office can be traced in unbroken succession to the original apostles of Christ.

[16]*Lumen Gentium* 21, 27.

[17]See Joseph Komonchak, "The Local Realization of the Church," and Adrien

Nocent, "The Local Church as Realization of the Church of Christ and Subject of the Eucharist," in *The Reception of Vatican II*, ed. Giuseppe Alberigo et al. (Washington, D.C.: Catholic University of America Press, 1987), 77-90 and 215-229.

[18]*Familiaris Consortio* 49.

[19]National Conference of Catholic Bishops, *Follow the Way of Love* (Washington, D.C.: USCC, 1994), 8.

[20]Karl Rahner is one of few prominent representatives of ecclesiology to write about domestic churches. His statements extending the notion of "local church" to the "church of the home" are brief, but significant. In *The Church and the Sacraments*, he writes, "We have already said how remarkable the relationship between individual parish (local community) and the whole Church is. The local community is not only a member, a province of the whole Church. The whole Church is not only the sum of the parishes. Rather in the local church and its active accomplishment and self-realization, the whole Church in a true sense is manifested as a totality. What happens in the individual parish, especially in the celebration of the Eucharist, renders unmistakably and really present, in its ground (the redemptive death of the Lord), the existence of the whole Church as the grace-giving presence of God. It testifies unambiguously to it and guarantees her nature and reality in the world. In view of this, and seeing that matrimony is an image of the alliance between Christ and the Church, we can say in a true sense of marriage that in it the Church is present; to the extent to which marriage realizes its own nature, as a valid marriage, sanctified by grace and lived in holiness. It is the smallest community but, for all that, a genuine community of the redeemed and sanctified, whose unity can build on the same foundation as that on which the Church is founded, the smallest of local churches, but a true one, the Church in miniature" (*The Church and the Sacraments* [New York: Herder & Herder, 1963], 111-112). See also "Marriage as a Sacrament," *Theological Investigations*, vol. 10 (New York: Seabury Press, 1977), 212, 221; "The Sacramental Basis for the Role of the Layman in the Church," *Theological Investigations,* vol. 8 (New York: Seabury Press, 1977), 70; *Foundations of Christian Faith* (New York: Seabury Press, 1978), 420-421.

The only other essay I've found that treats this subject is Provencher, "Vers une Théologie de la Famille," 33. Provencher says the Christian family is *not* a local or particular church as Vatican II defines it; its proclamation of the word is not officially authorized and it does not celebrate Eucharist in union with a bishop. Nevertheless, he says, the Christian family is a true cell of the church, because in it we recognize many realities essential to the constitution of the entire church—Christ's presence, the mission of evangelization, the life of prayer and charity. It represents in some manner a unity fundamental to the church, and realizes her presence concretely in a determinate milieu.

[21]Fahey recounts the interventions of Bishop Pietro Fiordella, recorded in *Acta*: "In his ecclesiological remarks Fiordella argued that the universal church comprised a vast number of local churches or dioceses, but the diocese was not the last subdivision of Church. Christian families should be conceived of as *minusculae ecclesiae* (mini-churches)," 87.

[22]See Mitch and Kathy Finley, *Christian Families in the Real World: Reflections*

on a Spirituality for the Domestic Church (Chicago: Thomas More Press, 1984), 11: "An important insight in the teachings of the Second Vatican Council has been neglected by virtually every major theologian whose subject has been theology of the church. Little if any awareness is found in their writings of the value of the conciliar teaching that the family constitutes 'the domestic church.' Theologians tend to ignore this idea, or mention it only in passing with a very limited understanding of its implications for both families and the church as a whole." Again, in "A Family Ecclesiology," *America* 149 (July 30, 1983): 50, Mitch Finley laments, "Search through the highly influential works of Hans Küng, Avery Dulles, and Richard McBrien. . . . As far as such theologians are concerned, the local church or parish is both structurally and theologically the bottom line."

An example of such oversight is seen in a recent book edited by Avery Dulles, S.J. and Patrick Granfield, *The Theology of Church: A Bibliography* (Mahwah, N.J.: Paulist Press, 1999). The book consists of 198 pages of bibliography in the field of ecclesiology, organized under 53 subject headings—without any heading for domestic church!

[23]A thorough survey of this concept is provided in Daniel J. Finucane's *Sensus Fidelium: The Use of a Concept in the Post-Vatican II Era* (Madison, Conn.: Catholic Scholars Press, 1996).

[24]*Lumen Gentium* 12; see also 25; and *Catechism of the Catholic Church* 91-93; *Familiaris Consortio* 5.

[25]Finucane's *Sensus Fidelium* reveals debate about the use of social scientific tools (such as opinion polls) in determining the *sensus fidelium*. Theologians seem to agree that the *sensus fidelium* reflects the voice of Christians of the past as well as the present. But there is no way to poll the spiritual knowledge of Christians past in a way that would satisfy the methodology of the contemporary social sciences. What records we have of past belief are largely the records of a demographically limited group—theologians and pastors. The beliefs of the illiterate masses are not well documented, compared to the beliefs of the laity today.

Moreover, magisterial texts (such as *Familiaris Consortio* 5) insist that the *sensus fidelium* is not necessarily the same as majority opinion. Opinions must be weighed (in conversation with theological tradition), not just counted.

[26]Boelen, "Church Renewal and the Christian Family," 369.

[27]This phrase was used by Pope John XXIII in his opening address to the Second Vatican Council. See Xavier Rynne, *Vatican Council II* (Maryknoll, N.Y.: Orbis Books, 1999), 47.

[28]Among these difficulties, we might cite transient populations who are not tied to a particular parish, time constraints of average families, lack of researchers trained in social sciences *and* in theology, large numbers of believers whose families drop out of institutional religious affiliation because of canonically invalid marriages, interdenominational marriages, dissent with church teaching, a bad experience with a minister, and so forth.

[29]Wendy Wright, "Living the Already But Not Yet: The Spiritual Life of the American Catholic Family." Warren Lecture Series in Catholic Studies, no. 25 (University of Tulsa, March 21, 1993), 4-5.

[30]Wendy Wright, *Sacred Dwelling: A Spirituality of Family Life* (New York: Crossroad, 1989), 24.

[31]Heaney-Hunter, "Domestic Church," 62.

[32]The NCCB Committee on Marriage and Family notes, "[O]ur prevailing theology of domestic church has arisen historically from a reflection on the sacramentality of marriage. This method is a deductive one. However, within our contemporary culture, we tend to reason inductively. We would start with the 'givenness' of family by examining the many ways in which people consider themselves to be families. We would look for patterns within the total phenomenon that disclose an ecclesial meaning. There is clearly an unresolved tension between the two approaches and, consequently, within our theologizing about family as domestic church" ("A Theological and Pastoral Colloquium: The Christian Family, A Domestic Church,"11).

[33]See especially Willie Teague, "What *Is* a Christian Family?" *Weavings* 5 (January-February 1988): 26-32; also Rosemary Haughton, *Beginning Life in Christ: Gospel Bearings of Christian Education* (Westminster, Md.: Newman Press, 1966). Authors such as these reflect upon events like Mary's unexpected pregnancy, Joseph's worries about her infidelity and their reputations, Elizabeth's sharing in the emotional roller-coaster of infertility and late-in-life pregnancy, the family's experience of homelessness and political exile, strange cousin John who is loved despite his idiosyncrasies, Jesus as the young adult whose family did not always understand the demands of his work, Joseph's apparent absence during Jesus' adult life, Mary as the mother of a death-row inmate, and Jesus' concern to provide for his mother after his death.

[34]See Bernard Häring, "The Christian Family as a Community for Salvation," in *Man Before God* (New Providence, N.J.: P. J. Kenedy & Sons, 1966), 146-158; Denis Edwards, "The Open Table: Theological Reflections on the Family," *Australasian Catholic Record* (July 1995), 327-339; Frederick Parella, "Towards a Spirituality of the Family," *Communio* 9, no. 2 (Summer 1982): 127-141.

[35]See especially Donald Miller, *Concepts of Family Life in Modern Catholic Theology: From Vatican II through Christifideles Laici* (Madison, Conn.: Catholic Scholars Press, 1996), 163-164; Gregory Konerman, "The Family as Domestic Church," in *Church Divinity*, ed. J. Morgan (Bristol, Ind.: Wyndam Hall Press, 1990-91), 58-67; and Maureen Gallagher, "Family as Sacrament," in *The Changing Family*, ed. Stanley Saxton et al. (Chicago: Loyola University Press, 1984), 5-13.

[36]Timothy Lincoln, "Ecclesiology, Marriage, and Historical Consciousness: The Domestic Church as an Ecumenical Opportunity," *New Theology Review* 8, no. 1 (February 1995): 63. See also Ernest Falardeau, "The Church, the Eucharist, and the Family," *One in Christ* 33, no. 1 (1997): 20-30; idem, "Mutual Recognition of Baptism and Pastoral Care of Interchurch Marriages," *Journal of Ecumenical Studies* 28, no. 1 (Winter 1991): 63-73; George Kilcourse, *Double Belonging: Interchurch Families and Christian Unity* (New York: Paulist Press, 1992); Ladislas Örsy, "Interchurch Families and the Eucharist," *Doctrine and Life* 47, no. 1 (January 1997), 10-13; idem, "Interchurch Marriages and Reception of the Eucharist," *America* 175, no. 10 (October 12, 1996): 18-19.

Examining the Role of the Emotions in the Moral Life

Thomas Aquinas and Neuropsychology

William C. Mattison, III

An inquiry into the role of the passions in the moral life may seem antiquated.[1] After all, who speaks of "passions" today anyway? Yet note the following excerpts from the recent *Catechism of the Catholic Church.*[2]

> The term "passions" belongs to Christian patrimony. Feelings or passions are emotions or movements of the sensitive appetite that incline us to act or not act in regard to something felt or imagined to be good or evil. (1763)
>
> In the passions . . . there is neither moral good nor evil. But insofar as they engage reason and the will, there is moral good or evil in them. (1773)
>
> Emotions and feelings can be taken up in the virtues or perverted by the vices. (1774)
>
> Moral perfection consists in man's being moved to the good not by his will alone, but also by his sensitive appetite, as in the words of the psalm: "My heart and flesh sing for joy to the living God." (1770)

The passions figure prominently in the most recent catechism. As will be demonstrated below, they are also a topic of contemporary scientific research. Yet despite the recent Thomistic revival in Catholic moral theology, there is little theological work on his understanding of the passions.[3] This is all the more surprising since the length of Thomas' treatment of the passions in the *Summa Theologiae* dwarfs his other treatments of habits, law, and grace.

One difficulty when trying to discuss the passions is definitional. The *Catechism* simply equates "passion" with "emotion." This paper also equates the two.[4] The terms "passion" and "emotion," however, have been understood quite differently by various schools of thought.[5] Discussion of the moral significance of passion or emotion is easily thwarted by disagreement over exactly what constitutes such phenomena. Defining emotion is not the purpose of this paper. Nevertheless, the discussion of Thomas' vision of the morality of the passions below, combined with the referenced material, will define emotions adequately enough for the main theses of this article.

Moral theology and philosophy may ignore the passions partly because of their focus on those features of action that are distinctively human, such as free will and reason. Do the passions pertain to free will? It would seem they do not. The very term "passion" indicates they are not fully under one's control. Do the passions pertain to reason? Again, it would seem they do not. "Emotion" and "reason" are often adduced as examples of opposites. Indeed, entire moral theories have centered on isolating reason from the adulterating influence of passion, in order that one might act most "rationally." The passions, therefore, are commonly assumed to be relevant to moral theology only to the extent that they might interfere with those more distinctively human features of action such as reason and free will.[6]

This was not Thomas' position. He not only followed Aristotle in claiming that virtue concerns both interior actions *and* passions; he also insisted, as we will see, that the passions could participate in reason. Hence the passions are an essential component of moral theology.

The paper will proceed as follows. The first section will offer three broad approaches for explaining the moral relevance of the passions. The third approach, exemplified by Thomas, claims that the passions are essential for virtuous action. The next section of the paper will more closely examine Thomas' argument for the moral importance of the passions. It will first explore why Thomas thought the passions to be essential to virtuous action and then explore how Thomas substantiates this claim with a particular understanding of the relationship between reason and passion. The third section of the paper will examine Damasio's research on that same relationship. The essay will then conclude with synthesizing thoughts and suggestions for further research.

The Passions and their Role (or Lack Thereof) in Virtuous Action

Consider three approaches to the role of the passions in the moral life. The first may be labeled the "Stoic extirpation of the passions."[7] The Stoic approach considers passions to be irrational attachments to external goods. In this view, the passions are always contrary to reason, and are ideally eradicated from the wise person.

A second and different approach agrees with the Stoics that the passions are non-rational movements of the "lower" parts of the soul. This second approach, therefore, views the passions with suspicion. But it differs from the Stoic position in that it does not claim that the passions are necessarily contrary to reason. Reason may "rein in" the passions, much as one would an unruly horse. Proponents of this position, such as Plato or Kant, accept the possibility that the passions may be tamed by reason so as to actually support the wise person in virtuous action (*contra* the Stoics). However, even when controlled by reason, the passions themselves in no way participate in reason. Furthermore, passion may support the virtuous person's good act, but an equally good act is possible without passion.

Although proponents of the second approach depart from the Stoics by stating that passions can support the wise person in virtuous acts, they give the same negative answers to the following three diagnostic questions of the Stoics.

1. Does a lack of passion render a virtuous action imperfect?
2. Can reason inform passion? In other words, are the actual passions a virtuous person "feels" shaped (not merely reined in or controlled) by that person's reason?
3. Can passion inform reason?

This third question is different from the first. Rather than asking merely whether a virtuous action might be incomplete without some accompanying passion, this question further inquires whether the virtuous action itself may somehow be positively informed by passion. Obviously non-virtuous acts are frequently shaped by passions. But to imply that passions actually contribute positively to the content of a reasonable act would make a very strong statement about the importance of the passions for moral theology and their relationship to reason.

Proponents of the second, Platonic, approach answer "no" to each of the three diagnostic questions. The second approach says that the passions may be channeled or controlled to support virtuous actions, but virtuous acts without any passion at all are still *fully* virtuous acts. Thomas, however, exemplifies a third position. He responds to the first question with a "yes." According to this view, the virtues always concern both interior actions and passions. The moral good is most perfectly achieved by one's actions and passions working together. Thus a virtuous act is less perfect if lacking in passion.

Like proponents of the second approach, however, Thomas still insists that reason is the standard for human virtue. So Thomas needs to elaborate the connection between reason and emotion. His position will be more carefully examined below. The superiority of this third approach will emerge through an examination of the work of both Thomas and Damasio.

Thomas on the Passions and Reason

Thomas' writings portray the passions as truly central in the Christian moral life. The *locus classicus* for Thomas' thought on the role of the passions in the moral life is the so-called "Treatise on the Passions," comprised of Questions Twenty-Two to Forty-Eight in the Prima Secunda of the *Summa Theologiae*. The length of this treatment alone suggests the importance Thomas places on the passions.

Thomas addresses "good and evil in the passions" in Question Twenty-Four. Leading up to the crucial third article, the first article responds affirmatively to the question of whether there can be good and evil in the passions. Thomas claims that as non-rational movements of the sensitive appetite, the passions are not good or evil in themselves. However, since they may be subject to the will and reason, there can be good and evil in them. The second article then asks if the passions, while morally significant, are always evil. Thomas notes that the Stoics claim the passions are always evil; they are "diseases of the soul."[8]

Thomas replies that the passions do indeed incline to sin if they are "contrary to the order of reason;" however, "in so far as they are controlled by reason, they pertain to virtue."[9] (We would insert a middle claim that insofar as the passions are able to be controlled by reason, they pertain either to virtue or to vice.) This article, therefore, places Thomas squarely beyond the Stoic position, the first of the three approaches to the passions in the moral life. Not only are the passions morally significant as potentially subject to reason, but they might also be good instead of evil if they are controlled by reason.

It is the third article in Question Twenty-Four, however, wherein Thomas distinguishes his position from the second (Platonic) approach described above. He asks whether passion increases or decreases the goodness or malice of an act. He has already established that passions can be good or evil. Now he asks whether passion makes an otherwise good act any more or less good (or, vice versa, an evil act any more or less evil). Thomas himself offers a fine example of what is at stake in the question: "Who merits the more, he who helps a poor man with a certain compassion of pity, or he who does it without any passion solely because of a judgment of reason?"[10] For Thomas, the person who acts *with passion* (here, pity) deserves more merit. His answer reveals that the passions are not to be understood as a non-essential component of the moral life, in other words, relevant but superfluous. Thomas agrees with the second approach that since the passions "can obey reason . . . [they belong] to the perfection of moral or human good, that the passions themselves should . . . be controlled by reason."[11] But Thomas goes further: it belongs to the *perfection* of moral good that the person should be moved to the good not only by the will, but also by the passions.[12] Therefore, even a virtuous act without such emotional involvement is imperfect.

Thomas holds two ideas. One is that a decision is said to be morally good inasmuch as it is an act of reason—a deliberate choice of the good. The other is that passion is an essential component of a fully virtuous act. Thomas is not just saying that the passions can be controlled by reason and thus not get in the way. He is saying they positively contribute to the goodness of the moral act. Thomas must offer more guidance as to how this is possible. He makes a crucial antecedent/consequent distinction that serves precisely that need. This reply is worth quoting in its entirety:

> The passions of the soul stand in twofold relation to the judgment of reason. First antecedently: and thus, since they obscure the judgment of reason, on which the goodness of the moral act depends, they diminish the goodness of the act; for it is more praiseworthy to do an act of charity from the judgment of reason than from the mere passion of pity. In the second place, consequently: and this in two ways. First, by way of redundance: because, when the higher part of the soul is intensely moved to anything, the lower part also follows that movement; and thus the passion that results in consequence, in the sensitive appetite, is a sign of the intensity of will, and so indicates greater moral goodness. Secondly, by way of choice; when a man, by the judgment of his reason, chooses to be affected by a passion to work more promptly with the co-ordination of the sensitive appetite. And thus a passion of the soul increases the goodness of an action.[13]

Thomas makes this distinction even more clear in *De Veritate*. There he claims that one may act either *from* passion or *with* passion. The former is "antecedent" passion. It diminishes the goodness of a good act (or, for that matter, increases the wrongness of an evil one) because such antecedent passion diminishes the role of reasoned deliberation in the act.[14] In fact, for Thomas an act is truly human only to the extent that it is rational. If passion diminishes the role of reason in the act, that makes the act even less "human." We could call a passionless act of almsgiving, for example, less fully human, since Thomas claims that it belongs to the perfection of a person's moral good that the person should be moved to the good not only by the will, but also by the passions. An act arising "out of reason" and "with [consequent] passion" constitutes the standard for Thomas' understanding of perfect human action. He thus respects reason as the rule of human action, and simultaneously insists that only reasonable action with passion is complete.

Thomas thus illuminates some of our common moral judgments concerning the emotions. Antecedent emotions are often exculpatory, *diminishing* our moral responsibility, as when we say, "Yes, he did something bad, but he was so scared" (or angry, or desperate, and so forth) or, "Yes, she kindly gave that person on the street some money, but only because she was so scared or uncomfortable." By contrast consequent passions can *augment* our moral evaluations, as when we further inculpate an evildoer who also seems to enjoy her act, or admire a nurse even more who compassionately cares for each of his patients. Thomas' antecedent/consequent distinction enables him to secure the moral importance of the passions, even while recognizing that they may at times hinder the use of reason.

Returning to our three diagnostic questions concerning the importance of the passions in moral theology, Thomas offers a resoundingly affirmative response to the first question, which asks whether a virtuous act without passion is somehow deficient. This answer places Thomas squarely beyond the second approach, which claims that the emotions may facilitate virtuous action, but are not themselves essential to the fully virtuous act.

Thomas insists on the moral importance of the passions precisely because he understood them to be more closely related to reason than is implied in the second approach. It is not just because the passions might mislead reason, though they might. Nor is it only because they are divinely created components of human nature, as important as this is.[15] The passions are crucial to moral theology because they can participate in reason.

Of course, human passions are not purely cognitive; one's passions may defy what one believes, as when a concerned parent still worries despite knowing that a child is surely safe. Later in article three of Question Twenty-Four Thomas uses a famous Aristotelian analogy to elucidate how reason can both command and fail to control the passions. Thomas claims reason may be said to command the *body* like a despot, since the members of the body cannot resist the command of the soul. Yet reason rules the *passions* as a political ruler.[16] But the passions might not obey reason since they "have something of their own."[17] He describes this "something of their own" as imagination and sense, which also hold sway over the passions, often against the command of reason. Hence the passions are not rational essentially, but rather "by participation."[18]

The political analogy is most illustrative here. The passions are ruled not as slaves, but as subjects. Certainly they are not to be extirpated, as the Stoics suggest. Yet neither are they merely to be reined in, as the famous Platonic horseman image suggests. While the Platonic image is similar to Thomas' analogy in that there is a lack of full control over the passions, it is also different. Platonic control implies domestication and not governance by reason. Thomas' political analogy suggests the passions may participate in the rule of law, which for Thomas is always the rule of reason.[19] For Thomas, reason actually informs the content of one's passions; one "feels" the way one does in part due to the cognitive beliefs one holds.

While passion and reason are quite different powers of the human person, Thomas' quasi-cognitive understanding of passion leads him to claim that reason can inform the passions. Hence, it is appropriate to pose our third diagnostic question again at this point: can the passions inform reason? In her *Choosing to Feel*, Diana Fritz Cates briefly examines Thomas' position on this question. She concludes cautiously that Thomas never speaks of passion as a source of morally relevant knowledge, but that it would not be grossly inconsistent with his thought had he done so.[20] She suggests this may provide an occasion to extend Thomas' thought, and her own book exemplifies such an effort. We will return below to possible reasons why Thomas does not directly claim that passion informs reason. With Cates we press the question of whether the emotions inform reason by seeking other sources that might confirm, reject, or complement Thomas' thought.

As empirical phenomena, the emotions lend themselves readily to scientific investigation. Hence we turn to the work of contemporary neuropsychologist Antonio Damasio. Damasio's work is a particularly fruitful source, for two reasons: first, he has worked extensively on precisely this question of the relationship between emotion and reason; second, his inductive experimentation is not only methodologically distinct from Thomas' own thought, but Damasio approaches this same subject matter from the opposite direction as Thomas. He proposes that emotion contributes to *reasonable* decision-making.

Antonio Damasio on Reason and Emotion

Antonio Damasio's 1994 book, *Descartes' Error: Emotion, Reason, and the Human Brain*, relies on psychological and neurobiological experimentation to address the question of the relationship between reason and emotion.[21] The book begins wonderfully—albeit somewhat disturbingly—with the stories of nineteenth-century railworker Phineas Gage and Damasio's own patient named Elliot. Each man suffered severe damage to subcortical areas of his brain, though the neocortex remained relatively undamaged. Scientists have long associated the neocortex, an area of the brain evolutionarily "recent" and disproportionately large in humans, with "higher reasoning" abilities such as conscious memory, calculation, language, and so on. Cortical and subcortical areas of the brain, including evolutionary elders such as the brain stem and limbic system, are commonly associated with sensory ability, body regulation, basic drives, and emotions. This description is grossly simplified, but will suffice for the purposes of this paper.[22]

Though having suffered severe subcortical damage to their brains, both men appeared at first glance to be largely functional. Motor and language abilities were unharmed. They performed well on tests of mathematical, verbal, and other intellectual abilities. Even when presented with scenarios to test moral reasoning, the patients performed admirably. Yet, in their "real lives" the men were far from functional. They could not hold jobs. They had become not only socially tactless, but also offensive to others due to their language and behavior. They would neglect obvious responsibilities and spend hours on insignificant tasks. In laboratory situations, they could articulate appropriate response options to complex moral situations and even consider the consequences of each option. Yet they could not make decisions about such situations in "real life." In short, while it seemed each had reasoning abilities and even "knew" what to do in a given moral situation, their actions outside the laboratory did not reflect such knowledge. Damasio offers a telling quote from one experimental session in which Elliot successfully articulated a variety of estimable options for action. Elliot smiled, proud of his imagination, but added, "And after all this, I still wouldn't know what to do!"[23]

How could each patient's brain damage account for these deficiencies when the distinctively human "higher reasoning" abilities were intact? In order to answer this question, Damasio examined which parts of the brain were damaged. He found the most extensive damage to those parts of the brain normally associated with emotional activity. Indeed, each man did experience a striking reduction in emotion. Damasio describes this realization concerning his own patient, Elliot. Never an overly emotional man, after his illness Elliot seemed to approach life on a "neutral note."[24] Damasio claims he never saw a "tinge of emotion" in Elliot despite hours of conversation. Elliot would dispassionately describe the illness that had wreaked havoc in his life as if he were an impartial observer. He was given psychological tests to gauge emotional response. Such response was virtually non-existent. And astonishingly enough, Elliott *knew* this, commenting after the test that the disturbing images he had just been shown would have evoked strong emotion before his illness. Damasio asks the reader to image the horror: Elliot not only did not feel joy, anger, or other emotions, but he also *knew* he did not feel those emotions. "We might summarize Elliot's predicament as *to know but not to feel*."[25] Damasio suspected that this emotional defect was deeply involved in Elliot's behavioral problems, that "the cold-bloodedness of Elliot's reasoning prevented him from assigning different values to different options, and made his decision-making landscape hopelessly flat."[26]

Further study of twelve other patients with similarly rare brain damage confirmed this hypothesis. Damasio's basic claim is *not* that emotion never disrupts rational decision-making. There is wisdom in advice to monitor one's emotions while making important decisions. Damasio would agree with Thomas that emotions have "something of their own" that often defies the command of reason. His point is this: "*Reduction in emotion may constitute an equally important source of irrational behavior.* The counterintuitive connection between absent emotion and warped behavior may tell us something about the biological machinery of reason."[27] Damasio's study goes on to probe that biological machinery and examine its ramifications on how we understand the relationship between reason and the passions. He rejects the following popular (mis)understanding of brain structure and function:

> In simple terms: The old brain core handles basic biological regulation down in the basement, while up above the neocortex deliberates with wisdom and subtlety. Upstairs in the cortex there is reason and willpower, while downstairs in the subcortex there is emotion and all that weak, fleshy stuff.[28]

Damasio claims that the very apparatus of rationality, often assumed to be solely neocortical, does not work without subcortical regulation. "[T]he apparatus of rationality [is built] not just on top of the apparatus of biological regulation, but also *from* it and *with* it."[29] The emotions serve as a "bridge" between the "rational" neocortical structures and the "nonrational" subcortical structures. At this point his analysis sounds similar to Thomas' understanding of the emotions as nonrational in themselves, but able to participate in reason.

Damasio suggests that the problematic "common view" of how the brain operates parallels an equally inaccurate "common view" of proper moral decision-making. He calls it the "high reason" view, one we can recognize as rather Stoic in its approach. It asserts that: "Formal logic will, by itself, get us to the best available solution for any problem. [T]o obtain the best results, emotions must be kept out. Rational processing must be unencumbered by passion."[30] Damasio's research indicates that emotionless decision-making has far more to do with the way patients with prefrontal brain damage go about deciding than with how healthy people act rationally. He grants that the healthy individual does react to a situation by rapidly creating scenarios of possible response options and related outcomes. But he adds that "your mind is not blank at the start of the reasoning process."[31] Visceral reactions accompany our consideration of the various possible actions and outcomes. These visceral reactions are emotional attachments or repulsions to different alternatives, (ideally) increasing the accuracy and efficiency of our deliberation process. Emotional attachments do not deliberate for us. But they do illuminate the salient features of a decision, enabling us to choose more quickly and appropriately.[32]

Damasio thus argues for the necessity of emotional involvement in order to think rationally. Like Thomas, he affirms that the passions are not just morally relevant or even important though non-essential; rather, they are a critical part of the rational, and hence moral, life. But Damasio finds himself in the same predicament as Thomas. Having established the importance of the passions, Damasio might be asked, as is Thomas in I-II 24, 3, ob. 1, what if our emotions incline us wrongly? Granting that an aberrant lack of emotion incapacitates one's decision-making ability, aren't we also frequently misled by our emotional attachments? Like Thomas, Damasio is aware of the objection. He even cites a few common irrational fears that seem to hinder rational thought. Unlike Thomas, he offers no way of discerning which ones are an obstacle to reason (such as Thomas' antecedent passions). He simply notes that though it may seem bizarre that emotions can be both beneficial and pernicious, they by no means represent the only biological phenomenon that may be positive or negative in varying degrees and circumstances.

Concluding Thoughts and Further Questions

Damasio's research confirms the Thomastic claims regarding the importance of the emotions in the moral life, over and against the

Stoic or Platonic approaches. Damasio's patients tragically personify the Stoic extirpation of the passions. The ramifications of this condition are disastrous. Damasio's research also contradicts the second (Platonic) claim that the passions are non-essential, though sometimes helpful, components of the virtuous act. His work suggests that the purported crux of inner human action, reason, relies on emotional attachments in order to function properly. If emotions of some degree or sort are indeed a precondition for rational thought, the second approach is based upon an inadequate understanding of the "hydraulics" of human decision-making.

While Damasio agrees with Thomas' insistence on the close relationship between reason and passions, they are not in full agreement. Thomas articulates this relationship by describing how reason informs emotion; Damasio argues that the emotions also inform reason. The two positions are not, of course, mutually exclusive. Damasio's exploration of how emotion may inform reason should not be taken as a rejection of the possibility of reason informing emotion. In fact, portions of his book allude to the cognitive character of passions in a fashion most consistent with Thomas' thought.[33] Yet, it is doubtful that the same reciprocity may be attributed to Thomas' work on reason and passion. Thomas seems to purposely limit his treatment to the way reason informs passion, and not vice versa.

As noted, however, Thomas offers a distinction between antecedent and consequent emotions. This distinction allows Thomas to place reason prior to passion in the virtuous act. If this distinction is interpreted to mean only *logical* antecedence and consequence, they merely reflect Thomas' insistence that, despite the importance of passion, reason is the standard of human action. Damasio might agree, despite his hypothesis concerning reason's reliance on emotional attachments. However, the *temporal* connotations of Thomas' terms render them easily interpreted as implying that one must first make an emotionless reasonable decision and then allow emotional resolve to help carry it out. Certain texts seem to support this interpretation. In I-II 24, 3 ad. 1, Thomas claims that consequent passion reflects a movement of the lower appetite that "follows" the intense movement of the higher part of the soul. He speaks of a person who, by the judgment of reason, chooses to be affected by a passion in order to work more promptly.

Damasio's hypothesis challenges Thomas' analysis. Damasio's findings should not be accepted as simple fact. But if Damasio is right that reason requires antecedent emotion, Thomas' analysis appears inaccurate. His interpretation would seem to imply that each virtuous action is to be performed without antecedent emotion. This model certainly lies in tension with Damasio's findings.

It is also arguably inconsistent, however, on Thomas' own terms. First, Thomas clearly claims a virtuous action is perfect only when it is performed with passion. A temporal interpretation of Thomas' distinction would have him exhorting the virtuous person to continually make reasonable decisions *with passion*, only to keep quelling that passion in order to prepare for the next reasonable decision *with passion*. This fragmented vision of the moral life would be problematic. Furthermore, such a position might also be internally inconsistent for Thomas, since his entire argument for *how* reason and emotions are related prevents him from espousing any strict dichotomy between the two. Passions are governed, according to Thomas, precisely by rational deliberation. Such reasoning does not domesticate the passions, but rather shapes their content. Hence, in reflecting on Adam's sin one may be filled with sorrow. In contemplating the resurrection one may be filled with joy. One cannot reflect or contemplate, and then discharge or liberate, a subsequent passion as one would an unruly horse from a stable. The very passion itself exists partially due to the reasonable deliberation and has taken its form from the content of the deliberation. Given Thomas' understanding of the close relationship between reason and emotion, he could espouse *logically* consequent emotion without dichotomizing these two powers of the single human soul.[34] While the staunchest proponent of reason, Thomas is clearly no advocate of some emotionless "pure" reason as his standard.[35]

Finally, Thomas' discussion of passions as subjects of moral virtue may further illuminate the antecedent/consequent distinction. By claiming that passions can be the subject of moral virtue, Thomas can claim that passions previously habituated (by rational deliberation) can indeed inform the rational deliberation that follows. Rather than raw surges of affect devoid of any rational content or influence, emotions are cognitive phenomena with a history, a history shaped by rational deliberation. Such passions may be exactly the sort that Damasio claims illuminate (or cloud) the morally salient features of a situation.

Future research on the importance of the passions in moral theology will benefit from further investigation of the question in light of

Thomas' understanding of habituated passion. However, since the passions always contain "something of their own" that may defy the governance of reason, an understanding of prior habituation will provide no simple solution to the question of whether passion informs reason. Future research will also have to expand the present analysis of the "hydraulics" of human action to include the will, which is beyond the scope of this piece. Finally, more research is required of social scientists to determine the scope and accuracy of Damasio's theory.

The question of the relationship between reason and the passions will provide an outstanding opportunity for continued dialogue between the social sciences and moral theology. But one firm conclusion may be drawn already. The emotions are an essential component of the virtuous life. No matter how they inform reason, they demand the attention of moral theologians.

Notes

[1]Mark Jordan claims that Thomas' teleological anthropology allows him to argue that human passions are "taken up" to participate in reason; any higher power is said to incorporate features of the lower one. Thus, Thomas' reason is not apathetic. See Jordan, "Aquinas' Construction of a Moral Account for the Passions" *Freiburger Zeitschrift für Philosophie und Theologie* 33 (1986): 93-97.

[2]*Catechism of the Catholic Church* (St. Louis: Liguori Publications, 1994). In fact, this latest catechism is the first ever to afford the passions their own distinctive section. (From a conversation with Fr. Servais Pinckaers, O.P., October 3, 2000.)

[3]There are exceptions. Four articles stand out. Mark Jordan examines the passions throughout Thomas' entire corpus. See "Aquinas' Construction of a Moral Account for the Passions," 71-97. Richard Mansfield focuses on the antecedent/consequent distinction of the *Summa Theologiae* and *De Veritate*. See "Antecedent Passion and the Moral Quality of Human Acts According to St. Thomas," *American Catholic Philosophical Quarterly* 71 (1997): 221-231. Servais Pinckaers, O.P., contrasts the notions of passion found in Aquinas and Descartes and notes the resulting differences in their moral significance. See "Les passions et la morale," *Révue Scholastique de Philosophie et Théologie* 74 (1991): 379-391. Finally, Judith Barad examines the character of passion in Thomas' work and, towards the end of her piece, turns to the morality of the passions. See "Aquinas on the Role of Emotion in Moral Judgment and Activity," *The Thomist* 55 (1991): 397-413. In terms of books, Diana Fritz Cates's *Choosing to Feel: Virtue, Friendship, and Compassion for Friends* (Notre Dame: University of Notre Dame Press, 1997) contains an outstanding discussion of the importance of the passions for Aristotle and Thomas, and their impact on practical wisdom. G. Simon Harak's *Virtuous Passions* (New

York: Paulist Press, 1993) is also worthy of note. Finally, Paul Wadell examines the nature of passion, specifically the passion of love, in his *Friends of God* (New York: Peter Lang, 1991).

[4]There is intuitive support for this equation due to the inner activities Thomas describes as passions. Some of the authors noted here nod toward this issue, but none examines it systematically in Thomas' work. The best examination of the relation between passion and emotion is found in Stephen Leighton, "Aristotle and the Emotions," in Amélie Rorty, ed., *Essays on Aristotle's Rhetoric* (Berkeley: University of California Press, 1980), 203-237.

[5]A renowned discussion of the passions is found in Augustine's *City of God*, IX.

[6]This suspicion of the passions is quite evident in the so-called manuals of moral theology, despite their reliance on Thomas. For instance, John A. McHugh, O.P. and Charles J. Callan, O.P., in their *Moral Theology: A Complete Course*, 2 vols. (New York: Joseph F. Wagner, Inc., 1958), 42-49, offer one of the more extended treatments of passion. Yet most of that discussion focuses on how the passions disturb judgment and need to be controlled. There is much on how to control morally dangerous passions, but little on how to foster proper passion.

[7]I borrow the phrase "extirpation of the passions" from Martha Nussbaum. See her *Therapy of Desire: Theory and Practice in Hellenistic Ethics* (Princeton: Princeton University Press, 1996). It is actually arguable whether the Stoics idealized *apatheia* in the completely emotionless sense of the word rightly caricatured by Augustine in *City of God,* XIV.9. A. A. Long, in his *Hellenistic Philosophers* (Cambridge: Cambridge University Press, 1987), suggests that despite their espousal of *apatheia*, the Stoics did maintain some (limited) place for what we might call emotions today. As Thomas notes in *Summa Theologiae* I-II 24, 2, the issue may be definitional: did the Stoics consider a passion under the command of reason no longer a passion? Regardless, their strong (to say the least) suspicion of passions as disturbances to reason rightly shunned by the wise still represents the most drastic position in the typology employed here.

[8]*Summa Theologiae* I-II, 24, 3, resp. (hereafter *ST*: all quotations are taken from the Fathers of the English Dominican Province translation, New York: Benziger Brothers, 1948).

[9]*ST* I-II 24, 2, ad 3.

[10]*De Veritate* XXVI, 7, Prologue.

[11]*ST* I-II 24, 3.

[12]*ST* I-II 24, 3, emphasis mine.

[13]*ST* I-II 24, 3, ad 1.

[14]Of course, the moral quality is diminished only if that inadequate deliberation is itself not a deliberate choice. See Thomas' discussion of ignorance for relevant distinctions, *ST* I-II, 19.6.

[15]This sense of the intelligibility of nature, and the resulting belief that nature provides nothing superfluous, is repeated throughout Thomas' *Summa*. For more on the thirteenth-century thinking of the intelligibility of creation, see Jean Porter, *Divine and Natural Law: Reclaiming the Tradition for Christian Ethics* (Grand

Rapids: Eerdmans, 1999). For the ramifications of articulating only virtues in the will and reason (to the exclusion of the passions), see Bonnie Dorrick Kent's *Virtues of the Will: The Transformation of Ethics in the Late Thirteenth Century* (Washington, D.C.: Catholic University Press of America, 1995).

[16]Thomas borrows this analogy from Aristotle's *Rhetoric*, I, 3. See *The Basic Works of Aristotle*, ed. Richard McKeon (New York: Random House, 1941), 1325-1451.

[17]*ST* I 81, 3, ad 2.

[18]Thomas claims this repeatedly throughout the *Summa*. See the citations in note 15 above.

[19]See *ST* I-II 90, 1.

[20]See Cates, *Choosing to Feel*, 24. Cates employs the model of the Aristotelian practical syllogism to note the ways that passion impacts choice. "Clearly, passion can derail the major or minor premises, by fostering inordinate desire for a lesser (or non-) good, or by distracting one from accurately grasping the salient features of a moral situation. Passion can also bolster the major premise for a good decision, as when one emotionally desires a true good. It is less clear, however, that passion can assist the person form a minor premise, constituted by a *belief* or a *perception* regarding what in the present situation best contributes to the desired end" (Cates, *Choosing to Feel*, 8, emphasis in original).

[21]Antonio Damasio, *Descartes' Error: Emotion, Reason, and the Human Brain* (New York: G. P. Putnam's Sons, 1994).

[22]For a complete account of the damage to their brains, see Damasio, *Descartes' Error*, 21-23, 38-39.

[23]Ibid., 49.

[24]Ibid., 45.

[25]Ibid., emphasis in original.

[26]Ibid., 51.

[27]Ibid., 53, emphasis in original.

[28]Ibid., 128.

[29]Ibid., 128, emphasis in original. The use of the terms "from" and "with" is ironic given Thomas' use of the terms. Of course, Thomas distinguished the two, whereas Damasio does not.

[30]Ibid., 171.

[31]Ibid., 170.

[32]Ibid., 175.

[33]See especially 128, and the following evaluation of William James's definition of emotion.

[34]See Servais Pinckaers, O.P., "Les passions et la morale," for a more detailed discussion of Descartes' impact in creating the impression of just such a dichotomy.

[35]Mark Jordan claims that Thomas' teleological anthropology allows him to argue that human passions are "taken up" to participate in reason; any higher power is said to incorporate features of the lower one. Thus, Thomas' reason is not apathetic. See Jordan, "Aquinas' Construction of a Moral Account for the Passions," 93-97.

Interpreting the Dreams of Perpetua: Psychology in the Service of Theology[1]

Felicidad Oberholzer

The classic definition of theology is faith seeking understanding. The range of tools at our disposal to attain an ever-deepening understanding of faith is, however, often underestimated, even though we ought to make full use of them. One discipline that has much to offer in pursuing this task is psychology. Just as with other related disciplines such as history and sociology, psychology can provide a unique and valuable access into the intricate context of a particular time, society, and culture (in this instance, as they relate to the human heart and psyche) and can help theology gain a fuller and broader grasp of faith. The application of these disciplines often results in hard questions for theology and the challenge to rethink and reformulate traditional interpretations. Such is often the case when, after a closer look at our great saints, what might seem like a less than exemplary profile emerges. We have to realize, however, that it is better to let human experience speak for itself with all its frailty and limitations, based on our conviction that truer profiles of faith and courage emerge when God's glory shows through human weakness as well as strength.

The purpose of this paper is to see how psychology can be of particular value to theology by examining the life and martyrdom of St. Perpetua vis-à-vis her dreams. It will show how a psychological analysis can deepen our knowledge of what happens in this complex and traumatic experience of self-sacrifice for Christ and will illustrate the limitations of theological discourse uninformed by these insights. By using a psychological approach and by setting aside the traditional theological interpretations to look afresh, I hope to allow Perpetua's humanness to speak more clearly and thus gain a more full and insightful theological perspective.

We can begin with a summary of the circumstances of Perpetua's martyrdom and the problem of interpreting her dreams. In 203, when Perpetua was a twenty-two-year-old well-educated and privileged Roman matron with an infant son, she died in the arena at Carthage for her Christian faith along with her pregnant slave Felicitas, their catechist Saturus, who voluntarily gave himself up so as to join them, and two others.[2] Her immediate family consisted of a father, mother, aunt, at least two brothers (one of whom was also a catechumen), and her infant son. She was accused of failure to obey the emperor Septimus Severus's edict forbidding conversion to Christianity and was held under house arrest while awaiting trial, during which time she completed her conversion by being baptized. Shortly after, she was moved to an overcrowded prison where she was terrified by the darkness and suffered greatly from the heat and ill treatment by the soldiers. After a hearing, at which she refused to deny that she was Christian, she was sentenced to die "by the beasts" in the arena as part of the games that were being held to celebrate the birthday of the emperor's son. Because two deacons bribed the soldiers, she was able to move to a better part of the prison as she awaited her execution. She records four emotionally heart-wrenching visits with her father in which he tried to convince her to offer sacrifice to the emperor or to deny that she was a Christian.

During her imprisonment, she wrote a diary traditionally titled *The Passion of Saints Perpetua and Felicity*, which is essentially a record of her thoughts, reflections, encounters with her family, and the events leading up to her death; it includes four dreams, or visions, that she had.[3] The diary was later redacted by an editor who added some details about her background, Saturus' record of a vision he had, and a description of the martyrs' deaths in the arena.

In the centuries following her death, this record was read on her feast day to congregations as a testimony of a faithful Christian's journey to excite fervor and passion in the hearts of the faithful. Although various interpretations were offered for different elements of the diary, the dreams recorded in the account drew special attention; Augustine, for example, preached three sermons on them.[4]

Many of the interpretations, especially those having to do with her dreams were, however, to a large extent impositions of what was thought to be a proper understanding of what had happened, and the original text has not easily been able to speak for itself. Following this early period and up to the present, many other attempts to explicate the experience of her final days have had a tendency to impose theological constructs or have lacked knowledge about dreams in making their interpretations.[5] Others have examined various elements in her account for historical and cultural knowledge of the second century, including the role of women under Roman patriarchy or the understanding of the body in the early church; however, they have often overlooked or sometimes even misunderstood the psychological dimension, which would have added to their research.[6]

Many psychological questions of interest arise from a careful reading of this text. What kind of person was Perpetua, and in what ways were her familial and cultural background formative in her development? What attracted her to Christianity? At this time when catechumens could easily have avoided persecution, why did she allow herself to be arrested knowing what the consequences would be? How did her relationship to her father affect her willingness to make this decision? Where was her husband, since no mention is made of him at all? What was her attachment to her baby? What was her relationship to Saturus other than catechumen to catechist? How ought the symbols in her dreams be interpreted (a ladder that ascends to a garden, a serpent on whose head she steps, a shepherd, her brother Dinocrates, her transformation into a man, among others)? These questions are very much key to understanding Perpetua and thus how God would have been at work in her transformation into a woman of faith and courage.

Although she is a martyr and a saint, Perpetua's personal testimony should not be expected to come from the standpoint of perfection. Like all of us, she must struggle with psychological woundedness, flaws, and imperfections, which ought not to be overlooked or distorted, since God works as much through our weaknesses as our strengths. Indeed, she could be a more powerful witness when seen this way than when held up as an example of holiness that precludes the kind of struggles that each of us in our own way must face throughout life.

The psychological approach I am taking begins from a few basic principles that will be worth briefly reviewing. A key to knowing ourselves is bringing into awareness how our unconscious affects who we are. The task of coming to wholeness involves the lifetime struggle to discover, understand, and accept all parts of ourselves. This includes recognizing our dark side, acknowledging our sinfulness, learning from our woundedness, and celebrating our gifts. Our unconscious is by definition unknown to us. It serves as a protection from what we are unable to bear, from what would be too overwhelming or threatening to our immature psyches, or from unpleasant and traumatic events and knowledge of our hidden selves. For these reasons, it is very difficult to face this deeper self-knowledge, which carries with it the powerful effects that were present when it was buried. If repressing it would simply solve our problems, then there would be no need to confront it.

The difficulty is that what has been repressed still affects our actions, our relationships, and much more: it leaks out. It is like burying nuclear waste products as a way of getting rid of them and then finding that they have polluted the environment. At least in this example, we would be cognizant of burying the waste; whereas, we are not aware that we are "burying" anything in our unconscious. The first manifestations of our unconscious are usually seen in difficulties that erupt in our lives or in our dreams. We have to learn to interpret these difficulties and our dreams to detect what is ready to be revealed to us when we have the courage to seek for it. Many of us do not want to participate in this process and even deny that such a task is possible. In a sense, we could say that the defenses some of us have built up to protect ourselves remain in place because we are too fragile to risk examining them or sometimes because the task seems too overwhelming or frightening. In theological language, we might say that the invitation that grace provides is refused.

The value of Perpetua's account is that her dreams give us a window into her unconscious and the possibility of understanding her much more fully. At the same time, any psychological explanations offered for Perpetua's experience must be tentative and open to regular reevaluation; such is the nature of the far from exact science of psychology. Accepting these limitations, however, does not mean we should not engage in a struggle to understand. Because of the constraints of time and space, I will simply excerpt her four visions, choose just one author's interpretation for each vision to illustrate its inadequacies, and then give a brief alternative interpretation of the visions to show what psychology can contribute.

Her first dream occurred after her brother asked her to pray for a vision to discover whether she was to be condemned or freed. She describes it as follows:

> I saw a ladder of tremendous height made of bronze, reaching all the way to the heavens, but it was so narrow that only one person

> could climb up at a time. To the sides of the ladder were attached all sorts of metal weapons: there were swords, spears, hooks, daggers, and spikes; so that if anyone tried to climb up carelessly or without paying attention, he would be mangled and his flesh would adhere to the weapons. At the foot of the ladder lay a dragon of enormous size, and it would attack those who tried to climb up and try to terrify them from doing so. And Saturus was the first to go up, he who was later to give himself up of his own accord. He had been the builder of our strength, although he was not present when we were arrested. And he arrived at the top of the staircase and he looked back and said to me: "Perpetua, I am waiting for you. But take care; do not let the dragon bite you." "He will not harm me," I said, "in the name of Christ Jesus." Slowly, as though he were afraid of me, the dragon stuck his head out from underneath the ladder. Then, using it as my first step, I trod on his head and went up. Then I saw an immense garden, and in it a grey-haired man sat in shepherd's garb; tall he was, and milking sheep. And standing around him were many thousands of people clad in white garments. He raised his head, looked at me, and said: "I am glad you have come, my child." He called me over to him and gave me, as it were, a mouthful of the milk (*caseo*)[7] he was drawing; and I took it into my cupped hands and consumed it. And all those who stood around said: "Amen!" At the sound of this word I came to, with the taste of something sweet still in my mouth. (*Passio* 4.3-10)

Let us first look at an interpretation of this vision offered by Alvyn Pettersen in his article "Perpetua—Prisoner of Conscience." An extended excerpt will be necessary to illustrate my point, and it will speak for itself.

> Nor did death carry a threat. For it was not that which effected separation from God but that which effected the transition to that existence where God alone was the ultimate horizon. Indeed, such a relinquishing of the fear that death was the final horizon in human life, and such an assumption of hope in God alone, is clearly manifest in Perpetua's first vision of her trials; therein a dragon tried to terrify her from stepping out upon the path to God. She however would not be terrified. Rather, claiming the name

of Jesus Christ, she rendered the once terrifying dragon terrified; and using it as her first step, she trod upon its head, and began her pilgrimage to God. . . .

Central to this inner discipline is Perpetua's desire to fulfil the church's sacramental motifs. These baptismal and eucharistic motifs appear mainly in the descriptions of her visions. The first vision is that which takes its form from that of Jacob in Genesis 28. The very form of the vision is baptismal: even as baptism entails the passage from death to self to life in God, so the ascending of the ladder involves the movement from man to God. The detail of the vision continues this theme: the dragon which tried to prevent any godward movement echoes the devil and all his pomp, renounced thrice in the baptismal rite. The same dragon was renounced *in nomine Jesu Christi.* Having thus overcome the dragon, Perpetua was then greeted by a grey haired man in shepherd's garb, who said, *bene venisti*, and *teuknon.* Common as the idea of the followers of Christ being *teukna* of God is, it yet recalls Tertullian's description of baptism in *De corona* 3.3: having been baptized "*then, when we are taken up (sc. as new born children), we taste first of all a mixture of milk and honey.*" Nor then is it inappropriate that in this vision Perpetua was called over by the grey haired old man and given "*as it were, a mouthful of the milk that he was drawing.*"

Here, however, motifs from the baptismal rite and from the Eucharist combine. For Perpetua took the milk into her cupped hands and consumed it. Those around her then said "Amen," at which she awoke from her vision, "*with the taste of something sweet still in her mouth.*"[8]

In his analysis, Pettersen has assumed that death was not seen as a threat to Perpetua because she would make a transition to where God alone was the ultimate horizon and that such an assumption of hope in God alone is manifest in her first dream. The implications are that she was not afraid of death and that a relationship with God after death was preferable to one with God in her normal life. Yet she has already spoken of being terrified of the dark hole of the prison and spoke of relief that her breasts weren't inflamed after the baby stopped nursing: certainly small sufferings compared to death by wild animals. There is no reason to think Perpetua did not struggle with fear in the face of death. Jesus himself was in agony before being executed and wanted his ordeal to pass from him while no doubt believing that his Father was on the other side of physical death.

Pettersen also stresses that Perpetua wished to fulfill the church's sacramental motifs, especially those of baptism and the Eucharist, which he thinks are described in her visions. I think it would be safe to say that as a healthy twenty-two-year-old with a new baby and a loving family, the sense of impending loss was great and that her unconscious was occupied at that moment with much more than fulfilling sacramental motifs. We need to remember that dream images are not just imaginative memories of real-life events; the depth and complexity of their symbolism defies a simple one-to-one correspondence with conscious experiences (such as Perpetua's baptism and participation in the Eucharist). The images could still be sacramental, but rather than seeing their source as the real-life symbols from the initiation rites, their more probable source would be the unconscious experience of conversion or transition, of which the "sacramental motifs" themselves are symbols.

This confusion is further illustrated by Pettersen's reference to the ladder from Jacob's dream in Genesis 28 (a popular association in the tradition of interpretation). We must be cautious about hearkening back to Jacob's ladder as if that is the prototype for its appearance in Perpetua's dream; more likely, there is something that commonly serves as a source for the ladder image for both Jacob and Perpetua.[9] We should approach both on equal terms as having dreams with ladder symbolism and even see how they could inform each other. It seems unlikely that a Roman woman whose life has been permeated with pagan imagery and who is new to Christianity would use dream images from Genesis. In fact, the idea of "using images" is itself misleading. The unconscious dream images do not behave in that way. The dreamer does not choose them; rather they emerge because they represent a thread, which if followed leads to the source of the conflict that has been hidden from the psyche to protect it.

Similarly, with the dragon at the foot of the ladder that Pettersen equates with the devil and all his pomp renounced thrice in the baptismal rite, rather than connect a dream symbol with a real-life liturgical symbol, we need to examine what underlying conflict or struggle generates the symbols in the first place. The devil in the baptismal rite might symbolize that which prevents godward movement, but in

Perpetua's dream, it could be a threat or obstacle in many other possible ways.

Finally, there are two difficulties with the treatment of the garden scene. First, Pettersen seems to imply that the grey-haired shepherd represents Christ, but the old man did not call Perpetua sister but child, as a father does. The second difficulty is an example of how the meaning of the text has been distorted. Because giving her milk fits better with associations to the custom of giving the newly baptized milk and honey, the word *caseum*, which is clearly cheese, is often changed to milk.[10] Some commentators have even remarked that when you milk sheep you get milk, not cheese, but in so opting for milk, they fail to understand dream imagery. The imagery is not intended to represent objective reality but uses spontaneous and unconscious images to convey the dreamer's inner state and psychic conflicts. The taking of cheese does not have to represent a baptismal motif in order to be significant.

Using Jungian dream interpretation and what knowledge we have of her personal life, let us reexamine this dream. As a component of her dream, Saturus would represent part of her psyche, "a builder of our strength," as Perpetua described him. In the dream, he has already ascended the ladder, apparently without trouble from the dragon, although he warns Perpetua that the dragon may bite. Thus, another part of her psyche represented by her standing at the foot of the ladder is hesitant and cautious in appraising the dangers of this journey. Remember that she is in prison, and although the trial has not yet taken place, she is well aware in her conscious psyche of the outcome that will follow if she does not deny that she is a Christian. This knowledge must have been frightening, yet it is still removed from full psychological realization. Her state would be like one fearfully contemplating the possibility of an operation pending test results, yet still not fully experiencing the fear until the verdict makes it a reality. Her ego, represented by herself in the dream, responds to Saturus, the animus part of her psyche (that part of the psyche in a woman, according to Jung, that initiates and is forward moving) by saying that she can do it because she has divine support in the name of Jesus Christ. We know that the name of Christ would carry weight because she had told her father in a struggle a few days before when he tried to shake her resolve that just as a vase could only be called by what it is so too she could only be called what she is, a Christian.[11]

The naming of something gives it a reality that cannot be denied.

The dragon, unlike the torturous weapons on the sides of the ladder, is a living obstacle; what in her psyche does this represent? Marie-Louise von Franz suggests the dragon is that part of her instinctive nature that does not want her to leave the ground (earth) to ascend to heavenly realms because clearly this is a dangerous ascent (climbing narrow ladders with sharp implements on either side is generally to be avoided).[12] Yet this obstacle does not seem to be that formidable because she could call on a suprapower to help her. In facing the trauma of impending martyrdom, Perpetua's struggle on a psychic level is tremendous. Since death would be sudden, the ascent would be straight up as compared to a lingering death, such as by illness. In contrast to the serpent, the other obstacles to her journey, represented by the implements, are stationary and more in her control to avoid. The stepping on the dragon represents her ability to step on and above the obstacle that could hinder her, and she is doing it by virtue of being a Christian. What is this obstacle? The day before she tells us of her father's pleas with her out of love not to call herself a Christian; his arguments are persuasive because she speaks of them as diabolical, that is, they are a terrifying temptation.[13] Thus, the dragon could represent the arguments presented by her father in person and echo her own temptations. Far from being ready and willing to die (which would possibly signal a suicidal or depressed condition), her deep struggle is evidence of a strong desire to live, a desire she heroically overcame in defense of her faith.

Although we do not know the details of her relationship with Saturus, it seems safe to assume that it was a very powerful one for her. He was her teacher and mentor. He was courageous, faithful, and ardent in his faith, and he sacrificed his life to be with her in prison and in death. In the dream, he is also a trailblazer and a protector. Contrast this with the fact that she makes no mention at all of her husband, either in real life or in her dreams, and the fact that the other important man in her life, her father, stands opposed to her, trying to draw her away from this suffering rather than support her in it. On the dream level Saturus could represent an important man who understands what she is doing and helps her achieve what she ultimately desires.

When she arrives at the top of the ladder, she finds an immense garden. Again, we should not make a hasty connection with Eden.

The garden could represent many things in ordinary terms—beauty, serenity, and peace—as well as symbolize paradise. The symbol of a garden as a kind of paradise is a very natural human symbol; it appears in the Genesis account for the same reason. For Perpetua, who would have been all too familiar with the noise, crowds, and dirt of Carthage, a serene and beautiful garden would represent peace, rest, and consolation after a struggle.

The shepherd could also represent many things, but on a personal level, we would have to associate this benevolent father figure who welcomes her, calls her his child, tells her he is glad she has come, and offers her a morsel of cheese, as representing her own father. The dream image seems to be compensatory for the previous battle with her father in which he did not welcome her ascent into paradise through martyrdom. Here she can make peace with the fact that she is breaking free from her father's disapproval and that he will understand. Her father is described as a grey-haired man, as is the man milking the sheep.

Since we cannot ask Perpetua herself what her associations are with cheese, we can only speculate on its significance. At least, we should consider the image as it appeared in the dream rather than what image might be more realistic or more theologically useful. One possible association might be to her nursing her son. The main image is that of being fed by a parental figure. But Perpetua could see herself as both an independent adult and a child, and the important idea of sustenance can be dually conveyed by milk, appropriate for a baby, and cheese, a more solid version of milk, appropriate for an adult. She tells us that her baby no longer needs breast milk so this too might represent comfort that the child will now be able to be nurtured on some form of solid food just as she is being fed by a nurturing figure. Presumably, her father had always been the source for meeting her physical needs, including food, thus she will now continue to be nurtured by a loving father, and her son, who is in her father's care, will be nurtured. The amen represents assent to this.

The second and third dreams form a diptych and concern her brother Dinocrates, whose memory she says had suddenly come to her mind, filling her with pain as she recalled his horrible death from cancer of the face when he was seven years old. Yet it should be noted that in the previous encounters with her father, he had told her, "think of your brothers, think of your mother and your aunt, think of your child who will not be able to live once you are gone."[14] Thinking of Dinocrates prompted her to begin to pray for him. She dreamt that night the first of these two dreams.

> I saw Dinocrates come out of a dark hole, where there were many others with him, very hot and thirsty, pale and dirty. On his face was the wound he had when he died. Now Dinocrates had been my brother according to the flesh; but he had died horribly of cancer of the face when he was seven years old, and his death was a source of loathing to everyone. Thus it was for him that I made my prayer. There was a great abyss between us: neither could approach the other. Where Dinocrates stood there was a pool full of water: and its rim was higher than the child's height, so that Dinocrates had to stretch himself up to drink. I was sorry that, though the pool had water in it, Dinocrates could not drink because of the height of the rim. Then I woke up, realizing that my brother was suffering. (*Passio* 7.4-8)

After awakening from this dream, she prays for him constantly that he may be helped in his trouble, "asking that this favor might be granted me" (*Passio* 7.10). She prays until she is transferred to the military prison and then she has the following dream.

> On the day we were kept in chains, I had this vision shown to me. I saw the same spot that I had seen before, but there was Dinocrates all clean, well dressed, and refreshed. I saw a scar where the wound had been, and the pool I had seen before now had its rim lowered to the level of the child's waist. And Dinocrates kept drinking water from it, and there above the rim was a golden bowl full of water. And Dinocrates drew close and began to drink from it, and yet the bowl remained full. And when he had drunk enough of the water, he began to play as children do. Then I awoke, and I realized that he had been delivered from his suffering. (*Passio* 8.1-4)

Let us first look at an example of a traditional interpretation from an article by Frederick Klawiter.

> The visions of both Perpetua and Saturus reveal that the imprisoned confessor possessed the priestly power of the keys. . . . Through Perpetua's intercessory prayers and tears, her brother

> was pardoned and given the full forgiveness of sins by the living water of baptism, the water which previously had been out of reach because he had died as a pagan.[15]

After noting that Musurillo's translation was "and I prayed for my brother day and night with tears and sighs that this favor might be granted me,"[16] Klawiter remarks that this left open what specifically the favor was. Concluding that Perpetua prayed for her brother and that he was pardoned, he says, "my translation seeks to bring out the sense of 'to pardon' in *donare* and assumes that the subject of the third person *donaretur* is *he*, which refers back to Dinocrates (*illo*)."[17]

These interpretations treat the dreams as if they were a consciously written-out exposition of a doctrine, in this case, on the value of intercessory prayer or the validation of the role of a martyr to pardon sins, rather than the unconscious spontaneous images springing from deep levels of Perpetua's psyche and reflecting her particular struggles. The dreams are not about Dinocrates; they are about Perpetua.

What part of her psyche or experience does Dinocrates represent? What inner struggle seems to be resolved with these two dreams? In his second visit to her, her father, worn out from suffering and sorrowing, pleads with her to change her mind, emotionally imploring her to remember her child and her brothers as well as her mother and aunt.[18] In all probability he was not thinking of Dinocrates, but that does not mean that this would not have prompted Perpetua to remember him, especially if there were unresolved issues around his death. He returns for his third visit when she is in the middle of a hearing before Hilarianus the governor and begs her again to have pity on her baby. Even the governor is moved by her father's appeal and asks her to have pity on her father and son and offer the sacrifice for the welfare of the emperor. She refuses and is sentenced, and when she asks her father to have her baby back, he refuses to give him to her.[19]

The two dreams of Dinocrates could very well be working through these heart-wrenching encounters with her father. He represents a wounded part of herself, possibly from the time she herself was seven years old. It is a part of herself that has not received healing. Surely, the events around the death of her brother profoundly affected her. As a child or teenager, she must have felt a sense of helplessness in the face of such suffering. She had no resources that a relationship with God might have provided for her family, and thus to her. It is unlikely that a belief in pagan gods would have served this purpose. Children, even adults, become fearful in the face of death especially when imaging their own deaths, often brought on by seeing a loved one die. Children often internalize a sense of guilt because of what is called the grandiose sense of self, by which they feel responsible for events happening around them (for example, children blame themselves for their parents' divorce). Now she is being held responsible for her baby's death by her father's taunt, "your child . . . will not be able to live once you are gone."[20]

Other associations with dying a horrifying death could easily be her own upcoming ordeal and impending death. Her need to stay strong is being challenged by her father with emotional pleas that pierce her. In the first dream, she sees Dinocrates coming out of a dark hole dirty, hot, and thirsty and having trouble drinking because the pool is too high. In the beginning of her diary, she talked about being in a dark hole, hot and no doubt thirsty; she was also separated from her baby, who was faint from hunger and thirst. In her dream, she talks about being separated from Dinocrates across an abyss, as she was and will be from her own child. Since his wound is on his face, it cannot be hidden or ignored; to be afraid and wounded in the arena cannot be hidden either. Will she be able to endure (to save face) in the face of the torture to come? The only favor she had asked the Spirit during her baptism was to be able to persevere in the flesh. She tells us that Dinocrates' death was a source of loathing to everyone. Does she not fear that her own death is a source of loathing to almost everyone, especially the faithful?

Perpetua prays that Dinocrates' suffering be alleviated. She did not say that he suffers because he was not baptized or is being punished for that or some other sin. She simply accepts that her dream describes him as suffering, and she associates this with his early childhood suffering, but his suffering is now being mirrored in her situation as well. In the second part of the dream sequence, he is in the same place as she had seen him before, but now he is not suffering. (If we accepted the interpretation that this was a place of punishment because he was not baptized, then it seems odd that heaven would be the same place.) He is clean, refreshed, and healed, and he drinks as much water as he wants from the golden bowl, which continues to be full, and then he begins to play. However, his state of renewal occurs *before* he goes near the pool. She had prayed, and those prayers had been effective.

She had not been able to help her brother when he suffered on earth, but she is now able to help him. Again, think of this as being part of her unconscious—the part that is dying horribly and the part that is sustaining her in physical death. In the same way, she was relieved of anxiety about her baby because he no longer seemed to need breast milk. Something in her psyche has shifted and her preparation for her upcoming ordeal has been strengthened. Whatever haunted her is now healed. This new confidence is reflected in the way that she is treated in prison, for she tells us that the prisoners are given great honor because the adjutant realized that they possessed great internal power.

On the day before her death, she has her last vision.

> Pomponius the deacon came to the prison gates and began to knock violently. I went out and opened the grate for him. He was dressed in an unbelted white tunic, wearing elaborate sandals. And he said to me: "Perpetua, come; we are waiting for you." Then he took my hand and we began to walk through rough and broken country. At last, we came to the amphitheater out of breath, and he led me into the center of the arena. Then he told me: "Do not be afraid. I am here, struggling with you." Then he left. I looked at the enormous crowd who watched in astonishment. I was surprised that no beasts were let loose on me; for I knew that I was condemned to die by the beasts. Then out came an Egyptian against me, of vicious appearance, together with his seconds, to fight with me. There also came up to me some handsome young men to be my seconds and assistants.
>
> My clothes were stripped off, and suddenly I was a man. My seconds began to rub me down with oil (as they are wont to do before a contest). Then I saw the Egyptian on the other side rolling in the dust. Next, there came forth a man of marvelous stature, such that he rose above the top of the amphitheater. He was clad in a beltless purple tunic with two stripes (one on either side) running down the middle of his chest. He wore sandals that were wondrously made of gold and silver, and he carried a wand like an athletic trainer and a green branch on which there were golden apples. And he asked for silence and said: "If this Egyptian defeats her he will slay her with the sword. But if she defeats him, she will receive this branch." Then he withdrew. We

> drew close to one another and began to let our fists fly. My opponent tried to get hold of my feet, but I kept striking him in the face with the heels of my feet. Then I was raised up into the air and I began to pummel him without, as it were, touching the ground. Then when I noticed there was a lull, I put my two hands together linking the fingers of one hand with those of the other and thus I got hold of his head. He fell flat on his face and I stepped on his head. The crowd began to shout and my assistants started to sing psalms. Then I walked up to the trainer and took the branch. He kissed me and said to me: "Peace be with you, my daughter!" I began to walk in triumph towards the Gate of Life. Then I awoke. I realized that it was not with wild animals that I would fight but with the Devil, but I knew that I would win the victory. (*Passio* 10.1-14)

Let us look at a few examples of interpretation of Perpetua's fourth vision from Cecil M. Robeck.

> The shoes that Pomponius wore may be significant. They may be made of gold and silver . . . or they may be white. In either case, they again may remind Perpetua of a picture derived from the *Shepherd of Hermas*. The white haired virgin whom he identified with the church confronted Hermas. This took place shortly after his confrontation with the monster that he overcame. In his description, the virgin wore white sandals. In this case, then, Pomponius may be reminiscent of the church that will watch as Perpetua meets the Egyptian.[21]

> There is one further note of interest that Perpetua recorded in her description of the Egyptian before the wrestling match. She notes that it is was the custom before such matches for the contestants to receive a rubdown with oil. The Egyptian, however, did not receive such a rubdown, but rather rolled himself in the dust. This activity may once again be related to an event recorded in the *Shepherd of Hermas*. When Hermas met the monster, it was busy stirring up the dust. One cannot help but recollect the probable background to each of these events that may be played by Gen 3:14, where the serpent was cursed and told that he would eat dust all the days of his life.[22]

> If the Egyptian motif is intriguing, Perpetua herself is equally so. She noted that she received the customary rubdown by her assistants. However, when she was stripped, she "became a man" (10.7). This bizarre turn of events has no clear precedent in Scripture. . . . David Scholer is even more helpful when he suggests that, through gender transformation, Perpetua may be viewed as a "positive example of women's empowerment in the early church." Needless to say, in a patriarchal society such as that which existed in Carthage during Perpetua's lifetime, the vision in which she was transformed into a man could enable her leadership to be accepted by hers and future generations through her courageous example as confessor and martyr, even if these congregations were patriarchal.[23]

In the first example, Robeck thought the shoes might remind Perpetua of the shepherd of Hermas. Again it seems unlikely that the image of the virgin in the *Shepherd of Hermas* would be one that was present in her psyche at the time of this wrenching inner struggle to win free from the pain of leaving her father and baby, although by this point she has been able to achieve more detachment as she has worked through the conflicts in her dreams and through her prayers. Each of the dreams (considering two and three to be one) has ended with very positive effect of winning through. She has been nurtured with cheese, water, and now the apples of victory.

Again, Robeck associates the dream image of the Egyptian rolling in the dust as similar to the monster Hermas met that stirred up dust and then associated this with the serpent in Genesis 3:14. This seems to me to be a projection of Robeck's associations on the dreams rather than what would have been a reflection of Perpetua's conflict.

Lastly, Robeck remarks that something is bizarre about the image of "became a man" and says there is no precedent in scripture. This seems to imply that the dream images should have associations with scripture rather than asking first what the images meant to Perpetua and then drawing conclusions. The claim that Perpetua's gender transformation gave a positive example of women's empowerment in the early church because she was a man seems illogical. The dream makes it very clear that she does not lose her female identity and, hence, her leadership role would not come about by taking on male power. In other words, she did not have to become male to be accepted as a leader; she did so in her own right as a powerful woman.

Keeping in mind that dream sequences have themes that run through and connect them, since the psyche is usually struggling over deeper issues continuously, how might we interpret this last dream that occurred the night before she died? Pomponius, who had helped in relieving her suffering in prison by bribing the guards, now appears in this dream as a person who comes to lead her through rough country to the arena and greets her by telling her, "We are waiting for you." The psychic journey to the arena and what that represents has been rough, but Pomponius represents what relieves suffering and stays with her.

The enemy that she must combat in the dream is a vicious looking Egyptian who rolls in the dust while she is stripped and rubbed down with oil by handsome young men. It is at this point that she says she has become a man, yet when the trainer, the man who rose above the top of the amphitheater, announces the conditions of the contest, he says that if this Egyptian defeats *her* he will slay her with the sword, and if *she* is victorious she will be given the bough.

Perhaps the key to this transformation can be found in the redactor's description of her when on the day of her execution, she was stripped naked and sent into the arena: the crowd was horrified when they saw that she was a "delicate young girl."[24] The contest in the dream represented as a physical fight would have not allowed these two to be equal physically, so the compensatory part of the dream gives her the physical strength needed for the combat, while she was already possessed of great psychic strength. She puts on the masculine body as a person might put on armor for a battle. There is nothing in the dream that indicates that she loses her own feminine identity but only that she takes on the physical male body to help her in the physical contest. When she wins the fight, she walks up to the trainer who gives her the branch, kisses her, and says, "Peace be with you, my daughter!" We have a larger than life male who judges the contest and finds her successful. Think of the Egyptian representing that part of herself (as well as the diabolical arguments of her father) that is brought to heel by her strength fully actualized. She is blessed by a man who addresses her as daughter, a father figure who is satisfied now and represents the divine power that tells her she will win through in the end. Thus, whatever strength to undergo the upcoming ordeal had been lacking or underdeveloped in her psychic journey has now emerged, giving her the confidence she will need for the "combat" the following day. The struggle for her was not about whether she was physically prepared for the ordeal that would be involved in her martyrdom; there was never any question that she, or anyone, could hope to contend with the wild animals in the arena. Rather, the battle concerned only whether she could persevere in this trial with courage and dignity. The victory in the dream represented her successful preparation. The devil she speaks of upon awakening from the last dream is her fears, anxieties, and temptations, but now she knows she will have the spiritual strength to contend victoriously with these. The trainer's offer of a father's blessing of peace at victory seems also to be related to her struggle to detach from her father, which can fairly be called a battle. We noted how she had described as diabolical his arguments to persuade her to deny that she was a Christian. He had come again to plead with her before she had her dream, and his pain, sorrow, and sense of abandonment were enough to "move all creation."[25] He was not Christian, so there was nothing to sustain him or to make intelligible the loss of his favorite child with whom he was deeply enmeshed. It must have seemed utterly meaningless to him. Here too the struggle with the "devil" would be not to let the terror of the situation in any way undermine her fidelity to Christianity.

Her relationship with her father appears to be a key to understanding these dreams and her struggles. Where does her strength of character come from? Clearly, she is strong-headed, independent, and courageous before being imprisoned; she took risks in becoming a catechumen. However, something was missing from her life (although all indications are that on many levels she led a privileged life), and whatever attracted her to Christianity met those needs and took hold of her in a deep and permanent way. Her father loved and favored her even over his sons, as he himself tells her. It seems probable that the very strengths that she shows now as an adult were developed and nurtured by this strong relationship in her childhood. It is not hard to think of God as a loving parent and Christ as a brother when your early childhood experiences have provided some evidence of this. Although the culture she lives in is strongly patriarchal, the authorities that order her to submit do not intimidate her. She is able to make her final journey to the arena knowing that she will be victorious and able to die with courage and integrity for the sake of her faith.

Having analyzed her dreams based on what we know about her

personal life, the next step then is to articulate what can be said theologically. An act of martyrdom is an act of heroism. A person's courage, founded on faith, sustains his or her quest for union with God in the face of life-threatening obstacles. Traditionally, we have recounted the "acts of the martyrs" in a way that shows them in the best possible light, highlighting their triumphs more than their struggles. As inspiring as these stories may have been in contemporary times, there is a sense of detachment from such accounts as if they do not connect with our own lives and struggles and they seem unreal. However, if we can see the saints and martyrs as people like ourselves who were not perfect, who struggled with their own inner conflicts, personal temptations, and relationships, who felt the range of emotions from fear to joy as they experienced God's transforming grace, then we too might find it easier to identify with them and be inspired by their lives. There is no doubt about Perpetua's heroic stand in the arena, but we now have some insight into the personal journey that led her there. We saw reflected in the deeper layers of her unconscious how she transcended the struggles and conflicts of her journey by her faith, prayer, and God's transforming grace.

Notes

[1]I would like to thank Saint Mary's College whose generous contribution from their faculty development fund enabled me to present this paper.

[2]Secundulus, the sixth member of the group, died in prison.

[3]I have used the text and translation from Herbert Musurillo, *The Acts of the Christian Martyrs* (Oxford: Clarendon Press, 1972), 106-131, hereafter referred to as *Passio*.

[4]Sermons 280-282.

[5]Peter Dronke and Patricia Cox Miller have both pointed out this problem, but being neither psychologists or theologians, have not offered solutions. See Patricia Cox Miller, *Dreams in Late Antiquity: Studies in the Imagination of a Culture* (Princeton, N.J.: Princeton University Press, 1994), 154-55, and Peter Dronke, *Women Writers of the Middle Ages: A Critical Study of Texts from Perpetua (d. 203) to Marguerite Porete (d. 1310)* (Cambridge; New York: Cambridge University Press, 1984), 6-7.

[6]Some very interesting recent studies include Judith Perkins, *The Suffering Self: Pain and Narrative Representation in Early Christianity* (London; New York: Routledge, 1995); Maureen Tilley, "One Woman's Body: Repression and Expression in the *Passio Perpetuae*," in *Ethnicity, Nationality and Religious Experience*, ed. Peter C. Phan, College Theology Society Annual Vol. 37 (Lanham, Md.:

University Press of America, 1995), 57-71; Joyce E. Salisbury, *Perpetua's Passion: The Death and Memory of a Young Roman Woman* (New York: Routledge, 1997), 228.

[7]The word *caseum* actually means cheese; see below.

[8]Alvyn Pettersen, "Perpetua—Prisoner of Conscience," *Vigiliae Christianae* 41 (1987): 147-48.

[9]See Dronke, *Women Writers of the Middle Ages*, 8.

[10]See Miller, *Dreams in Late Antiquity*, 157, and Musurillo, *The Acts of the Christian Martyrs*, 113 with n. 8.

[11]*Passio* 3.1-2.

[12]Marie-Louise von Franz, *The Passion of Perpetua* (Irving, Tex.: Spring Publications, 1980), 21-25.

[13]*Passio* 3.1-3.

[14]*Passio* 5.3.

[15]Frederick Klawiter, "The Role of Martyrdom and Persecution in Developing the Priestly Authority of Women in Early Christianity: A Case Study of Montanism," *Church History* 49, no. 3 (1980): 257.

[16]*Passio* 7.10: *et feci pro illo orationem die et nocte gemens et lacrimans ut mihi donaretur.*

[17]Klawiter, "The Role of Martyrdom and Persecution," 258 n. 24. His translation is "I prayed for him day and night, sighing and shedding tears, that he might be pardoned for me."

[18]*Passio* 5.1-4.

[19]*Passio.*

[20]*Passio* 5.3.

[21]Cecil M. Robeck, *Prophecy in Carthage: Perpetua, Tertullian, and Cyprian* (Cleveland, Ohio: Pilgrim Press, 1992), 60.

[22]Ibid., 63.

[23]Ibid., 64-65.

[24]*Passio* 20.2.

[25]*Passio* 9.2.

Contributors

Michael Horace Barnes is professor of religious studies and holds the Alumni Chair in Humanities at the University of Dayton. His most recent book, *Stages of Thought* (Oxford University Press, 2000), deals with the evolution of cognitive styles through cultural history and compares its impact on both religious thought and science. His introductory textbook, *In the Presence of Mystery: An Introduction to the Story of Religion* (Twenty-Third Publications, 1984, 1990, 2001) presents a broader but simpler picture of the evolution of religion.

Gregory G. Baum holds degrees in mathematics and physics, theology, and sociology. He is professor emeritus at McGill University and long-time professor of theology and later sociology at St. Michael's College, University of Toronto. He is the author of more than twenty books, many on theology and the social sciences including the influential *Religion and Alienation: A Theological Reading of Sociology* (Paulist, 1975) and the more recent collection of essays, *The Twentieth Century: A Theological Overview* (Orbis Books, 2000). Since 1962 he has been editor of *The Ecumenist*, and he served on the editorial board of *Concilium* from 1970 to 1990. He is the recipient of numerous honorary doctorates, and is an "Officer of the Order of Canada."

Michael J. Baxter, C.S.C. is assistant professor of theology at the University of Notre Dame. He received his Ph.D. in Theology and Ethics at Duke University (1996). He was awarded the Charlotte Newcombe Dissertation Fellowship (1993-94) and was a fellow at the Center for the Study of American Religion at Princeton University (1995-96). His articles have appeared in the *De Paul Law Review*, *Pro Ecclesia*, *Communio*, *The Thomist*, and *Modern Theology*. He is currently working on a collection of essays, entitled *American Catholics to the Rescue.*

Boyd Blundell is a doctoral student in theological ethics at Boston College. His current research is on the hermeneutical theme of personal identity in the recent work of Paul Ricoeur. His upcoming dissertation, "Philosophical Hermeneutics and Theological Identity," examines how philosophical hermeneutics is imported into the theological ethics of William Schweiker and Klaus Demmer.

Florence Caffrey Bourg is assistant professor of religious and pastoral studies at the College of Mount St. Joseph, Cincinnati. She serves as convenor of the College Theology Society's Marriage and Family interest group. Other articles by Dr. Bourg on family and domestic church are forthcoming in *INTAMS*, the journal of the International Academy of Marital Spirituality, as well as the *Josephinum Journal of Theology*.

John A. Coleman, S.J. is the Charles Casassa Professor of Social Values at Loyola Marymount University in Los Angeles. Among his books are *The Evolution of Dutch Catholicism*, *An American Strategic Theology*, *One Hundred Years of Catholic Social Teaching*, and *Religion and Nationalism*. Coleman is the recipient of the 2000 Luzbetak Award for outstanding research on the American Catholic Church given by the Center for Applied Research in the Apostolate.

James D. Davidson is professor of sociology at Purdue University and visiting distinguished professor of religious studies at the University of Dayton in spring 2001. He is co-author of *American Catholics* (Alta Mira, 2001), *The Search for Common Ground* (Our Sunday Visitor, 1997), and *Laity: American and Catholic* (Sheed & Ward, 1996). He has been president of the Religious Research Association and North Central Sociological Association, editor of the *Review of Religious Research*, and executive secretary of the Society for the Scientific Study of Religion.

Carol J. Dempsey, O.P. is associate professor of theology (biblical studies) at the University of Portland, Oregon, and has been named a National Regional Scholar of the Society of Biblical Literature. She is the author of *The Prophets: A Liberation Critical Reading* (Fortress, 2000), co-editor and contributor to the volume *All Cre-*

ation Is Groaning: An Interdisciplinary Vision for Life in a Sacred Universe (Liturgical Press, 1999), and *Hope Amid the Ruins: The Ethic of Israel's Prophets* (Chalice Press, 2000). She is an associate editor of the *Catholic Biblical Quarterly* and a member of the Board of Directors of the College Theology Society.

Jeannine Hill Fletcher is completing a doctorate in theology at Harvard Divinity School. Her dissertation, titled "Ultimacy and Identity: Karl Rahner and George Lindbeck on Religious Pluralism," analyzes the contemporary discourse on religious pluralism within Christian theology, drawing on post-colonial and feminist theory. Publications include "Reason, Holiness and Diversity: Fides et Ratio Through the Lens of Religious Pluralism," *Philosophy & Theology*, 12.1 (2000).

Reid B. Locklin is a graduate student in systematic and comparative theology at Boston College. He has recently returned from India, where he studied under the guidance of an Advaitin teacher. He is currently working on a dissertation entitled "A First Course in Salvation: Sankara, Augustine, and the Ongoing Creation of Religious Community."

Victor H. Matthews is professor of religious studies at Southwest Missouri State University, a specialist in Hebrew Bible and the social world of the ancient Near East. He has published eight books and numerous articles, including *Old Testament Themes* (Chalice Press, 2000), *The Old Testament: Text and Context* (James Moyer, co-author; Hendrickson, 1997), *Old Testament Parallels: Stories and Laws from the Ancient Near East* (co-author, D. C. Benjamin; Paulist, 1997), and *The Social World of Ancient Israel* (D. C. Benjamin, co-author; Hendrickson, 1993).

William C. Mattison, III is a doctoral candidate in moral theology and Christian ethics at the University of Notre Dame. He is spending this year in Fribourg, Switzerland, on a Fulbright Fellowship. His primary areas of study are Catholic moral theology and virtue ethics, focusing on Thomas Aquinas and the relation of emotions to virtue. His dissertation will explore Christian anger as a lens into these larger interests.

Judith A. Merkle is a member of the religious studies faculty at Niagara University. She writes and speaks on church and society, social ethics, and the theology of religious life. Among her publications are *Committed by Choice* (Liturgical Press, 1992), *A Different Touch: A Study of the Vows in Religious Life* (Liturgical Press, 1998), and "Social Ethics in the New Millennium" in *Ethical Dilemmas in the New Millennium (I)*, ed. Francis A. Eigo (Villanova University Press, 2000).

Felicidad Oberholzer is professor of religious studies at Saint Mary's College of California and adjunct professor at the Jesuit School of Theology in Berkeley. She has a Ph.D. in theology and personality sciences from the Graduate Theological Union in Berkeley. She is a licensed clinical psychologist and a marriage, family, and child counselor, and has completed postgraduate work at the C. G. Jung Institute in San Francisco.

Peter C. Phan holds an S.T.D. from the Universitas Pontificia Salesiana and Ph.D. and an earned D.D. from the University of London. He is the Warren-Blanding Professor of Religion and Culture in the Department of Religion and Religious Education at the Catholic University of America, Washington, D.C. He has written or edited seven books, including *Christianity and the Wider Ecumenism* (Paragon House, 1990), *Social Thought* (Michael Glazier, 1984), and *Eternity in Time: A Study of Karl Rahner's Eschatology* (Associated University Presses, 1988), as well as numerous articles.

Mathew N. Schmalz is presently an Edward Bennett Williams Fellow and assistant professor of religious studies at the College of the Holy Cross in Worcester, Massachusetts. He is completing an ethnographic study of Catholic communities in North India. He has received a grant from the Wabash Center to develop an interactive website on a North Indian village, which will be available for use as a teaching tool in undergraduate religious studies courses.

Terrence W. Tilley is chair and professor, Department of Religious Studies, the University of Dayton. He is the author of six books, most recently *Inventing Catholic Tradition* (Orbis, 2000), scores of professional articles and essays, and co-editor of two other books. He is a past president of the CTS (1996-98).

James K. Voiss, S.J. completed his Ph.D. in systematic theology at the University of Notre Dame in December 1999. His dissertation was entitled "A Comparison and Analysis of Karl Rahner and Hans Urs von Balthasar on Structural Change in the Church." In addition to undergraduate systematic theology courses, he teaches a graduate course on the modern European interplay between theology and philosophy at St. Louis University. During his studies he contributed several articles to the *Encyclopedia of Catholicism* edited by Richard McBrien.

Patricia Wittberg, S.C., a Sister of Charity of Cincinnati, is associate professor of sociology at Indiana University in Indianapolis. Her books include *Pathways to Recreating Religious Communities* (Paulist Press, 1996), *The Rise and Decline of Catholic Religious Orders: A Social Movement Perspective* (Paulist Press, 1996), and *Creating a Future for Religious Life: A Sociological Perspective* (Paulist Press, 1991), as well as articles such as "Religion and Families" (in *Handbook on Marriage and the Family*, ed. Marvin Sussman et al., Plenum, 1999) and "Called to Service: The Changing Institutional Identities of American Denominations" (in *Nonprofit and Voluntary Sector Quarterly* 29, no. 3, 2000).